The

19.

Sta

Bu.

Ha

GW00455813

December 1995

British Bus Publishing

1996 Stagecoach Bus Handbook

The 1996 Stagecoach Bus Handbook is the third edition of this Bus Handbook dedicated to the various fleets of Stagecoach Holdings, both within the United Kingdom and overseas.

Although this book has been produced with the encouragement of, and in co-operation with, Stagecoach management, it is not an official Stagecoach fleet list and the vehicles included are subject to variation, particularly as substantial new vehicle deliveries lead to older vehicles being 'cascaded' to other subsidiaries. Some vehicles listed are no longer in regular use on service but are retained for special purposes or preserved by the company. The services operated and the allocation of vehicles to subsidiary companies are subject to variation at any time, although accurate at the time of going to print. The contents are correct to December 1995, and include the vehicles of Rodoviária de Lisboa which joined the group in January 1996 and enlarged East Midland and Western Scottish operations.

The publishers would be glad to hear from readers should any information be available which corrects or enhances that given in this publication, or to receive any suitable photographs for use in future editions, particularly those covering the overseas operations.

Principal Editors: David Donati and Bill Potter
Acknowledgements:
We are grateful to Mark Jameson, Colin Lloyd, Brian Pritchard, Richard Smiles, Buses Worldwide, the PSV Circle and the Management and officials of Stagecoach Holdings and their operating companies for their kind assistance and co-operation in the compilation of this book.
To keep up to date with the fleets we recommend *Buses*, published monthly by Ian Allan Ltd and for more in-depth information the news sheets of the PSV Circle.

The front cover photo is by Bill Potter
The rear cover photographs are by Stagecoach International and Tony Wilson

ISBN 1 897990 23 5
Published by *British Bus Publishing* Ltd
The Vyne, 16 St Margarets Drive, Wellington,
Telford, Shropshire, TF1 3PH
© British Bus Publishing Ltd, January 1996

Stagecoach

The Stagecoach Group is the largest private sector operator of buses in the United Kingdom. This Bus Handbook details the latest fleets of constituent companies, both in Britain and overseas in Africa, Hong Kong, Portugal and New Zealand.

Stagecoach can trace its roots back to a small self-drive caravan and caravanette rental business which was formed in Perth in 1976. Trading as Gloagtrotter (later GT Coaches), the business expanded a couple of years later to include minibus private hire under the original partnership of Ann Gloag, now Executive Director of Stagecoach Holdings, and her husband, Robin. Her brother, Brian Souter, now Executive Chairman (an accountant by profession), joined the fledgling organisation in 1980 just prior to its starting regular long distance services at which time the Stagecoach name was adopted, at the suggestion of Ann's other brother, David. This move into regular services was made possible by coach deregulation, introduced in the 1980 Transport Act.

Stagecoach was born out of deregulation and privatisation. The freedom of deregulation and the opportunities of privatisation have facilitated the rapid growth of Stagecoach.

The first service began in October 1980, an overnight run from Dundee to London. Subsequently further legs were added that brought in Aberdeen and Glasgow to form a network of coach services. Soon a network of express services was developed that operated throughout Scotland and ran south of the border to London via Manchester and Birmingham. The quality of vehicle provided on these services quickly improved, exotic foreign double deck coaches becoming the norm from 1982 onwards in marked contrast to the traditional single deck coaches used by their main competitor - The Scottish Bus Group.

In December 1982 Mrs Gloag's husband left the business and set up his own company trading as Highwayman Coaches at Errol near Perth. In tandem with the coach service expansion, a number of school contracts had been secured. These were operated primarily with second hand Bristol Lodekkas and, by the mid 1980s, Stagecoach was the largest operator of that type, with a fleet of over 20. In December 1980 Stagecoach took its first step into regular bus service operation when the Perth to Errol route of A & C McLennan of Spittalfield was taken over. It was this route which five years later was to see the start of the 'Provincial Routemaster Revival' which was started by Stagecoach when it introduced Routemasters between Perth and Errol in the spring of 1985. In the early 1980s a number of other Scottish coach operations were absorbed into Stagecoach including Adamson & Low of Edinburgh and Bennetts of Kilwinning in Ayrshire, although both were subsequently disposed of. After a period of consolidation, a further expansion into local bus services was achieved when, in November 1985, the remaining business of McLennan's of Spittalfield was purchased. This gave the Stagecoach company a significant presence in the Tayside region, and most importantly McLennans extensive workshops and engineering facilities at Spittalfield which were needed to maintain the ever-growing express coach fleet.

The 1985 Transport Act resulted in the deregulation of bus services outside of London. As the implementation of the Act drew near, the Stagecoach company prepared its plans for a major expansion in the bus market. A new company was formed called Magicbus, and on 26th October 1986 it commenced operating a number of services in Glasgow. The vehicles utilised were primarily Routemasters formerly with London Buses or Northern General and these vehicles brought back conductor operation to the city along with the Routemasters of Kelvin and Clydeside. At the same time there was some expansion of services in Tayside, Stagecoach taking over a number of rural routes not registered commercially by Strathtay Scottish, including the routes north of Perth to Aberfeldy and Pitlochry.

With established operations in Tayside and Glasgow, and an extensive network of express services, the Stagecoach team considered for the first time acquiring operators outside its native Scotland, and took an interest in the pending privatisation of National Bus Company's subsidiaries. An unsuccessful bid for City of Oxford did not deter the directors who turned their attention to Hampshire Bus. A new holding company, Skipburn Limited, was formed by directors Brian Souter and Ann Gloag together with their uncle Fraser McColl and the General Manager of Hampshire Bus. Hampshire Bus together with Pilgrim Coaches were successfully purchased on 2nd April 1987. The new owners did not waste time in rationalising their new acquisition, with Pilgrim Coaches, which had been loss-making from the outset, closing down on 26th April 1987. By 3rd October, the Southampton area operations had been sold to Southern Vectis who formed a new company, trading as Solent Blue Line, to operate the routes. The residual Hampshire Bus operation continues as part of the Stagecoach South company with depots at Andover, Basingstoke and Winchester.

In 1987 Derek Scott joined the board as Finance Director, and has subsequently paid a key role in shaping the growth of the group. While still digesting Hampshire Bus, the Stagecoach board turned its attention to the acquisition of a second NBC subsidiary. This time Cumberland was the target and, following a successful offer, Stagecoach took control of Cumberland Motor Services on 23rd July 1987. The Cumberland operations were based at Whitehaven with depots in Carlisle, Penrith,

To coincide with Coach and Bus '95 Stagecoach announced substantial new vehicle orders totalling over 1000 buses to be delivered to its UK and overseas subsidiaries during 1996. Commenting on this massive order, Brian Souter said: "This level of investment in new vehicles demonstrates our commitment to maintain our operating costs at the lowest possible levels, while at the same time offering our customers the highest standards of safety and comfort". Brian Souter (right) is seen at the driving seat of Fife's Alexander Ultra-bodied Volvo B10L with Sandy Glennie, Managing Director of Volvo Bus.

Keswick, Workington and Millom. The new owners quickly recast the Carlisle city network and introduced crew-operated Routemasters to that city. The Cumberland company acquired a number of its competitors during 1988 including Yeowart's of Whitehaven and Kirkpatrick of Brigham, near Cockermouth.

In July 1987 the McColl interests in Skipburn were acquired and Fraser McColl returned to Canada. However, further expansion of the group was still being sought. Under the NBC privatisation rules only three subsidiaries could be acquired by any purchaser. However, Hampshire Bus and Pilgrim Coaches had been classed as one unit, Cumberland a second and, therefore, Stagecoach was able to acquire United Counties as its third NBC company. The area of operation encompassed Bedford, Corby, Huntingdon, Kettering and Northampton and was the group's first presence in the Midlands. As with Cumberland, it was not long before the potential of Routemasters was realised and the Corby and Bedford networks received a fleet of these vehicles soon after the Stagecoach acquisition.

During 1988 Ewan Brown joined the board of directors in a non-executive capacity. Being a Merchant Banker by profession, and a former director of the Scottish Bus Group, he brought valuable skills and knowledge to the management team.

Up to this point the Stagecoach Group had acquired three NBC companies. All were operating a typical mix of National Bus Company standard vehicles which primarily consisted of Leyland Nationals and Leopards, and Bristol VRTs. Additionally, the fleet in Scotland was mainly secondhand Routemasters and Bristol Lodekkas together with Volvo B58 and Neoplan coaches for the express network. Vehicles in Scotland were in the now standard Stagecoach livery of white with blue, red and mustard (later to become orange) stripes and it was decided that in order to provide flexibility and enable vehicles to be transferred between fleets, all vehicles in the group would be painted in this corporate style. Very quickly the new livery began to appear on all three English fleets.

New vehicle purchases had to be made in order that the bus companies could maintain and develop their business into the 1990s and early purchases of Alexander-bodied Mercedes 709 minibuses and Leyland Olympians were to be a portent of large numbers of vehicles of these types in years to come. The importance of investing in new vehicles, and its consequent increase in patronage and reduction of maintenance costs, has continued to the present.

The most significant event of 1988 was the private placing of a quantity of Stagecoach shares with institutional investors. This raised £5 million and set the financial scene for Stagecoach to develop into a major force within the bus industry. It was also a sign of things to come, that is the Stock Market floatation five years later.

1989 saw the first Stagecoach acquisition overseas when, in March of that year, it purchased a 51% share in United Transport Malawi Limited from United Transport International. The vehicles operated in Africa are somewhat strange to British eyes with large numbers of ERF Trailblazer and Leyland Victory single deckers, all built to meet the rough African conditions where much mileage is run on dirt roads. Stagecoach did, however, introduce double decker operation to the Malawi fleet with Daimler CVG6 double deckers previously operated in Hong Kong by the Kowloon Motor Bus Company. Several of these, together with a Bristol FLF, are now withdrawn as the company has taken delivery of Dennis Dragons. City services and long distance express routes are operated from four depots based in Blantyre (Makata Road, Chichiri), Lilongwe and Mzuzu.

Having ventured into Africa, Stagecoach soon returned to the acquisition trail in England. East Midland Motor Services had been sold to its management by NBC, but in April 1989 the management decided to sell its entire share holding, Stagecoach being the purchaser. The operation was conducted under East Midland, Mansfield & District, and Rainworth Travel names in the East Midland area, and in addition there were two Frontrunner operations, one based in Essex and the other in north west Derbyshire and eastern Greater Manchester. The Frontrunner South East operation was quickly sold on to Ensign Bus of Purfleet while the Derbyshire/Manchester operation was absorbed by Ribble. This left the East Midland management to concentrate in its own territory and soon its coaching operations were consolidated into Rainworth Travel which was renamed Midland Travel. The bus operations are based on Worksop, Chesterfield and Mansfield and, as with other acquisitions, former London Routemasters were again tried, this time in Mansfield where Routemaster operation lasted until 1991. In May 1993 the Midland Travel coaching operation was sold to Skills of Nottingham.

Only a matter of days after the East Midland acquisition, a further company was acquired from its management. Ribble Motor Services Limited, based in the north west of England, had been bought by its management team and had subsequently purchased, from United Transport, the Bee Line Buzz Company - a large minibus operation based in Manchester, together with the Zippy minibus operation based in Preston.

Having added two major bus companies in North West England to one it already owned, Stagecoach embarked upon a reorganisation and rationalisation of its interests in the area. The Barrow-in-Furness municipal undertaking had been in financial difficulties for some time, following heavy competition with Ribble, and its services and depot were acquired in May 1989. For operational control reasons, and to align with the county boundaries, Ribble's South Cumbrian and Lake District operations were transferred to Cumberland Motor Services which also took control in Barrow. This concentrated Cumberland into the county of Cumbria and Ribble into Lancashire and Greater Manchester. In September of 1989 Ribble sold its Bee Line Buzz subsidiary and some of its own Ribble Manchester operations to the Drawlane Group though it retained the Preston-based Zippy minibuses, a name now used for all Ribble minibus operations. Having lost depots at Barrow, Ulverston and Kendal to Cumberland and the Manchester operation passing to Drawlane, Ribble was left to concentrate on the central area which consists of the old Lancashire towns of Blackburn, Bolton, Chorley, Clitheroe, Fleetwood, Lancaster, Morecambe and Preston, the largest expansion being at Bolton.

Despite the activity in England there were still changes taking place in Scotland during 1989. On 19th June new bus services in and around the cities of Perth and Dundee were introduced, primarily in competition with Strathtay Scottish, whose managing director, Neil Renilson was recruited by the group at the same time. This new network was branded Perth Panther and, after a prolonged period of competition, in which both operators used Routemasters on Perth City services, Strathtay closed their Crieff depot and operations in 1991 and their Perth depot and operations in the summer of 1993.

Perhaps the most surprising development of 1989 was the decision by Stagecoach to sell the express coach operations that had been the genesis of the company. On 4th August 1989 the company announced the sale of its express network to National Express who re-branded the operation as Caledonian Express. With this sale Stagecoach clearly indicated that it was to concentrate on local bus operations in future. The Scottish operations saw further expansion when Inverness Traction was purchased from receivership in November. Inverness Traction had been competing with Highland Scottish on town services in Inverness since 1987. Stagecoach placed this Inverness operation under the Magicbus and Perth Panther management, and renamed the Magicbus company Stagecoach Scotland Ltd as the holding company for its Glasgow, Tayside and Inverness operations. All of these operations were carving out their market through head to head competition with established state-owned operators, whereas in England established operators had been purchased, and competitive pressures were the other way round.

The south coast of England was not neglected either. In August 1989 the management of Southdown decided to sell out to Stagecoach. This brought a sixth former NBC subsidiary into the fold and Stagecoach then acquired, in October, the operations of Portsmouth City Bus from Southampton City Bus who held 75% and a workers co-operative which owned the remaining 25%. In December 1989 Hastings and District was added when the management sold the company which it had bought from NBC.

In 1990 there was expansion overseas with the purchase of Gray Coach Lines of Toronto, Canada. This brought to the Stagecoach Group an extensive network of express coach services throughout eastern Canada together with Niagara Falls sightseeing tours and the Toronto City/Airport express coach service. The venture proved to be unsuccessful in financial terms and the Group's interest in Gray Coach Lines was sold to Greyhound Lines of Canada in December 1992, but not before a number of Stagecoach Scotland Bristol FLFs had been transferred for sightseeing tour work.

One result of the large expansion on the south coast of England was an inquiry by the Monopolies and Mergers Commission that subsequently instructed Stagecoach to divest themselves of Portsmouth City Bus, and this operation was subsequently sold to Transit Holdings in January 1991. The South of England subsidiaries that remained were then restructured and consolidated in April 1992 when a new company, Stagecoach South Limited, was given overall control of Hastings Buses, Southdown and Hampshire Bus. As part of the reorganisation

Southdown was split into two operating companies, Sussex Coastline Buses and South Coast Buses, the latter also taking in Hastings Buses. The Southdown name was discontinued, and South Coast Buses operates at Eastbourne and Hastings with Coastline Buses trading from Chichester, Havant and Worthing.

Following on from the privatisation of NBC the Government decided to extend privatisation to the Scottish Bus Group. It was decreed that only two companies could be acquired by any one purchaser and Stagecoach completed its quota with the purchase of Bluebird Northern and Fife Scottish during the first half of 1991. Bluebird is based in Aberdeen and also has depots at Ballater, Elgin, Fyvie, Macduff, Peterhead and Stonehaven, together with several outstations. Bluebird was acquired in March and its archaic legal company name of Northern Scottish Omnibuses Ltd was quickly changed to Bluebird Buses Ltd. Bluebird was placed under common management with Stagecoach Scotland Ltd and its fleet renumbered into a single series.

By July of 1991 the Fife company was also under the Stagecoach umbrella. In line with the company name operations are concentrated in the Kingdom of Fife with depots at Aberhill (Methil), Cowdenbeath, Dunfermline, Glenrothes, Kirkcaldy and St Andrews. In the autumn of 1991 Stagecoach Scotland further expanded when it took over the remaining Inverness and Easter Ross area operations from Highland, adding some 30 extra buses to the Inverness Traction Fleet, plus the former Highland depot at Tain. With two former SBG companies now under its wing, plus the Perth and Inverness operations, Stagecoach had established a strong presence on the eastern side of Scotland. In line with Stagecoach policy the corporate colours started to appear on the newly-acquired fleets and fleet renewal commenced, primarily involving Alexander-bodied Mercedes minibuses and Leyland Olympians. There were also transfers north of the border of vehicles from the English companies which resulted in some unfamiliar types of vehicles being introduced into Scotland, especially ECW-bodied Bristol VRTs. The VRT had been despised by SBG with all its examples being exchanged for NBC-owned Bristol FLFs.

November 1991 saw further expansion in Africa. British Electric Traction (BET) had decided to divest themselves of local bus operations throughout the world and Stagecoach saw potential in acquiring its Kenya operations. As a result of the deal Stagecoach now has a 75% share of Kenya Bus Services (Nairobi), and a 51% share in Kenya Bus Services (Mombassa). The remaining share holdings are held by the local city councils and both operations are maintained under franchising arrangements. As in Malawi the ERF Trailblazer and Leyland Victory tend to dominate the fleets though there are a number of unusual vehicles including some manufactured by Isuzu in Japan.

There is one company in the Stagecoach Group which plays a large part in the UK transport system as a whole, but operates no buses! National Transport Tokens was formed in the 1970s to manufacture and distribute concessionary travel tokens to various bodies, mostly local authorities. The aluminium tokens produced by National Transport Tokens are accepted by a variety of operators in lieu of cash fares, including bus companies, taxi firms and rail services. Stagecoach bought a controlling interest in the company in March 1992 and its headquarters were moved from Manchester to Preston.

In October 1992 Brian Cox, Managing Director of Stagecoach South, and Barry Hinkley, Managing Director of Cumberland joined the main board as executive appointments while Muir Russell and Barry Sealey formed two additional non-executive directorships in December, Muir Russell resigning in January 1995 following his promotion within the Scottish Office.

It came as a significant surprise in April 1992 when Stagecoach decided to sell another of its initial operations. Having disposed of the express network the deal was now to sell the Glasgow-based Magicbus operation to Kelvin Central Buses. The vehicles transferred included some newly-delivered Dennis Darts and a substantial number of Bristol VRTs and Routemasters, and the Glasgow depot was also acquired by Kelvin. The Magicbus name and Stagecoach livery continued in use with Kelvin Central until 1993 as part of the deal.

1992 also saw further expansion of the southern fleet when Stagecoach acquired Alder Valley's operations based at depots in Aldershot, Alton and Hindhead. Alder Valley had been through a particularly disturbed time having had a number of owners since privatisation from NBC and suffering from subsequent fragmentation. The Alder Valley operation acquired by Stagecoach was placed under the Stagecoach South umbrella and is operated under the brand name Hants & Surrey.

Having seen the deregulation and privatisation process in the United Kingdom the New Zealand Government decided to embark on a similar course of action. In October 1992 the Wellington City Transport undertaking was privatised and Stagecoach was the successful bidder. There are three companies involved: Wellington City Transport, with a depot at Karori and an outstation at Kilbirnie; Cityline Auckland based at Papakura and Cityline Hutt Valley with depots at Lower Hutt and Stokes Valley. With its new undertaking, Stagecoach now has experience of operating MAN and Hino vehicles but more interestingly, is now operating electric traction. The Wellington City Transport fleet contains over seventy Volvo trolleybuses while Wellington City Transport's share in Harbour City Cable Car Limited has resulted in Stagecoach having an operating interest in this funicular railway.

Overseas developments in 1992 were not confined to Africa and New Zealand. For some time Stagecoach had held a stake in Speedybus Enterprises Limited of Hong Kong, whose primary functions were to sell advertising space on double deckers it supplied to Chinese municipal bus companies, and to import vehicles to China through Hong Kong. Speedybus also supplied Hong Kong double deckers to Stagecoach Malawi. In 1992 Stagecoach Hong Kong Ltd was formed to operate bus services in Hong Kong, and to gain an operating base in the colony. (Speedybus was primarily a bus dealer and bus advertising contractor rather than an operator, and was disposed of in 1993). In 1994 the company commenced operating services on two commuter routes with five Volvo B10Ms. These vehicles are almost the same as the Stagecoach standard Alexander PS-bodied Volvo B10Ms except that they are fitted with air conditioning to cope with the humid Hong Kong climate. In 1995 six tri-axle Volvo Olympians joined the operation and a second residents route was introduced.

In the spring of 1992 Lancaster City Council expressed an intention to sell its municipal bus undertaking, much of the network operated comprised joint services with Ribble. As Ribble already had a substantial presence in Lancaster and the surrounding area, Stagecoach was not expected to be a bidder for the operation. However, in order to protect its interests in the area, Ribble registered many of Lancaster City's routes and subsequently the City Council decided to liquidate their undertaking, selling the depot and some twelve buses to Ribble during 1993. As a result of this acquisition Ribble was able to close its own, smaller, depot in Morecambe and move into the former council depot in Heysham.

Expansion in the south of England continued in 1993 when the management of East Kent sold their company. This is yet another former NBC subsidiary that was purchased by a management team. Again the new acquisition had been placed under the control of Stagecoach South and it now trades under the Stagecoach East Kent name. The East Kent purchase brought with it depots at Ashford, Canterbury, Thanet (Westwood), Dover, Folkestone and Herne Bay and contained a typical mix of former NBC vehicles with Leyland Nationals, Bristol Vrs and Olympians together with a substantial number of minibuses. In addition it contained several MCW and Scania products. In 1994 East Kent purchased four Dennis low-floor vehicles with Berkhof bodies for the Canterbury Park and Ride service, these being the first such vehicles in the Stagecoach Group.

While the Government has not legislated for the privatisation of municipal bus companies, a number of councils took the opportunity to sell before the end of 1993 to allow the income from the sale to be used on other projects. Grimsby Cleethorpes Transport was jointly owned by the Boroughs of Grimsby and Cleethorpes and the two councils decided to sell the undertaking through a competitive tendering process and Stagecoach were the successful bidder. The deal was completed in November 1993 and has now brought the Stagecoach livery to South Humberside. The vehicles acquired are of a typical municipal nature and included substantial numbers of Dennis Dominators and Lances. The last of the five Lances delivered in 1993 was painted into Stagecoach livery before delivery. Grimsby Cleethorpes is operated as a division of the East Midland company.

The 1000th new bus to join Stagecoach was handed over to Ann Gloag and Brian Souter on the opening day of Coach & Bus 93; this was a Volvo B6 destined for United Counties. Stagecoach has been the largest UK purchaser of new buses in recent years, and has invested heavily in renewing its fleet and offering passengers modern, comfortable vehicles. The order for new vehicles for delivery in 1995 was the largest annual order for buses in the UK since privatisation began in the 1980s. Purchasing policy continued to be based on Volvo double and single deck chassis together with Mercedes minibuses, though Dennis have supplied the Dart and Javelin in significant numbers. Alexander are the preferred bus body builder with Plaxton as the coach body supplier, although some vehicles have been bodied by Northern Counties, particularly for the Groups urban operations.

December 1993 saw a further major acquisition by Stagecoach Holdings. Western Travel Ltd was formed on the privatisation of the Cheltenham and Gloucester company from NBC. Cheltenham and Gloucester operates in both the cities mentioned in its title together with services in Swindon and the Cotswolds based on Stroud. Western Travel itself went on the acquisition trail as part of the NBC privatisation process and acquired the Midland Red South company which brought with it operations in Leamington Spa, Nuneaton, Rugby, Stratford-upon-Avon and Warwick. Western Travel had also secured the eastern part of the National Welsh operation trading as Red & White, adding operations around the Red & White historical base of Monmouthshire and the eastern valleys of South Wales. A further 650 vehicles were added to the Stagecoach Group with this purchase, the first being painted into corporate colours during December 1993, under the Stagecoach West name.

1993 also saw the company become listed on the London Stock Exchange. The successful 1993 share flotation attracted much publicity and the proceeds gave the group access to considerable additional funds with which to expand. Some 80% of Stagecoach UK employees are now shareholders.

1994 saw the bus industry's consolidation accelerate and Stagecoach's development move into the larger metropolitan markets of which it has previously only had limited experience. The year opened with the launch of Stagecoach Manchester at the end of January. Although a division within Ribble, it traded separately under its own brand name on the long established 192 route from central Manchester to Hazel Grove south of Stockport. Originally set up as a unit with sixteen B6s, rapid passenger growth called for more and larger vehicles, and the year finished with 23 B10Ms allocated to the route. In the autumn of 1995 this operation with the vehicles was sold to EYMS Group Ltd who also operated south Manchester services through their Finglands subsidiary.

The first full scale acquisition of 1994 was of Western Scottish, a former SBG company, which was sixty-eight per cent owned by its employees. Western is based at Kilmarnock with depots at Ayr, Cumnock, Dumfries and Stranraer, and a number of sub-depots both on the mainland and on the Isles of Arran and Bute. The operating area runs from the southern outskirts of Glasgow right down to Annan where the services meet those of Stagecoach North West's Cumberland division while the fleet comprised 340 vehicles, including a large number of different chassis and bodies.

In July 1994 Busways Travel Services Ltd became a subsidiary company of Stagecoach. Busways Travel Services Ltd was a private limited company established by the Transport Act 1985 to acquire the bus undertaking of Tyne and Wear Passenger Transport Executive.

Busways commenced trading in October 1986 under the ownership of the PTA, though its origins can be found in the municipal transport undertakings in Newcastle upon Tyne, South Shields and Sunderland, and also the private companies acquired in 1973 (Armstrong and Galley) and 1975 (Economic). In May 1989 the management/employee buyout was successfully completed. Fifty-one per cent of the shares were purchased by the management of ten while 49% were purchased for employees through the ESOP. The Tyne and Wear Omnibus Company Ltd was acquired in November 1989 and in August 1993 Busways acquired a majority shareholding in Welcome Passenger Transport Ltd.

With a fleet of 590 buses and coaches Busways provides mainly urban local bus services in the Newcastle upon Tyne, South Shields and Sunderland areas whose combined population is approximately half a million. The acquisition represented an important development for the group because Busways mainly provides services in the densely populated metropolitan area of Tyne and Wear. Stagecoach had not previously had a significant presence in a metropolitan area and this development further strengthened the group due to the high usage of public transport in the Tyne and Wear area. A further important feature is that Busways was an Employee Share Ownership Plan (ESOP) company and before the acquisition could proceed, some 1700 employee shareholders had to approve the merger. In the event 99.65% of votes were cast in favour.

Because of the strength of the brand names in the local market the group readily agreed that Busways should retain its distinctive liveries once Busways joined the group and the presentation of trading names was revised to include reference to group membership. However, during 1995 corporate livery was introduced following a locally made decision after market research showed the group livery to have a more modern image.

Also in the summer of 1994, Stagecoach announced its intention to buy a 20% share in Mainline, the former South Yorkshire PTE bus operation based on Sheffield, Doncaster and Rotherham. In October, however, the Office of Fair Trading decided to investigate this purchase the result being a requirement for Stagecoach to divest its interest. While a sale to FirstBus was agreed, an appeal against the principal of forced divestment is still pending in the Scottish courts.

The breakthrough into London bus operation was achieved at the beginning of September 1994 when the purchase of London Buses' subsidiaries East London and Selkent were announced as part of the privatisation of the capital's red bus fleets. In the case of East London this returned Stagecoach operations to that area of the city following the disposal of East Midland's Frontrunner South East in 1989 to Ensign Bus of Purfleet. Both companies run local suburban services in their respective areas of London as well as trunk routes into the central area. East London's fleet comprises 600 buses operating out of depots at Leyton, Barking, East Ham and Stratford, while Selkent's has 450 buses operating from depots at Bromley, Catford, Plumstead and Orpington.

A few weeks later saw further expansion in the urban areas of the north east of England, with the acquisition of Cleveland Transit early in the month, and along with it 51% of the share capital of formerly troubled Kingston upon Hull City Transport. The remaining 49% of Kingston upon Hull City transport owned by the ESOP was also acquired. Days later, Darlington City Transport ceased trading after Busways established a competing network of services in the town, and with it the birth of Stagecoach Darlington. In the middle of the month Hartlepool Transport joined Stagecoach in an agreed sale. Hartlepool, also based in the county of Cleveland, employed some 145 staff and operated 68 vehicles. In 1995 the management of the Darlington operation was transferred from Busways to Cleveland.

November 1994 was planned to see the return of Stagecoach into Glasgow with the introduction of Stagecoach Glasgow, a 69 vehicle quality operation, in similar fashion to the Manchester unit. However, two days before Stagecoach Glasgow was due to commence operations, Strathclyde Buses announced they would sell 20% of their shares to

Stagecoach in a similar style deal to the Mainline share exchange, and the Stagecoach Glasgow operation, staff and 18 Volvo B10Ms passed to SBL. Like the Mainline operation, this holding attracted the attention of the Monopolies and Mergers Commission who, after investigation, instructed divestment. A legal appeal against the decision is to be heard early in 1996.

Further expansion in 1995 commenced in January with the acquisition of A1 Service. This was a complex sale in that Ayrshire Bus Owners was the last Scottish co-operative bus company and was owned by nine separate members. Stagecoach took 75 vehicles with the purchase, not all constituent members sold all their vehicles and Stagecoach declined to purchase some of the most elderly vehicles. As a result of this and an urgent need to replace many of those acquired, Leyland Titans and Bristol VRs were transferred from other companies to ensure operational needs were met. During the year no less than 21 new Volvo Olympians and many modern mid-life vehicles were placed with this operation to replace the very elderly A1 fleet which had been the subject of a Traffic Commissioners hearing and warning shortly prior to the sale to Stagecoach.

Despite the small scale of this operation the purchase the Monopolies and Mergers Commission directed the Secretary of State for Trade and Industry to inquire into the purchase. Much criticism of the MMC has been voiced over this inquiry as each investigation costs the taxpayer a considerable amount of money and consumes valuable management time and energy. It was remarked at the time that often larger acquisitions by other groups were being cleared without referral. In November the report was published allowing the retention of the operation providing certain conditions on fares and service levels were adhered to.

June 1995 saw the announcement of a joint venture with Montague Private Equity to buy part of Rodoviária de Lisboa, the main operator in and around the Portuguese capital. The main towns served are Cascais, Estoril and Sintra, with the 900mm gauge Sintra tram operation included. Some 75 buses and 260 staff from two depots and associated services transfer on 1st January 1996. This purchase brings many AECs and early Volvo products including bendi-buses into the group, though many of the older examples will be replaced in the next year with the arrival of fifty new Scania single-deck buses.

In New Zealand Stagecoach acquired the operations of Cesta Travel in Wellington, which borough one additional vehicle to the fleet and Stokes Valley Coaches of Upper Hutt. The Runcimans Motors business was acquired with bus services taken into the Cityline Hutt Valley operation initially while the remaining contract and hire business has been acquired, retaining a local identity.

In July 1995 Stagecoach confirmed the acquisition of ailing Chesterfield Transport following an Extraordinary General Meeting at which 99% of Chesterfield's employees voted in favour of the take over. The Chesterfield operation was placed under East Midlands management who moved its local depot to Stonegravels depot off Sheffield Road. This acquisition too has become the subject of a Monopolies and Mergers Commission enquiry with only a few vehicles repainted and the arrival of ten much travelled B10Ms from Ribble. As we go to press a ruling is still awaited. Meanwhile integration of the operation - including a much needed vehicle renumbering - has not been able to progress.

October brought Coach and Bus 95 at which four Stagecoach buses were exhibited by various suppliers. Mercedes-Benz displayed the 800th 709D for the group, destined for Cumberland. On the Northern Counties stand was the last of 53 Volvo Olympians destined for Selkent from the 1995 order. Also in red livery was an Alexander-bodied Dennis Dart for East London but the main Stagecoach attraction was the first Volvo B10L for the group. Now in the Fife Scottish fleet, it is to be used along side new B10Ms and features the Säffle-designed body built by Alexander as its Ultra model.

The investment in new vehicles continues with some 500 new vehicles delivered within 1995. This represented a total expenditure in excess of £40 million. At Coach and Bus 95 substantial corporate orders were announced totalling over 1000 buses for delivery during 1996. In a statement Brian Souter said "The level of investment in new vehicles demonstrates our continued commitment to maintain our operating costs at the lowest possible levels, while at the same time offering our customers the highest standard of safety and comfort."

The delivery programme consists of 400 Mercedes-Benz 709Ds with Alexander AM bodywork; 240 Volvo Olympians comprising both the 9.6m and 10.3m versions of which 140 will be bodied by Northern Counties and 100 by Alexander; 100 Dennis Darts with Alexander Dash bodywork; 60 Alexander PS bodied B10Ms; 10 Plaxton Expressliners on Volvo B10M and 70 B10Ms with Plaxton Interurban bodies of which 10 will be the articulated variant. For the record these will not actually be the first articulated vehicles for the group. In the winter of 1991, Gray Coach Lines operated a Quebec-built Provost articulated coach on demonstration on its routes between Toronto, Guelph and Kitchener. In January Stagecoach inherits articulated Volvo B10Ms with the Portuguese services. In addition to the principal programme other vehicles will be added for specific needs. This includes five Dennis Lance buses with Berkhof bodywork for Ribble's use on the M10 service in Manchester and two further B10M articulated express vehicles with Jonckheere bodywork for Fife Scottish.

Stagecoach have bid for a number of British Rail franchises which if successful may well achieve their ambitions earlier than 2000! In late December 1995 Stagecoach was awarded the South West Trains (SWT) rail franchise for a seven year period. SWT operates urban and main line passenger rail services from London Waterloo to over 200 stations principally in south west London, Surrey, Hampshire and Dorset using 1022 vehicles, mainly electric multiple units and Class 159 diesel rail cars. Stagecoach's franchise plan includes the provision of dedicated bus feeder services, initially servicing the Romsey and Bordon areas and investment in improving station facilities and information.

1995 ended with the announcement that an agreement had been reached to acquire the entire issued share capital of Cambus Holdings which currently employees some 780 staff and operates around 370 buses and coaches. Cambus Holdings and its subsidiaries provide bus and coach services in Cambridge, Peterborough and Milton Keynes, and also operate coach tours throughout the UK and overseas. The acquisition gives Stagecoach a presence for the first time in Cambridgeshire and Milton Keynes areas.

As 1996 commenced the corporate livery of white with orange, red and blue stripes is now a familiar sight throughout the United Kingdom and is also highly visible in a number of countries overseas. The company strives to develop its policy of expansion within the whole sphere of transport and the stated ambition of the group is to develop into a truly global surface transport provider, with a turnover of £1 billion by the year 2000.

Of one thing we can be certain. When writing the 1997 edition there will be a lot of further developments to report. Growth and development have been one of the hallmarks of Stagecoach for the past fifteen years, and surely will be so for 1996 as well!

BLUEBIRD

Bluebird Buses Ltd, Guild Street, Aberdeen, Grampian, AB9 2DR

Depots : King Street, Aberdeen; Montgarrie Road, Alford; Golf Road, Ballater; Castleton Place, Braemar; March Road, Buckie; Stirling Road, Crieff; Pinefield, Elgin; North Road, Forres; Hanover Street, Fraserburgh; Schoolhill, Fyvie; Burnett Road, Inverness; Union Road, Macduff; Longside Road, Mintlaw; Ruthvenfield Road, Perth; St Peter Street, Peterhead; Spittalfield; Spurryhillock Ind Est, Stonehaven; Bellabeg, Strathdon and Scotsburn Road, Tain. **Outstations** : Ellon and Inverurie.

002-007

Leyland Olympian ONLXB/1R   Alexander RL   H45/32F   1981

002	SSA2X	004	SSA4X	005	SSA5X	006	SSA6X	007	SSA7X
003	SSA3X								

008	K508ESS	Leyland Olympian ON2R50G13Z4	Alexander RL	DPH43/27F	1992
009	K509ESS	Leyland Olympian ON2R50G13Z4	Alexander RL	DPH43/27F	1992
010	K510ESS	Leyland Olympian ON2R50G13Z4	Alexander RL	DPH43/27F	1992
011	K511ESS	Leyland Olympian ON2R50G13Z4	Alexander RL	DPH43/27F	1992
012	TSO12X	Leyland Olympian ONLXB/1R	Eastern Coach Works	H45/32F	1982	Ex Stagecoach, 1994
013	TSO13X	Leyland Olympian ONLXB/1R	Eastern Coach Works	H45/32F	1982	Ex Stagecoach, 1994
014	TSO14X	Leyland Olympian ONLXB/1R	Eastern Coach Works	H45/32F	1982	Ex Stagecoach, 1994
015	K515ESS	Leyland Olympian ON2R50G13Z4	Alexander RL	DPH43/27F	1992
016	TSO16X	Leyland Olympian ONLXB/1R	Eastern Coach Works	H45/32F	1982	Ex Stagecoach, 1994
017	TSO17X	Leyland Olympian ONLXB/1R	Eastern Coach Works	H45/32F	1982	Ex Stagecoach, 1994
018	K518ESS	Leyland Olympian ON2R50G13Z4	Alexander RL	DPH43/27F	1992
019	OMS910W	Leyland Olympian B45-6LXB	Eastern Coach Works	H45/32F	1981	Ex Stagecoach, 1994

020-025

Leyland Olympian ONLXB/1R   Eastern Coach Works   H45/32F   1982   Ex Stagecoach, 1994

020	TSO20X	022	9492SC	023	TSO23X	024	TSO24X	025	TSO15X
021	TSO21X								

026	L26JSA	Volvo Olympian YN2RV18Z4	Northern Counties Palatine I	DPH43/25F	1993
027	L27JSA	Volvo Olympian YN2RV18Z4	Northern Counties Palatine I	DPH43/25F	1993
028	L28JSA	Volvo Olympian YN2RV18Z4	Northern Counties Palatine I	DPH43/25F	1993
029	TSO29X	Leyland Olympian ONLXB/1R	Eastern Coach Works	H45/32F	1982	Ex Stagecoach, 1994
030	TSO30X	Leyland Olympian ONLXB/1R	Eastern Coach Works	H45/32F	1982	Ex Stagecoach, 1994
031	TSO31X	Leyland Olympian ONLXB/1R	Eastern Coach Works	H45/32F	1982	Ex Stagecoach, 1994
032	TSO32X	Leyland Olympian ONLXB/1R	Eastern Coach Works	H45/32F	1982	Ex Stagecoach, 1994

033-060

Leyland Olympian ONLXB/1R*   Alexander RL   H45/32F*   1983-85   *044 is DPH41/29F
*049 has a 5LXCT engine

033	YSO33Y	039	YSO39Y	045	A45FRS	051	B351LSO	056	B356LSO
034	YSO34Y	040	YSO40Y	046	A46FRS	052	B352LSO	057	B357LSO
035	YSO35Y	041	YSO41Y	047	A47FRS	053	B353LSO	058	B358LSO
036	YSO36Y	042	YSO42Y	048	B348LSO	054	B354LSO	059	B359LSO
037	YSO37Y	043	YSO43Y	049	B349LSO	055	B355LSO	060	B360LSO
038	YSO38Y	044	A44FRS	050	B350LSO				

061-066

Leyland Olympian ONLXB/1RV   Alexander RL   DPH43/27F   1986

061	C461SSO	063	C463SSO	064	MHS4P	065	MHS5P	066	C466SSO
062	C462SSO								

067-071

Leyland Olympian ONLXB/1RV   Alexander RL   H47/30F   1986

067	C467SSO	068	C468SSO	069	C469SSO	070	C470SSO	071	GSO1V

076	MAU146P	Bristol VRT/SL3/6LX	Eastern Coach Works	H39/31F	1976	Ex Stagecoach, 1992
082	OCY910R	Bristol VRT/SL3/501	Eastern Coach Works	H43/31F	1977	Ex East Midland, 1992

Opposite: **Bluebird operate in the Grampian Region of Scotland and retain the attractive Bluebird motif which dates back to the 1930s. Shown here are 589, M589OSO, an example of the Stagecoach standard single deck - the Alexander-bodied Volvo B10M and Olympian 003, SSA3X. Bluebird operate both Alexander and Eastern Coach Works-bodied examples of early Leyland Olympian production.** *Phillip Stephenson*

085-089

Leyland Olympian ONLXB/1RV   Alexander RL   DPH43/27F 1987

| 085 | D385XRS | 086 | D386XRS | 087 | D387XRS | 088 | D388XRS | 089 | D389XRS |

090-099

Leyland Olympian ON2R56G13Z4 Alexander RL   DPH47/27F 1991-92

| 090 | J120XHH | 092 | J122XHH | 097 | J197YSS | 098 | J198YSS | 099 | J199YSS |
| 091 | J121XHH | 096 | J196YSS | | | | | | |

100	L100JLB	Volvo Olympian YN2RV18Z4	Northern Counties Palatine I	DPH43/25F	1993		
101	L101JSA	Volvo Olympian YN2RV18Z4	Northern Counties Palatine I	DPH43/25F	1993		
102	L102JSA	Volvo Olympian YN2RV18Z4	Northern Counties Palatine I	DPH43/25F	1993		
103	FDV810V	Bristol VRT/SL3/6LXB	Eastern Coach Works	H43/31F	1980	Ex Stagecoach, 1994	
104	JAK209W	Bristol VRT/SL3/6LXB	Eastern Coach Works	H43/31F	1980	Ex Western Scottish, 1995	
105	FDV816V	Bristol VRT/SL3/6LXB	Eastern Coach Works	H43/31F	1980	Ex Stagecoach, 1994	
106	UWV608S	Bristol VRT/SL3/6LXB	Eastern Coach Works	CO43/31F	1977	Ex Stagecoach, 1991	
107	FDV819V	Bristol VRT/SL3/6LXB	Eastern Coach Works	H43/31F	1980	Ex Stagecoach, 1994	
108	UWV609S	Bristol VRT/SL3/6LXB	Eastern Coach Works	CO43/31F	1977	Ex Stagecoach, 1991	
109	FDV840V	Bristol VRT/SL3/6LXB	Eastern Coach Works	H43/31F	1980	Ex Stagecoach, 1994	
110	JAK210W	Bristol VRT/SL3/6LXB	Eastern Coach Works	H43/31F	1980	Ex Stagecoach, 1994	
111	KWA213W	Bristol VRT/SL3/6LXB	Eastern Coach Works	H43/31F	1981	Ex Western Scottish, 1995	
112	JAK212W	Bristol VRT/SL3/6LXB	Eastern Coach Works	H43/31F	1980	Ex Stagecoach, 1994	
113	HWG207W	Bristol VRT/SL3/6LXB	Eastern Coach Works	H43/31F	1980	Ex Western Scottish, 1995	
114	KWA219W	Bristol VRT/SL3/6LXC	Eastern Coach Works	H43/31F	1981	Ex Western Scottish, 1995	
115	FAO429V	Bristol VRT/SL3/6LXB	Eastern Coach Works	H43/31F	1980	Ex Western Scottish, 1995	
116	EWE205V	Bristol VRT/SL3/6LXB	Eastern Coach Works	H43/31F	1980	Ex Western Scottish, 1995	
117	KKY222W	Bristol VRT/SL3/6LXB	Eastern Coach Works	H43/31F	1981	Ex Western Scottish, 1995	
120	SAO410R	Bristol VRT/SL3/501	Eastern Coach Works	H43/31F	1977	Ex Cumberland, 1991	
122	SAO412R	Bristol VRT/SL3/501	Eastern Coach Works	H43/31F	1977	Ex Cumberland, 1991	
123	EWE202V	Bristol VRT/SL3/6LXB	Eastern Coach Works	H43/31F	1980	Ex Western Scottish, 1995	
124	KWA215W	Bristol VRT/SL3/6LXC	Eastern Coach Works	H43/31F	1981	Ex Western Scottish, 1995	
125	KWA216W	Bristol VRT/SL3/6LXC	Eastern Coach Works	H43/31F	1981	Ex Western Scottish, 1995	
126	KRM430W	Bristol VRT/SL3/6LXB	Eastern Coach Works	H43/31F	1980	Ex Western Scottish, 1995	
128	RJT155R	Bristol VRT/SL3/6LXB	Eastern Coach Works	H43/31F	1977	Ex Stagecoach, 1992	
131	RRS46R	Leyland Leopard PSU3E/4R	Duple Dominant I	C49F	1977		
132	RRS47R	Leyland Leopard PSU3E/4R	Duple Dominant I	C49F	1977		
133	RRS48R	Leyland Leopard PSU3E/4R	Duple Dominant I	C49F	1977		
134	PRA109R	Leyland Leopard PSU3C/4R	Alexander AT	C49F	1976	Ex East Midland, 1995	
135	RRS50R	Leyland Leopard PSU3E/4R	Duple Dominant I	C49F	1977		
136	PRA110R	Leyland Leopard PSU3C/4R	Alexander AT	C49F	1976	Ex East Midland, 1995	
137	PRA112R	Leyland Leopard PSU3C/4R	Alexander AT	C49F	1976	Ex East Midland, 1995	
138	RRS53R	Leyland Leopard PSU3E/4R	Duple Dominant I	C49F	1977		

139-144

Leyland Leopard PSU3E/4R   Alexander AT   DP49F 1979

| 139 | CRS60T | 141 | CRS62T | 142 | CRS63T | 143 | CRS68T | 144 | CRS69T |
| 140 | CRS61T | | | | | | | | |

145	CRS70T	Leyland Leopard PSU3E/4R	Duple Dominant I	C49F	1979	
146	CRS71T	Leyland Leopard PSU3E/4R	Duple Dominant I	C49F	1979	
147	CRS73T	Leyland Leopard PSU3E/4R	Duple Dominant I	C49F	1979	
148	CRS74T	Leyland Leopard PSU3E/4R	Duple Dominant I	C49F	1979	
149	OSJ635R	Leyland Leopard PSU3C/3R	Alexander AY	B53F	1977	Ex East Midland, 1995
150	OSJ643R	Leyland Leopard PSU3C/3R	Alexander AY	B53F	1977	Ex East Midland, 1995
151	OSJ644R	Leyland Leopard PSU3C/3R	Alexander AY	B53F	1977	Ex East Midland, 1995

152-158

Leyland Leopard PSU3E/4R   Alexander AYS   DP49F*   1980   Ex Stagecoach, 1994
*155/7 are B53F

| 152 | GSO89V | 154 | GSO91V | 156 | GSO93V | 157 | GSO94V | 158 | GSO95V |
| 153 | GSO90V | 155 | GSO92V | | | | | | |

159	KRS529V	Leyland Leopard PSU3E/4R	Duple Dominant II Express	C49F	1980	
160	KRS531V	Leyland Leopard PSU3E/4R	Duple Dominant II Express	C49F	1980	
161	KRS532V	Leyland Leopard PSU3E/4R	Duple Dominant II Express	C49F	1980	
162	OSJ634R	Leyland Leopard PSU3C/3R	Alexander AY	B53F	1977	Ex East Midland, 1995
163	JSA101V	Leyland Leopard PSU3F/4R	Alexander AT	DP49F	1980	
164	JSA102V	Leyland Leopard PSU3F/4R	Alexander AT	DP49F	1980	
165	JSA103V	Leyland Leopard PSU3F/4R	Alexander AT	DP49F	1980	
166	JSA104V	Leyland Leopard PSU3F/4R	Alexander AT	DP49F	1980	

Perthshire operations continue to use the Stagecoach name displayed in the traditional type face. Above is Northern Counties-bodied Volvo Olympian 101, L101JSA seen on the Aberfeldy and Dunkeld group of services. Below is 169, OVL473, a Leyland Leopard with Duple Dominant II Express bodywork with a healthy mid-day load as it operates the 15 service from Perth to Comrie through Crieff.

R A Smith/Phillip Stephenson

167-171

| | | Leyland Leopard PSU3G/4R | Duple Dominant II Express | C49F | 1981 | Ex Stagecoach, 1994 |

167	4585SC	168	145CLT	169	OVL473	170	LSK528	171	866NHT

No.	Reg	Chassis	Body	Type	Year	History
172	GTO798V	Leyland Leopard PSU3E/4R	Duple Dominant II Express	C53F	1980	Ex Western Scottish, 1995
173	OSJ636R	Leyland Leopard PSU3C/3R	Alexander AY	B53F	1977	Ex East Midland, 1995
188	DWF188V	Bristol VRT/SL3/6LXB	Eastern Coach Works	H43/31F	1979	Ex Stagecoach, 1994
190	DWF190V	Bristol VRT/SL3/6LXB	Eastern Coach Works	H43/31F	1979	Ex Stagecoach, 1994
191	DWF191V	Bristol VRT/SL3/6LXB	Eastern Coach Works	H43/31F	1979	Ex Stagecoach, 1994
193	DWF193V	Bristol VRT/SL3/6LXB	Eastern Coach Works	H43/31F	1979	Ex Stagecoach, 1994
213	HNE252V	Leyland Leopard PSU5C/4R	Duple Dominant II Express	C53F	1980	Ex Stagecoach, 1994
214	HNE254V	Leyland Leopard PSU5C/4R	Duple Dominant II Express	C53F	1980	Ex Stagecoach, 1994
215	JND260V	Leyland Leopard PSU5C/4R	Duple Dominant II Express	C53F	1980	Ex Stagecoach, 1994
216	XRM772Y	Leyland Leopard PSU5C/4R	Duple Dominant III	C57F	1983	Ex Hardie's Coaches, Aberchirder, 1994
217	D523KSE	Bedford YNV Venturer	Duple 320	C57F	1986	Ex Hardie's Coaches, Aberchirder, 1994
221	WFS135W	Leyland Leopard PSU3F/4R	Alexander AYS	B53F	1980	Ex Stagecoach, 1994
223	WFS137W	Leyland Leopard PSU3F/4R	Alexander AYS	B53F	1980	Ex Stagecoach, 1994
225u	G133USE	Leyland DAF 400	Leyland DAF	M16	1990	Ex Scotravel, Elgin, 1995
226u	G568UAS	Peugeot-Talbot Pullman	Dormobile	B14F	1990	Ex Scotravel, Elgin, 1995
230	D435RYS	Mercedes-Benz 609D	Scott	C24F	1987	Ex Airpark, Linwood, 1990
231	D436RYS	Mercedes-Benz 609D	Scott	C24F	1987	Ex Airpark, Linwood, 1990
233	E364YGB	Mercedes-Benz 609D	Scott	C24F	1988	Ex Airpark, Linwood, 1990
234	E842KAS	Mercedes-Benz 609D	Reeve Burgess	C23F	1988	Ex Glenlivet & District, 1990
235	E947BHS	Mercedes-Benz 609D	Scott	C24F	1988	Ex Whitelaw, Stonehouse, 1990
236	F77HAU	Mercedes-Benz 609D	Scott	C24F	1988	Ex Skills, Sheffield, 1990
237	F164XCS	Mercedes-Benz 609D	Scott	C24F	1989	Ex Clyde Coast, Ardrossan, 1990
238	F862FWB	Mercedes-Benz 609D	Whittaker	C24F	1989	Ex Metcalfe, Ferryhill, 1990
239	D322MNC	Mercedes-Benz 609D	Made-to-Measure	DP25F	1986	Ex Fife Scottish, 1994
240	B875GSG	Mercedes-Benz L608D	Northern Scottish	C24F	1984	Ex Fife Scottish, 1994
241	C901HWF	Mercedes-Benz L608D	Reeve Burgess	DP19F	1985	Ex Fife Scottish, 1994

251-292

| | | Mercedes-Benz 709D | Alexander Sprint | B25F* | 1990 | Ex Stagecoach, 1991-94 |

*279-292 are B23F

251	G251TSL	258	G258TSL	272	G272TSL	279	G279TSL	287	G287TSL
252	G252TSL	259	G259TSL	273	G273TSL	282	G282TSL	288	G288TSL
253	G253TSL	260	G260TSL	274	G274TSL	283	G283TSL	289	G289TSL
254	G254TSL	261	G261TSL	275	G275TSL	284	G284TSL	290	G290TSL
255	G255TSL	262	G262TSL	276	G276TSL	285	G285TSL	291	G291TSL
256	G256TSL	270	G270TSL	277	G277TSL	286	G286TSL	292	G292TSL
257	G257TSL	271	G271TSL	278	G278TSL				

No.	Reg	Chassis	Body	Type	Year	History
293	E713LYU	Mercedes-Benz 811D	Optare StarRider	B26F	1988	Ex Western Scottish, 1995
294	E714LYU	Mercedes-Benz 811D	Optare StarRider	B26F	1988	Ex Western Scottish, 1995
295	F169FWY	Mercedes-Benz 811D	Optare StarRider	B26F	1989	Ex Western Scottish, 1995
296	F177FWY	Mercedes-Benz 811D	Optare StarRider	B26F	1989	Ex Western Scottish, 1995
297	F180FWY	Mercedes-Benz 811D	Optare StarRider	B26F	1989	Ex Western Scottish, 1995
298	G86KUB	Mercedes-Benz 811D	Optare StarRider	B26F	1989	Ex Western Scottish, 1995
301	L301JSA	Mercedes-Benz 709D	Alexander Sprint	DP25F	1993	
302	L302JSA	Mercedes-Benz 709D	Alexander Sprint	DP25F	1993	
303	L303JSA	Mercedes-Benz 709D	Alexander Sprint	DP25F	1993	

304-314

| | | Mercedes-Benz 709D | Alexander Sprint | DP25F | 1990 | Ex Stagecoach, 1991-94 |

304	G193PAO	307	G196PAO	309	G198PAO	311	G200PAO	313	G202PAO
305	G194PAO	308	G197PAO	310	G199PAO	312	G201PAO	314	G203PAO
306	G195PAO								

315-321

| | | Mercedes-Benz 709D | Alexander Sprint | DP25F | 1993-94 | |

315	L315JSA	317	M317RSO	319	M319RSO	320	M320RSO	321	M321RSO
316	L316JSA	318	M318RSO						

No.	Reg	Chassis	Body	Type	Year	History
421	A116ESA	Leyland Tiger TRBTL11/2R	Alexander P	B52F	1983	
422	A117ESA	Leyland Tiger TRBTL11/2R	Alexander P	B52F	1983	
423	A118ESA	Leyland Tiger TRBTL11/2R	Alexander P	B52F	1983	

424-430

| | | Leyland Tiger TRBLXB/2RH | Alexander P | B52F | 1984 | |

424	A121GSA	426	A123GSA	428	A125GSA	429	A126GSA	430	A127GSA
425	A122GSA	427	A124GSA						

IT markings are used for the Inverness Traction operation with some 38 vehicles allocated to the city with Dennis Darts and Mercedes-Benz 709Ds dominating. One of the latter is 282, G282TSL, seen outside the famous Arnotts store while boarding passengers for Milton Crescent. *R A Smith*

431u	PES190Y	Leyland Tiger TRCTL11/3R	Duple Laser	C55F	1983	Ex Fife Scottish, 1994
432	PSO177W	Leyland Tiger TRCTL11/3R	Duple Dominant IV	C53F	1981	Ex Kelvin Scottish, 1989
433u	A940XGG	Leyland Tiger TRCTL11/3R	Duple Laser	C51F	1984	Ex Fife Scottish, 1994
434	A941XGG	Leyland Tiger TRCTL11/3R	Duple Laser	C51F	1984	Ex Fife Scottish, 1994
435u	A942XGG	Leyland Tiger TRCTL11/3R	Duple Laser	C51F	1984	Ex Fife Scottish, 1994

442-446

		Leyland Tiger TRCTL11/2RP	Alexander TC	C51F*	1985	*443 is C49F; 446 is C47F

442	TSV718	**443**	TSV719	**444**	TSV720	**445**	TSV721	**446**	TSV722

447	126ASV	Leyland Tiger TRBTL11/2R	Alexander TE	C51F	1983	Ex Kelvin Scottish, 1986
448	127ASV	Leyland Tiger TRBTL11/2R	Alexander TE	C51F	1983	Ex Kelvin Scottish, 1986
449	128ASV	Leyland Tiger TRBTL11/2R	Alexander TE	C51F	1983	Ex Kelvin Scottish, 1986

450-454

		Leyland Tiger TRCTL11/3RH	Alexander TC	C57F	1987	

450	D744BRS	**451**	LSK547	**452**	LSK548	**453**	147YFM	**454**	BSK756

455	HSK760	Leyland Tiger TRCLXC/2RH	Duple 320	C53F	1986	Ex Central Scottish, 1989
456	C111JCS	Leyland Tiger TRCLXC/2RH	Duple 320	C53F	1986	Ex Central Scottish, 1989
458	WAO643Y	Leyland Tiger TRCTL11/2R	Alexander TE	C47F	1983	Ex Ribble, 1994
459	A40XHE	Leyland Tiger TRCTL11/2R	Alexander TE	DP49F	1983	Ex East Midland, 1991

460-465

		Leyland Tiger TRCTL11/3R	Duple Laser	C53F	1984	Ex National Welsh, 1992

460	AAX600A	**462**	AKG232A	**463**	AAX589A	**464**	AAX601A	**465**	AKG162A
461	AAX631A								

466	NIB4138	Leyland Tiger TRCTL11/3R	Duple Laser	C51F	1984	Ex Stagecoach, 1994
467	NIB5455	Leyland Tiger TRCTL11/3R	Duple Laser	C51F	1984	Ex Stagecoach, 1994
468	A663WSU	Leyland Tiger TRBTL11/2RP	Alexander TE	DP53F	1983	Ex Kelvin Central, 1993
469	NIB5232	Leyland Tiger TRCTL11/3RH	Plaxton Paramount 3200 II	C51F	1985	Ex Stagecoach, 1994
470	NIB5233	Leyland Tiger TRCTL11/3RH	Plaxton Paramount 3200 II	C51F	1985	Ex Stagecoach, 1994

Photographed on Union Street in Aberdeen at the end of its journey from Peterhead is Interurban 532, M532RSO. This Plaxton product is used extensively within the group for Stagecoach Express services and will be joined in 1996 by ten longer versions of the Plaxton body based on the Volvo B10M articulated chassis for the Stagecoach Express operations. *Tony Wilson*

501-512   Dennis Dart 9.8SDL3017   Alexander Dash   B41F   1992

501	J501FPS	504	J504FPS	507	J507FPS	509	J509FPS	511	J511FPS
502	J502FPS	505	J505FPS	508	J508FPS	510	J510FPS	512	J512FPS
503	J503FPS	506	J506FPS						

513-522   Dennis Dart 9.8SDL3017   Alexander Dash   B40F   1993

513	K101XHG	515	K103XHG	517	K105XHG	519	K107XHG	521	K109XHG
514	K102XHG	516	K104XHG	518	K106XHG	520	K108XHG	522	K110XHG

527-544   Volvo B10M-62   Plaxton Premiére Interurban DP51F   1994

527	M527RSO	531	M531RSO	535	M535RSO	539	M539RSO	542	M542RSO
528	M528RSO	532	M532RSO	536	M536RSO	540	M540RSO	543	M543RSO
529	M529RSO	533	M533RSO	537	M537RSO	541	M541RSO	544	M544RSO
530	M530RSO	534	M534RSO	538	M538RSO				

545	1412NE	Volvo B10M-61	Van Hool Alizée	C53F	1986	Ex Hardie's Coaches, Aberchirder, 1994
546	TSV778	Volvo B10M-61	Van Hool Alizée	C53F	1986	Ex Hardie's Coaches, Aberchirder, 1994
547	TSV779	Volvo B10M-61	Van Hool Alizée	C53F	1987	Ex Rainworth Travel, 1992
548	TSV780	Volvo B10M-61	Van Hool Alizée	C53F	1987	Ex Shearings, 1991
549	TSV781	Volvo B10M-61	Van Hool Alizée	C53F	1987	Ex Shearings, 1991
550	CSU920	Volvo B10M-61	Van Hool Alizée	C53F	1987	Ex Rainworth Travel, 1992
551	CSU921	Volvo B10M-61	Van Hool Alizée	C53F	1987	Ex Shearings, 1991
552	CSU922	Volvo B10M-61	Van Hool Alizée	C53F	1987	Ex Shearings, 1991
553	CSU923	Volvo B10M-61	Van Hool Alizée	C53F	1987	Ex Shearings, 1991
554	F277WAF	Volvo B10M-61	Duple 320	C53F	1989	Ex Scotravel, Elgin, 1995
555	DDZ8844	Volvo B10M-61	Duple 320	C53F	1989	Ex Scotravel, Elgin, 1995

561-570

Volvo B10M-60 — Plaxton Premiére Interurban DP51F — 1993 — 561/70 ex Stagecoach, 1994

| 561 | K561GSA | 563 | K563GSA | 565 | K565GSA | 567 | K567GSA | 569 | K569GSA |
| 562 | K562GSA | 564 | K564GSA | 566 | K566GSA | 568 | K568GSA | 570 | K570GSA |

571-578

Volvo B10M-55 — Alexander PS — B49F — 1993 — Ex Stagecoach, 1994

| 571 | K571LTS | 573 | K573LTS | 575 | K575LTS | 577 | K577LTS | 578 | K578LTS |
| 572 | K572LTS | 574 | K574LTS | 576 | K576LTS | | | | |

579-588

Volvo B10M-60 — Plaxton Premiére Interurban DP51F — 1993

| 579 | L579JSA | 581 | L581JSA | 586 | L586JSA | 587 | L587JSA | 588 | L588JSA |
| 580 | L580JSA | 585 | L585JSA | | | | | | |

589-598

Volvo B10M-55 — Alexander PS — DP48F — 1994

| 589 | M589OSO | 591 | M591OSO | 593 | M593OSO | 595 | M595OSO | 597 | M597OSO |
| 590 | M590OSO | 592 | M592OSO | 594 | M594OSO | 596 | M596OSO | 598 | M598OSO |

No.	Reg.	Chassis	Body	Seating	Year	Notes
601	UYJ654	AEC Routemaster R2RH	Park Royal	H36/28R	1962	Ex Stagecoach, 1994
602	EDS50A	AEC Routemaster R2RH	Park Royal	H36/28R	1960	Ex Stagecoach, 1994
603	NSG636A	AEC Routemaster R2RH	Park Royal	H36/28R	1962	Ex Stagecoach, 1994
604	YTS820A	AEC Routemaster 2R2RH	Park Royal	H36/28R	1963	Ex Stagecoach, 1994
605	USK625	AEC Routemaster R2RH	Park Royal	H36/28R	1961	Ex Stagecoach, 1994
606	ALD968B	AEC Routemaster 2R2RH	Park Royal	H36/28R	1964	Ex Stagecoach, 1994
609	XSL596A	AEC Routemaster 2R2RH	Park Royal	H36/28R	1962	Ex Stagecoach, 1994
614	LDS210A	AEC Routemaster R2RH	Park Royal	H36/28R	1962	Ex Stagecoach, 1994
618	N618USS	Volvo B10M-62	Plaxton Expressliner 2	C44FT	1995	
619	N619USS	Volvo B10M-62	Plaxton Expressliner 2	C44FT	1995	
620	N620USS	Volvo B10M-62	Plaxton Expressliner 2	C44FT	1995	
621	J917LEM	Volvo B10M-61	Plaxton Paramount 3500 III	C46FT	1991	Ex Express Travel, 1994
622	J919LEM	Volvo B10M-61	Plaxton Paramount 3500 III	C46FT	1991	Ex Express Travel, 1994
623	J455FSR	Volvo B10M-61	Plaxton Paramount 3500 III	C46FT	1991	Ex Express Travel, 1994
624	J456FSR	Volvo B10M-61	Plaxton Paramount 3500 III	C46FT	1992	Ex Speedlink, 1994
651u	NMY643E	AEC Routemaster R2RH2	Park Royal	H32/24F	1967	Ex Kelvin Scottish, 1993
696	UWV605S	Bristol VRT/SL3/6LXB	Eastern Coach Works	CO43/31F	1977	Ex East Midland, 1992

Liveries: 618-24 National Express

Previous Registrations:

126ASV	BMS511Y	KRS531V	HSA97V, CSU921
127ASV	BMS513Y	KRS532V	HSA98V, CSU922
128ASV	BMS515Y	L100JLB	L110JSA
1412NE	C325DND	LDS201A	607DYE
145CLT	ORS107W, TSV719, PSO28W	LSK528	ORS109W, TSV721, PSO31W
147YFM	D439XRS	LSK547	D437XRS
4585SC	ORS106W, TSV718, PSO27W	LSK548	D438XRS
866NHT	ORS110W, TSV722, PSO32W	MHS4P	C464SSO
9492SC	TSO19X	MHS5P	C465SSO
A663WSU	A120GLS, WLT976	NIB4138	A45YAK
A940XGG	A507PST, GSU344	NIB5232	B47DWE
A941XGG	A505PST, GSU342	NIB5233	B48DWE
A942XGG	A506PST, GSU343	NIB5455	A46YAK
AAX589A	A216VWO	NSG636A	164CLT
AAX600A	A219VWO	OVL473	ORS108W, TSV720, PSO29W
AAX601A	A218VWO	PES190Y	VTY130Y, GSU341
AAX631A	A222VWO	PSO177W	BSG549W, 630DYE, WGB175W, CSU920
AKG162A	A223VWO	TSV718	B328LSA
AKG232A	A229VWO	TSV719	B329LSA
BSK/56	E640BRS	TSV720	B330LSA
CSU920	D550MVR	TSV721	B331LSA
CSU921	D551MVR	TSV722	B332LSA
CSU922	D552MVR	TSV778	C330DND
CSU923	D553MVR	TSV779	D547MVR
D744BRS	D436XRS, BSK744	TSV780	D548MVR
DDZ8844	F27LTO	TSV781	D549MVR
EDS50A	WLT560	USK625	WLT980
GSO1V	C471SSO	UYJ654	224CLT
HSK760	C110JCS	XSL596A	289CLT
KIW8504	WIA20, A930WYS	YTS820A	599CLT
KRS529V	HSA96V, CSU920		

The 1996 Stagecoach Bus Handbook

BUSWAYS

Busways Travel Services Ltd, Manors, Newcastle-upon-Tyne, NE1 2EL

Depots : Shields Road, Byker (Armstrong Galley, Blue Bus, Newcastle Busways); Unit 8, Catherine Road, Herrington Burn; Stamfordham Road, Slatyford Lane, Slatyford (Newcastle Busways); Wheatsheaf depot, North Bridge Street, Sunderland (Sunderland Busways and Favourite); Dean Road, Chichester, South Shields (Economic, South Shields).

3	ONL645X	Leyland Leopard PSU5D/4R	Plaxton Supreme V	C53F	1982	Ex Jumbulance project, 1986
4	KSU454	Leyland Tiger TRCTL11/3R	Van Hool Alizée	C50FT	1985	
5	KSU455	Leyland Tiger TRCTL11/3R	Van Hool Alizée	C50FT	1985	
6	KSU456	Leyland Tiger TRCTL11/3R	Van Hool Alizée	C53F	1985	
7	KSU457	Leyland Tiger TRCTL11/3RZ	Plaxton Paramount 3500 III	C53F	1988	
8	KSU458	Leyland Royal Tiger RT	Van Hool Alizée	C49FT	1986	
9	KSU459	Leyland Tiger TRCTL11/3RH	Van Hool Alizée	C48FT	1986	
14	644HKX	Leyland Tiger TRCTL11/3R	Plaxton Paramount 3500 II	C53F	1985	Ex Fowler, Holbeach, 1989
15	1JVK	Leyland Tiger TRCTL11/3RH	Plaxton Paramount 3500 III	C53F	1987	
16	2JVK	Leyland Tiger TRCL10/3ARZM	Plaxton Paramount 3200 III	C53F	1988	Ex Shearings, 1993
17	491JVX	Leyland Tiger TRCL10/3ARZM	Plaxton Paramount 3200 III	C53F	1988	Ex Shearings, 1993
18	552UTE	Leyland Tiger TRCL10/3ARZM	Plaxton Paramount 3200 III	C53F	1988	Ex Shearings, 1993
19	813VPU	Volvo B10M-60	Plaxton Excalibur	C46FT	1993	Ex Park's, 1993
21	HIL8426	DAF SB2305DHS585	Van Hool Alizée	C51FT	1987	Ex East Midland, 1995
22	HIL8427	DAF SB2305DHS585	Van Hool Alizée	C51FT	1988	Ex East Midland, 1995
51	A305DCU	MCW Metroliner DR130/5	MCW	CH53/16DT	1984	
60	KSU460	Volvo B10M-60	Van Hool Alizeé	C51FT	1991	Ex Park's, 1994
61	HTY139W	Leyland Leopard PSU3E/4R	Duple Dominant II Express	C49F	1980	Ex Grey-Green, 1988
62	HTY137W	Leyland Leopard PSU3E/4R	Duple Dominant II Express	C49F	1980	Ex Grey-Green, 1988
63	HTY138W	Leyland Leopard PSU3E/4R	Duple Dominant II Express	C49F	1980	Ex Grey-Green, 1988
65	TBC1X	Leyland Leopard PSU3F/4R	Plaxton Supreme IV Express	C53F	1981	Ex Nottingham, 1988
66	TBC2X	Leyland Leopard PSU3F/4R	Plaxton Supreme IV Express	C53F	1981	Ex Nottingham, 1988
71	CMJ447T	Leyland Leopard PSU3E/4R	Plaxton Supreme III Express	C53F	1979	Ex Southend, 1988
81	L81YBB	Volvo B10M-62	Plaxton Expressliner 2	C44FT	1993	
82	L82YBB	Volvo B10M-62	Plaxton Expressliner 2	C46FT	1994	
83	L83YBB	Volvo B10M-62	Plaxton Expressliner 2	C46FT	1994	
84	L84YBB	Volvo B10M-62	Plaxton Expressliner 2	C46FT	1994	
85	KSU462	Volvo B10M-60	Plaxton Excalibur	C46FT	1992	Ex Park's, 1993
86	KSU463	Volvo B10M-60	Plaxton Excalibur	C46FT	1992	Ex Park's, 1993
87	KSU464	Volvo B10M-60	Plaxton Excalibur	C46FT	1992	Ex Park's, 1993
88	M808JTY	Volvo B10M-62	Plaxton Excalibur	C44FT	1995	
90	E317BRM	MCW MetroRider MF150/36	MCW	C25F	1988	Ex Cumberland, 1995

101-125

		Leyland Lynx LX112L10ZR1S	Leyland	B49F	1988-89

101	F101HVK	106	F106HVK	111	F111HVK	116	F116HVK	121	F121HVK
102	F102HVK	107	F107HVK	112	F112HVK	117	F117HVK	122	F122HVK
103	F103HVK	108	F108HVK	113	F113HVK	118	F118HVK	123	F123HVK
104	F104HVK	109	F109HVK	114	F114HVK	119	F119HVK	124	F124HVK
105	F105HVK	110	F110HVK	115	F115HVK	120	F120HVK	125	F125HVK

126	H126ACU	Leyland Lynx LX2R11C15Z4S	Leyland	DP47F	1990
127	H127ACU	Leyland Lynx LX2R11C15Z4S	Leyland	DP47F	1990

204-223

		Leyland Atlantean AN68A/2R	Alexander AL	H49/37F	1980

204	EJR104W	209	EJR109W	212	EJR112W	215	EJR115W	219	EJR119W
205	EJR105W	210	EJR110W	213	EJR113W	217	EJR117W	222	EJR122W
207	EJR107W	211	EJR111W	214	EJR114W	218	EJR118W	223	EJR123W
208	EJR108W								

Opposite top: **Newly repainted by Busways for the National Express Air Link service to London Heathrow and Gatwick is 86, KSU463. This coach is one of three formerly with Park's that feature the Plaxton Excalibur body design. It was photographed in Leicester.** *Tony Wilson*
Opposite bottom: **During 1995 Busways decided to introduce the corporate livery to the fleet. One of the early repaints was 901, F901JRG which also carries dedicated vinyls for the MetroCentre Shuttle service.** *Tony Wilson*

247-312
Leyland Atlantean AN68A/2R   Alexander AL   H49/37F   1978

247	SCN247S	259	SCN259S	275	SCN275S	286	SCN286S	298	UVK298T
248	SCN248S	262	SCN262S	276	SCN276S	287	UVK287T	299	UVK299T
249	SCN249S	263	SCN263S	277	SCN277S	288	UVK288T	300	UVK300T
250	SCN250S	264	SCN264S	278	SCN278S	289	UVK289T	302	VCU302T
251	SCN251S	266	SCN266S	279	SCN279S	290	UVK290T	303	VCU303T
252	SCN252S	267	SCN267S	280	SCN280S	291	UVK291T	304	VCU304T
254	SCN254S	268	SCN268S	281	SCN281S	292	UVK292T	309	VCU309T
255	SCN255S	270	SCN270S	282	SCN282S	294	UVK294T	310	VCU310T
256	SCN256S	271	SCN271S	283	SCN283S	295	UVK295T	312	VCU312T
258	SCN258S	273	SCN273S	285	SCN285S	297	UVK297T		

314-363
Leyland Atlantean AN68A/2R   Alexander AL   H49/37F   1980

314	AVK134V	323	AVK143V	333	AVK153V	344	AVK164V	356	AVK176V
315	AVK135V	324	AVK144V	334	AVK154V	347	AVK167V	357	AVK177V
316	AVK136V	325	AVK145V	336	AVK156V	348	AVK168V	358	AVK178V
317	AVK137V	326	AVK146V	337	AVK157V	349	AVK169V	359	AVK179V
318	AVK138V	327	AVK147V	338	AVK158V	350	AVK170V	360	AVK180V
319	AVK139V	328	AVK148V	339	AVK159V	351	AVK171V	361	AVK181V
320	AVK140V	329	AVK149V	340	AVK160V	352	AVK172V	362	AVK182V
321	AVK141V	330	AVK150V	341	AVK161V	354	AVK174V	363	AVK183V
322	AVK142V	331	AVK151V	342	AVK162V				

421-430
Scania N113DRB   Alexander RH   H47/29F   1990

421	H421BNL	423	H423BNL	425	H425BNL	427	H427BNL	429	H429BNL
422	H422BNL	424	H424BNL	426	H426BNL	428	H428BNL	430	H430BNL

500-564
Leyland Atlantean AN68A/2R   Alexander AL   H48/33F*   1976   *500/40-4 are H48/34F

500	MVK500R	540	MVK540R	543	MVK543R	558	MVK558R	563	MVK563R
521	MVK521R	541	MVK541R	544	MVK544R	561	MVK561R	564	MVK564R
532	MVK532R	542	MVK542R	551	MVK551R				

601-665
Leyland Olympian ONLXB/1R   Alexander RH   H45/31F   1985-86

601	C601LFT	615	C615LFT	628	C628LFT	641	C641LFT	654	C654LFT
602	C602LFT	616	C616LFT	629	C629LFT	642	C642LFT	655	C655LFT
603	C603LFT	617	C617LFT	630	C630LFT	643	C643LFT	656	C656LFT
604	C604LFT	618	C618LFT	631	C631LFT	644	C644LFT	657	C657LFT
605	C605LFT	619	C619LFT	632	C632LFT	645	C645LFT	658	C658LFT
606	C606LFT	620	C620LFT	633	C633LFT	646	C646LFT	659	C659LFT
608	C608LFT	621	C621LFT	634	C634LFT	647	C647LFT	660	C660LFT
609	C609LFT	622	C622LFT	635	C635LFT	648	C648LFT	661	C661LFT
610	C610LFT	623	C623LFT	636	C636LFT	649	C649LFT	662	C662LFT
611	C611LFT	624	C624LFT	637	C637LFT	650	C650LFT	663	C663LFT
612	C612LFT	625	C625LFT	638	C638LFT	651	C651LFT	664	C664LFT
613	C613LFT	626	C626LFT	639	C639LFT	652	C652LFT	665	C665LFT
614	C614LFT	627	C627LFT	640	C640LFT	653	C653LFT		

667-676
Leyland Olympian ON2R50C13Z4   Northern Counties Palatine   H47/30F   1990-91

667	H667BNL	669	H669BNL	671	H671BNL	673	H673BNL	675	H675BNL
668	H668BNL	670	H670BNL	672	H672BNL	674	H674BNL	676	H676BNL

677-697
Leyland Olympian ONLXB/1RH   Northern Counties   H43/30F   1988   Ex London Buses, 1991

677	E901KYR	682	E909KYR	686	E914KYR	690	E919KYR	694	E923KYR
678	E905KYR	683	E910KYR	687	E915KYR	691	E920KYR	695	E924KYR
679	E906KYR	684	E911KYR	688	E917KYR	692	E921KYR	696	E925KYR
680	E907KYR	685	E912KYR	689	E918KYR	693	E922KYR	697	E927KYR
681	E908KYR								

Sunderland Busways used green relief in the livery, represented here by Olympian 663, C663LFT. The delivery of seventeen new Volvo B10Ms to the city has seen a reduction in the number of Daimler Fleetlines that remain, and also the transfer of the former London Buses Olympians from Sunderland to Newcastle. *Tony Wilson*

701-740

Volvo Olympian YN2RV18Z4   Alexander RL   H47/29F   1995

701	N701LTN	709	N709LTN	717	N717LTN	725	N725LTN	733	N733LTN
702	N702LTN	710	N710LTN	718	N718LTN	726	N726LTN	734	N734LTN
703	N703LTN	711	N711LTN	719	N719LTN	727	N727LTN	735	N735LTN
704	N704LTN	712	N712LTN	720	N720LTN	728	N728LTN	736	N736LTN
705	N705LTN	713	N713LTN	721	N721LTN	729	N729LTN	737	N737LTN
706	N706LTN	714	N714LTN	722	N722LTN	730	N730LTN	738	N738LTN
707	N707LTN	715	N715LTN	723	N723LTN	731	N731LTN	739	N739LTN
708	N708LTN	716	N716LTN	724	N724LTN	732	N732LTN	740	N740LTN

803-838

Leyland Fleetline FE30AGR   Alexander AL   H44/30F   1977

803	OCU803R	817	OCU817R	822	OCU822R	828	RCU828S	833	RCU833S
807	OCU807R	818	OCU818R	824	OCU824R	829	RCU829S	834	RCU834S
814	OCU814R	819	OCU819R	825	OCU825R	830	RCU830S	835	RCU835S
815	OCU815R	820	OCU820R	826	RCU826S	831	RCU831S	837	RCU837S
816	OCU816R	821w	OCU821R	827	RCU827S	832	RCU832S	838	RCU838S

901-920

Scania N113CRB   Alexander PS   B51F*   1988-89   *901-6 are B49F

901	F901JRG	905	F905JRG	909	F909JRG	913	F913JRG	917	F917JRG
902	F902JRG	906	F906JRG	910	F910JRG	914	F914JRG	918	F918JRG
903	F903JRG	907	F907JRG	911	F911JRG	915	F915JRG	919	F919JRG
904	F904JRG	908	F908JRG	912	F912JRG	916	F916JRG	920	F920JRG

921-926

Scania N113CRB   Alexander PS   B51F*   1989-90   *926 is B49F

921	G921TCU	923	G923TCU	924	G924TCU	925	G925TCU	926	G926TCU
922	G922TCU						

927	G113SKX	Scania N113CRB	Alexander PS	B49F	1989	Ex Scania demonstrator, 1991

Four Scania L113s operate with Busways as part of an evaluation of low floor single-deck buses. Two carry Alexander Strider bodywork while the other pair, including 951, M951DRG, carry Northern Counties Paladin bodywork. *Phillip Stephenson*

928-937

						Scania N113CRB		Alexander PS		B51F	1991

928	H428EFT	930	H430EFT	932	H432EFT	934	H434EFT	936	H436EFT
929	H429EFT	931	H431EFT	933	H433EFT	935	H435EFT	937	H437EFT

938	G108CEH	Scania N113CRB	Alexander PS	B49F	1990	Ex Stevensons, 1993

951	M951DRG	Scania L113CRL	Northern Counties Paladin	B49F	1994	
952	M952DRG	Scania L113CRL	Northern Counties Paladin	DP49F	1994	
953	M953DRG	Scania L113CRL	Alexander Strider	B51F	1994	
954	M954DRG	Scania L113CRL	Alexander Strider	B51F	1994	
1201	M201DRG	Dennis Lance 11SDA3113	Plaxton Verde	B49F	1994	
1202	M202DRG	Dennis Lance 11SDA3113	Plaxton Verde	B49F	1994	
1203	M203DRG	Dennis Lance 11SDA3113	Plaxton Verde	B49F	1994	
1204	M204DRG	Dennis Lance 11SDA3113	Optare Sigma	B47F	1994	
1218	KBB118D	Leyland Atlantean PDR1/1R	MCW	O44/34F	1966	
1227	SVK627G	Leyland Atlantean PDR1A/1R	Alexander J	O44/30F	1969	

1401-1460

						Mercedes-Benz 709D		Reeve Burgess Beaver		B20F*	1987-88	*1431/49/51/3 are B23F
												*1444 is DP22F

1401	D401TFT	1413	D413TFT	1425	E425AFT	1437	E437AFT	1449	E449AFT
1402	D402TFT	1414	D414TFT	1426	E426AFT	1438	E438AFT	1450	E450AFT
1403	D403TFT	1415	D415TFT	1427	E427AFT	1439	E439AFT	1451	E451AFT
1404	D404TFT	1416	D416TFT	1428	E428AFT	1440	E440AFT	1452	E452AFT
1405	D405TFT	1417	D417TFT	1429	E429AFT	1441	E441AFT	1453	E453AFT
1406	D406TFT	1418	D418TFT	1430	E430AFT	1442	E442AFT	1454	E454AFT
1407	D407TFT	1419	D419TFT	1431	E431AFT	1443	E443AFT	1455	E455AFT
1408	D408TFT	1420	D420TFT	1432	E432AFT	1444	E444AFT	1456	E456AFT
1409	D409TFT	1421	E421AFT	1433	E433AFT	1445	E445AFT	1457	E457AFT
1410	D410TFT	1422	E422AFT	1434	E434AFT	1446	E446AFT	1458	E458AFT
1411	D411TFT	1423	E423AFT	1435	E435AFT	1447	E447AFT	1459	E459AFT
1412	D412TFT	1424	E424AFT	1436	E436AFT	1448	E448AFT	1460	E460AFT

The 1996 Stagecoach Bus Handbook

One of the Dennis Darts now in corporate livery is 1705, K705PCN, seen here allocated to the South Shields operation. *Andrew Jarosz*

1621-1640

1621-1640		Renault-Dodge S56		Alexander AM		B25F	1987			

1621	E621BVK	1625	E625BVK	1629	E629BVK	1633	E633BVK	1637	E637BVK
1622	E622BVK	1626	E626BVK	1630	E630BVK	1634	E634BVK	1638	E638BVK
1623	E623BVK	1627	E627BVK	1631	E631BVK	1635	E635BVK	1639	E639BVK
1624	E624BVK	1628	E628BVK	1632	E632BVK	1636	E636BVK	1640	E640BVK

1642	G22CSG	Renault-Dodge S56	Reeve Burgess Beaver	B25F	1989	Ex Fife Scottish, 1994
1643	G23CSG	Renault-Dodge S56	Reeve Burgess Beaver	B25F	1989	Ex Fife Scottish, 1994
1644	E127KYW	MCW MetroRider MF150/38	MCW	B25F	1987	Ex Stagecoach Selkent, 1995
1645	E146KYW	MCW MetroRider MF150/38	MCW	B25F	1987	Ex Stagecoach Selkent, 1995
1653	F653KNL	Iveco Daily 49-10	Carlyle Dailybus 2	B23F	1989	
1658	F658KNL	Iveco Daily 49-10	Carlyle Dailybus 2	B23F	1989	
1659	F659KNL	Iveco Daily 49-10	Carlyle Dailybus 2	B23F	1989	
1661	F661KNL	Iveco Daily 49-10	Carlyle Dailybus 2	B23F	1989	

1679-1693

1679-1693	Optare MetroRider	Optare	B29F	1991-92 Ex Welcome, 1993

1679	J371BNW	1682	J374BNW	1685	J377BNW	1688	J380BNW	1691	K164FYG
1680	J372BNW	1683	J375BNW	1686	J378BNW	1689	K162FYG	1692	K165FYG
1681	J373BNW	1684	J376BNW	1687	J379BNW	1690	K163FYG	1693	K166FYG

1694-1700

1694-1700	Iveco 59.12	Dormobile Routemaker	B27F	1992 Ex Welcome, 1993

1694	K330RCN	1696	K332RCN	1698	K335RCN	1699	K336RCN	1700	K337RCN
1695	K331RCN	1697	K334RCN						

Fleet	Reg	Chassis	Body	Seating	Year	Notes
1701	J701KCU	Dennis Dart 9.8SDL3017	Plaxton Pointer	B40F	1992	
1702	J702KCU	Dennis Dart 9.8SDL3017	Plaxton Pointer	B40F	1992	

1703-1743

Dennis Dart 9.8SDL3017*   Alexander Dash   B40F   1992-93
*1723-28 are 9.8SDL3025; 1729-43 are 9.8SDL3035

1703 K703PCN	1712 K712PCN	1720 K720PCN	1728 K728PNL	1736 L736VNL
1704 K704PCN	1713 K713PCN	1721 K721PCN	1729 L729VNL	1737 L737VNL
1705 K705PCN	1714 K714PCN	1722 K722PCN	1730 L730VNL	1738 L738VNL
1706 K706PCN	1715 K715PCN	1723 K723PNL	1731 L731VNL	1739 L739VNL
1707 K707PCN	1716 K716PCN	1724 K724PNL	1732 L732VNL	1740 L740VNL
1708 K708PCN	1717 K717PCN	1725 K725PNL	1733 L733VNL	1741 L741VNL
1709 K709PCN	1718 K718PCN	1726 K726PNL	1734 L734VNL	1742 L742VNL
1710 K710PCN	1719 K719PCN	1727 K727PNL	1735 L735VNL	1743 L743VNL
1711 K711PCN				

1744-1759

Dennis Dart 9.8SDL3035   Plaxton Pointer   B40F   1993

1744 L744VNL	1748 L748VNL	1751 L751VNL	1754 L754VNL	1757 L757VNL
1745 L745VNL	1749 L749VNL	1752 L752VNL	1755 L755VNL	1758 L758VNL
1746 L746VNL	1750 L750VNL	1753 L753VNL	1756 L756VNL	1759 L759VNL

1760-1765

Dennis Dart 9.8SDL3040   Alexander Dash   B40F   1994

1760 L760ARG	1762 L762ARG	1763 L763ARG	1764 L764ARG	1765 L765ARG
1761 L761ARG				

1766-1771

Dennis Dart 9.8SDL3040   Plaxton Pointer   B40F   1994

1766 M766DRG	1768 M768DRG	1769 M769DRG	1770 M770DRG	1771 M771DRG
1767 M767DRG				

Fleet	Reg	Chassis	Body	Seating	Year	Notes
1800	RAH681F	Bristol RESL6G	Eastern Coach Works	B53F	1968	Ex Buckinghamshire RC, 1994
1801	ECU201E	Bristol RESL6L	Eastern Coach Works	B45D	1967	Ex Bickers, Coddenham, 1988
1802	TRY118H	Bristol RELL6L	Eastern Coach Works	B48F	1969	Ex Ipswich, 1988
1803	LPU452J	Bristol RELL6L	Eastern Coach Works	B53F	1971	Ex Buckinghamshire RC, 1994
1804	EHU383K	Bristol RELL6L	Eastern Coach Works	B50F	1972	Ex Buckinghamshire RC, 1994
1805	EPW516K	Bristol RELL6G	Eastern Coach Works	B53F	1972	Ex Buckinghamshire RC, 1994
1806	PVT221L	Bristol RELL6L	Eastern Coach Works	B53F	1972	Ex Buckinghamshire RC, 1994
1808	HPW522L	Bristol RELL6L	Eastern Coach Works	B53F	1972	Ex Buckinghamshire RC, 1994

1810-1816

Bristol RELL6L   Eastern Coach Works   B49F*   1972   Ex Colchester, 1988
*1810/2 are B53F

1810 YWC16L	1812 OWC720M	1814 OWC723M	1815 SWC25K	1816 SWC26K
1811 YWC18L	1813 OWC722M			

1817-1821

Bristol RESL6G   Eastern Coach Works   B43F   1975   Ex Thamesdown, 1987-88

1817 JMW166P	1818 JMW167P	1819 JMW168P	1820 JMW169P	1821 JMW170P

Fleet	Reg	Chassis	Body	Seating	Year	Notes
1822	TDL567K	Bristol RELL6G	Eastern Coach Works	B53F	1971	Ex Catch-a-Bus, 1993
1823	NKG246M	Bristol RESL6G	Eastern Coach Works	B44F	1973	Ex Buckinghamshire RC, 1994
1824u	OCK363K	Bristol RESL6G	Eastern Coach Works	B47F	1972	Ex Buckinghamshire RC, 1994
1825u	OCK369K	Bristol RESL6G	Eastern Coach Works	B47F	1972	Ex Buckinghamshire RC, 1994
1826u	KTX242L	Bristol RESL6G	Eastern Coach Works	B47F	1973	Ex Buckinghamshire RC, 1994
1832	LBN201P	Leyland Leopard PSU3C/4R	Plaxton Elite III Express	C51F	1976	Ex Southend, 1987
1833	LBN202P	Leyland Leopard PSU3C/4R	Plaxton Elite III Express	C51F	1976	Ex Southend, 1988
1847	MTE16R	Leyland Leopard PSU3D/2R	Plaxton Derwent	B48F	1976	Ex GM Buses, 1987
1863	ESU263	Leyland Tiger TRCTL11/3R	Plaxton Paramount 3500	C49FT	1984	Ex Armchair, Brentford, 1992
1864	FYX824W	Leyland Leopard PSU3E/4R	Duple Dominant II Express	C49F	1980	Ex Grey-Green, 1988
1868	AHN388T	Leyland Leopard PSU3E/4R	Plaxton Supreme IV Express	DP55F	1978	Ex Cleveland Transit, 1990
1869	AHN389T	Leyland Leopard PSU3E/4R	Plaxton Supreme IV Express	DP55F	1978	Ex Cleveland Transit, 1990
1870	AHN390T	Leyland Leopard PSU3E/4R	Plaxton Supreme IV Express	DP55F	1978	Ex Cleveland Transit, 1990
1872	CMJ450T	Leyland Leopard PSU3E/4R	Plaxton Supreme III Express	C51F	1978	Ex Southend, 1988
1876	CBB476V	Leyland Leopard PSU3F/4R	Duple Dominant I	C53F	1980	
1877	CBB477V	Leyland Leopard PSU3F/4R	Duple Dominant I	C47F	1980	
1895	OTD824R	Leyland Leopard PSU3E/4R	Plaxton Supreme III Express	C51F	1977	Ex GM Buses, 1987
1896	OTD825R	Leyland Leopard PSU3E/4R	Plaxton Supreme III Express	C51F	1977	Ex GM Buses, 1987
1901	M901DRG	Volvo B10B	Alexander Strider	B51F	1994	
1902	M902DRG	Volvo B10B	Alexander Strider	B51F	1994	

2123	SNS822W	Leyland National 2 NL116AL11/1R		B52F	1980	Ex Ribble, 1994
2126	WAO397Y	Leyland National 2 NL116HLXB/1R		B52F	1983	Ex Ribble, 1994
2128	SNS828W	Leyland National 2 NL116AL11/1R		B52F	1980	Ex Ribble, 1994

2201-2217

Volvo B10M-55 Alexander PS DP49F 1995

2201	N201LTN	2205	N205LTN	2209	N209LTN	2212	N212LTN	2215	N215LTN
2202	N202LTN	2206	N206LTN	2210	N210LTN	2213	N213LTN	2216	N216LTN
2203	N203LTN	2207	N207LTN	2211	N211LTN	2214	N214LTN	2217	N217LTN
2204	N204LTN	2208	N208LTN						

Allocations:

Armstrong   Galley: 3-9/14-22/81-8

Blue Bus Services: 61/3/5/6, 268/73/7, 302/3/12/33/57, 500/21/32/41-4/51/8,
1401-3/6/11/5/9/20/2/4/5/37/47/52, 1642/3/61/89-91, 1701/2/44-6, 1800/5/8/10/11-21/32/3/68

Favourite: 71, 262/86/8/97, 334/7/8, 540/61/4, 1444, 1634-40, 1713-5/48/70/1, 1863

Newcastle - Byker: 90, 205/64, 347/50/61, 421-30, 601-6/8-19/5/42/77-83/90-7, 701-30, 906/18-20/28/9/33-7/51-4,
1412/6/21/3/6-30/2-6/8-43/55.

Newcastle - Slatyford: 207-15/7/49/51/2/5/9/94, 310/4-30, 620-4/6-41/3-9/84-9, 901-5/7-17/21-7/30/1/2/8,
1204, 1417, 1644/5/79-88/92/3, 1802.

South Shields: 115-27, B140, 267/70/1/9/80/2/3/7/9/90/2/5/9, 300, 675/6, 731-40, 1201/2/27,
1404/5/7-9/14/18/31/45/6/8-51/3/4/6-60, 1703-12/40-3/49-59/66-9, 1801/72.

Sunderland: 101-14, 223, 650-65/7-74, 824-29/32-5/7/8, 1203/18,
1621-33/94-99, 1700/16-39/60-5, 1864, 1901/2, 2201-17

Reserve or unallocated: remainder

Previous registrations:

1JVK	F900JRG	KSU455	B105DVK
2JVK	F715ENE	KSU456	B103DVK
491JVX	F716ENE	KSU457	From new
552UTE	F717ENE	KSU458	C110PCU
644HKX	E664JAV	KSU459	C109PCU
813VPU	J423HDS	KSU460	J691LGE
A305DCU	A751CRG, KSU461	KSU462	J420HDS
ESU263	A829PPP	KSU463	J422HDS
HIL8426	D274XCX, 5516PP, D397EDX	KSU464	J424HDS
HIL8427	E666KXC	KSU465	C155LJR
HTY137W	FYX820W, KSU464	KSU466	C103DYE
HTY138W	FYX821W, KSU463	LCU112	From new
HTY139W	FYX819W, KSU460	ONL645X	MCN827X, 813VPU, ONL450X, 813VPU
KSU454	B104DVK		

The Economic operation at South Shields is to continue and will use the fleetname Stagecoach Economio, with the first of the repaints appearing during December 1995. Shown in the maroon and ivory scheme is Plaxton-bodied Dart 1752, L752VNL.
Colin Clarke

CAMBUS

Cambus Ltd, 3-5 Dukes Court, Newmarket Road, Cambridge CB5 8DY
Premier Travel Services Ltd, Kilmaine Close, Kings Hedges Road,
Cambridge, CB4 2PH
Viscount Bus and Coach Co Ltd, 351 Lincoln Road, Peterborough,
Cambridgeshire, PE1 2PG
MK Metro Ltd, Snowdon Drive, Winterhill, Milton Keynes, MK6 1AD

Depots: Cowley Road, Cambridge; Kilmaine Close, Cambridge; Wisbech Road, March; Snowdon Drive, Winterhill, Milton Keynes; Depot Road, Newmarket; and Lincoln Road, Peterborough. Outstations: Crowland; Market Deeping; Stamford and Wisbech.

01-45

Mercedes-Benz L608D Robin Hood* B20F* 1986 *29 is Dormobile(1990) and B25F

01	D101VRP	10	D110VRP	19	D119VRP	28	D128VRP	37	D137VRP
02	D102VRP	11	D111VRP	20	D120VRP	29	D129VRP	38	D138VRP
03	D103VRP	12	D112VRP	21	D121VRP	30	D130VRP	39	D139VRP
04	D104VRP	13	D113VRP	22	D122VRP	31	D131VRP	40	D140VRP
05	D105VRP	14	D114VRP	23	D123VRP	32	D132VRP	41	D141VRP
06	D106VRP	15	D115VRP	24	D124VRP	33	D133VRP	42	D142VRP
07	D107VRP	16	D116VRP	25	D125VRP	34	D134VRP	43	D143VRP
08	D108VRP	17	D117VRP	26	D126VRP	35	D135VRP	44	D144VRP
09	D109VRP	18	D118VRP	27	D127VRP	36	D136VRP	45	D145VRP

47-64

Mercedes-Benz L608D Alexander AM DP19F* 1986 *55/6/64 are B20F

47	D147VRP	48	D148VRP	55	D155VRP	56	D156VRP	64	D164VRP

66-73

Mercedes-Benz 709D Robin Hood B25F 1988

66	E66MVV	68	E68MVV	70	E70MVV	72	E72MVV	73	E73MVV
67	E67MVV	69	E69MVV	71	E71MVV				

77	D177VRP	Mercedes-Benz L608D	Dormobile (1990)	B25F	1986
81	D181VRP	Mercedes-Benz L608D	Alexander AM	B20F	1986
83	D183VRP	Mercedes-Benz L608D	Alexander AM	B20F	1986
92	D192VRP	Mercedes-Benz L608D	Alexander AM	B20F	1986

93-99

Mercedes-Benz 709D Dormobile Routemaker B29F 1989-90

93	G93ERP	96	G96ERP	97	G97ERP	98	G98NBD	99	G99NBD
94	G94ERP								

100	G100NBD	Mercedes-Benz 709D	Dormobile Routemaker	B29F	1990

155-169

Volvo B6-9M Marshall C32 B32F 1993

155	L655MFL	158	L658MFL	161	L661MFL	164	L664MFL	168	L668MFL
156	L656MFL	159	L659MFL	162	L662MFL	165	L665MFL	169	L669MFL
157	L657MFL	160	L660MFL	163	L663MFL	167	L667MFL		

201	J201JRP	Mercedes-Benz 709D	Plaxton Beaver	B27F	1991	
202	J202JRP	Mercedes-Benz 709D	Plaxton Beaver	B27F	1991	
203	J203JRP	Mercedes-Benz 709D	Plaxton Beaver	B27F	1991	
204	J204JRP	Mercedes-Benz 709D	Plaxton Beaver	B27F	1991	
304	PEX620W	Leyland National 2 NL116AL11/1R		B49F	1981	Ex Viscount, 1990
305	PEX621W	Leyland National 2 NL116AL11/1R		B49F	1981	Ex Viscount, 1990
307	UVF623X	Leyland National 2 NL116AL11/1R		B49F	1981	Ex Eastern Counties, 1984
310	F167SMT	Leyland Lynx LX112L10ZR1S	Leyland Lynx	B49F	1989	Ex Miller, Foxton, 1992
311	F168SMT	Leyland Lynx LX112L10ZR1S	Leyland Lynx	B49F	1989	Ex Miller, Foxton, 1992
312	F171SMT	Leyland Lynx LX112L10ZR1S	Leyland Lynx	B49F	1989	Ex Miller, Foxton, 1992
359	F359GKN	Mercedes-Benz 811D	Dormobile Routemaker	B29F	1989	Ex Dormobile demonstrator, 1989
389	F107NRT	Volvo B10M-61	Plaxton Paramount 3500 III	C49FT	1988	Ex Viscount, 1990
390	F108NRT	Volvo B10M-61	Plaxton Paramount 3500 III	C49FT	1988	Ex Viscount, 1990
391	HSV196	Volvo B10M-61	Plaxton Paramount 3500 III	C49FT	1988	Ex Viscount, 1990

1995 ended with the announcement that an agreement had been reached to acquire the entire issued share capital of Cambus Holdings which employed some 780 staff and operates around 370 buses and coaches. One of the coaches with Premier is 414, J448HDS, seen while operating a holiday tour.
R A Smith

400	ESU920	Scania K92CRB	Van Hool Alizée	C55F	1988	Ex Miller, Foxton, 1992
401	ESU913	Scania K92CRB	Van Hool Alizée	C53F	1988	Ex Miller, Foxton, 1992
402	H402DEG	Volvo B10M-60	Plaxton Paramount 3500 III	C51F	1990	
403	H403DEG	Volvo B10M-60	Plaxton Paramount 3500 III	C51F	1990	
404	HSV194	Volvo B10M-61	Plaxton Paramount 3500 III	C49FT	1988	Ex Wallace Arnold, 1991
405	HSV195	Volvo B10M-61	Plaxton Paramount 3500 III	C49FT	1988	Ex Wallace Arnold, 1991
406	H406GAV	Volvo B10M-60	Plaxton Paramount 3500 III	C51F	1991	
407	H407GAV	Volvo B10M-60	Plaxton Paramount 3500 III	C53F	1991	
408	J408TEW	Volvo B10M-60	Plaxton Paramount 3500 III	C53F	1992	
409	J409TEW	Volvo B10M-60	Plaxton Paramount 3500 III	C49FT	1992	
410	F947NER	Scania K112CRB	Plaxton Paramount 3500 III	C49FT	1988	Ex Miller, Foxton, 1993
411	F948NER	Scania K112CRB	Plaxton Paramount 3500 III	C49FT	1988	Ex Miller, Foxton, 1993
412	F252OFP	Volvo B10M-60	Plaxton Paramount 3500 III	C49FT	1989	On loan
413	J447HDS	Volvo B10M-60	Plaxton Premiére 350	C49FT	1992	Ex Park's, 1993
414	J448HDS	Volvo B10M-60	Plaxton Premiére 350	C49FT	1992	Ex Park's, 1993
421	K911RGE	Volvo B10M-60	Jonckheere Deauville P599	C49FT	1993	Ex Park's, 1994
422	K912RGE	Volvo B10M-60	Jonckheere Deauville P599	C49FT	1993	Ex Park's, 1994
424	K96OGA	Toyota Coaster HDB30R	Caetano Optimo II	C21F	1992	Ex Morrow, Glasgow, 1993
425	G525LWU	Volvo B10M-60	Plaxton Paramount 3500 III	C49FT	1990	Ex Wallace Arnold, 1994
426	G526LWU	Volvo B10M-60	Plaxton Paramount 3500 III	C49FT	1990	Ex Wallace Arnold, 1994
427	G527LWU	Volvo B10M-60	Plaxton Paramount 3500 III	C49FT	1990	Ex Wallace Arnold, 1994
428	K458PNR	Volvo B10M-60	Plaxton Premiére 350	C49FT	1993	Ex Supreme, Hadleigh, 1994
429	K457PNR	Volvo B10M-60	Plaxton Premiére 350	C49FT	1993	Ex Supreme, Hadleigh, 1994
430	G520LWU	Volvo B10M-60	Plaxton Paramount 3500 III	C49FT	1990	Ex Wallace Arnold, 1994

431-435		Volvo B10M-60	Plaxton Paramount 3500 III	C48FT	1991	Ex Wallace Arnold, 1994
						*431 is C49FT

431	H649UWR	432	H642UWR	433	H643UWR	434	H652UWR	435	H653UWR

437-444		Volvo B10M-60	Plaxton Premiére 350	C48FT	1992	Ex Wallace Arnold, 1994

737	J702CWT	439	J739CWT	441	J741CWT	443	J743CWT	444	J744CWT
738	J706CWT	440	J740CWT	442	J742CWT				

The striped livery style introduced during National Bus days continues in use with several operators. Using a scheme of two blues and white is the sole remaining Bristol VR in the Cambus operation with high-back seating, 741, RAH268W. *Phillip Stephenson*

445-452				Volvo B10M-62		Plaxton Expressliner II		C49FT		1995	
445	N445XVA	447	N447XVA	449	N449XVA	451	N451XVA	452	N452XVA		
446	N446XVA	448	N448XVA	450	N450XVA						

481	A681KDV	Leyland Olympian ONLXB/1R	Eastern Coach Works	H45/32F	1983	Ex Southern National, 1995
483	A683KDV	Leyland Olympian ONLXB/1R	Eastern Coach Works	H45/32F	1983	Ex Southern National, 1995
500	E500LFL	Leyland Olympian ONLXCT/1RH	Optare	DPH43/27F	1988	
501	E501LFL	Leyland Olympian ONLXCT/1RH	Optare	DPH43/27F	1988	
503	UWW3X	Leyland Olympian ONLXB/1R	Roe	H47/29F	1982	Ex West Yorkshire PTE, 1987
504	UWW4X	Leyland Olympian ONLXB/1R	Roe	H47/29F	1982	Ex West Yorkshire PTE, 1987
505	UWW8X	Leyland Olympian ONLXB/1R	Roe	H47/29F	1982	Ex West Yorkshire PTE, 1987

512-517				Leyland Olympian ONLXB/1RZ		Northern Counties		H45/30F		1989	
512	F512NJE	514	F514NJE	515	F515NJE	516	F516NJE	517	F517NJE		
513	F513NJE										

518	N518XER	Volvo Olympian YN2RV18Z4	Northern Counties Palatine	DPH45/31F	1995	
519	N519XER	Volvo Olympian YN2RV18Z4	Northern Counties Palatine	DPH45/31F	1995	
520	N520XER	Volvo Olympian YN2RV18Z4	Northern Counties Palatine	DPH45/31F	1995	
552	JAH552D	Bristol FLF6G	Eastern Coach Works	O38/32F	1966	Ex Eastern Counties, 1984
703	NAH138P	Bristol VRT/SL3/501(6LXB)	Eastern Coach Works	H43/31F	1976	Ex Eastern Counties, 1984

709-718				Bristol VRT/SL3/6LXB		Eastern Coach Works		H43/31F		1976-77 Ex Eastern Counties, 1984	
709	OPW179P	712	OPW182P	716	PEX386R	717	PVF353R	718	TEX405R		
710	OPW180P	715	WPW200S								

The 1996 Stagecoach Bus Handbook

719-729

Bristol VRT/SL3/6LXB — Eastern Coach Works — H43/31F — 1978-79 — Ex Eastern Counties, 1984
724 ex Green, Kirkintilloch, 1991

| 719 | YNG209S | 721 | YNG212S | 723 | BCL213T | 725 | DEX228T | 727 | DNG232T |
| 720 | YNG210S | 722 | YWY830S | 724 | FRP905T | 726 | DEX231T | 729 | DNG234T |

730-737

Bristol VRT/SL3/6LXB — Eastern Coach Works — H43/31F — 1979-81 — Ex York City & District, 1990

| 730 | FWR216T | 732 | FWR218T | 734 | NUM341V | 736 | SUB794W | 737 | SUB795W |
| 731 | FWR217T | 733 | JUB650V | 735 | PWY37W | | | | |

| 738 | RAH260W | Bristol VRT/SL3/6LXB | Eastern Coach Works | H43/31F | 1980 | Ex Eastern Counties, 1984 |
| 739 | URP943W | Bristol VRT/SL3/501 | Eastern Coach Works | H43/31F | 1981 | Ex United Counties, 1986 |

740-746

Bristol VRT/SL3/6LXB — Eastern Coach Works — H43/31F* — 1980-81 — Ex Eastern Counties, 1984
*741 is DPH42/24F

| 740 | RAH265W | 742 | VEX295X | 744 | VEX296X | 745 | VEX303X | 746 | VEX304X |
| 741 | RAH268W | 743 | VEX300X | | | | | | |

747	STW24W	Bristol VRT/SL3/6LXB	Eastern Coach Works	H39/31F	1981	Ex Green, Kirkintilloch, 1991
748	STW30W	Bristol VRT/SL3/6LXC	Eastern Coach Works	H39/31F	1981	Ex Green, Kirkintilloch, 1991
749	DBV28W	Bristol VRT/SL3/6LXB	Eastern Coach Works	H43/31F	1980	Ex Ribble, 1993
750	ONH927V	Bristol VRT/SL3/6LXB	Eastern Coach Works	H43/31F	1980	Ex United Counties, 1993
751	VEX298X	Bristol VRT/SL3/6LXB	Eastern Coach Works	H43/31F	1981	Ex Eastern Counties, 1984
753	VEX289X	Bristol VRT/SL3/6LXB	Eastern Coach Works	H43/31F	1981	Ex Eastern Counties, 1984
755	VEX293X	Bristol VRT/SL3/6LXB	Eastern Coach Works	H43/31F	1981	Ex Eastern Counties, 1984
761	PTT92R	Bristol VRT/SL3/6LXB	Eastern Coach Works	H43/31F	1976	Ex Red Bus, 1986
762	XDV607S	Bristol VRT/SL3/6LXB	Eastern Coach Works	H43/31F	1978	Ex Red Bus, 1986
763	YVV896S	Bristol VRT/SL3/6LXB	Eastern Coach Works	H43/31F	1978	Ex Green, Kirkintilloch, 1991
764	WWY130S	Bristol VRT/SL3/6LXB	Eastern Coach Works	H43/31F	1978	Ex Eastern Counties, 1984
899	E461TEW	Volkswagen LT55	Optare City Pacer	B25F	1987	
911	E911LVE	Volkswagen LT55	Optare City Pacer	B25F	1988	
912	E912LVE	Volkswagen LT55	Optare City Pacer	B25F	1988	
913	E913NEW	Volkswagen LT55	Optare City Pacer	B25F	1988	
922	E42RDW	Volkswagen LT55	Optare City Pacer	DP25F	1987	Ex Taff Ely, 1988
923	E43RDW	Volkswagen LT55	Optare City Pacer	DP25F	1987	Ex Taff Ely, 1988
924	E44RDW	Volkswagen LT55	Optare City Pacer	DP25F	1987	Ex Taff Ely, 1988
925	E45RDW	Volkswagen LT55	Optare City Pacer	DP25F	1987	Ex Taff Ely, 1988
926	E46RDW	Volkswagen LT55	Optare City Pacer	DP25F	1987	Ex National Welsh, 1989
927	E750VWT	Volkswagen LT55	Optare City Pacer	DP25F	1987	Ex National Welsh, 1989

960-974

Optare MetroRider — Optare — B29F — 1992-93

960	J960DWX	963	K963HUB	966	K966HUB	969	K969HUB	972	K972HUB
961	J961DWX	964	K964HUB	967	K967HUB	970	K970HUB	973	K973HUB
962	J962DWX	965	K965HUB	968	K968HUB	971	K971HUB	974	K974HUB

975-979

Optare MetroRider — Optare — B29F — 1995

| 975 | M975WWR | 976 | M976WWR | 977 | M977WWR | 978 | M978WWR | 979 | M979VWY |

990	K390TCE	Optare MetroRider	Optare	B29F	1993	
2036	C336SFL	Ford Transit 190	Carlyle	DP16F	1986	
2618	PEX618W	Leyland National 2 NL116L11/1R		B49F	1980	Ex Eastern Counties, 1984
2619	PEX619W	Leyland National 2 NL116L11/1R		B49F	1980	Ex Eastern Counties, 1984
2622	PEX622W	Leyland National 2 NL116L11/1R		B49F	1980	Ex Eastern Counties, 1984
3009	CBV9S	Bristol VRT/SL3/501(6LXB)	Eastern Coach Works	H43/31F	1977	Ex Ribble, 1993
3019	CBV19S	Bristol VRT/SL3/501(6LXB)	Eastern Coach Works	H43/31F	1977	Ex Ribble, 1993
3034	NJT34P	Bristol VRT/SL3/6LX	Eastern Coach Works	H43/31F	1976	Ex Wilts & Dorset, 1993
3136	NAH136P	Bristol VRT/SL3/6LXB	Eastern Coach Works	H43/31F	1976	Ex Eastern Counties, 1984
3137	NAH137P	Bristol VRT/SL3/6LXB(501)	Eastern Coach Works	H43/31F	1976	Ex Eastern Counties, 1984
3233	DNG233T	Bristol VRT/SL3/6LXB	Eastern Coach Works	H43/31F	1979	Ex Eastern Counties, 1984
3282	MDM282P	Bristol VRT/SL3/6LXB	Eastern Coach Works	H43/31F	1975	Ex Happy Days, Woodseaves, 1993
3307	NRU307M	Bristol VRT/SL2/6LX	Eastern Coach Works	H43/31F	1974	Ex Wilts & Dorset, 1993
3310	NRU310M	Bristol VRT/SL2/6LX	Eastern Coach Works	H43/31F	1974	Ex Wilts & Dorset, 1993
3311	NRU311M	Bristol VRT/SL2/6LX	Eastern Coach Works	H43/31F	1974	Ex Wilts & Dorset, 1993
3353	YTU353S	Bristol VRT/SL3/501	Eastern Coach Works	H43/31F	1977	Ex Happy Days, Woodseaves, 1993
3436	OUD436M	Bristol VRT/SL2/6LX	Eastern Coach Works	H43/34F	1974	Ex Western National, 1993
3441	JJT441N	Bristol VRT/SL3/6LX	Eastern Coach Works	H43/31F	1975	Ex Wilts & Dorset, 1993
3556	MEL556P	Bristol VRT/SL3/6LXB	Eastern Coach Works	H43/31F	1976	Ex Wilts & Dorset, 1993
3559	MEL559P	Bristol VRT/SL3/6LXB	Eastern Coach Works	H43/31F	1976	Ex Wilts & Dorset, 1993
3575	GNJ575N	Bristol VRT/SL2/6LX	Eastern Coach Works	H43/31F	1975	Ex Brighton & Hove, 1988

The Viscount fleet will shortly be renumbered to bring it in line with the remainder of the Cambus fleet. Currently it operates with prefix letters. Shown here is B6, F506NJE, a Leyland Olympian with Northern Counties bodywork. *Phillip Stephenson*

3711	GNG711N	Bristol VRT/SL3/6G	Eastern Coach Works	H43/31F	1975	Ex Eastern Counties, 1984
3724	LOD724P	Bristol VRT/SL3/501	Eastern Coach Works	DPH31/29F	1975	Ex Southern National, 1993
3725	LOD725P	Bristol VRT/SL3/501	Eastern Coach Works	DPH31/29F	1975	Ex Southern National, 1993
3826	URB826S	Bristol VRT/SL3/501(6LXB)	Eastern Coach Works	H43/31F	1977	Ex Trent, 1992
3937	MCL937P	Bristol VRT/SL3/6LXB	Eastern Coach Works	H43/31F	1976	Ex Eastern Counties, 1994
3942	URP942W	Bristol VRT/SL3/6LXB	Eastern Coach Works	H43/31F	1981	Ex United Counties, 1986

Viscount

B1	VEX291X	Bristol VRT/SL3/6LXB	Eastern Coach Works	DPH41/25F	1981	Ex Eastern Counties, 1984
B2	E502LFL	Leyland Olympian ONLXCT/1RH	Optare	DPH43/27F	1988	Ex Eastern Counties, 1984
B3	H473CEG	Leyland Olympian ON2R50G13Z4	Leyland	H47/31F	1990	
B4	H474CEG	Leyland Olympian ON2R50G13Z4	Leyland	H43/27F	1990	
B5	H475CEG	Leyland Olympian ON2R50G13Z4	Leyland	H47/31F	1990	

B6-B11

		Leyland Olympian ONLXB/1R	Northern Counties	H45/30F	1988

B6	F506NJE	**B8**	F508NJE	**B9**	F509NJE	**B10**	F510NJE	**B11**	F511NJE
B7	F507NJE						

B12	A561KWY	Leyland Olympian ONLXB/1R	Eastern Coach Works	H45/32F	1983	Ex Selby & District, 1995
B36	DEX227T	Bristol VRT/SL3/6LXB	Eastern Coach Works	H43/31F	1979	Ex Eastern Counties, 1984
B37	HAH237V	Bristol VRT/SL3/6LXB	Eastern Coach Works	H43/31F	1979	Ex Eastern Counties, 1984
B38	YNG208S	Bristol VRT/SL3/6LXB	Eastern Coach Works	H43/31F	1978	Ex Eastern Counties, 1984
B39	PWY39W	Bristol VRT/SL3/6LXB	Eastern Coach Works	H43/31F	1980	Ex York City & District, 1990
B40	PWY40W	Bristol VRT/SL3/6LXB	Eastern Coach Works	H43/31F	1980	Ex York City & District, 1990

B41-B52
Bristol VRT/SL3/6LXB   Eastern Coach Works   H43/31F   1977-81   Ex Eastern Counties, 1984

B41	WPW201S	**B44**	RAH264W	**B47**	KVF247V	**B49**	KVF249V	**B51**	VEX301X
B42	WPW202S	**B45**	KVF245V	**B48**	KVF248V	**B50**	KVF250V	**B52**	VEX299X
B43	VPW85S	**B46**	KVF246V						

B57	BFX570T	Bristol VRT/SL3/6LXB	Eastern Coach Works	H43/31F	1979 Ex Wilts & Dorset, 1993
B58	VAH278X	Bristol VRT/SL3/6LXB	Eastern Coach Works	H43/31F	1981 Ex Eastern Counties, 1984
B59	VAH279X	Bristol VRT/SL3/6LXB	Eastern Coach Works	H43/31F	1981 Ex Eastern Counties, 1984
B60	VAH280X	Bristol VRT/SL3/6LXB	Eastern Coach Works	H43/31F	1981 Ex Eastern Counties, 1984

B66-B73
Bristol VRT/SL3/6LXB   Eastern Coach Works   H43/31F   1979-81   Ex York City & District, 1990

B66	LWU466V	**B68**	LWU468V	**B70**	LWU470V	**B72**	SUB792W
B67	LWU467V	**B69**	FWR219T	**B71**	SUB791W	**B73**	SUB793W

B74-B80
Bristol VRT/SL3/6LXB   Eastern Coach Works   H43/31F   1981   Ex Keighley & District, 1990

B74	SUB790W	**B76**	PWY46W	**B78**	PWY48W	**B79**	PWY49W
B75	PWY45W	**B77**	PWY47W			**B80**	PWY50W

FLF453	JAH553D	Bristol FLF6G	Eastern Coach Works	H38/32F	1966 Ex Eastern Counties, 1984

S1-7
Optare MetroRider   Optare   B29F   1992-93

1	K391KUA	**3**	K393KUA	**5**	J805DWW	**6**	J806DWW	**7**	J807DWW
2	K392KUA	**4**	K975HUB						

S8	M808WWR	Optare MetroRider	Optare	B27F	1995
S9	M809WWR	Optare MetroRider	Optare	B27F	1995
S10	M810WWR	Optare MetroRider	Optare	B27F	1995

S71-S77
Iveco 59-12   Marshall C31   B25F   1992-93

S71	K171CAV	**S73**	K173CAV	**S75**	K175CAV	**S76**	K176CAV
S72	K172CAV	**S74**	K174CAV			**S77**	K177CAV

WM1	E664RVP	MCW MetroRider MF150/17	MCW	B25F	1987	On loan from West Midlands Travel
WM2	D642NOE	MCW MetroRider MF150/4	MCW	B25F	1987	On loan from West Midlands Travel
WM7	D647NOE	MCW MetroRider MF150/4	MCW	B25F	1987	On loan from West Midlands Travel
WM9	D645NOE	MCW MetroRider MF150/4	MCW	B25F	1987	On loan from West Midlands Travel
WM10	E657RVP	MCW MetroRider MF150/17	MCW	B25F	1987	On loan from West Midlands Travel
WM12	D631NOE	MCW MetroRider MF150/4	MCW	B25F	1987	On loan from West Midlands Travel
WM13	D603NOE	MCW MetroRider MF150/4	MCW	B25F	1987	On loan from West Midlands Travel
WM15	D640NOE	MCW MetroRider MF150/4	MCW	B25F	1987	On loan from West Midlands Travel
WM16	D604NOE	MCW MetroRider MF150/4	MCW	B25F	1987	On loan from West Midlands Travel
WM17	D605NOE	MCW MetroRider MF150/4	MCW	B25F	1987	On loan from West Midlands Travel
W001	D632NOE	MCW MetroRider MF150/4	MCW	B25F	1987	On loan from West Midlands Travel
W002	D648NOE	MCW MetroRider MF150/4	MCW	B25F	1987	On loan from West Midlands Travel

Milton Keynes Community Transport

CT419	K419FAV	Mercedes-Benz 709D	Marshall C19	DP18FL	1993	
CT426	K426FAV	Mercedes-Benz 709D	Marshall C19	DP18FL	1993	
CT428	K428FAV	Mercedes-Benz 709D	Marshall C19	DP18FL	1993	
CT447	C447NNV	Renault-Dodge S56	Harrops Wellfair	M16L	1986	
CT448	C448NNV	Renault-Dodge S56	Harrops Wellfair	M16L	1986	

Previous Registrations:

461TEW	E814SUM, ESU913	ESU920	F950NER	HSV195	F905UNW
ESU913	F951NER	HSV194	E904UNW	HSV196	E315OEG

For allocations of vehicles to operations and current vehicle livery varients please refer to the Eastern Bus Handbook.

CHELTENHAM & GLOUCESTER

Cheltenham & Gloucester Omnibus Company Ltd
Cheltenham District Traction Company Ltd,
Swindon & District Bus Company Ltd,
3/4 Bath Street, Cheltenham, GL50 1YE
Circle Line, Abbey Road Depot, Hempsted, Gloucester GL2 6HU

Depots : Lansdowne Ind Est, Gloucester Road, Cheltenham; Forrest Road Ind Est, Cinderford; Cirencester; London Road, Gloucester; London Road, Stroud and Eastcott Road, Swindon. **Outstation:** Love Lane, Gloucester.

101-105		Leyland Olympian ONLXB/2RZ	Alexander RL			H51/36F	1990		
101	G101AAD	**102**	G102AAD	**103**	G103AAD	**104**	G104AAD	**105**	G105AAD

106-111		Leyland Titan TNLXB/1RF	Park Royal			H47/26F	1979-80 Ex Thames Transit, 1990		
106	GNF6V	**108**	GNF8V	**109**	GNF9V	**110**	GNF10V	**111**	GNF11V

112-124		Leyland Olympian ONLXB/1R	Roe			H47/29F	1982-83 Ex Bristol, 1983		
							113 ex Yorkshire Rider, 1987		
112	JHU899X	**115**	LWS33Y	**118**	LWS36Y	**121**	LWS39Y	**123**	LWS41Y
113	UWW7X	**116**	LWS34Y	**119**	LWS37Y	**122**	LWS40Y	**124**	NTC132Y
114	JHU912X	**117**	LWS35Y	**120**	LWS38Y				

201	JOU160P	Bristol VRT/SL3/501(6LXB)	Eastern Coach Works	H43/28F	1975	Ex Bristol, 1983
202	MUA872P	Bristol VRT/SL3/6LX	Eastern Coach Works	H43/31F	1975	Ex Bristol, 1983

204-213		Bristol VRT/SL3/6LXB		Eastern Coach Works		H43/28F	1976-77 Ex Bristol, 1983		
204	MOU739R	**205**	NHU670R	**208**	NWS288R	**211**	REU309S	**213**	REU311S

214	RFB617S	Bristol VRT/SL3/6LXB	Eastern Coach Works	H43/31F	1978	Ex Bristol, 1983

215-219		Bristol VRT/SL3/6LXB		Eastern Coach Works		H43/31F*	1978 Ex Devon General, 1987		
							*215 is H43/29F		
215	XDV602S	**216**	XDV606S	**217**	VOD593S	**218**	VOD596S	**219**	VOD597S

222	TWS906T	Bristol VRT/SL3/6LXB	Eastern Coach Works	H43/28F	1979	Ex Bristol, 1983
223	TWS913T	Bristol VRT/SL3/6LXB	Eastern Coach Works	H43/28F	1979	Ex Bristol, 1983
224	TWS914T	Bristol VRT/SL3/6LXB	Eastern Coach Works	H43/28F	1979	Ex Bristol, 1983

225-231		Bristol VRT/SL3/680*	Eastern Coach Works		H43/31F	1981	Ex Bristol, 1983	
							*225-30 fitted with 6LXB engines	
225	DHW350W	**227**	EWS740W	**229**	EWS746W	**230**	EWS748W	**231** EWS751W
226	DHW352W	**228**	EWS743W					

301-313		Leyland National 11351A/1R(DAF)	B52F*			1977-79	Ex Bristol, 1983		
							*301 is B25DL/B52F		
301	467WYA	**305**	PHW989S	**307**	SAE752S	**309**	SAE754S	**311**	SAE756S
302	YFB973V	**306**	PHW988S	**308**	TAE642S	**310**	VEU231T	**312**	TAE644S
303	TAE641S								

314	YFB972V	Leyland National 11351A/1R(DAF)		B52F	1979	Ex Bristol, 1983
322w	GOL406N	Leyland National 11351/1R		B49F	1975	Ex Midland Red South, 1992
323w	HEU120N	Leyland National 11351/1R		B52F	1975	Ex Badgerline, 1991

Opposite, top: **Extended Leyland Olympian 103, G103AAD is currently the only Alexander-bodied example with Stroud Valleys names, other Olympians at Stroud having Roe bodywork.**
Opposite bottom: **The introduction of new Volvo B10Ms on service 51 from Swindon to Cheltenham and the doubling of frequency has also seen a doubling of passengers carried. Shown loading passengers outside the Corn Hall, Cirencester is 402, N402LDF, complete with Stagecoach Cirencester names.** *both, Richard Godfery*

361-375

Leyland National 2 NL116L11/1R — B52F* — 1980 — Ex Bristol, 1983
*368 B52FL (variable)

361	AAE644V	364	AAE648V	367	AAE651V	370	AAE660V	373	BHY997V
362	HIL6075	365	AAE649V	368	YJV806	371	AAE665V	374	BHY998V
363	511OHU	366	AAE650V	369	AAE659V	372	BHY996V	375	BOU6V

376	ARN892Y	Leyland National 2 NL116HLXB/1R	DP52F	1983	Ex Ribble, 1994
377	RHG880X	Leyland National 2 NL116AL11/1R	B52F	1982	Ex Ribble, 1994
378	NHH382W	Leyland National 2 NL116AL11/1R	B52F	1981	Ex Ribble, 1994
379	SHH389X	Leyland National 2 NL116AL11/1R	B52F	1982	Ex Ribble, 1994
380	RRM385X	Leyland National 2 NL116AL11/1R	B52F	1981	Ex Ribble, 1995
381	SNS825W	Leyland National 2 NL116AL11/1R	B52F	1980	Ex Ribble, 1995
382	KHH376W	Leyland National 2 NL116AL11/1R	B52F	1980	Ex Ribble, 1995
391	LFR860X	Leyland National 2 NL106AL11/1R	B44F	1981	Ex Ribble, 1995
392	LFR861X	Leyland National 2 NL106AL11/1R	B44F	1981	Ex Midland Red, 1995
393	LFR873X	Leyland National 2 NL106AL11/1R	B44F	1981	Ex Midland Red, 1995

401-409

Volvo B10M-55 — Alexander PS — DP48F — 1995

401	N401LDF	403	N403LDF	405	N405LDF	407	N407LDF	409	N409LDF
402	N402LDF	404	N404LDF	406	N406LDF	408	N408LDF		

500	VAE499T	Leyland National 10351B/1R	B44F	1978	Ex Bristol, 1983
501w	VAE501T	Leyland National 10351B/1R	B44F	1979	Ex Bristol, 1983
503	VAE507T	Leyland National 10351B/1R	B44F	1979	Ex Bristol, 1983
533	G533LWU	Volvo B10M-60	Plaxton Paramount 3500 III	C48FT	1990	Ex Wallace Arnold, 1993
534	G534LWU	Volvo B10M-60	Plaxton Paramount 3500 III	C48FT	1990	Ex Wallace Arnold, 1993
546	G546LWU	Volvo B10M-60	Plaxton Paramount 3500 III	C48FT	1990	Ex Wallace Arnold, 1993
547	G547LWU	Volvo B10M-60	Plaxton Paramount 3500 III	C48FT	1990	Ex Wallace Arnold, 1993
548	G548LWU	Volvo B10M-60	Plaxton Paramount 3500 III	C48FT	1990	Ex Wallace Arnold, 1993
601	F53RFS	MCW MetroRider MF150/98	MCW	B25F	1988	Ex Fife Scottish, 1995
602	F54RFS	MCW MetroRider MF150/98	MCW	B25F	1988	Ex Fife Scottish, 1995

621-645

Ford Transit 190 — Alexander AM — B16F — 1985

621w	C621SFH	631	C631SFH	636	C636SFH	641	C641SFH	644	C644SFH
626	C626SFH	632	C632SFH	637	C637SFH	642	C642SFH	645	C645SFH
630w	C630SFH	633	C633SFH	640	C640SFH	643	C643SFH		

649-662

Mercedes-Benz L608D — Alexander AM — B20F — 1986

649	C649XDF	652	C652XDF	655	C655XDF	658	C658XDF	661	C661XDF
650	C650XDF	653	C653XDF	656	C656XDF	659	C659XDF	662	C662XDF
651	C651XDF	654	C654XDF	657	C657XDF	660	C660XDF		

663	E663JAD	MCW MetroRider MF150/43	MCW	B25F	1987	
667	E667JAD	MCW MetroRider MF150/43	MCW	B25F	1987	
674w	E674KDG	MCW MetroRider MF150/60	MCW	B25F	1988	
676	E676KDG	MCW MetroRider MF150/61	MCW	DP25F	1988	
677	F677PDF	Mercedes-Benz 709D	PMT	B25F	1988	
678	F311DET	Mercedes-Benz 709D	Reeve Burgess Beaver	B25F	1988	Ex Reeve Burgess demonstrator, 1989

679-684

Mercedes-Benz 709D — PMT — B25F — 1989

679	G679AAD	681	G681AAD	682	G682AAD	683	G683AAD	684	G684AAD
680	G680AAD								

686-703

Mercedes-Benz 709D — Alexander Sprint — B25F — 1994

686	L686CDD	690	L690CDD	694	L694CDD	697	M697EDD	701	M701EDD
687	L687CDD	691	L691CDD	695	L695CDD	698	M698EDD	702	M702EDD
688	L688CDD	692	L692CDD	696	L696CDD	699	M699EDD	703	M703EDD
689	L689CDD	693	L693CDD						

704-717

Mercedes-Benz 709D — Alexander Sprint — B25F* — 1995 — *704 is DP25F

704	M704JDG	707	M707JDG	710	M710JDG	713	M713FMR	716	N716KAM
705	M705JDG	708	M708JDG	711	M711FMR	714	M714FMR	717	N717KAM
706	M706JDG	709	M709JDG	712	M712FMR	715	M715FMR		

Bunting adorned the streets of Cirencester when this picture of 601, F53RFS, was taken. New to Fife Scottish, 601 arrived with Cheltenham & Gloucester during 1995 and is based in Cirencester.
Robert Edworthy

Stroud Valleys replaced early Leyland Nationals with later examples from other fleets. Previously with Ribble was 381, SNS825W, a 1980 National 2 seen passing under a railway bridge at Stroud.
Richard Godfrey

The Metro name continues for many of the minibus operations. Seen in Gloucester is 707, M707JDG with Alexander Sprint bodywork. While Alexander classify all minibuses as AM-type, only the coachbuilt version is known as the Sprint. *Richard Godfrey*

801	K801OMW	Mercedes-Benz 811D	Wright NimBus	B33F	1993
802	K802OMW	Mercedes-Benz 811D	Wright NimBus	B33F	1993
803	L803XDG	Mercedes-Benz 811D	Marshall C16	B33F	1993
804	L804XDG	Mercedes-Benz 811D	Marshall C16	B33F	1993
805	L805XDG	Mercedes-Benz 811D	Marshall C16	B33F	1993
806	L806XDG	Mercedes-Benz 811D	Marshall C16	B33F	1993
807	L330CHB	Mercedes-Benz 811D	Marshall C16	B33F	1993 Ex Red & White, 1994
808	K308YKG	Mercedes-Benz 811D	Wright NimBus	B33F	1992 Ex Red & White, 1995

831-845

		Volvo B6-9.9M	Alexander Dash	B40F 1994

831	L831CDG	834	L834CDG	837	L837CDG	840	L840CDG	843	M843EMW
832	L832CDG	835	L835CDG	838	L838CDG	841	L841CDG	844	M844EMW
833	L833CDG	836	L836CDG	839	L839CDG	842	L842CDG	845	M845EMW

846	L248CCK	Volvo B6-9.9M	Alexander Dash	DP40F	1993 Ex Ribble, 1995
847	M847HDF	Volvo B6-9.9M	Alexander Dash	B40F	1994
848	L709FWO	Volvo B6-9.9M	Alexander Dash	B40F	1994 Ex Red & White, 1995
849	L710FWO	Volvo B6-9.9M	Alexander Dash	B40F	1994 Ex Red & White, 1995
850	L711FWO	Volvo B6-9.9M	Alexander Dash	B40F	1994 Ex Red & White, 1995
851	L712FWO	Volvo B6-9.9M	Alexander Dash	B40F	1994 Ex Red & White, 1995

Circle-Line:

1065	KKW65P	Leyland Leopard PSU3C/4R	Alexander AY	DP43DL	1975 Ex South Yorkshire's Transport, 1992
1102	E102OUH	Freight Rover Sherpa	Carlyle	B20F	1987 Ex Red & White, 1994
1114	NFB114R	Bristol VRT/SL3/6LXB	Eastern Coach Works	H43/27D	1976 Ex City Line, 1993
1266	LEU266P	Bristol VRT/SL3/6LXB	Eastern Coach Works	H43/27D	1976 Ex Ashby, Gloucester, 1991
1267	LEU267P	Bristol VRT/SL3/6LXB	Eastern Coach Works	H43/27D	1976 Ex Ashby, Gloucester, 1991
1289	NWS289R	Bristol VRT/SL3/6LXB	Eastern Coach Works	H43/28F	1977
1310	REU310S	Bristol VRT/SL3/6LXB	Eastern Coach Works	H43/28F	1977
1439	B439WTC	Ford Transit 190	Dormobile	B16F	1985 Ex Badgerline, 1993
1443	B443WTC	Ford Transit 190	Dormobile	B16F	1985 Ex Badgerline, 1993
1468	PPH468R	Bristol VRT/SL3/501	Eastern Coach Works	H43/31F	1977 Ex Swanbrook, Cheltenham, 1991
1469	A469TUV	Leyland Cub CU335	Wadham Stringer Vanguard	B21FL	1984 Ex LB of Wandsworth, 1992

1480	C480BFB	Ford Transit 190	Dormobile	B16F	1986	Ex Badgerline, 1993
1499	C499BFB	Ford Transit 190	Dormobile	B16F	1986	Ex Badgerline, 1993
1505	JOX505P	Leyland National 11351A/1R		B49F	1976	Ex Stagecoach Midland Red, 1995
1511	LUL511X	Leyland Cub CU335	Wadham Stringer Vanguard	B21FL	1982	Ex London Residuary Body, 1994
1515w	PEU515R	Bristol VRT/SL3/6LXB	Eastern Coach Works	H43/31F	1977	Bristol, 1983
1532	KRW532V	Volvo B58-61	Duple Dominant	C54F	1980	Ex Lloyd, Nuneaton, 1993
1545	DNE545Y	Dodge G10	Wadham Stringer	DP30CL	1983	Ex Community Routes, Hattersley, 1993
1581	D581VBV	Freight Rover Sherpa	Dormobile	B16F	1988	Ex Lane, Churchdown, 1994
1598	VOD598S	Bristol VRT/SL3/6LXB	Eastern Coach Works	H43/31F	1978	Ex Devon General, 1987
1603	NFB603R	Leyland National 11351A/1R		B52F	1977	Ex Bristol, 1983
1604	D604HTC	Iveco 79-14	Robin Hood	B30FL	1987	Ex Gloucestershire CC, 1992
1605	D605HTC	Iveco 79-14	Robin Hood	B30FL	1987	Ex Gloucestershire CC, 1992
1617	C617SFH	Ford Transit 190	Alexander AM	B16F	1985	
1639	C639SFH	Ford Transit 190	Alexander AM	B16F	1985	
1665	E665JAD	MCW MetroRider MF150	MCW	B25F	1987	
1693	C693VAD	Leyland Cub CU435	Wadham Stringer Vanguard	B32FL	1986	Ex Gloucestershire CC, 1992
1694	C694VAD	Leyland Cub CU435	Wadham Stringer Vanguard	B32FL	1986	Ex Gloucestershire CC, 1992
1696	C696VAD	Leyland Cub CU435	Wadham Stringer Vanguard	B32FL	1986	Ex Gloucestershire CC, 1992
1697	C697VAD	Leyland Cub CU435	Wadham Stringer Vanguard	B32FL	1986	Ex Gloucestershire CC, 1992
1710	SND710X	Leyland Tiger TRCTL11/3R	Plaxton Supreme V Express	C53F	1982	Ex Cumberland, 1994
1713	WLT713	Leyland Tiger TRCTL11/3RH	Duple Laser 2	C46F	1984	Ex Cumberland, 1994
1726	LHT726P	Bristol VRT/SL3/6LXB	Eastern Coach Works	H43/27D	1976	Ex City Line, 1993
1738	C738CUC	Leyland Cub CU335	Wadham Stringer	B21FL	1986	Ex LB of Wandsworth, 1992
1740	MOU740R	Bristol VRT/SL3/501(6LXB)	Eastern Coach Works	H43/27D	1975	Ex City Line, 1993
1838	LOA838X	Leyland Leopard PSU3F/4R	Willowbrook 003	C49F	1982	Ex Vanguard, Bedworth, 1995
1841	ASD841T	Seddon Pennine 7	Alexander AY	B53F	1979	Ex Stevensons, 1992
1842	OBD842P	Bristol VRT/SL3/501(6LXB)	Eastern Coach Works	H43/31F	1976	Ex United Counties, 1994
1848	BSD848T	Seddon Pennine 7	Alexander AY	B53F	1979	Ex Stevensons, 1992
1875	WBD875S	Bristol VRT/SL3/6LXB	Eastern Coach Works	H43/31F	1977	Ex United Counties, 1994
1977	DSD977V	Seddon Pennine 7	Alexander AT	C49F	1979	Ex Western Scottish, 1995
2693	PHY693S	Bristol VRT/SL3/6LXB	Eastern Coach Works	H43/27D	1977	Ex Ashby, Gloucester, 1991

Operating Units:

Circle-Line:	1065-2693.
Cheltenham District:	119, 201/2/4/5/16/25, 301/6/12/4/61/4-7/74/5/92, 404-9, 533/4/46-8, 631/3/6/7/40-3/9/50/2-4/63/7/76/83/6/9-98, 705-10.
Cirencester:	117, 211/4/5, 401-3, 601/2.
Gloucester Citybus:	114/21-3, 213/23/4, 302/3/5/7/8/10/1/22/3, 391/3, 503, 626/56-9/61/2/80-2/4/7/8/99, 701-3, 831-42/8-51.
Stroud Valleys:	103/15/8/20, 226-31, 362/3/8/76-9/81/2, 500, 621/32/44/5/51/5/60/77-9, 704, 803-8
Swindon & District:	101/2/4-6/8-13/6/24, 208/18/9/22, 309/69-73/80, 501, 674, 711-7, 801/2/43-5.

Previous Registrations:

467WYA	TAE645S	HIL6075	AAE646V	WLT713	B108HAO
511OUH	AAE647V	YJV806	AAE658V		

Circle-Line use a livery of green and white. Shown here in Cheltenham is 1977, DSD977V, a Seddon Pennine 7 with Alexander AT-type bodywork. The sphere of operation has moved westwards in recent years with much work carried out in the Forest of Dean.
Robert Edworthy

CUMBERLAND

Cumberland Motor Services, PO Box 17, Tangier Street, Whitehaven, Cumbria, CA28 7XF

Depots : Walney Road, Barrow; Willowholme Industrial Estate, Carlisle; Station Road, Kendal; and Lillyhall, Workington.
Outstations Ambleside, Appleby, Askam, Grange, Haverthwaite, Millom, Orton, Penrith, Sedbergh and Ulverston.

1-15
Mercedes-Benz 709D   Alexander Sprint   B23F   1995

1	N201UHH	4	N204UHH	7	N207UHH	10	N210UHH	13	N213UHH
2	N202UHH	5	N205UHH	8	N208UHH	11	N211UHH	14	N214UHH
3	N203UHH	6	N206UHH	9	N209UHH	12	N212UHH	15	N215UHH

35-46
Mercedes-Benz L608D   Reeve Burgess   B20F   1986-87

35	D35UAO	37	D37UAO	39	D39UAO	43	D43UAO	45	D45UAO
36	D36UAO	38	D38UAO	42	D42UAO	44	D44UAO	46	D46UAO

47-53
Mercedes-Benz 709D   Alexander Sprint   B25F   1988   51-53 ex Hampshire Bus, 1989

47	E47CHH	49	E49CHH	51	E510PVV	52	E511PVV	53	E512PVV
48	E48CHH	50	E50CHH						

54-70
Mercedes-Benz 709D   Alexander Sprint   B23F*   1990-91   55-70 ex Magicbus, 1990-91
*57-9/61-4 are B25F

54	G178PAO	58	G268TSL	61	G263TSL	64	G266TSL	67	G295TSL
55	G299TSL	59	G269TSL	62	G264TSL	65	G297TSL	68	G294TSL
56	G300TSL	60	G296TSL	63	G265TSL	66	G298TSL	70	G293TSL
57	G267TSL								

71-78
Mercedes-Benz 709D   Alexander Sprint   B25F   1993

71	K871GHH	73	K873GHH	75	K875GHH	77	K877GHH	78	K878GHH
72	K872GHH	74	K874GHH	76	K876GHH				

79-86
Mercedes-Benz 709D   Alexander Sprint   B25F   1993   Ex Ribble, 1994

79	K626UFR	81	K622UFR	83	K121XHG	85	L123DRN	86	K113XHG
80	K623UFR	82	K114XHG	84	L126DRN				

Cumberland have recently taken delivery of five Volvo B10Ms with Expressliner 2 bodywork for services between London, the north west and Scotland. Seen entering Grasmere on the early morning run south is 130, **N130VAO.** *Bill Potter*

Tourism plays an important role in the English Lake District, and Stagecoach Cumberland operate appropriate summer services. These are marketed as Lakeland Experience and consist of open-top services between Grasmere and Bowness, and services to Coniston and Borrowdale with single decks and minibuses all painted in a livery based on the old Southdown colours. Seen in Grasmere is Leyland Atlantean 1928 ERV251D. *Tony Wilson*

101	109DRM	Leyland Tiger TRCTL11/2R	Duple Laser	C50F	1984	
102	A102DAO	Leyland Tiger TRCTL11/2R	Duple Laser	C50F	1984	
103	B103HAO	Leyland Tiger TRCTL11/3RH	Duple Laser 2	C50F	1984	
105	B105HAO	Leyland Tiger TRCTL11/3RH	Duple Laser 2	C53F	1984	
106	B106HAO	Leyland Tiger TRCTL11/3RH	Duple Laser 2	C49FT	1984	
107	TCK841	Leyland Tiger TRCTL11/3RH	Duple Laser 2	C46FT	1984	
109	WLT706	Leyland Tiger TRCTL11/3RH	Plaxton Paramount 3500 II	C48FT	1986	
110	WLT824	Leyland Tiger TRCTL11/3RH	Plaxton Paramount 3500 II	C46FT	1986	
111	VRR447	Leyland Tiger TRCTL11/3RH	Plaxton Paramount 3500 II	C48FT	1985	Ex Hampshire Bus, 1988
114	PSU787	Leyland Tiger TRCTL11/3RZ	Duple Caribbean 2	C49FT	1986	Ex East Midland, 1995
120	J120AHH	Volvo B10M-60	Plaxton Expressliner	C46FT	1991	
121	J121AHH	Volvo B10M-60	Plaxton Expressliner	C46FT	1991	
125	L125NAO	Volvo B10M-62	Plaxton Expressliner 2	C46FT	1994	
126	L126NAO	Volvo B10M-62	Plaxton Expressliner 2	C46FT	1994	
127	L127NAO	Volvo B10M-62	Plaxton Expressliner 2	C46FT	1994	
128	N128VAO	Volvo B10M-62	Plaxton Expressliner 2	C44FT	1995	
129	N129VAO	Volvo B10M-62	Plaxton Expressliner 2	C44FT	1995	
130	N130VAO	Volvo B10M-62	Plaxton Expressliner 2	C44FT	1995	
131	N131VAO	Volvo B10M-62	Plaxton Expressliner 2	C44FT	1995	
132	N132VAO	Volvo B10M-62	Plaxton Expressliner 2	C44FT	1995	
153	LJC800	Volvo B10M-61	Van Hool Alizée	C48F	1982	Ex Magicbus, 1988
156	PCK335	Leyland Tiger TRCTL11/3RH	Duple Laser 2	C53F	1985	Ex Ribble, 1989
158	DSV943	Volvo B10M-61	Plaxton Paramount 3500 III	C48FT	1987	Ex Wallace Arnold, 1990
159	LJY145	Volvo B10M-61	Plaxton Paramount 3500 III	C48FT	1987	Ex Ribble, 1995
160	YDG616	Volvo B10M-61	Plaxton Paramount 3500 III	C48FT	1987	Ex Ribble, 1995
161	JPU817	Volvo B10M-61	Plaxton Paramount 3500 III	C53F	1987	Ex Wallace Arnold, 1990
162	B162WRN	Leyland Tiger TRCTL11/3RH	Duple Laser 2	C53F	1985	Ex Ribble, 1991
251	F251JRM	Leyland Lynx LX112L10ZR1	Leyland	B51F	1989	
252	F252JRM	Leyland Lynx LX112L10ZR1	Leyland	B51F	1989	
253	F253KAO	Leyland Lynx LX112L10ZR1	Leyland	B51F	1989	
254	E709MFV	Leyland Lynx LX112L10ZR1	Leyland	B51F	1988	Ex Leyland Bus, 1989
255	C544RAO	Leyland Lynx LX1126LXCTFR1 (Cummins) Leyland		B51F	1986	Ex Ribble, 1991

270-282 — Volvo B6-9.9M · Alexander Dash · B40F · 1993

270	L270LHH	272	L272LHH	274	L274LHH	276	L276JAO	282	L282JAO
271	L271LHH	273	L273LHH	275	L275JAO				

420-437 — Bristol VRT/SL3/6LXB · Eastern Coach Works · H43/31F · 1980

420	FAO420V	424	FAO424V	427	FAO427V	432	KRM432W	435	KRM435W
421	FAO421V	425	FAO425V	428	FAO428V	433	KRM433W	436	KRM436W
422	FAO422V	426	FAO426V	431	KRM431W	434	KRM434W	437	KRM437W
423	FAO423V								

505u	LUA273V	Leyland Leopard PSU3F/4R	Plaxton Supreme IV	C51F	1980	Ex Yeowart, Whitehaven, 1988	
509	ORY640	DAF SB2305DHTD585	Plaxton Paramount 3200 III	C53F	1988	Ex Yeowart, Whitehaven, 1988	
520	D520RCK	Mercedes-Benz L608D	Reeve Burgess	DP19F	1986	Ex Ribble, 1989	

525-560 — Mercedes-Benz L608D · Reeve Burgess · B20F · 1986 · Ex Ribble, 1989

525	D525RCK	529	D529RCK	531	D531RCK	534	D534RCK	559	D559RCK
528	D528RCK	530	D530RCK	533	D533RCK	558u	D558RCK	560	D560RCK

569u	LUA275V	Leyland Leopard PSU3E/4R	Plaxton Supreme IV	C51F	1980	Ex Kirkpatrick, Brigham, 1988
625u	GRM625V	Leyland Leopard PSU3F/4R	Duple Dominant II	C49F	1980	

699-788 — Volvo B10M-55 · Alexander PS · B49F* · 1992-93 · *772-788 are DP48F

699	K699ERM	717	K717DAO	735	K735DAO	754	K754DAO	771	K771DAO
700	K700DAO	718	K718DAO	736	K736DAO	755	K755DAO	772	K772DAO
701	K701DAO	719	K719DAO	737	K737DAO	756	K756DAO	773	K773DAO
702	K702DAO	720	K720DAO	738	K738DAO	757	K757DAO	774	K774DAO
703	K703DAO	721	K721DAO	739	K739DAO	758	K758DAO	775	K775DAO
704	K704ERM	722	K722DAO	740	K740DAO	759	K759DAO	776	K776DAO
705	K705DAO	723	K723DAO	741	K741DAO	760	K760DAO	777	K777DAO
706	K706DAO	724	K724DAO	742	K742DAO	761	K761DAO	778	K778DAO
707	K707DAO	725	K725DAO	743	K743DAO	762	K762DAO	779	K779DAO
708	K708DAO	726	K726DAO	744	K744DAO	763	K763DAO	780	K780DAO
709	K709DAO	727	K727DAO	745	K745DAO	764	K764DAO	781	K781DAO
710	K710DAO	728	K728DAO	746	K746DAO	765	K765DAO	783	K783DAO
711	K711DAO	729	K729DAO	748	K748DAO	766	K766DAO	784	K784DAO
712	K712DAO	730	K730DAO	749	K749DAO	767	K767DAO	785	K785DAO
713	K713DAO	731	K731DAO	750	K750DAO	768	K768DAO	786	K786DAO
714	K714DAO	732	K732DAO	751	K751DAO	769	K769DAO	787	K787DAO
715	K715DAO	733	K733DAO	752	K752DAO	770	K770DAO	788	K788DAO
716	K716DAO	734	K734DAO	753	K753DAO				

789	N789NRM	Volvo B10M-55	Alexander PS	DP48F	1995	
790	N790NRM	Volvo B10M-55	Alexander PS	DP48F	1995	
810	TRN810V	Leyland National 10351B/1R		B44F	1979	Ex Ribble, 1986
1001	URM801Y	Leyland Olympian ONLXB/1R	Eastern Coach Works	DPH45/30F	1982	
1002	URM802Y	Leyland Olympian ONLXB/1R	Eastern Coach Works	H45/32F	1982	

1003-1011 — Leyland Olympian ONLXB/2RZ · Alexander RL · H51/36F · 1988

1003	F803FAO	1005	F805FAO	1007	F807FAO	1009	F809FAO	1011	F811FAO
1004	F804FAO	1006	F806FAO	1008	F808FAO	1010	F810FAO		

1012-1019 — Leyland Olympian ON2R56G13Z4 · Alexander RL · H51/34F · 1990

1012	H112SAO	1014	H114SAO	1016	H116SAO	1018	H118SAO	1019	H119SAO
1013	H113SAO	1015	H115SAO	1017	H117SAO				

Opposite, top: **Penrith is an outstation of Carlisle and normally home for the five Leyland Lynx in the Cumberland fleet. These include two of the prototype examples, more details of which can be found in the recently published Leyland Lynx Handbook. Shown here is 253, F253KAO.** *Richard Godfrey*
Opposite, bottom: **The majority of the original order for Alexander-bodied Volvo B10Ms were placed in service by Cumberland who replaced almost all of their Leyland Nationals as a result. Seen on Carlisle city service is 733, K733DAO.** *Richard Godfrey*

1020-1027 Leyland Olympian ON2R56G13Z4 Alexander RL   DPH47/27F 1991

| 1020 | J120AAO | 1022 | J122AAO | 1024 | J124XHH | 1026 | J126XHH | 1027 | J127XHH |
| 1021 | J121AAO | 1023 | J123XHH | 1025 | J125XHH | | | | |

1028-1035 Leyland Olympian ON2R50G13Z4 Alexander RL   DPH43/27F 1992

| 1028 | K128DAO | 1030 | K130DAO | 1032 | K132DAO | 1034 | K134DAO | 1035 | K135DAO |
| 1029 | K129DAO | 1031 | K131DAO | 1033 | K133DAO | | | | |

1090	C382SAO	Leyland Olympian ONLXB/1RV	Alexander RL	H47/30F	1986	Ex Bluebird, 1991
1091	C383SAO	Leyland Olympian ONLXB/1RV	Alexander RL	H47/30F	1986	Ex Bluebird, 1991
1092	D384XAO	Leyland Olympian ONLXB/1RV	Alexander RL	H47/30F	1987	Ex Bluebird, 1991
1093	D380XRS	Leyland Olympian ONLXB/1RV	Alexander RL	H47/30F	1987	Ex Bluebird, 1992
1094	D381XRS	Leyland Olympian ONLXB/1RV	Alexander RL	H47/30F	1987	Ex Bluebird, 1992
1103	KRN103T	Leyland Leopard PSU3E/4R	Duple Dominant II	C47F	1978	Ex Ribble, 1989
1105	KRN105T	Leyland Leopard PSU3E/4R	Duple Dominant II	C47F	1978	Ex Ribble, 1989
1113	KRN113T	Leyland Leopard PSU3E/4R	Duple Dominant II	C47F	1979	Ex Ribble, 1989
1119	KRN119T	Leyland Leopard PSU3E/4R	Duple Dominant II	C47F	1979	Ex Ribble, 1986
1151	B151WRN	Leyland Tiger TRCTL11/2RH	Duple Laser 2	C49F	1985	Ex Ribble, 1991
1153	B153WRN	Leyland Tiger TRCTL11/2RH	Duple Laser 2	C49F	1985	Ex Ribble, 1991
1154	B154WRN	Leyland Tiger TRCTL11/2RH	Duple Laser 2	C49F	1985	Ex Ribble, 1991
1155	B43MAO	Leyland Tiger TRCTL11/3RH	Duple Laser 2	C53F	1985	Ex Ribble, 1991
1162	WLT380	Volvo B10M-61	Plaxton Paramount 3500 II	C48F	1986	Ex Ribble, 1994
1175	MRJ275W	Leyland Leopard PSU5D/4R	Plaxton Supreme IV	C50F	1981	Ex Ribble, 1989
1199	FDV799V	Leyland Leopard PSU3E/4R	Plaxton Supreme IV Express	C49F	1980	Ex Ribble, 1989
1201	F201FHH	Leyland Olympian ONLXCT/3RZ	Alexander RL	DPH55/41F	1989	
1202	F202FHH	Leyland Olympian ONLXCT/3RZ	Alexander RL	DPH55/41F	1989	
1253	HNE253V	Leyland Leopard PSU5C/4R	Duple Dominant II	C53F	1980	Ex Ribble, 1989
1928	ERV251D	Leyland Atlantean PDR1/1 MkII	Metro Cammell	O43/31F	1966	Ex Southdown, 1991
2002	CBV2S	Bristol VRT/SL3/501 (6LXB)	Eastern Coach Works	O43/31F	1977	Ex Ribble, 1986
2024	DBV24W	Bristol VRT/SL3/6LXB	Eastern Coach Works	H43/31F	1980	Ex Ribble, 1986
2032	DBV32W	Bristol VRT/SL3/6LXB	Eastern Coach Works	H43/31F	1980	Ex Ribble, 1986
2035	UWV610S	Bristol VRT/SL3/6LXB	Eastern Coach Works	O43/31F	1977	Ex Southdown, 1990
2036	UWV612S	Bristol VRT/SL3/6LXB	Eastern Coach Works	O43/31F	1977	Ex Southdown, 1990
2037	UWV618S	Bristol VRT/SL3/6LXB	Eastern Coach Works	O43/31F	1978	Ex Southdown, 1990
2038	UWV620S	Bristol VRT/SL3/6LXB	Eastern Coach Works	O43/31F	1978	Ex Southdown, 1990
2075	XRR175S	Bristol VRT/SL3/6LXB	Eastern Coach Works	O43/31F	1980	Ex Ribble, 1995
2076	UWV622S	Bristol VRT/SL3/6LXB	Eastern Coach Works	O43/31F	1980	Ex Ribble, 1996
2134	DBV134Y	Leyland Olympian ONLXB/1R	Eastern Coach Works	H45/32F	1983	Ex Ribble, 1989
2175	C175ECK	Leyland Olympian ONLXB/1R	Eastern Coach Works	DPH42/30F	1985	Ex Ribble, 1989
2176	C176ECK	Leyland Olympian ONLXB/1R	Eastern Coach Works	DPH42/30F	1985	Ex Ribble, 1989
2177	C177ECK	Leyland Olympian ONLXB/1R	Eastern Coach Works	DPH42/30F	1986	Ex Ribble, 1989

Previous Registrations:

109DRM	A101DAO	LJY145	D205LWX
B43MAO	B155WRN, PCK335	ORY640	E986AHH
C382SAO	C473SSO, GSO3V	PCK335	B156WRN
C383SAO	C474SSO, GSO4V	PSU787	C495LJV
D384XAO	D375XRS, GSO5V	TCK841	B107HAO
D560RCK	D561RCK	VRR447	B180RLJ
DSV943	D203LWX	WLT380	C105DWR
E709MFV	E709MFV, BMN88G	WLT706	C109OHH
JPU817	D207LWX	WLT824	C110OHH
LJC800	From new	YDG616	D206LWX

Livery variations:
Coachline: 109/11/4, 153/8/60/1, 1153.
Lakeland Experience: 276/82, 520/58/60, 810, 1928, 2002/35-8/75/6.
National Express: 120/1/5-32.

Named vehicles: 520 *William Wordsworth*, 558 *John Ruskin*, 560 *Beatrix Potter*.

EAST LONDON

East London Bus & Coach Company Ltd, 16-20 Clements Road, Ilford,
Essex, IG1 1BA

Depots : Longbridge Road, Barking; Fairfield Road, Bow; High Road, Leyton; North Street, Romford; Waterden Road, Stratford and Redclyffe Road, Upton Park.

| **DA10** | G684KNW | DAF SB220LC550 | | Optare Delta | | B36D | 1989 | Ex London Buses, 1994 |

DA11-35

DAF SB220LC550 — Optare Delta — B40D — 1992-93 Ex London Buses, 1994

11	J711CYG	16	J716CYG	21	J721CYG	26	J726CYG	31	K631HWX
12	J712CYG	17	J717CYG	22	J722CYG	27	J727CYG	32	K632HWX
13	J713CYG	18	J718CYG	23	J723CYG	28	J728CYG	33	K633HWX
14	J714CYG	19	J719CYG	24	J724CYG	29	J729CYG	34	K634HWX
15	J715CYG	20	J720CYG	25	J725CYG	30	K630HWX	35	K635HWX

DAL1-27

Dennis Dart 9.8SDL3054 — Alexander Dash — B36F — 1995

1	N301AMC	7	N307AMC	13	N313AMC	18	N318AMC	23	N323AMC
2	N302AMC	8	N308AMC	14	N314AMC	19	N319AMC	24	N324AMC
3	N303AMC	9	N309AMC	15	N315AMC	20	N320AMC	25	N325AMC
4	N304AMC	10	N310AMC	16	N316AMC	21	N321AMC	26	N326AMC
5	N305AMC	11	N311AMC	17	N317AMC	22	N322AMC	27	N327AMC
6	N306AMC	12	N312AMC						

DRL109-138

Dennis Dart 9SDL3024 — Plaxton Pointer — B34F — 1993 Ex London Buses, 1994

109	K109SRH	115	K115SRH	121	K121SRH	127	K127SRH	133	K133SRH
110	K110SRH	116	K116SRH	122	K122SRH	128	K128SRH	134	K134SRH
111	K211SRH	117	K117SRH	123	K123SRH	129	K129SRH	135	K135SRH
112	K112SRH	118	K118SRH	124	K124SRH	130	K130SRH	136	L136VRH
113	K113SRH	119	K119SRH	125	K125SRH	131	K131SRH	137	L137VRH
114	K114SRH	120	K120SRH	126	K126SRH	132	K132SRH	138	L138VRH

DRL139-146

Dennis Dart 9SDL3034 — Plaxton Pointer — B34F — 1993 Ex London Buses, 1994

139	L139VRH	141	L141VRH	143	L143VRH	145	L145VRH	146	L146VRH
140	L140VRH	142	L142VRH	144	L144VRH				

During October 1995 DA25, J725CYG, is seen wearing the now-standard all red livery in Ilford. Within the group the DAF-based Optare Delta can be found only with East London and Stagecoach South in both cases the vehicles were acquired with the fleets.
Richard Godfrey

DWL15-26

Dennis Dart 9SDL3016 | Wright Handy-bus | B35F | 1993 | Ex London Buses, 1994

15	NDZ3015	18	NDZ3018	21	NDZ3021	23	NDZ3023	25	NDZ3025
16	NDZ3016	19	NDZ3019	22	NDZ3022	24	NDZ3024	26	NDZ3026
17	NDZ3017	20	NDZ3020								

DW133-159

Dennis Dart 8.5SDL3015 | Wright Handy-bus | B29F | 1993 | Ex London Buses, 1994

133	NDZ3133	139	NDZ3139	145	NDZ3145	150	NDZ3150	155	NDZ3155
134	NDZ3134	140	NDZ3140	146	NDZ3146	151	NDZ3151	156	NDZ3156
135	NDZ3135	141	NDZ3141	147	NDZ3147	152	NDZ3152	157	NDZ3157
136	NDZ3136	142	NDZ3142	148	NDZ3148	153	NDZ3153	158	NDZ3158
137	NDZ3137	143	NDZ3143	149	NDZ3149	154	NDZ3154	159	NDZ3159
138	NDZ3138	144	NDZ3144								

LA1-16

Dennis Lance 11SDA3101 | Alexander PS | B39D | 1992 | Ex Selkent, 1995

1	J101WSC	5	J105WSC	8	J108WSC	11	J411WSC	14	J114WSC
2	J102WSC	6	J106WSC	9	J109WSC	12	J112WSC	15	J115WSC
3	J103WSC	7	J107WSC	10	J110WSC	13	J113WSC	16	J116WSC
4	J104WSC								

MR16	D476PON	MCW MetroRider MF150/14	MCW	B23F	1987	Ex London Buses, 1994
RMA5	NMY635E	AEC Routemaster R2RH2	Park Royal	H32/24F	1967	Ex London Buses, 1994
RMA8	NMY640E	AEC Routemaster R2RH2	Park Royal	H32/24F	1967	Ex London Buses, 1994
RM613	WLT613	AEC Routemaster R2RH	Park Royal	H36/28R	1960	Ex London Buses, 1994
RML886	WLT886	AEC Routemaster R2RH1(C)	Park Royal	H36/28R	1961	Ex London Buses, 1994
RML890	XFF814	AEC Routemaster R2RH1(C)	Park Royal	H40/32R	1961	Ex London Buses, 1994
RML898	XFF813	AEC Routemaster R2RH1	Park Royal	H40/32R	1961	Ex London Buses, 1994
RMC1456	LFF875	AEC Routemaster R2RH	Park Royal	H32/25RD	1962	Ex London Buses, 1994
RMC1461	461CLT	AEC Routemaster R2RH	Park Royal	H32/25RD	1962	Ex London Buses, 1994
RMC1485	485CLT	AEC Routemaster R2RH	Park Royal	H32/25RD	1962	Ex London Buses, 1994
RM1527	527CLT	AEC Routemaster 2R2RH	Park Royal	H36/28R	1963	Ex London Buses, 1994

RML2272-2592

AEC Routemaster R2RH1 | Park Royal | H40/32R | 1965-66 | Ex London Buses, 1994
2272/86/311/445/456/495-581 have Cummins engines

2272	CUV272C	2399	JJD399D	2444	JJD444D	2470	JJD470D	2497	JJD497D
2286	CUV286C	2402	JJD402D	2445	JJD445D	2481	JJD481D	2541	JJD541D
2300	CUV300C	2415	JJD415D	2450	JJD450D	2488	JJD488D	2550	JJD550D
2303	CUV303C	2429	JJD429D	2451	JJD451D	2493	JJD493D	2565	JJD565D
2311	CUV311C	2435	JJD435D	2456	JJD456D	2495	JJD495D	2581	JJD581D
2392	JJD392D	2437	JJD437D	2462	JJD462D	2496	JJD496D	2592	JJD592D

RML2607-2760

AEC Routemaster R2RH1 | Park Royal | H40/32R | 1967-68 | Ex London Buses, 1994
2610/6/39-42/61/70/1/96/705/23/43/8 have Cummins engines

2607	NML607E	2641	NML641E	2665	SMK665F	2705	SMK705F	2743	SMK743F
2610	NML610E	2642	NML642E	2670	SMK670F	2709	SMK709F	2748	SMK748F
2616	NML616E	2657	NML657E	2671	SMK671F	2723	SMK723F	2749	SMK749F
2624	NML624E	2661	SMK661F	2696	SMK696F	2738	SMK738F	2760	SMK760F
2639	NML639E								

S22-29

Scania N113DRB | Alexander RH | H47/31F | 1991 | Ex London Buses, 1994

22	J822HMC	24	J824HMC	26	J826HMC	28	J828HMC	29	J829HMC
23	J823HMC	25	J825HMC	27	J827HMC						

S30	J230XKY	Scania N113DRB	Northern Counties Palatine	H47/33F	1991	Ex London Buses, 1994
S31	J231XKY	Scania N113DRB	Northern Counties Palatine	H47/33F	1991	Ex London Buses, 1994

Opposite: **After a period using loaned Volvo B10Ms for the 247 service, East London received new Dennis Darts during 1995. Seen at Romford station is DAL3, N303AMC complete with East London Hoppa names. Stratford bus station is the location for this picture of Scania S22, J822HMC. Eight of the fifty operated carry Alexander bodywork, the remainder feature Northern Counties Palatine bodies.** *Tony Wilson/Malc McDonald*

RMC1461, 461CLT, carries traditional Green Line livery as seen in this picture taken during an enthusiasts event. Special purpose vehicles are retained within the Stagecoach group where they can be justified, others being donated or loaned to recognised establishments for continued preservation.
Phillip Stephenson

S32-71

		Scania N113DRB		Northern Counties Palatine		H41/25D		1991-92 Ex London Buses, 1994		

32	J132HMT	40	J140HMT	48	K848LMK	56	K856LMK	64	K864LMK
33	J133HMT	41	J141HMT	49	K849LMK	57	K857LMK	65	K865LMK
34	J134HMT	42	J142HMT	50	K850LMK	58	K858LMK	66	K866LMK
35	J135HMT	43	J143HMT	51	K851LMK	59	K859LMK	67	K867LMK
36	J136HMT	44	J144HMT	52	K852LMK	60	K860LMK	68	K868LMK
37	J137HMT	45	J145HMT	53	K853LMK	61	K861LMK	69	K869LMK
38	J138HMT	46	K846LMK	54	K854LMK	62	K862LMK	70	K870LMK
39	J139HMT	47	K847LMK	55	K855LMK	63	K863LMK	71	K871LMK

SLW15-30

		Scania N113CRL		Wright Pathfinder 320		B37D		1994		

15	RDZ6115	19	RDZ6119	22	RDZ6122	25	RDZ6125	28	RDZ6128
16	RDZ6116	20	RDZ6120	23	RDZ6123	26	RDZ6126	29	RDZ6129
17	RDZ6117	21	RDZ6121	24	RDZ6124	27	RDZ6127	30	RDZ6130
18	RDZ6118								

SP2	K302FYG	DAF DB250WB505	Optare Spectra	H44/23D	1992	Ex London Buses, 1994
SR1	E155CGJ	Mercedes-Benz 811D	Optare StarRider	B26F	1988	Ex London Buses, 1994
SR2	E712LYU	Mercedes-Benz 811D	Optare StarRider	B26F	1988	Ex London Buses, 1994

The East London Line all-stations replacement bus service between Whitechapel and Surrey Quays is operated by Stagecoach. Seen at Whitechapel station in the white and orange livery used for this contract is SR91, G91KUB. Six of the Optare StarRiders went to Bluebird Buses at Stonehaven during December. *Tony Wilson*

SR12-119

Mercedes-Benz 811D — Optare StarRider — B26F — 1988-89 Ex London Buses, 1994

12	F912YWY	60	F160FWY	72	F172FWY	76	F176FWY	105	G105KUB
13	F913YWY	65	F165FWY	73	F173FWY	78	F178FWY	106	G106KUB
32	F32CWY	66	F166FWY	74	F174FWY	79	F179FWY	107	G107KUB
50	F50CWY	70	F170FWY	75	F175FWY	91	G91KUB	119	G119KUB
56	F156FWY	71	F171FWY						

T1-230

Leyland Titan TNLXB2RRSp — Park Royal — H44/26D* — 1978-80 Ex London Buses, 1994
*'63/80 are DPH44/26F, many H44/22D; 230 is H44/24D

1	THX401S	12	WYV12T	22	WYV22T	34	WYV34T	80	CUL80V
2	THX402S	13	WYV13T	23	WYV23T	35	WYV35T	140	CUL140V
3	WYV3T	14	WYV14T	24	WYV24T	36	WYV36T	163	CUL163V
4	WYV4T	15	WYV15T	25	WYV25T	37	WYV37T	175	CUL175V
6	WYV6T	16	WYV16T	26	WYV26T	38	WYV38T	193	CUL193V
7	WYV7T	17	WYV17T	28	WYV28T	39	WYV39T	214	CUL214V
8	WYV8T	18	WYV18T	30	WYV30T	40	WYV40T	222	CUL222V
9	WYV9T	19	WYV19T	31	WYV31T	63	WYV63T	223	CUL223V
10	WYV10T	20	WYV20T	32	WYV32T	66	WYV66T	230	EYE230V
11	WYV11T	21	WYV21T	33	WYV33T				

T260	GYE260W	Leyland Titan TNLXB2RR	Park Royal/Leyland	H44/26D	1981	Ex London Buses, 1994
T261	GYE261W	Leyland Titan TNTL112RR	Park Royal/Leyland	H44/26D	1981	Ex London Buses, 1994
T262	GYE262W	Leyland Titan TNLXB2RR	Park Royal/Leyland	H44/26D	1981	Ex London Buses, 1994
T263	GYE263W	Leyland Titan TNLXB2RR	Park Royal/Leyland	H44/26D	1981	Ex London Buses, 1994

T264-549

Leyland Titan TNLXB2RR   Leyland   H44/24D*   1981-82   Ex London Buses, 1994
266/85, 311/20/31 are H44/26D; 282 is H44/26F; 512 is O44/24D; 282 ex Selkent, 1995

264	GYE264W	379	KYV379X	456	KYV456X	496	KYV496X	526	KYV526X
266	GYE266W	380	KYV380X	458	KYV458X	497	KYV497X	527	KYV527X
268	GYE268W	386	KYV386X	460	KYV460X	498	KYV498X	529	KYV529X
270	GYE270W	387	KYV387X	461	KYV461X	500	KYV500X	531	KYV531X
273	GYE273W	394	KYV394X	462	KYV462X	501	KYV501X	532	KYV532X
282	KYN282X	395	KYV395X	465	KYV465X	502	KYV502X	533	KYV533X
285	KYN285X	403	KYV403X	466	KYV466X	503	KYV503X	535	KYV535X
286	KYN286X	404	KYV404X	467	KYV467X	504	KYV504X	536	KYV536X
298	KYN298X	406	KYV406X	469	KYV469X	505	KYV505X	537	KYV537X
306	KYN306X	428	KYV428X	470	KYV470X	506	KYV506X	539	KYV539X
311	KYV311X	434	KYV434X	471	KYV471X	508	KYV508X	540	KYV540X
318	KYV318X	437	KYV437X	473	KYV473X	512	KYV512X	541	KYV541X
320	KYV320X	439	KYV439X	476	KYV476X	513	KYV513X	542	KYV542X
326	KYV326X	441	KYV441X	480	KYV480X	514	KYV514X	543	KYV543X
331	KYV331X	444	KYV444X	486	KYV486X	515	KYV515X	544	KYV544X
334	KYV334X	445	KYV445X	488	KYV488X	517	KYV517X	545	KYV545X
340	KYV340X	446	KYV446X	490	KYV490X	521	KYV521X	546	KYV546X
360	KYV360X	448	KYV448X	492	KYV492X	522	KYV522X	548	KYV548X
366	KYV366X	453	KYV453X	495	KYV495X	525	KYV525X	549	KYV549X
378	KYV378X	454	KYV454X						

T550-675

Leyland Titan TNLXB2RR   Leyland   H44/24D   1982-83   Ex London Buses, 1994

550	NUW550Y	575	NUW575Y	598	NUW598Y	626	NUW626Y	650	NUW650Y
551	NUW551Y	576	NUW576Y	600	NUW600Y	627	NUW627Y	651	NUW651Y
552	NUW552Y	577	NUW577Y	601	NUW601Y	629	NUW629Y	652	NUW652Y
553	NUW553Y	578	NUW578Y	602	NUW602Y	630	NUW630Y	653	NUW653Y
554	NUW554Y	579	NUW579Y	603	NUW603Y	631	NUW631Y	654	NUW654Y
555	NUW555Y	580	NUW580Y	604	NUW604Y	632	NUW632Y	657	NUW657Y
556	NUW556Y	581	NUW581Y	605	NUW605Y	633	NUW633Y	658	NUW658Y
557	NUW557Y	582	NUW582Y	606	NUW606Y	634	NUW634Y	659	NUW659Y
558	NUW558Y	583	NUW583Y	608	NUW608Y	636	NUW636Y	660	NUW660Y
559	NUW559Y	584	NUW584Y	609	NUW609Y	637	NUW637Y	662	NUW662Y
560	NUW560Y	585	NUW585Y	610	NUW610Y	639	NUW639Y	663	NUW663Y
562	NUW562Y	586	NUW586Y	613	NUW613Y	640	NUW640Y	664	NUW664Y
563	NUW563Y	587	NUW587Y	614	NUW614Y	641	NUW641Y	665	NUW665Y
564	NUW564Y	588	NUW588Y	615	NUW615Y	642	NUW642Y	666	NUW666Y
565	NUW565Y	589	NUW589Y	617	NUW617Y	643	NUW643Y	668	NUW668Y
566	NUW566Y	590	NUW590Y	619	NUW619Y	644	NUW644Y	669	NUW669Y
568	NUW568Y	591	NUW591Y	621	NUW621Y	645	NUW645Y	670	NUW670Y
569	NUW569Y	592	NUW592Y	622	NUW622Y	646	NUW646Y	671	NUW671Y
571	NUW571Y	593	NUW593Y	623	NUW623Y	647	NUW647Y	672	NUW672Y
572	NUW572Y	595	NUW595Y	624	NUW624Y	648	NUW648Y	673	NUW673Y
573	NUW573Y	597	NUW597Y	625	NUW625Y	649	NUW649Y	675	NUW675Y
574	NUW574Y								

T686-971

Leyland Titan TNLXB2RR   Leyland   H44/24D   1983-84   Ex London Buses, 1994
802-970 are H44/26D

686	OHV686Y	731	OHV731Y	784	OHV784Y	846	A846SUL	935	A935SYE
688	OHV688Y	738	OHV738Y	789	OHV789Y	849	A849SUL	944	A944SYE
691	OHV691Y	743	OHV743Y	802	OHV802Y	867	A867SUL	945	A945SYE
697	OHV697Y	744	OHV744Y	819	RYK819Y	873	A873SUL	949	A949SYE
699	OHV699Y	749	OHV749Y	826	A826SUL	902	A902SYE	953	A953SYE
702	OHV702Y	751	OHV751Y	827	A827SUL	905	A905SYE	960	A960SYE
719	OHV719Y	759	OHV759Y	832	A832SUL	921	A921SYE	965	A965SYE
724	OHV724Y	761	OHV761Y	840	A840SUL	922	A922SYE	971	A971SYE
729	OHV729Y	769	OHV769Y						

T1022	A622THV	Leyland Titan TNLXB2RR	Leyland	H44/24D	1984	Ex London Buses, 1994
T1026	A626THV	Leyland Titan TNLXB2RR	Leyland	H44/24D	1984	Ex London Buses, 1994
T1050	A650THV	Leyland Titan TNLXB2RR	Leyland	H44/24D	1984	Ex London Buses, 1994
T1128	486CLT	Leyland Titan TNLXB1RF	Leyland	DPH43/29F	1979	Ex London Buses, 1994

The main double deck bus for the former London Buses fleets is still the Leyland Titan. Photographed on Leyton Green Road is T873, A873SUL one of those built by Leyland at Lillyhall. The initial thirteen Titans built in Cumbria before full production commenced there were built on the site now occupied by the Cumberland depot.
Richard Godfrey

Sixteen Dennis Lance operate with East London and form the LA Class, the A signifying Alexander bodywork. Seen heading for Ilford is LA2, J102WSC, the entire class having transferred from Selkent over the summer of 1995.
Richard Godfrey

VP4	H654UWR	Volvo B10M-60	Plaxton Paramount 3500 III	C49FT	1991	Ex Wallace Arnold, 1995
VP5	H655UWR	Volvo B10M-60	Plaxton Paramount 3500 III	C49FT	1991	Ex Wallace Arnold, 1995
VP7	H657UWR	Volvo B10M-60	Plaxton Paramount 3500 III	C51F	1991	Ex Wallace Arnold, 1995

Previous Registrations:

461CLT	From new	E155CGJ	E711LYU, WLT461	WLT886	From new
485CLT	From new	LFF875	456CLT	XFF814	WLT890
486CLT	WDA3T	WLT613	From new	XFF813	WLT898
527CLT	From new				

Livery: Red; Green(1962 Green Line) RMC1461.

On order: 26 Volvo Olympians

Named Vehicles: RMA5 *King Charles II*; RMC1456 *Prince Albert*; RMC1461 *Sir Christopher Wren*; RMC1485 *King William I*; T512 *Phoenix*; T1128 *The Ranger*

EAST MIDLAND

East Midland Motor Services Ltd, New Street, Chesterfield, S40 2LQ
Grimsby Cleethorpes Transport Ltd, Victoria Street, Grimsby, DN31 1NS
Chesterfield Transport Ltd, New Street, Chesterfield, S40 2LQ

Depots : Stonegravels, Sheffield Road, Chesterfield; Victoria Street, Grimsby; Sutton Road, Mansfield and Hardy Street, Worksop.

Chesterfield:

12-19				Mercedes-Benz 811D		Alexander AM		B33F	1992	Ex Chesterfield, 1995	
12	J213AET	**15**	J215AET	**17**	J217AET			**18**	J218AET	**19**	J219AET
14	J214AET	**16**	J216AET								

20	JAO477V	Leyland National 10351A/2R			B44F	1980	Ex Chesterfield, 1995
21	EKY21V	Leyland National 2 NL116L11/1R			B52F	1980	Ex Chesterfield, 1995
22	EKY22V	Leyland National 2 NL116L11/1R			B52F	1980	Ex Chesterfield, 1995
23	EKY23V	Leyland National 2 NL116L11/1R			B52F	1981	Ex Chesterfield, 1995

24-29				Leyland National 2 NL106L11/1R				B44F	1980	Ex Chesterfield, 1995	
24	EKY24V	**26**	EKY26V	**27**	EKY27V			**28**	EKY28V	**29**	EKY29V
25	EKY25V										

30-34				Leyland National 2 NL116AL11/1R				B52F	1981	Ex Chesterfield, 1995	
30	OWB30X	**31**	OWB31X	**32**	OWB32X			**33**	OWB33X	**34**	OWB34X

35-41				Leyland National 11351A/1R				B49F	1979	Ex Chesterfield, 1995	
35u	ABA25T	**37**	WBN477T	**39**	WBN479T			**40**	WBN480T	**41**	WBN469T
36	WBN484T	**38**	WBN482T								

42	GOL420N	Leyland National 11351/1R			B49F	1975	Ex Chesterfield, 1995
43	GOL436N	Leyland National 11351/1R			B49F	1975	Ex Chesterfield, 1995
49	GFJ665N	Leyland National 11351/1R			B49F	1974	Ex Chesterfield, 1995

50-55				Leyland National 2 NL116HLXCT/1R				B52F*	1984	Ex Chesterfield, 1995 *50/1 are DP47F	
50	B150DHL	**52**	B152DHL	**53**	B153DHL			**54**	B154DHL	**55**	B155DHL
51	B151DHL										

56u	GOL398N	Leyland National 11351/1R			B49F	1975	Ex Chesterfield, 1995
60	E60WDT	Leyland Lynx LX112TL11ZR1	Leyland Lynx		DP45F	1987	Ex Chesterfield, 1995
61	E61WDT	Leyland Lynx LX112TL11ZR1	Leyland Lynx		DP45F	1987	Ex Chesterfield, 1995

71-80				Leyland National 11351A/1R*				B49F	1978	Ex Chesterfield, 1995 73 fitted with Volvo engine	
71	VKU71S	**73u**	VKU73S	**75**	VKU75S	**77w**	VKU77S	**79u**	VKU79S
72u	VKU72S	**74**	VKU74S	**76u**	VKU76S	**78**	VKU78S	**80**	VKU80S

81-87				Leyland National 11351A/1R				B49F	1977-79	Ex Chesterfield, 1995	
81	PTD668S	**83**	ABA13T	**85**	WBN468T			**86**	WBN470T	**87**	WBN473T
82	RBU180R	**84**	ABA18T								

89	H257THL	Mercedes-Benz 709D		Reeve Burgess Beaver	B25F	1991	Ex Chesterfield, 1995

Opposite: **East Midland currently employ three fleet numbering series. One is the original East Midland series, the second is for the Grimsby-Cleethorpes subsidiary represented here by open-top Leyland Fleetline 113, MBE613R. A third sequence encompasses the former Chesterfield Transport fleet that is currently the subject of a Monopolies and Mergers Commission enquiry. Several vehicles with this operation are in Stagecoach corporate livery with East Midland names including ten much-travelled B10Ms from Ribble and as seen here, Leyland National 52, B152DHL.**
David Longbottom/Tony Wilson

90-98

						Mercedes-Benz 709D	Alexander AM	B25F*	1988	Ex Chesterfield, 1995
										*97/8 are DP25F

90	E90YWB	92	E92YWB	94	E94YWB	96	E96YWB	98	E98YWB
91	E91YWB	93	E93YWB	95	E95YWB	97	E97YWB		

101	KHT121P	Leyland National 11351/1R(Volvo)		B52F	1976	Ex Chesterfield, 1995
102	OAH552M	Leyland National 1151/1R/0401(Volvo)		B52F	1973	Ex Chesterfield, 1995
103	PTF762L	Leyland National 1151/1R/0401(Volvo)		B52F	1973	Ex Chesterfield, 1995
104	UHG741R	Leyland National 11351A/1R(Volvo)		B49F	1976	Ex Chesterfield, 1995
105	URA605S	Leyland National 11351A/1R(Volvo)		B49F	1977	Ex Chesterfield, 1995
106	VKE566S	Leyland National 11351A/1R(Volvo)		B49F	1977	Ex Chesterfield, 1995
107	RAU597R	Leyland National 11351A/1R(Volvo)		B49F	1976	Ex Chesterfield, 1995
130	KWJ130P	Daimler Fleetline CRG6LX	Roe	H42/29D	1976	
143	NKY143R	Leyland Fleetline FE30ALR	Roe	H42/29D	1977	
146	NKY146R	Leyland Fleetline FE30ALR	Roe	H42/29D	1977	
148	NKY148R	Leyland Fleetline FE30ALR	Roe	H42/29D	1977	
149	NKY149R	Leyland Fleetline FE30ALR	Roe	H42/29D	1977	

150-159

						Leyland Fleetline FE30AGR	Roe	H42/29D	1978	Ex Chesterfield, 1995

150	UWA150S	152	UWA152S	154	UWA154S	157	UWA157S	159	UWA159S
151	UWA151S	153	UWA153S	155	UWA155S	158	UWA158S		

161	TWF201Y	Leyland Olympian ONLXB/1R	Roe	H47/29F	1982	Ex Chesterfield, 1995
162	TWF202Y	Leyland Olympian ONLXB/1R	Roe	H47/29F	1982	Ex Chesterfield, 1995
163	NNU123M	Daimler Fleetline CRL6	Roe	H42/29D	1973	
165	PTD641S	Leyland Fleetline FE30AGR	Northern Counties	H43/32F	1977	Ex Chesterfield, 1995
166w	PTD652S	Leyland Fleetline FE30AGR	Northern Counties	H43/32F	1978	Ex Chesterfield, 1995
167	SUA123R	Leyland Atlantean AN68/1R	Roe	H43/33F	1977	Ex Chesterfield, 1995
168	LUG98P	Leyland Atlantean AN68/1R	Roe	H43/33F	1975	Ex Chesterfield, 1995
169	LUG96P	Leyland Atlantean AN68/1R	Roe	H43/33F	1975	Ex Chesterfield, 1995
170	LUG104P	Leyland Atlantean AN68/1R	Roe	H43/33F	1975	Ex Chesterfield, 1995
193w	ENU93H	Leyland Panther PSUR1A/1	Northern Counties	B49F	1969	Ex Chesterfield, 1995
194w	ARB528T	Bedford YMT	Plaxton Supreme III Express	C49F	1978	Ex Chesterfield, 1995
195w	JKJ277V	Bedford YMT	Duple Dominant II	C53F	1979	Ex Chesterfield, 1995
201	RHL174X	Leyland Tiger TRCTL11/3R	Duple Dominant IV	C53F	1982	Ex Chesterfield, 1995
213	MTV754P	Leyland Leopard PSU3C/4R	Duple Dominant	DP53F	1976	Ex Chesterfield, 1995
215	CPY704T	Leyland Leopard PSU3E/4R	Plaxton Supreme IV Express	DP55F	1979	Ex Chesterfield, 1995
216	FDC413V	Leyland Leopard PSU3E/4R	Plaxton Supreme IV Express	DP55F	1979	Ex Chesterfield, 1995
217	FDC408V	Leyland Leopard PSU3E/4R	Plaxton Supreme IV Express	DP55F	1979	Ex Chesterfield, 1995
302	YPD129Y	Leyland Tiger TRCTL11/2R	Duple Dominant IV Express	DP53F	1983	Ex Chesterfield, 1995
303	YPD133Y	Leyland Tiger TRCTL11/2R	Duple Dominant IV Express	DP53F	1983	Ex Chesterfield, 1995
309	THX179S	Leyland National 10351A/2R		B38D	1978	Ex Chesterfield, 1995
310	AYR322T	Leyland National 10351A/2R		B38D	1979	Ex Chesterfield, 1995
320w	E71XKW	Mercedes-Benz 609D	Reeve Burgess	C19F	1988	Ex Chesterfield, 1995
322w	B707FWA	Ford Transit	Mellor	M12	1985	Ex Chesterfield, 1995

591-600

						Volvo B10M-55	Alexander PS	DP48F	1994	Ex Ribble, 1995

591	L341KCK	593	L343KCK	595	L339KCK	597	M411RRN	599	M413RRN
592	L342KCK	594	L344KCK	596	L340KCK	598	M412RRN	600	M414RRN

752-761

						Mercedes-Benz 709D	Alexander Sprint	B25F	1995

752	N752CKU	754	N754CKU	756	N756CKU	758	N758CKU	760	N760CKU
753	N753CKU	755	N755CKU	757	N757CKU	759	N759CKU	761	N761CKU

The Daimler Fleetline was the favoured double-deck of Chesterfield Transport. Here is shown 158, UWA158S, an example with Roe bodywork, waiting time in the centre of Chesterfield. *Tony Wilson*

Stagecoach Grimsby-Cleethorpes:

| **1-9** | | Dennis Lance 11SDA3106* | East Lancashire EL2000 | B45F | 1993 | 1-7 ex Grimsby Cleethorpes, 1993 *5-9 are type 11SDA3111 |

| 1 | K701NDO | 3 | K703NDO | 5 | L705HFU | 7 | L707HFU | 9 | L709HFU |
| 2 | K702NDO | 4 | K704NDO | 6 | L706HFU | 8 | L708HFU | | |

27	E927PBE	Leyland Tiger TRBLXCT/2RH	Alexander P	DP51F	1987	Ex Grimsby Cleethorpes, 1993
28	E928PBE	Leyland Tiger TRBLXCT/2RH	Alexander P	DP51F	1987	Ex Grimsby Cleethorpes, 1993
29	E929PBE	Leyland Tiger TRBLXCT/2RH	Alexander P	DP51F	1987	Ex Grimsby Cleethorpes, 1993
30	E930PBE	Leyland Tiger TRBLXCT/2RH	Alexander P	DP51F	1987	Ex Grimsby Cleethorpes, 1993
31	EJV31Y	Dennis Falcon H SDA411	Wadham Stringer Vanguard	B42F	1983	Ex Grimsby Cleethorpes, 1993
32	EJV32Y	Dennis Falcon H SDA411	Wadham Stringer Vanguard	B42F	1983	Ex Grimsby Cleethorpes, 1993
33	EJV33Y	Dennis Falcon H SDA411	Wadham Stringer Vanguard	B42F	1983	Ex Grimsby Cleethorpes, 1993
34	EJV34Y	Dennis Falcon H SDA411	Wadham Stringer Vanguard	B42F	1983	Ex Grimsby Cleethorpes, 1993

| **45-49** | | MCW MetroRider MF150/94 | MCW | B23F | 1988 | Ex Grimsby Cleethorpes, 1993 |

| 45 | E45HFE | 46 | E46HFE | 47 | E47HFE | 48 | E48HFE | 49 | E49HFE |

50	E50HFE	MCW MetroRider MF150/94	MCW	B23F	1988	Ex Grimsby Cleethorpes, 1993
51	E51HFE	MCW MetroRider MF150/94	MCW	B23F	1988	Ex Grimsby Cleethorpes, 1993
56	E56HFE	MCW MetroRider MF150/94	MCW	DP23F	1988	Ex Grimsby Cleethorpes, 1993
57	E57HFE	MCW MetroRider MF150/94	MCW	DP23F	1988	Ex Grimsby Cleethorpes, 1993
58	E58HFE	MCW MetroRider MF150/94	MCW	DP23F	1988	Ex Grimsby Cleethorpes, 1993

59-70

| | | | | | | | | | Leyland Fleetline FE30AGR | Roe | H45/29D | 1979-80 | Ex Grimsby Cleethorpes, 1993 |

59w	TFU59T	62w	TFU62T	65w	WFU465V	67u	WFU467V	69w	WFU469V
60w	TFU60T	63w	TFU63T	66u	WFU466V	68w	WFU468V	70w	WFU470V
61	TFU61T	64w	TFU64T						

71	A71GEE	Leyland Olympian ONTL11/1R	Eastern Coach Works	H45/31F	1983	Ex Grimsby Cleethorpes, 1993
72	A72GEE	Leyland Olympian ONTL11/1R	Eastern Coach Works	H45/31F	1983	Ex Grimsby Cleethorpes, 1993
73	A73GEE	Leyland Olympian ONTL11/1R	Eastern Coach Works	H47/28D	1983	Ex Grimsby Cleethorpes, 1993
74	A74GEE	Leyland Olympian ONTL11/1R	Eastern Coach Works	H47/28D	1983	Ex Grimsby Cleethorpes, 1993
75	F75TFU	Dennis Dominator DDA1021	Alexander RH	H45/33F	1989	Ex Grimsby Cleethorpes, 1993
76	F76TFU	Dennis Dominator DDA1021	Alexander RH	H45/33F	1989	Ex Grimsby Cleethorpes, 1993
77	F77TFU	Dennis Dominator DDA1021	Alexander RH	H45/33F	1989	Ex Grimsby Cleethorpes, 1993
78	F78TFU	Dennis Dominator DDA1022	Alexander RH	H45/33F	1989	Ex Grimsby Cleethorpes, 1993
79	G79VFW	Dennis Dominator DDA1028	Alexander RH	H45/33F	1990	Ex Grimsby Cleethorpes, 1993
80	G80VFW	Dennis Dominator DDA1028	Alexander RH	H45/33F	1990	Ex Grimsby Cleethorpes, 1993
81	G81VFW	Dennis Dominator DDA1029	Alexander RH	H45/33F	1990	Ex Grimsby Cleethorpes, 1993

82-94

| | | | | | | | | | Dennis Dominator DDA1034* | East Lancashire | H45/33F | 1991-92 | Ex Grimsby Cleethorpes, 1993 |
| | | | | | | | | | | | | | *91-4 are DDA1036 |

82	H482BEE	84	H484BEE	91	J91DJV	93	J93DJV	94	J94DJV
83	H483BEE	85	H485BEE	92	J92DJV				

103	BJV103L	Daimler Fleetline CRG6LX	Roe	O45/29D	1973	Ex Grimsby Cleethorpes, 1993
113	MBE613R	Leyland Fleetline FE30AGR	Roe	O45/29D	1976	Ex Grimsby Cleethorpes, 1993

120-129

| | | | | | | | | | Leyland Fleetline FE30AGR | Roe | H45/29D | 1977-80 | Ex Grimsby Cleethorpes, 1993 |

120u	OJV120S	122w	OJV122S	124w	OJV124S	126w	XFU126V	128w	XFU128V
121w	OJV121S	123w	OJV123S	125	XFU125V	127w	XFU127V	129w	XFU129V

130-144

| | | | | | | | | | Volvo Olympian YN2RV18Z4 | Alexander RL | H47/29F | 1995 |

130	N130AET	133	N133AET	136	N136AET	139	N139AET	142	N142AET
131	N131AET	134	N134AET	137	N137AET	140	N140AET	143	N143AET
132	N132AET	135	N135AET	138	N138AET	141	N141AET	144	N144AET

159	BFW136W	Ford R1114	Plaxton Supreme IV	C53F	1981	
172	XGS736S	Leyland Leopard PSU3E/4R	Plaxton Supreme III	C53F	1978	Ex Grimsby Cleethorpes, 1993
173	BHO441V	Leyland Leopard PSU5C/4R	Duple Supreme II	C55F	1980	Ex Grimsby Cleethorpes, 1993
174	MRJ270W	Leyland Leopard PSU5C/4R	Plaxton Supreme IV	C41DL	1980	Ex Grimsby Cleethorpes, 1993
175	EFU935Y	Leyland Leopard PSU5C/4R	Duple Dominant I	C53F	1983	Ex Grimsby Cleethorpes, 1993
176	OJL823Y	Leyland Leopard PSU5C/4R	Duple Dominant III	C53F	1983	Ex Grimsby Cleethorpes, 1993
177	OJL822Y	Leyland Leopard PSU5C/4R	Duple Dominant III	C49F	1983	Ex Grimsby Cleethorpes, 1993
183	PJI4314	Leyland Tiger TRCTL11/2R	Plaxton Paramount 3200 E	C47F	1983	
187	PYE841Y	Leyland Tiger TRCTL11/3R	Duple Laser	C53F	1983	Ex Grimsby Cleethorpes, 1993
188	PYE842Y	Leyland Tiger TRCTL11/3R	Duple Laser	C53F	1983	Ex Grimsby Cleethorpes, 1993
189	PSU764	Leyland Tiger TRCTL11/3R	Duple Laser	C53F	1983	Ex Grimsby Cleethorpes, 1993
190	PSU443	Leyland Tiger TRCTL11/3R	Duple Laser	C53F	1983	Ex Grimsby Cleethorpes, 1993
191	A243YGF	Leyland Tiger TRCTL11/3RH	Duple Laser	C57F	1984	Ex Grimsby Cleethorpes, 1993
192	PS2743	Leyland Tiger TRCTL11/3RH	Duple Laser	C57F	1984	Ex Grimsby Cleethorpes, 1993
193	PS3696	Leyland Tiger TRCTL11/3RH	Duple Laser	C57F	1984	Ex Grimsby Cleethorpes, 1993
644	J746CWT	Volvo B10M-60	Plaxton Premiére 350	C50F	1992	Ex Wallace Arnold, 1995
645	J748CWT	Volvo B10M-60	Plaxton Premiére 350	C50F	1992	Ex Wallace Arnold, 1995

East Midland:

31	SKY31Y	Leyland Tiger TRCTL11/3R	Eastern Coach Works B51	C51F	1983
32	SKY32Y	Leyland Tiger TRCTL11/3R	Eastern Coach Works B51	C51F	1983
37	PJI4316	Leyland Tiger TRCTL11/2R	Duple Dominant IV	C47F	1983
38	PJI4317	Leyland Tiger TRCTL11/2R	Duple Dominant IV	C47F	1983

39-44

| | | | | | | | | | Leyland Tiger TRCTL11/2R | Alexander TE | DP45F* | 1983-84 | *42/3 are DP49F |

39	A39XHE	41	A41XHE	42	A42XHE	43	A43XHE	44	A44XHE

49	B49DWE	Leyland Tiger TRCTL11/2RH	Alexander TE	DP49F	1984
52	B52DWE	Leyland Tiger TRCTL11/2RH	Alexander TE	DP49F	1984
53	B53DWJ	Leyland Tiger TRCTL11/2RH	Alexander TE	DP49F	1985
54	B54DWJ	Leyland Tiger TRCTL11/2RH	Alexander TE	DP49F	1985

101-109

Volvo Olympian YN2RV18Z4   Northern Counties Palatine   H47/29F   1993

101	K101JWJ	103	K103JWJ	105	K105JWJ	107	K107JWJ	109	L109LHL
102	K102JWJ	104	K104JWJ	106	K106JWJ	108	L108LHL		

197w	C712LWE	Bedford YNT		Plaxton Paramount 3200 II	C53F	1986	Ex Chesterfield, 1995
198	K546RJX	DAF SB3000DKVF601		Van Hool Alizée	C53F	1993	Ex Hallmark, Luton, 1995
199	L557EHD	DAF SB3000WS601		Van Hool Alizée	C53F	1994	Ex Burton, Fellbeck, 1995

203-224

Bristol VRT/SL3/6LXB*   Eastern Coach Works   H43/31F   1980-81   *218 is type 6LXC

203	EWE203V	211	JAK211W	218	KWA218W	223	KWA223W	224	KWA224W
206	EWE206V	214	KWA214W	221	KWA221W				

301-325

Leyland Olympian ONLXB/1R   Eastern Coach Works   H45/32F   1981-84

301	NHL301X	306	SHE306Y	311	SHE311Y	316	A316XWG	321	A321YWJ
302	NHL302X	307	SHE307Y	312	UDT312Y	317	A317XWG	322	A322AKU
303	NHL303X	308	SHE308Y	313	UDT313Y	318	A318XWG	323	A323AKU
304	NHL304X	309	SHE309Y	314	A314XWG	319	A319YWJ	324	A324AKU
305	NHL305X	310	SHE310Y	315	A315XWG	320	A320YWJ	325	A325AKU

326-330

Leyland Olympian ONLXB/1R   Eastern Coach Works   CH40/32F   1985

326	C326HWJ	327	C327HWJ	328	C328HWJ	329	C329HWJ	330	C330HWJ

331-336

Leyland Olympian ONLXB/1R   Eastern Coach Works   H45/32F   1986

331	C331HWJ	333	C333HWJ	334	C334HWJ	335	C335HWJ	336	C336HWJ
332	C332HWJ								

337	GSO8V	Leyland Olympian ONLXB/1RV	Alexander RL	H45/32F	1987	Ex United Counties, 1992

339-343

Leyland Olympian ON6LXB/2RZ   Alexander RL   DPH51/31F 1989

339	G339KKW	340	G340KKW	341	G341KKW	342	G342KKW	343	G343KKW

344-353

Leyland Olympian ON25R6G13Z4 Alexander RL   DPH51/31F* 1990-91   *349-353 are DPH47/27F

344	H344SWA	346	H346SWA	348	H348SWA	350	J350XET	352	J352XET
345	H345SWA	347	H347SWA	349	J349XET	351	J351XET	353	J353XET

354-358

Leyland Olympian ON2R50G13Z4 Northern Counties Palatine H47/29F   1992

354	K354DWJ	355	K355DWJ	356	K356DWJ	357	K357DWJ	358	K358DWJ

359-363

Leyland Olympian ON2R54G13Z4   Alexander RL   DPH43/27F 1992

359	K359DWJ	360	K360DWJ	361	K361DWJ	362	K362DWJ	363	K363DWJ

412	DWF22V	Leyland Leopard PSU3E/4R	Duple Dominant(1985)	B55F	1979
413	DWF23V	Leyland Leopard PSU3E/4R	Duple Dominant(1985)	B51F	1979
414	DWF24V	Leyland Leopard PSU3E/4R	Alexander P(1985)	B52F	1979
415w	DWF25V	Leyland Leopard PSU3E/4R	Duple Dominant(1985)	B51F	1980
416	DWF26V	Leyland Leopard PSU3E/4R	Duple Dominant(1985)	B55F	1980

425-433

Leyland Tiger TRCTL11/2RH   Alexander P   B52F   1985

425	B625DWF	427	B627DWF	429	B629DWF	431	B631DWF	433	B633DWF
426	B626DWF	428	B628DWF	430	B630DWF	432	B632DWF		

435-453

Volvo B6-9.9M   Alexander Dash   B40F   1993

435	L435LWA	439	L439LWA	443	L443LWA	448	L448LWA	451	L451LWA
436	L436LWA	440	L440LWA	445	L445LWA	449	L449LWA	452	L452LWA
437	L437LWA	441	L441LWA	446	L446LWA	450	L450LWA	453	L453LHL
438	L438LWA	442	L442LWA	447	L447LWA				

The Grimsby to Sheffield Stagecoach Express service has gained considerable favour with the travelling public with frequencies improving as more and more passengers are carried. The vehicles used are Plaxton-bodied Volvo B10Ms including 640, L640LDT. *Tony Wilson*

601-609   Volvo B10M-55   Alexander PS   DP48F   1995

601	M601VHE	603	M603VHE	605	M605VHE	607	M607VHE	609	M609WET
602	M602VHE	604	M604VHE	606	M606VHE	608	M608WET		

614	EKW614V	Leyland National 2 NL106L11/1R		B44F	1980
615	EKW615V	Leyland National 2 NL106L11/1R		B44F	1980
616	EKW616V	Leyland National 2 NL106L11/1R		B44F	1980

617-621   Leyland National 2 NL116L11/1R   B49F   1980

617	GWE617V	618	GWE618V	619	GWE619V	620	HWJ620W	621	HWJ621W

622	MWG622X	Leyland National 2 NL116AL11/1R	B49F	1981	
623	MWG623X	Leyland National 2 NL116AL11/1R	B49F	1981	
624	MWG624X	Leyland National 2 NL116AL11/1R	B49F	1981	
625	LAG188V	Leyland National 2 NL116L11/1R	B49F	1980	Ex East Yorkshire, 1988
626	LAG189V	Leyland National 2 NL116L11/1R	B49F	1980	Ex East Yorkshire, 1988
627	NRP580V	Leyland National 2 NL116L11/1R	B49F	1980	Ex United Counties, 1992
628	SVV586W	Leyland National 2 NL116L11/1R	B49F	1981	Ex United Counties, 1992
634	VWA34Y	Leyland National 2 NL116HLXB/1R	DP47F	1983	
635	VWA35Y	Leyland National 2 NL116HLXB/1R	DP47F	1983	
636	VWA36Y	Leyland National 2 NL116HLXB/1R	DP47F	1983	

637-643   Volvo B10M-62   Plaxton Premiére Interurban   DP51F   1993

637	L637LDT	639	L639LDT	641	L641LDT	642	L642LDT	643	L643LDT
638	L638LDT	640	L640LDT				

650	H658UWR	Volvo B10M-60	Plaxton Paramount 3500 III C51F	1991	Ex Wallace Arnold, 1995
651	H659UWR	Volvo B10M-60	Plaxton Paramount 3500 III C51F	1991	Ex Wallace Arnold, 1995

700-710

		Mercedes-Benz L608D	Reeve Burgess	B20F*	1986	Ex Cumberland, 1995
						*702/6/8-10 are DP19F

700	D34UAO	702	D511RCK	705	D522RCK	707	D539RCK	709	D519RCK
701	D503RCK	703	D547RCK	706	D504RCK	708	D518RCK	710	D561RCK

720-727

		Mercedes-Benz 811D	Reeve Burgess Beaver	B31F	1989-90

720	G820KWF	722	G822KWF	724	G824KWF	726	G826KWF	727	G827KWF
721	G821KWF	723	G823KWF	725	G825KWF				

728	E721BVO	Mercedes-Benz 811D	Optare StarRider	B33F	1988	Ex Maun, Mansfield, 1990
729	E880DRA	Mercedes-Benz 811D	Optare StarRider	B33F	1988	Ex Maun, Mansfield, 1990
730	E481DAU	Mercedes-Benz 811D	Optare StarRider	B33F	1988	Ex Maun, Mansfield, 1990

731-751

		Mercedes-Benz 709D	Alexander Sprint	B25F	1993

731	L731LWA	735	L735LWA	739	L739LWA	743	L743LWA	748	L748LWA
732	L732LWA	736	L736LWA	740	L740LWA	744	L744LWA	749	L749LWA
733	L733LWA	737	L737LWA	741	L741LWA	745	L745LWA	750	L750LWA
734	L734LWA	738	L738LWA	742	L742LWA	746	L746LWA	751	L751LHL

915u	G915KWF	Iveco Daily 49.10	Reeve Burgess Beaver	B25F	1989
916u	G916KWF	Iveco Daily 49.10	Reeve Burgess Beaver	B25F	1989

Previous Registrations:

A243YGF	A601HVT, PS2045	PJI4317	UHE38Y
GSO8V	D378XRS	PS2743	A602HVT
OJL822Y	SSG321Y, PS2945	PS3696	A603HVT
OJL823Y	EJV419Y, PS2743	PSU443	A844SYR
PJI4314	UWJ33Y	PSU764	PYE843Y
PJI4316	UHE37Y	RHL174X	OHE278X, 563UM

Several vehicles are currently on loan to other operations within the East Midland management.

East Midland received Leyland Tigers with Alexander P-type bodywork as part of their 1985 NBC allocation, the latest single decks until new Volvos supplied in 1993. Seen at Chesterfield during 1995 is 431, B631DWF.
Richard Godfrey

FIFE SCOTTISH

Fife Scottish Omnibuses Ltd, Esplanade, Kirkcaldy, Fife, KY1 1SP

Depots : Methilhaven Road, Methil (Aberhill); Broad Street, Cowdenbeath; St Leonard's Street, Dunfermline; Flemington Road, Glenrothes; Esplanade, Kirkcaldy and City Road, St Andrews.

50-69

MCW MetroRider MF150/98 — MCW — B25F* — 1988 — *50/67-9 are MF150/102 and DP25F 62 is MF150/99; 66 is MF150/101.

50	F790PSN	57	F57RFS	61	F61RFS	66	F66RFS	68	F68RFS
55	F55RFS	58	F58RFS	62	F62RFS	67	F67RFS	69	F69RFS
56	F56RFS	60	F60RFS						

70-76

Mercedes-Benz 709D — Alexander Sprint — B25F — 1994

70	M770TFS	72	M772TFS	74	M774TFS	75	M775TFS	76	M776TFS
71	M771TFS	73	M773TFS						

77	VLT77	Mercedes-Benz 811D	Reeve Burgess Beaver	DP33F	1989	Ex Selkent, 1994
78	M778TFS	Mercedes-Benz 709D	Alexander Sprint	B25F	1994	
79	M779TFS	Mercedes-Benz 709D	Alexander Sprint	B25F	1994	
80	G280TSL	Mercedes-Benz 709D	Alexander Sprint	B23F	1990	Ex Bluebird, 1992
81	G281TSL	Mercedes-Benz 709D	Alexander Sprint	B23F	1990	Ex Bluebird, 1992
82	M780TFS	Mercedes-Benz 709D	Alexander Sprint	B25F	1994	

85-94

Mercedes-Benz 709D — Alexander Sprint — B25F — 1993

85	K485FFS	87	K487FFS	89	K489FFS	91	K491FFS	93	K493FFS
86	K486FFS	88	K488FFS	90	K490FFS	92	K492FFS	94	K494FFS

104	TMS404X	Leyland Leopard PSU3G/4R	Alexander AYS	B53F	1982	Ex Ribble, 1992
122	XMS422Y	Leyland Leopard PSU3G/4R	Alexander AYS	B53F	1982	Ex Ribble, 1992
123	XMS423Y	Leyland Leopard PSU3G/4R	Alexander AYS	B53F	1982	Ex Ribble, 1992

138-160

Leyland Leopard PSU3F/4R* — Alexander AYS — B53F — 1980-81 — *159/60 are PSU3G/4R

138	WFS138W	141	WFS141W	148	WFS148W	150	WFS150W	159	CSF159W
139	WFS139W	142	WFS142W	149	WFS149W	158	CSF158W	160	CSF160W
140	WFS140W	147	WFS147W						

180-189

Leyland Leopard PSU3G/4R — Alexander AYS — B53F — 1982

180	PSX180Y	182	PSX182Y	184	PSX184Y	186	PSX186Y	188	PSX188Y
181	PSX181Y	183	PSX183Y	185	PSX185Y	187	PSX187Y	189	PSX189Y

200	XMS420Y	Leyland Leopard PSU3G/4R	Alexander AYS	DP49F	1982	Ex Ribble, 1992
205	TMS405X	Leyland Leopard PSU3G/4R	Alexander AYS	DP49F	1982	Ex Ribble, 1992
206	TMS406X	Leyland Leopard PSU3G/4R	Alexander AYS	DP49F	1982	Ex Ribble, 1992
207	TMS407X	Leyland Leopard PSU3G/4R	Alexander AYS	DP49F	1982	Ex Ribble, 1992
261	CSF161W	Leyland Leopard PSU3G/4R	Alexander AYS	DP49F	1981	
262	CSF162W	Leyland Leopard PSU3G/4R	Alexander AYS	DP47F	1981	

263-269

Leyland Leopard PSU3F/4R — Alexander AYS — DP49F — 1981

263	CSF163W	265	CSF165W	267	CSF167W	268	CSF168W	269	CSF169W
264	CSF164W	266	CSF166W						

270-279

Leyland Leopard PSU3G/4R — Alexander AT — DP49F — 1982

270	NFS170Y	272	NFS172Y	274	NFS174Y	276	NFS176Y	278	NFS178Y
271	NFS171Y	273	NFS173Y	275	NFS175Y	277	NFS177Y	279	NFS179Y

282	GSO82V	Leyland Leopard PSU3E/4R	Alexander AYS	DP53F	1980	Ex Stagecoach, 1994
283	GSO83V	Leyland Leopard PSU3E/4R	Alexander AYS	DP49F	1980	Ex Stagecoach, 1994
284	GSO84V	Leyland Leopard PSU3E/4R	Alexander AYS	DP53F	1980	Ex Stagecoach, 1994

For many years the standard bus for the Scottish Bus Group was the Leyland Leopard with Alexander Y-type bodywork. This was supplied with bus and high-back seating, long and narrow windows and, for some time, as a coach with hinged doorway. Seen heading for Kirkcaldy is Fife Scottish 266, CSF166W. *Phillip Stephenson*

290-294

Leyland Leopard PSU3G/4R   Alexander AT   DP49F   1982

290	RSC190Y	291	RSC191Y	292	RSC192Y	293	RSC193Y	294	RSC194Y

301-310

Volvo B10M-55   Alexander PS   B49F   1994

301	L301PSC	303	L303PSC	305	L305PSC	307	L307PSC	309	L309PSC
302	L302PSC	304	L304PSC	306	L306PSC	308	L308PSC	310	L310PSC

314-330

Volvo B10M-55   Alexander PS   B49F*   1995   *314/5 are DP48F

314	M314PKS	318	N318VMS	322	N322VMS	325	N325VMS	328	N328VMS
315	M315PKS	319	N319VMS	323	N323VMS	326	N326VMS	329	N329VMS
316	N316VMS	320	N320VMS	324	N324VMS	327	N327VMS	330	N330VMS
317	N317VMS	321	N321VMS						

392	YSX929W	Leyland National 2 NL106L11/1R		B44F	1980
393	YSX930W	Leyland National 2 NL106L11/1R		B44F	1981
399	N141VDU	Volvo B10L	Alexander Ultra	B44F	1995

412-419

Leyland Tiger TRCTL11/3RH   Alexander P   B61F   1986-87

412	D512CSF	414	D614ASG	416	D516DSX	418	D518DSX	419	D519DSX
413	D713CSC	415	D615ASG	417	D517DSX				

420-424

Leyland Tiger TRBTL11/2RH   Alexander P   B57F   1987

420	D520DSX	421	D521DSX	422	D522DSX	423	D523DSX	424	D524DSX

441-445

Leyland Tiger TRCTL11/2RH   Alexander TC   C47F   1985

441	GSU341	442	GSU342	443	GSU343	444	GSU344	445	MSU445

466-470

Leyland Tiger TRBTL11/2R   Alexander TE   DP49F*   1983   Ex Kelvin Central, 1989   *470 is DP47F

466	MNS6Y	467	MNS7Y	468	MNS8Y	469	MNS9Y	470	MNS10Y

477	D277FAS	Leyland Tiger TRCTL11/3RH	Alexander TE	DP53F	1987	Ex Highland Scottish, 1987
478	D278FAS	Leyland Tiger TRCTL11/3RH	Alexander TE	DP53F	1987	Ex Highland Scottish, 1987
479	D279FAS	Leyland Tiger TRCTL11/3RH	Alexander TE	DP53F	1987	Ex Highland Scottish, 1987
499	MSU499	Leyland Tiger TRCTL11/3RZ	Duple 340	C48FT	1987	Ex Kelvin Central, 1990
504	IIL3504	Volvo B10M-61	Van Hool Alizée	C49FT	1988	Ex Rainworth Travel, 1993
506	IIL3506	Volvo B10M-61	Van Hool Alizée	C49FT	1988	Ex Rainworth Travel, 1993
512	M102CDD	Dennis Javelin 11SDL2133	Plaxton Premiere Interurban	DP47F	1994	Ex Stagecoach South, 1995
513	M103CDD	Dennis Javelin 11SDL2133	Plaxton Premiere Interurban	DP47F	1994	Ex Stagecoach South, 1995
514	M104CDD	Dennis Javelin 11SDL2133	Plaxton Premiere Interurban	DP47F	1994	Ex Stagecoach South, 1995

542-556

Volvo B10M-62 — Plaxton Premiére 320 — C53F — 1994

542	M942TSX	545	M945TSX	548	M948TSX	551	M951TSX	554	M954TSX
543	M943TSX	546	M946TSX	549	M949TSX	552	M952TSX	555	M955TSX
544	M944TSX	547	M947TSX	550	M950TSX	553	M953TSX	556	M956TSX

576	K576DFS	Volvo B10M-60	Plaxton Premiére 320	C53F	1993
577	K577DFS	Volvo B10M-60	Plaxton Premiére 320	C53F	1993

578-590

Volvo B10M-60 — Plaxton Premiére Interurban DP51F — 1993

578	L578HSG	581	L581HSG	584	L584HSG	587	L587HSG	589	L589HSG
579	L579HSG	582	L582HSG	585	L585HSG	588	L588HSG	590	L590HSG
580	L580HSG	583	L583HSG	586	L586HSG				

601-605

Dennis Dart 9.8SDL3017 — Alexander Dash — B40F — 1992

601	K601ESH	602	K602ESH	603	K603ESH	604	K604ESH	605	K605ESH

623-628

Volvo B6-9.9M — Alexander Dash — B40F — 1993 — Ex Ribble, 1994

623	L423MVV	625	L425MVV	626	L426MVV	627	L427MVV	628	L428MVV
624	L424MVV								

651-659

Volvo B6-9.9M — Alexander Dash — B40F — 1993-94

651	L651HKS	653	L653HKS	655	L655HKS	657	L657HKS	659	L659HKS
652	L652HKS	654	L654HKS	656	L656HKS	658	L658HKS		

667	L267CCK	Volvo B6-9.9M	Alexander Dash	B40F	1993	Ex Ribble, 1994
668	L268CCK	Volvo B6-9.9M	Alexander Dash	B40F	1993	Ex Ribble, 1994
669	L269CCK	Volvo B6-9.9M	Alexander Dash	B40F	1993	Ex Ribble, 1994
670	M670SSX	Volvo B6-9.9M	Alexander Dash	B40F	1994	
671	M671SSX	Volvo B6-9.9M	Alexander Dash	B40F	1994	
672	M672SSX	Volvo B6-9.9M	Alexander Dash	B40F	1994	
673	M673SSX	Volvo B6-9.9M	Alexander Dash	B40F	1994	

701-725

Leyland Olympian ON2R50G13Z4 Alexander RL — H47/32F — 1992

701	J801WFS	704	J804WFS	707	J807WFS	720	K720ASC	723	K723ASC
702	J802WFS	705	J805WFS	718	K718ASC	721	K721ASC	724	K724ASC
703	J803WFS	706	J806WFS	719	K719ASC	722	K722ASC	725	K725ASC

737	G337KKW	Leyland Olympian ON2R56G13Z4 Alexander RL	DPH51/31F	1989	Ex East Midland, 1992
738	G338KKW	Leyland Olympian ON2R56G13Z4 Alexander RL	DPH51/31F	1989	Ex East Midland, 1992
806	KSF6N	Ailsa B55-10	Alexander AV	H44/35F	1975	Ex Highland Scottish, 1990
810	LSX10P	Ailsa B55-10	Alexander AV	H44/35F	1975	Ex Highland Scottish, 1990
816	LSX16P	Ailsa B55-10	Alexander AV	H44/35F	1975	
817	LSX17P	Ailsa B55-10	Alexander AV	H44/35F	1975	
832	LSX33P	Ailsa B55-10	Alexander AV	H44/35F	1975	
834	NSP334R	Ailsa B55-10	Alexander AV	H44/31D	1976	Ex Western Scottish, 1995
838	LSX38P	Ailsa B55-10	Alexander AV	H44/35F	1975	

Opposite, top: **Stagecoach Express workings have proved very successful with modern vehicles and improved frequencies.** Seen in George Street, Edinburgh is Fife Scottish 544, M944TSX, a Volvo B10M with Plaxton Interurban bodywork. 1996 will see a major development at Fife with the introduction of articulated express vehicles for use on the services over the Forth Road Bridge that are often restricted to single-deck operation due to high winds. *Tony Wilson*
Opposite, bottom: Three Northern Counties-bodied Volvo B10M double decks were transferred from Stagecoach South during 1991. These are fitted with high-back seating for the limited stop services.

847-866 · Ailsa B55-10 MkII · Alexander AV · H44/35F · 1979

847	OSC47V	851	OSC51V	855	OSC55V	861	OSC61V	864	OSC64V
848	OSC48V	852	OSC52V	856	OSC56V	862	OSC62V	865	OSC65V
849	OSC49V	853	OSC53V	857	OSC57V	863	OSC63V	866	OSC66V
850	OSC50V	854	OSC54V	860	OSC60V				

867-874 · Volvo B55-10 MkIII · Alexander RV · H44/37F · 1984

867	A967YSX	869	A969YSX	871	A971YSX	873	A973YSX	874	A974YSX
868	A968YSX	870	A970YSX	872	A972YSX				

875	UFS875R	Ailsa B55-10	Alexander AV	H44/35F	1977
876	UFS876R	Ailsa B55-10	Alexander AV	H44/35F	1977
877	UFS877R	Ailsa B55-10	Alexander AV	H44/35F	1977
878	UFS878R	Ailsa B55-10	Alexander AV	H44/35F	1977

901-920 · Volvo Citybus B10M-50 · Alexander RV · DPH47/33F* 1985-87 · 908 ex Volvo demonstrator, 1986 · *909/10 are DPH45/35F

901	C801USG	907	C807USG	910	E910KSG	915	C795USG	919	C799USG
905	C805USG	908	B108CCS	914	C794USG	918	C798USG	920	C800USG
906	C806USG	909	E909KSG						

940	F310MYJ	Volvo Citybus B10M-50	Northern Counties	DPH43/33F	1989	Ex Southdown, 1991
941	F311MYJ	Volvo Citybus B10M-50	Northern Counties	DPH43/33F	1989	Ex Southdown, 1991
942	F312MYJ	Volvo Citybus B10M-50	Northern Counties	DPH43/33F	1989	Ex Southdown, 1991

972-997 · Volvo Citybus B10M-50 · Alexander RV · H47/37F · 1985-86

972	C802USG	979	B179FFS	984	B184FFS	988	C788USG	992	C792USG
973	C803USG	980	B180FFS	985	B185FFS	989	C789USG	993	C793USG
974	C804USG	981	B181FFS	986	B186FFS	990	C790USG	996	C796USG
977	B177FFS	982	B182FFS	987	C787USG	991	C791USG	997	C797USG
978	B178FFS	983	B183FFS						

1102	ABV669A	Leyland Atlantean PDR1/1	Metro Cammell	O44/31F	1961	Ex Cumberland, 1992
1107	UWV617S	Bristol VRT/SL3/6LXB	Eastern Coach Works	CO43/31F	1978	Ex Stagecoach South, 1994
1110	OVV850R	Bristol VRT/SL3/501(6LX)	Eastern Coach Works	H43/31F	1976	Ex Stagecoach, 1994
1111	VTV167S	Bristol VRT/SL3/6LXB	Eastern Coach Works	H43/31F	1978	Ex Stagecoach, 1994
1112	RJT153R	Bristol VRT/SL3/6LXB	Eastern Coach Works	H43/31F	1977	Ex Stagecoach, 1994
1113	VPR487S	Bristol VRT/SL3/6LXB	Eastern Coach Works	H43/31F	1978	Ex Stagecoach, 1994
1114	XAP643S	Bristol VRT/SL3/6LXB	Eastern Coach Works	H43/31F	1978	Ex Stagecoach, 1994
1115	EWE204V	Bristol VRT/SL3/6LXB	Eastern Coach Works	H43/31F	1980	Ex East Midland, 1994
1116	HWG208W	Bristol VRT/SL3/6LXB	Eastern Coach Works	H43/31F	1980	Ex East Midland, 1994
1117	RTH924S	Bristol VRT/SL3/6LXB	Eastern Coach Works	H43/31F	1977	Ex East Midland, 1994
1118	KWA217W	Bristol VRT/SL3/6LXC	Eastern Coach Works	H43/31F	1981	Ex East Midland, 1994
1119	KKY220W	Bristol VRT/SL3/6LXB	Eastern Coach Works	H43/31F	1981	Ex East Midland, 1994
1120	DWF198V	Bristol VRT/SL3/501	Eastern Coach Works	H43/31F	1980	Ex East Midland, 1994
1121	DWF199V	Bristol VRT/SL3/501	Eastern Coach Works	H43/31F	1980	Ex East Midland, 1994
1122	DWF200V	Bristol VRT/SL3/501	Eastern Coach Works	H43/31F	1980	Ex East Midland, 1994
1123	RVB973S	Bristol VRT/SL3/6LXB	Willowbrook	H43/31F	1978	Ex Stagecoach South, 1994
1124	RVB974S	Bristol VRT/SL3/6LXB	Willowbrook	H43/31F	1978	Ex Stagecoach South, 1994
1125	RVB978S	Bristol VRT/SL3/6LXB	Willowbrook	H43/31F	1978	Ex Stagecoach South, 1994
1126	TFN990T	Bristol VRT/SL3/6LXB	Willowbrook	H43/31F	1978	Ex Stagecoach South, 1994
1127	PRU917R	Bristol VRT/SL3/6LXB	Eastern Coach Works	H43/31F	1977	Ex Bluebird, 1994
1128	RPR716R	Bristol VRT/SL3/6LXB	Eastern Coach Works	H43/31F	1977	Ex Bluebird, 1994
1129	WHH415S	Bristol VRT/SL3/501	Eastern Coach Works	H43/31F	1978	Ex Bluebird, 1994
1136	LEO736Y	Leyland Atlantean AN68D/1R	Northern Counties	H43/32F	1983	Ex Ribble, 1995
1144	SCN244S	Leyland Atlantean AN68A/2R	Alexander AL	H49/37F	1978	Ex Busways, 1995
1157	SCN257S	Leyland Atlantean AN68A/2R	Alexander AL	H49/37F	1978	Ex Busways, 1995
1161	SCN261S	Leyland Atlantean AN68A/2R	Alexander AL	H49/37F	1978	Ex Busways, 1995

Previous Registrations:

ABV669A	927GTA		
F790PSN	F70RFS, MSU463	GSU345	B211FFS, MSU445
GSU341	B207FFS	IIL3504	E626UNE, GIL2967, E937XSB
GSU342	B208FFS	IIL3506	E624UNE, MIB658, E931XSB
GSU343	B209FFS	MSU499	D319SGB
GSU344	B210FFS	VLT77	F396DHL

KINGSTON UPON HULL

Kingston-upon-Hull City Transport Ltd, Lombard Street,
Kingston-upon-Hull, HU2 8QN

42	BUT24Y	Dennis Dorchester SDA801	Plaxton Paramount 3200	C49F	1983	Ex Leicester, 1987
43	BUT25Y	Dennis Dorchester SDA801	Plaxton Paramount 3200	C49F	1983	Ex Leicester, 1987
50	IIL1319	Volvo B10M-61	Plaxton Paramount 3200 II	C50FT	1986	
51	IIL1321	Volvo B10M-61	Plaxton Paramount 3200 III	C50FT	1986	
52	E52WAG	Volvo B10M-61	Plaxton Paramount 3200 III	C50FT	1988	
53	F53EAT	Dennis Javelin SDA1907	Plaxton Paramount 3200 III	C48FT	1989	
55	F55EAT	Dennis Javelin SDA1907	Plaxton Paramount 3200 III	C49FT	1989	
56	G56SAG	Volvo B10M-61	Plaxton Paramount 3500 III	C48FT	1990	
60	B60WKH	Leyland National 2 NL116HLXCT/1R		B24DL	1984	
61	YAY21Y	Dennis Lancet SD506	Duple Dominant	B25DL	1982	Ex Leicester, 1987
71	H71XKH	Leyland Swift ST2R44C97A4	Reeve Burgess Harrier	C34FT	1990	
72	K572DFS	Volvo B10M-60	Plaxton Premiére 320	C53F	1993	Ex East Midland, 1995
73	K573DFS	Volvo B10M-60	Plaxton Premiére 320	C53F	1993	Ex East Midland, 1995
74	J749CWT	Volvo B10M-60	Plaxton Premiére 350	C53F	1992	Ex Wallace Arnold, 1995
75	K571DFS	Volvo B10M-60	Plaxton Premiére 320	C53F	1993	Ex East Midland, 1995

106-110

Dennis Dominator DDA904   Alexander RL   H43/32F   1984

106	B106UAT	107	B107UAT	108	B108UAT	109	B109UAT	110	B110UAT

111	C111CAT	Dennis Dominator DDA1007	East Lancashire	H43/28F	1986
112	C112CAT	Dennis Dominator DDA1007	East Lancashire	H43/28F	1986
113	C113CAT	Dennis Dominator DDA1007	East Lancashire	DPH43/28F	1986

122-131

Dennis Dominator DDA1006   East Lancashire   H45/30F   1985-86

122	C122CAT	124	C124CAT	126	C126CAT	128	C128CAT	131	C131CAT
123	C123CAT	125	C125CAT	127	C127CAT	129	C129CAT		

132	E132SAT	Dennis Dominator DDA1014	East Lancashire (1992)	H45/21D	1987

133-141

Dennis Dominator DDA1014   East Lancashire   H45/32F   1987

133	E133SAT	135	E135SAT	137	E137SAT	139	E139SAT	141	E141SAT
134	E134SAT	136	E136SAT	138	E138SAT	140	E140SAT		

142-151

Dennis Dominator DDA1016   East Lancashire   H45/31F   1988

142	E142BKH	144	E144BKH	146	E146BKH	148	E148BKH	150	E150BKH
143	E143BKH	145	E145BKH	147	E147BKH	149	E149BKH	151	E151BKH

Typical vehicles in the Kingston-upon-Hull operation are Dennis Dominators, the one shown here with East Lancashire bodywork. During 1996 the KHCT names are to be replaced with white on blue Stagecoach logos in a similar style to the white on red ones used in London. *Mike Fowler*

Above: In addition to the Volvo saloons, three Olympians joined the KHCT fleet during 1995. Pictured here is 817, M817KRH. *Tony Wilson*

Opposite, top: The blue and yellow livery is to be retained for the time being at Hull. Representing the minibus fleet is 609, D609MKH, with a Robin Hood City Nipper body style is built on the Iveco Daily chassis. *Tony Wilson*
Opposite, bottom: New Volvo B10Ms were placed in service during 1995 and these were fitted with Northern Counties Paladin bodywork. Arriving in the city centre is 712, M712KRH. *Tony Wilson*

152-157

Dennis Dominator DDA1027		East Lancashire		H47/33F		1989			

152	F152HAT	154	F154HAT	155	F155HAT	156	F156HAT	157	F157HAT
153	F153HAT								

192	PSO179W	Leyland Tiger TRCTL11/3R	Duple Dominant IV	C51F	1981	Ex Stagecoach Darlington, 1995
204	J204JKH	Volvo B10M-60	Plaxton Paramount 3500 III	C51FT	1992	Ex York Pullman, 1993
205	J205JKH	Volvo B10M-60	Plaxton Paramount 3500 III	C51FT	1992	Ex York Pullman, 1993

516-530

MCW Metrobus DR102	MCW	H43/30F	1981

516	SAG516W	519	SAG519W	522	SAG522W	525	SAG525W	528	SAG528W
517	SAG517W	520	SAG520W	523	SAG523W	526	SAG526W	529	SAG529W
518	SAG518W	521	SAG521W	524	SAG524W	527	SAG527W	530	SAG530W

601-615

Iveco Daily 49-10	Robin Hood City Nipper	B25F*	1987	*602 is B18F
			604/6 ex Stagecoach Darlington, 1995	

601	D601MKH	604	D604MKH	608	D608MKH	612	D612MKH	614	D614MKH
602	D602MKH	605	D605MKH	609	D609MKH	613	D613MKH	615	D615MKH
603	D603MKH	606	D606MKH	611	D611MKH				

701-706

Scania N112CRB	East Lancashire	DP49F*	1988	*703 is B50F

701	F701BAT	703	F703BAT	704	F704BAT	705	F705BAT	706	F706CAG
702	F702BAT								

707-718

Volvo B10M-55	Northern Counties Paladin	B48F	1995

707	M707KRH	710	M710KRH	713	M713KRH	715	M715KRH	717	M717KRH
708	M708KRH	711	M711KRH	714	M714KRH	716	M716KRH	718	M718KRH
709	M709KRH	712	M712KRH						

801-816

Scania N113DRB	East Lancashire	H51/37F	1989-90	*809-16 are H47/37F

801	G801JRH	805	G805JRH	808	G808LAG	811	H811WKH	814	H814WKH
802	G802JRH	806	G806JRH	809	H809WKH	812	H812WKH	815	H815WKH
803	G803JRH	807	G807LAG	810	H810WKH	813	H813WKH	816	H816WKH
804	G804JRH								

817	M817KRH	Volvo Olympian YN2RV18Z4	Northern Counties Palatine	H47/29F	1995
818	M818KRH	Volvo Olympian YN2RV18Z4	Northern Counties Palatine	H47/29F	1995
819	M819KRH	Volvo Olympian YN2RV18Z4	Northern Counties Palatine	H47/29F	1995

Previous Registrations:

IIL1319	C50FRH	IIL1321	D51ORH	PSO179W	BSG545W, CSU922

MIDLAND RED

Midland Red (South) Ltd, Railway Terrace, Rugby, Warwickshire, CV21 3HS

Depots : Canal Street, Banbury; Rowley Drive, Coventry; Station Approach, Leamington Spa; Newtown Road, Nuneaton; Railway Terrace, Rugby and Avenue Farm, Stratford-on-Avon.

1xxx operate as G & G Travel; 2xxx Vanguard; 3xxx David R Grasby.

1	A75NAC	Leyland Tiger TRCTL11/2R	Plaxton Paramount 3200 E	C47FT	1983	
3001	6267AC	Volvo B10M-61	Ikarus Blue Danube	C53F	1987	Ex David R Grasby, 1995
2	A76NAC	Leyland Tiger TRCTL11/2R	Plaxton Paramount 3200 E	C47FT	1983	
3002	3669DG	Volvo B10M-61	Plaxton Supreme V	C53F	1982	Ex David R Grasby, 1995
5	331HWD	Leyland Leopard PSU3E/4R	Plaxton Supreme IV Express	C49F	1980	Ex Midland Red North, 1981
6	3273AC	Leyland Leopard PSU3E/4R	Plaxton Supreme IV Express	C46FT	1980	Ex Midland Red North, 1981
3007	4012VC	Leyland Leopard PSU3E/4R	Plaxton Supreme IV Express	C53F	1979	Ex Premier Travel, 1991
9	BVP791V	Leyland Leopard PSU3E/4R	Willowbrook 003	C49F	1980	
3015	NPA230W	Leyland Leopard PSU3E/4R	Plaxton Supreme IV Express	C53F	1981	Ex East Midland, 1994
2016	YBO16T	Leyland Leopard PSU3E/2R	East Lancashire	B51F	1979	Ex G & G, Leamington, 1993
2018	YBO18T	Leyland Leopard PSU3E/2R	East Lancashire	B51F	1979	Ex G & G, Leamington, 1993
19	A848VML	Leyland Leopard PSU3E/4R	Duple Dominant IV (1983)	C53F	1979	Ex Grey-Green, 1987
20	TVC504W	Leyland Leopard PSU3E/4R	Eastern Coach Works	C53F	1981	
3021	B21AUS	DAF MB200DKFL600	Van Hool Alizée	C48FT	1985	Ex David R Grasby, 1995
3026	ELJ209V	Leyland Leopard PSU3E/4R	Plaxton Supreme IV Express	C53F	1979	Ex East Midland, 1994
27	JWA27W	Leyland Leopard PSU3E/4R	Willowbrook 003	C47F	1981	Ex East Midland, 1994
3028	C328DND	Volvo B10M-61	Van Hool Alizée	C53F	1986	Ex David R Grasby, 1995
29	NAK29X	Leyland Leopard PSU3F/4R	Duple Dominant IV	C47F	1981	Ex East Midland, 1994
1051	KIB8140	Leyland National 10351A/2R		B22DL	1978	Ex London Buses, 1991
1052	AIB4053	Leyland National 10351A/2R		B22DL	1978	Ex London Buses, 1991
1053	PIB8019	Leyland National 10351A/2R		B22DL	1978	Ex London Buses, 1991
1058	9984PG	Leyland Leopard PSU3E/4R	Duple Dominant II Express	C53F	1980	Ex Grey-Green, 1988
1059	E630KCX	DAF SB2305DHTD585	Duple 320	C53F	1988	Ex Gray, Hoyland Common, 1990

60-65

		Volvo B10M-60			Plaxton Paramount 3500 III	C48FT	1990	Ex Wallace Arnold, 1993	
60	G528LWU	62	G530LWU	63	G531LWU	64	G532LWU	65	G535LWU
61	G529LWU								

2066	3063VC	Volvo B10M-60	Plaxton Paramount 3500 III	C51FT	1990	Ex Wallace Arnold, 1993
2067	9258VC	Volvo B10M-60	Plaxton Paramount 3500 III	C51FT	1990	Ex Wallace Arnold, 1993
1068	WSU293	Volvo B10M-60	Plaxton Paramount 3200 III	C53F	1990	Ex Cheltenham & Gloucester, 1993
70	BIW4977	Leyland Tiger TRCTL11/3R	Plaxton Paramount 3200 E	C49FT	1984	
3073	491GAC	Leyland Tiger TRCTL11/3RH	Plaxton Paramount 3200 II	C51F	1984	
2074	4828VC	Leyland Tiger TRCTL11/3RH	Plaxton Paramount 3500 II	C51F	1985	Ex Sovereign, 1990
75	9737VC	Leyland Tiger TRCTL11/3R	Plaxton Paramount 3500 II	C51F	1985	Ex Sovereign, 1990
2076	6253VC	Leyland Tiger TRCTL11/3RH	Plaxton Paramount 3200 II	C51F	1986	Ex Thames Transit, 1991
2077	6804VC	Leyland Tiger TRCTL11/3RH	Plaxton Paramount 3200 II	C51F	1986	Ex Thames Transit, 1991
3086	MKV86V	Ford R1114	Plaxton Supreme IV Express	C53F	1980	Ex David R Grasby, 1995
3087	MKV87V	Ford R1014	Plaxton Supreme IV	C45F	1980	Ex David R Grasby, 1995
1087	498FYB	Leyland Tiger TRCTL11/3R	Plaxton Paramount 3200	C50F	1983	Ex Cheltenham & Gloucester, 1993
1088	A8GGT	Leyland Tiger TRCTL11/3R	Plaxton Paramount 3200 E	C57F	1983	Ex Cheltenham & Gloucester, 1993
1089	A7GGT	Leyland Tiger TRCTL11/3RH	Plaxton Paramount 3200	C51F	1984	
90	552OHU	Leyland Tiger TRCTL11/3R	Plaxton Paramount 3200	C57F	1983	Ex Cheltenham & Gloucester, 1990
91	420GAC	Leyland Tiger TRCTL11/3R	Plaxton Paramount 3200	C46FT	1983	Ex Cheltenham & Gloucester, 1991

201-216

		Volvo B10M-55			Alexander PS		DP48F*	1995	206-213 are B49F	
201	M201LHP	205	M205LHP	208	N208TDU	211	N211TDU	214	N214TDU
202	M202LHP	206	N206TDU	209	M209LHP	212	N212TDU	215	N215TDU
203	M203LHP	207	N207TDU	210	M210LHP	213	N213TDU	216	N216TDU
204	M204LHP								

Opposite, top: **Coventry Council House provides the background to Midland Red 206, N206TDU, one of sixteen added to the fleet during 1995. Interestingly, the batch is split with both bus and high-back seated examples.** *Richard Godfrey - Opposite, bottom:* **An interesting addition to the G&G Travel operation is 1803, TAE639S, a Leyland National. Displaying a National 3 badge, it is one of many extensively refurbished with DAF engines by Cheltenham & Gloucester from where it came in 1995. To identify vehicles and their operations Midland Red add a prefix to the main number which, in this case, is now numbered 803 following its transfer to Nuneaton.** *Richard Godfrey*

300	E433YHL	Mercedes-Benz 709D	Reeve Burgess Beaver	B25F	1988	Ex Loftys, Bridge Trafford, 1993
301	G301WHP	Mercedes-Benz 709D	PMT	B25F	1989	
302	G302WHP	Mercedes-Benz 709D	PMT	B25F	1989	
303	G303WHP	Mercedes-Benz 709D	PMT	B25F	1989	
304	J304THP	Mercedes-Benz 709D	Alexander Sprint	B25F	1992	
305	J305THP	Mercedes-Benz 709D	Alexander Sprint	B25F	1992	
306	K306ARW	Mercedes-Benz 709D	Wright NimBus	B25F	1992	
307	L307SKV	Mercedes-Benz 709D	Wright NimBus	B25F	1993	

308-330

Mercedes-Benz 709D   Alexander Sprint   B23F   1994

308	L308YDU	313	L313YDU	318	L318YDU	323	L323YDU	327	L327YKV
309	L309YDU	314	L314YDU	319	L319YDU	324	L324YDU	328	L328YKV
310	L310YDU	315	L315YDU	320	L320YDU	325	L325YDU	329	L329YKV
311	L311YDU	316	L316YDU	321	L321YDU	326	L326YKV	330	L330YKV
312	L312YDU	317	L317YDU	322	L322YDU				

331-346

Mercedes-Benz 709D   Alexander Sprint   B23F   1995

331	M331LHP	335	M335LHP	338	M338LHP	341	M341LHP	344	M344LHP
332	M332LHP	336	M336LHP	339	M339LHP	342	M342LHP	345	M345LHP
334	M334LHP	337	M337LHP	340	M340LHP	343	M343LHP	346	M346LHP

| 2345 | C102HKG | Ford Transit 190D | Robin Hood | B16F | 1986 | Ex Red & White, 1993 |

352-358

Ford Transit 190D   Alexander AM   B16F   1985   Ex Cheltenham & Gloucester, 1990

| 352 | C619SFH | 1353 | C620SFH | 354 | C622SFH | 355 | C623SFH | 358 | C628SFH |

361	C702FKE	Ford Transit 190D	Dormobile	B16F	1986	Ex East Kent, 1990
362	C703FKE	Ford Transit 190D	Dormobile	B16F	1986	Ex East Kent, 1990
364	C714FKE	Ford Transit 190D	Dormobile	B16F	1986	Ex East Kent, 1991
366	D313WPE	Ford Transit 190D	Carlyle	B16F	1986	Ex Alder Valley, 1991
367	D314WPE	Ford Transit 190D	Carlyle	B16F	1986	Ex Alder Valley, 1991
368	D315WPE	Ford Transit 190D	Carlyle	B16F	1986	Ex Alder Valley, 1991
369	D320WPE	Ford Transit 190D	Carlyle	B16F	1986	Ex Alder Valley, 1991
371	C729JJO	Ford Transit 190D	Carlyle	B16F	1986	Ex City of Oxford, 1991
373	C718FKE	Ford Transit 190D	Dormobile	B16F	1986	Ex East Kent, 1991
383	C618SFH	Ford Transit 190D	Alexander	B16F	1985	Ex Cheltenham & Gloucester, 1994
384	C627SFH	Ford Transit 190D	Alexander	B16F	1985	Ex Cheltenham & Gloucester, 1994
385	C629SFH	Ford Transit 190D	Alexander	B16F	1985	Ex Cheltenham & Gloucester, 1994
386	C716FKE	Ford Transit 190D	Dormobile	B16F	1986	Ex Stagecoach South, 1994
387	C634SFH	Ford Transit 190D	Alexander	B16F	1985	Ex Cheltenham & Gloucester, 1994
388	C635SFH	Ford Transit 190D	Alexander	B16F	1985	Ex Cheltenham & Gloucester, 1994
389	C638SFH	Ford Transit 190D	Alexander	B16F	1985	Ex Cheltenham & Gloucester, 1994
390	C705FKE	Ford Transit 190D	Dormobile	B16F	1986	Ex Stagecoach South, 1994
391	C715FKE	Ford Transit 190D	Dormobile	B16F	1986	Ex Stagecoach South, 1994
392	C724FKE	Ford Transit 190D	Dormobile	B16F	1986	Ex Stagecoach South, 1994
400	F71LAL	Mercedes-Benz 811D	Alexander AM	DP33F	1988	Ex Skills, Nottingham, 1991

401-418

Mercedes-Benz 811D   Wright NimBus   B33F*   1991   *402/4/7-12 are DP33F
   *405/6/13/7/8 are B31F

401	H401MRW	405	H495MRW	409	J409PRW	413	J413PRW	416	J416PRW
402	H402MRW	406	H406MRW	410	J410PRW	414	J414PRW	417	J417PRW
403	H403MRW	407	J407PRW	411	J411PRW	415	J415PRW	418	J418PRW
404	H404MRW	408	J408PRW	412	J412PRW				

| 419 | G115OGA | Mercedes-Benz 811D | Alexander AM | DP33F | 1988 | Ex Beaton, Blantyre, 1992 |

420-425

Mercedes-Benz 811D   Wright NimBus   B31F   1993

| 420 | K420ARW | 422 | K422ARW | 423 | K423ARW | 424 | K424ARW | 425 | K425ARW |
| 421 | K421ARW | | | | | | | | |

426	CSV219	Mercedes-Benz 811D	Optare StarRider	DP29F	1989	Ex Brents Coaches, Watford, 1993
1427	H912XGA	Mercedes-Benz 814D	Reeve Burgess Beaver	DP33F	1990	Ex Loftys, Bridge Trafford, 1993
3435	ANA435Y	DAF MB200DKTL600	Plaxton Paramount 3200	C53F	1983	Ex David R Grasby, 1995

Six Volvo B6s joined the Midland Red fleet in 1994. Seen at the northern end of the X18 Coventry to Stratford service is 455, L455YAC. *Richard Godfrey*

451-456

Volvo B6-9.9M   Alexander Dash   B40F   1994

451	L451YAC	453	L453YAC	454	L454YAC	455	L455YAC	456	L456YAC
452	L452YAC								

483	D273OOJ	Freight Rover Sherpa	Carlyle	B20F	1987	Ex Carlyle, 1988
1484	D271OOJ	Freight Rover Sherpa	Carlyle	B20F	1987	Ex Carlyle, 1988
1485	D735OOG	Freight Rover Sherpa	Carlyle	B18F	1987	Ex Carlyle, 1988
1486	D736OOG	Freight Rover Sherpa	Carlyle	B20F	1987	Ex Carlyle, 1988
1489	E77PUH	Freight Rover Sherpa	Carlyle Citybus 2	B20F	1987	Ex Red & White, 1991
1490	E95OUH	Freight Rover Sherpa	Carlyle Citybus 2	B20F	1987	Ex Red & White, 1991
1491	E99OUH	Freight Rover Sherpa	Carlyle Citybus 2	B20F	1987	Ex Red & White, 1991

502-590

Leyland National 11351A/1R   B49F*   1976-77   Ex Midland Red, 1981
582 is fitted with DAF engine; 504/90 are B49DL(variable); 554/87 ex Cheltenham & Gloucester, 1994-95

2502	JOX502P	2553	NOE553R	577	NOE577R	582	NOE582R	589	NOE589R
2503	JOX503P	554	NOE554R	578	NOE578R	586	NOE586R	590	NOE590R
504	JOX504P	2571	NOE571R	581	NOE581R	2587	NOE587R		

2507	XGR728R	Leyland National 11351A/1R (DAF)	B49F	1977	Ex United, 1993
2509	THX231S	Leyland National 10351A/2R	B36D	1978	Ex London Buses, 1991
2510	CBV780S	Leyland National 11351A/1R	B49F	1977	Ex Thames Transit, 1991
591	YEU446V	Leyland National 10351B/1R	B44F	1981	Ex Cheltenham & Gloucester, 1994
592	NOE551R	Leyland National 11351A/1R	B49F	1976	Ex Midland Red, 1981
593	KHT122P	Leyland National 11351/1R	B52F	1976	Ex Cheltenham & Gloucester, 1994
594	VAE502T	Leyland National 10351B/1R	B44F	1979	Ex Cheltenham & Gloucester, 1994
595	GOL426N	Leyland National 11351/1R	B49F	1975	Ex Cheltenham & Gloucester, 1994
596	GOL413N	Leyland National 11351/1R	B49F	1975	Ex Cheltenham & Gloucester, 1994
597	HEU122N	Leyland National 11351/1R	B52F	1975	Ex Cheltenham & Gloucester, 1994
598	KHT124P	Leyland National 11351/1R	B52F	1976	Ex Cheltenham & Gloucester, 1994
599	WFR392V	Leyland National 10351B/1R	B44F	1980	Ex Ribble, 1994
2600	SAE753S	Leyland National 11351A/1R	B52F	1978	Ex Cheltenham & Gloucester, 1994

602-772   Leyland National 11351A/1R(DAF)   B49F*   1977-80   Ex Midland Red, 1981
*624, 708 are B52F; 755/6 have LPG engines

602	NOE602R	622	PUK622R	627	PUK627R	708	TOF708S	755	XOV755T
603	NOE603R	623	PUK623R	628	PUK628R	709	TOF709S	756	XOV756T
604	NOE604R	624	PUK624R	629	PUK629R	710	TOF710S	760	XOV760T
605	NOE605R	625	PUK625R	664	SOA664S	753	XOV753T	771	BVP771V
606	NOE606R	626	PUK626R	707	TOF707S	754	XOV754T	772	BVP772V
621	PUK621R								

1802	SHH392X	Leyland National 2 NL116AL11/1R		B52F	1982	Ex Cheltenham & Gloucester, 1995
803	TAE639S	Leyland National 11351A/1R(DAF)		B52F	1978	Ex Cheltenham & Gloucester, 1995
1808	BVP808V	Leyland National 2 NL116L11/1R		B49F	1980	Ex North Western, 1991
1809	SVV589W	Leyland National 2 NL116L11/1R		B49F	1980	Ex Luton & District, 1991
816	BVP816V	Leyland National 2 NL116L11/1R (DAF)		B49F	1980	Ex Midland Red, 1981
817	BVP817V	Leyland National 2 NL116L11/1R (DAF)		B49F	1980	Ex Midland Red, 1981
818	BVP818V	Leyland National 2 NL116L11/1R (DAF)		B49F	1980	Ex Midland Red, 1981
1820	F660PWK	Leyland Lynx LX112L10ZR1R	Leyland	B51F	1988	
1821	F661PWK	Leyland Lynx LX112L10ZR1R	Leyland	B51F	1988	

821-830   Iveco Daily 49.10   Marshall C29   B23F   1993   Ex Selkent, 1995

821	K521EFL	823	K523EFL	825	K525EFL	827	K527EFL	829	K529EFL
822	K522EFL	824	K524EFL	826	K526EFL	828	K528EFL	830	K530EFL

834	D34KAX	Iveco Daily 49.10	Robin Hood City Nippy	B19F	1986	Ex Rhondda, 1992
843	D43KAX	Iveco Daily 49.10	Robin Hood City Nippy	B19F	1986	Ex Rhondda, 1992
845	D45KAX	Iveco Daily 49.10	Robin Hood City Nippy	B19F	1986	Ex Rhondda, 1992
847	D47KAX	Iveco Daily 49.10	Robin Hood City Nippy	B19F	1986	Ex Rhondda, 1992

851-862   Iveco Daily 49.10   Robin Hood City Nippy   B19F*   1986-87   *852 is B21F

851	D851CKV	853	D853CKV	856	D856CKV	858	D858CKV	862	D862CKV
852	D852CKV	854	D854CKV	857	D857CKV	859	D859CKV		

864-868   Iveco Daily 49.10   Robin Hood City Nippy   B19F   1988

864	F864PAC	865	F865PAC	866	F866PAC	867	F867PAC	868	F868PAC

871	F871UAC	Iveco Daily 49.10	Robin Hood City Nippy	B25F	1989	
872	F872UAC	Iveco Daily 49.10	Robin Hood City Nippy	B25F	1989	
873	G26XBK	Iveco Daily 49.10	Phoenix	B25F	1990	Ex Loftys, Bridge Trafford, 1993
885	D885CKV	Iveco Daily 49.10	Robin Hood City Nippy	DP19F	1986	
888	D888CKV	Iveco Daily 49.10	Robin Hood City Nippy	DP19F	1986	

902-912   Leyland Olympian ONLXB/1R   Eastern Coach Works   H45/32F   1983-84

1902	A542HAC	1904	A544HAC	1906	A546HAC	910	B910ODU	1912	B912ODU
1903	A543HAC	1905	A545HAC	1907	A547HAC	1911	B911ODU		

927	NHU671R	Bristol VRT/SL3/6LXB	Eastern Coach Works	H43/27D	1979	Ex Cheltenham & Gloucester, 1994
2928	LHT725P	Bristol VRT/SL3/501(6LXB)	Eastern Coach Works	H39/31F	1976	Ex Cheltenham & Gloucester, 1994
2929	NHU672R	Bristol VRT/SL3/6LXB	Eastern Coach Works	H43/27D	1979	Ex Cheltenham & Gloucester, 1994
1930	LHT724P	Bristol VRT/SL3/501(6LXB)	Eastern Coach Works	H43/31F	1976	Ex Swindon & District, 1992
1931	MAU145P	Bristol VRT/SL3/6LXB	Eastern Coach Works	H43/31F	1976	Ex Bluebird, 1993
931	CBV11S	Bristol VRT/SL3/501(6LXB)	Eastern Coach Works	H43/31F	1977	Ex Ribble, 1994
1932	ONH846P	Bristol VRT/SL3/6LXB	Eastern Coach Works	H43/31F	1976	Ex Bluebird, 1993
932	CBV16S	Bristol VRT/SL3/501(6LXB)	Eastern Coach Works	H43/31F	1977	Ex Ribble, 1994
1933	PEU516R	Bristol VRT/SL3/6LXB	Eastern Coach Works	H43/31F	1977	Ex Swindon & District, 1992
933	CBV20S	Bristol VRT/SL3/501(6LXB)	Eastern Coach Works	H43/31F	1977	Ex Ribble, 1994
935	DBV31W	Bristol VRT/SL3/6LXB	Eastern Coach Works	H43/31F	1980	Ex Ribble, 1994
936	URF661S	Bristol VRT/SL3/501	Eastern Coach Works	H43/31F	1977	Ex Ribble, 1994
937	DWF195V	Bristol VRT/SL3/6LXB	Eastern Coach Works	H43/31F	1979	Ex East Midland, 1994
938	DWF197V	Bristol VRT/SL3/6LXB	Eastern Coach Works	H43/31F	1979	Ex East Midland, 1994
2939	DWF194V	Bristol VRT/SL3/6LXB	Eastern Coach Works	H43/31F	1979	Ex East Midland, 1994
940	PEU511R	Bristol VRT/SL3/6LXB	Eastern Coach Works	DPH43/31F	1977	Ex Badgerline, 1993
2941	GTX746W	Bristol VRT/SL3/501	Eastern Coach Works	H43/31F	1980	Ex Red & White, 1993
943	GTX754W	Bristol VRT/SL3/501	Eastern Coach Works	H43/31F	1980	Ex Red & White, 1993
944	HUD475S	Bristol VRT/SL3/6LXB	Eastern Coach Works	H43/31F	1977	Ex City of Oxford, 1993
945	HUD480S	Bristol VRT/SL3/6LXB	Eastern Coach Works	H43/31F	1977	Ex City of Oxford, 1993
946	HUD479S	Bristol VRT/SL3/6LXB	Eastern Coach Works	H43/31F	1977	Ex City of Oxford, 1993
947	AET181T	Bristol VRT/SL3/6LXB	Eastern Coach Works	H43/31F	1979	Ex East Midland, 1994
3948	VTV170S	Bristol VRT/SL3/6LXB	Eastern Coach Works	H43/31F	1978	Ex East Midland, 1994

Pool Meadow bus station in Coventry is the location of this picture of Leyland Olympian 964, C964XVC, and one of five with high-back seating supplied to the fleet in the mid 1980s of which four are based at Stratford, the fifth working from Leamington. *Richard Godfrey*

3949	DWF189V	Bristol VRT/SL3/6LXB	Eastern Coach Works	H43/31F	1980	Ex East Midland, 1994
950	TWS903T	Bristol VRT/SL3/6LXB	Eastern Coach Works	H43/28F	1979	Ex Cheltenham & Gloucester, 1995
952	OUC44R	Leyland Fleetline FE30AGR	MCW	H44/29F	1976	Ex Stevenson's, 1989
953	OJD241R	Leyland Fleetline FE30AGR	MCW	H44/29F	1977	Ex Stevenson's, 1989
954	OUC42R	Leyland Fleetline FE30AGR	MCW	H44/29F	1976	Ex Stevenson's, 1990
955	OJD136R	Leyland Fleetline FE30AGR	Park Royal	H44/29F	1976	Ex Stevenson's, 1990
1958	WDA994T	Leyland Fleetline FE30AGR	MCW	H43/33F	1979	Ex West Midlands Travel, 1990
959	YNA363M	Daimler Fleetline CRG6LXB	Northern Counties	H43/32F	1974	Ex Greater Manchester PTE, 1988
960	B960ODU	Leyland Olympian ONLXB/1R	Eastern Coach Works	DPH42/30F	1984	
961	B961ODU	Leyland Olympian ONLXB/1R	Eastern Coach Works	DPH42/30F	1984	
962	C962XVC	Leyland Olympian ONLXB/1RH	Eastern Coach Works	DPH42/29F	1986	
963	C963XVC	Leyland Olympian ONLXB/1RH	Eastern Coach Works	DPH42/29F	1986	
964	C964XVC	Leyland Olympian ONLXB/1RH	Eastern Coach Works	DPH42/29F	1986	
3968	KUC968P	Leyland Fleetline FE30ALR	MCW	H44/28F	1976	Ex David R Grasby, 1995
970	SCN252S	Leyland Atlantean AN68A/2R	Alexander AL	H49/37F	1978	Ex Busways, 1995
971	SCN253S	Leyland Atlantean AN68A/2R	Alexander AL	H49/37F	1978	Ex Busways, 1995
972	SCN265S	Leyland Atlantean AN68A/2R	Alexander AL	H49/37F	1978	Ex Busways, 1995
973	UVK298T	Leyland Atlantean AN68A/2R	Alexander AL	H49/37F	1978	Ex Busways, 1995
974	VCU301T	Leyland Atlantean AN68A/2R	Alexander AL	H49/37F	1978	Ex Busways, 1995
975	VCU310T	Leyland Atlantean AN68A/2R	Alexander AL	H49/37F	1978	Ex Busways, 1995
976	AVK172V	Leyland Atlantean AN68A/2R	Alexander AL	H49/37F	1978	Ex Busways, 1995
977	EJR106W	Leyland Atlantean AN68A/2R	Alexander AL	H49/37F	1978	Ex Busways, 1995
978		Leyland Atlantean AN68A/2R	Alexander AL	H49/37F	1978	Ex Busways, 1996
979		Leyland Atlantean AN68A/2R	Alexander AL	H49/37F	1978	Ex Busways, 1996
980		Leyland Atlantean AN68A/2R	Alexander AL	H49/37F	1978	Ex Busways, 1996
981		Leyland Atlantean AN68A/2R	Alexander AL	H49/3/F	1978	Ex Busways, 1996

Previous Registrations:

3063VC	G543LWU	552OHU	A201RHT	A7GGT	B72OKV
3273AC	BVP788V	6253VC	YDK917, JPU817, C472CAP	A8GGT	A202RHT
331HWD	BVP787V	6267AC	E422KAC	A848VML	FRA64V
3669DG	YKV811X	6804VC	WVT618, C473CAP	AIB4053	THX186S
4012VC	KUB546V	9258VC	G544LWU	BIW4977	A70KDU
420GAC	CDG213Y	9737VC	C212PPE	CSV219	F846TLU
4828VC	C211PPE	9984PG	FYX815W	KIB8140	THX249S
491GAC	B73OKV	A75NAC	A190GVC, 420GAC	PIB8019	THX119S
498FYB	CDG207Y	A76NAC	A191GVC, 491GAC	WSU293	From New

RED & WHITE

Red & White Services Ltd; The Valleys Bus Company Ltd; Aberdare Bus Company Ltd,
1 St David's Road, Cwmbran, Gwent, NP44 1QX

Depots and outstations: Red & White - Mill Street, Abergavenny; Bishops Meadow, Brecon; Warwick Road, Brynmawr; Cinderford; Bulwark Road, Chepstow; Risca Road, Crosskeys; St David's Road, Cwmbran; Lydney; Ross on Wye; **The Valleys** - Merthyr Industrial Estate, Pant, Merthyr Tydfil; Commercial Street, Pengam; **Aberdare Bus** - Cwmbach New Road, Cwmbach, Aberdare.

11	E292TAX	Renault-Dodge S56	Northern Counties	DP25F	1988	Ex Cynon Valley, 1992
20	E931UBO	Renault-Dodge S56	Northern Counties	DP25F	1988	Ex Cynon Valley, 1992
22	G21CSG	Renault-Dodge S56	Reeve Burgess Beaver	B25F	1989	Ex Fife Scottish, 1994
25	G24CSG	Renault-Dodge S56	Reeve Burgess Beaver	B25F	1989	Ex Fife Scottish, 1994
281	D950UDY	Mercedes-Benz L608D	Alexander	DP19F	1986	Ex Stagecoach South, 1994
282	D544RCK	Mercedes-Benz L608D	Reeve Burgess	B25F	1986	Ex Ribble, 1994
283	D540RCK	Mercedes-Benz L608D	Reeve Burgess	B20F	1986	Ex Ribble, 1994
284w	C595SHC	Mercedes-Benz L608D	PMT Hanbridge	B20F	1986	Ex Stagecoach South, 1994
285w	C808SDY	Mercedes-Benz L608D	Alexander	B20F	1986	Ex Stagecoach South, 1994
286	C902HWF	Mercedes-Benz L608D	Reeve Burgess	B25F	1985	Ex Bluebird, 1994
287w	C820SDY	Mercedes-Benz L608D	Alexander	B20F	1986	Ex Stagecoach South, 1994
288	C596SHC	Mercedes-Benz L608D	PMT Hanbridge	B20F	1986	Ex Stagecoach South, 1994
289	C593SHC	Mercedes-Benz L608D	PMT Hanbridge	B20F	1986	Ex Stagecoach South, 1994
295	F958HTO	Iveco Daily 49.10	Robin Hood City Nippy	B23F	1988	Ex East Midland, 1994
296	G912KWF	Iveco Daily 49.10	Reeve Burgess Beaver	B25F	1989	Ex East Midland, 1994
297	G919KWF	Iveco Daily 49.10	Reeve Burgess Beaver	B25F	1989	Ex East Midland, 1994
298	G920KWF	Iveco Daily 49.10	Reeve Burgess Beaver	B25F	1989	Ex East Midland, 1994
299	G924KWF	Iveco Daily 49.10	Reeve Burgess Beaver	B25F	1989	Ex East Midland, 1994
300	H370PNY	Iveco Daily 49-10	Carlyle Dailybus	B25F	1991	Ex Cynon Valley, 1992

As we go to press the last of the large fleet of Freight Rover Sherpa minibuses have been withdrawn for disposal. Also diminishing is the number of Iveco products. Shown here is 300, H370PNY an example fitted with Carlyle Dailybus 2 body style. *Phillip Stephenson*

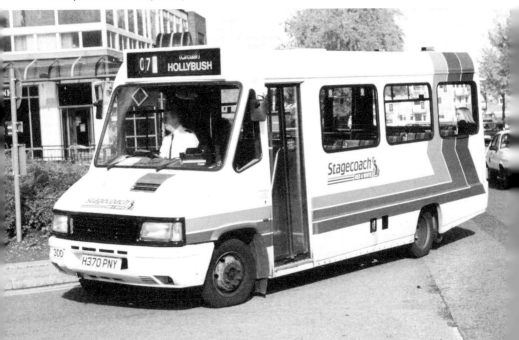

Merthyr bus station is the location for this view of Red & White 343, L343FWO. The Mercedes-Benz 709D with Alexander Sprint body continues as the preferred minibus type with a further 400 due for delivery to the group during 1996. *Richard Godfrey*

301	H301PAX	Mercedes-Benz 709D	PMT Ami	C25F	1991		
302	J302TUH	Mercedes-Benz 709D	PMT Bursley	B25F	1991		
303	J303TUH	Mercedes-Benz 709D	PMT Bursley	B25F	1991		

304-317   Mercedes-Benz 811D   Wright NimBus   B33F   1992

304	J304UKG	307	J307UKG	310	K310YKG	313	K313YKG	316	K316YKG
305	J305UKG	308	K308YKG	311	K311YKG	314	K314YKG	317	K317YKG
306	J306UKG	309	K309YKG	312	K312YKG	315	K315YKG		

318	K318YKG	Mercedes-Benz 709D	Wright NimBus	B25F	1992	
319	K319YKG	Mercedes-Benz 709D	Alexander Sprint	B25F	1992	
320	K320YKG	Mercedes-Benz 709D	Alexander Sprint	B25F	1992	
321	K321YKG	Mercedes-Benz 709D	Alexander Sprint	B25F	1992	
322	K322YKG	Mercedes-Benz 811D	Wright NimBus	B33F	1992	
323	K323YKG	Mercedes-Benz 811D	Wright NimBus	B33F	1992	
324	K324YKG	Mercedes-Benz 811D	Wright NimBus	B33F	1992	
325	K325YKG	Mercedes-Benz 811D	Wright NimBus	B33F	1992	
326	L326CHB	Mercedes-Benz 811D	Marshall C16	B33F	1993	
327	L327CHB	Mercedes-Benz 811D	Marshall C16	B33F	1993	
328	L328CHB	Mercedes-Benz 811D	Marshall C16	B33F	1993	
329	L329CHB	Mercedes-Benz 811D	Marshall C16	B33F	1993	
330	L685CDD	Mercedes-Benz 709D	Alexander Sprint	B25F	1994	Ex Cheltenham & Gloucester, 1994
331	L331CHR	Mercedes-Benz 811D	Marshall C16	B33F	1993	
332	H556TUG	Mercedes-Benz 709D	Dormobile Routemaker	DP27F	1990	Ex Graham's, Tredegar, 1994

334-360   Mercedes-Benz 709D   Alexander Sprint   B25F   1994

334	L334FWO	340	L340FWO	346	M346JBO	351	M351JBO	356	M356JBO
335	L335FWO	341	L341FWO	347	M347JBO	352	M352JBO	357	M357JBO
336	L336FWO	342	L342FWO	348	M348JBO	353	M353JBO	358	M358JBO
337	L337FWO	343	L343FWO	349	M349JBO	354	M354JBO	359	M359JBO
338	L338FWO	344	M344JBO	350	M350JBO	355	M355JBO	360	M360JBO
339	L339FWO	345	M345JBO						

361-371 — Mercedes-Benz 709D — Alexander Sprint — B25F — 1995

361	M361LAX	364	M364LAX	366	M366LAX	368	M368LAX	370	M370LAX
362	M362LAX	365	M365LAX	367	M367LAX	369	M369LAX	371	M371LAX
363	M363LAX								

391	GHB146N	Bristol RESL6L	Eastern Coach Works	B44F	1974	Ex Cynon Valley, 1992
392	HTG354N	Bristol RESL6L	Eastern Coach Works	B44F	1975	Ex Cynon Valley, 1992
393	GHB148N	Bristol RESL6L	Eastern Coach Works	B44F	1974	Ex Cynon Valley, 1992
394	D109NDW	Leyland Lynx LX112TL11ZR1	Leyland Lynx	B48F	1987	Ex Cynon Valley, 1992
395	E113RBO	Leyland Lynx LX112TL11ZR1	Leyland Lynx	B48F	1987	Ex Cynon Valley, 1992
396	E114SDW	Leyland Lynx LX112TL11ZR1	Leyland Lynx	B48F	1987	Ex Cynon Valley, 1992
397	E115SDW	Leyland Lynx LX112TL11ZR1	Leyland Lynx	B48F	1988	Ex Cynon Valley, 1992
398	F74DCW	Leyland Lynx LX2R11C15Z4R	Leyland Lynx 2	DP45F	1989	Ex Cynon Valley, 1992
420	NWO454R	Leyland National 11351A/1R/SC		DP48F	1977	Ex National Welsh, 1991
423	NWO457R	Leyland National 11351A/1R/SC		DP48F	1977	Ex National Welsh, 1991
427	NWO461R	Leyland National 11351A/1R/SC		DP48F	1977	Ex National Welsh, 1991
434	NWO468R	Leyland National 11351A/1R/SC		DP48F	1977	Ex National Welsh, 1991
442	UTX726S	Leyland National 10351A/1R		B44F	1978	Ex Cynon Valley, 1992
448	DDW433V	Leyland National 10351A/1R		B44F	1980	Ex Cynon Valley, 1992
449	DDW434V	Leyland National 10351A/1R		B44F	1980	Ex Cynon Valley, 1992
472	YBO147T	Leyland National 10351A/1R		B44F	1979	Ex National Welsh, 1991
500	YSX934W	Leyland National 2 NL106L11/1R		B44F	1981	Ex Fife Scottish, 1994
501	RSG814V	Leyland National 2 NL116L11/1R		B52F	1980	Ex Fife Scottish, 1994
502	YSX932W	Leyland National 2 NL106L11/1R		B44F	1981	Ex Fife Scottish, 1994
503	YSX933W	Leyland National 2 NL106L11/1R		B44F	1981	Ex Fife Scottish, 1994
504	MSO13W	Leyland National 2 NL116L11/1R		B52F	1980	Ex Fife Scottish, 1994
505	RSG815V	Leyland National 2 NL116L11/1R		B52F	1980	Ex Fife Scottish, 1994
506	WAS765V	Leyland National 2 NL116L11/1R		B52F	1980	Ex Fife Scottish, 1994
507	WAS767V	Leyland National 2 NL116L11/1R		D52F	1980	Ex Fife Scottish, 1994
508	MSO14W	Leyland National 2 NL116L11/1R		B52F	1980	Ex Fife Scottish, 1994
509	YSX926W	Leyland National 2 NL106L11/1R		B44F	1981	Ex Fife Scottish, 1994
510	YSX935W	Leyland National 2 NL106L11/1R		B44F	1981	Ex Fife Scottish, 1994
512	RSG824V	Leyland National 2 NL116L11/1R		B52F	1980	Ex Fife Scottish, 1994
513	RSG825V	Leyland National 2 NL116L11/1R		B52F	1980	Ex Fife Scottish, 1994
514	RSG823V	Leyland National 2 NL116L11/1R		B52F	1980	Ex Fife Scottish, 1995
515	DMS22V	Leyland National 2 NL116L11/1R		B52F	1980	Ex Fife Scottish, 1995
516	NLS987W	Leyland National 2 NL116L11/1R		B52F	1980	Ex Fife Scottish, 1995
517	DMS20V	Leyland National 2 NL116L11/1R		B52F	1980	Ex Fife Scottish, 1995

598-649 — Leyland National 11351A/1R — B49F — 1977-79 — Ex National Welsh, 1991

605/35/49 are fitted with Volvo engines, 619 DAF.

598	SKG908S	619	SKG923S	634	WUH167T	645w	BUH210V	647	BUH212V
605	SKG915S	633	WUH166T	635	WUH168T	646	BUH211V	649	BUH214V

651	NOE552R	Leyland National 11351A/1R	B49F	1976	Ex Cheltenham & Gloucester, 1991
652	NOE573R	Leyland National 11351A/1R(Volvo)	B49F	1976	Ex Midland Red South, 1992
653	NOE572R	Leyland National 11351A/1R(DAF)	B49F	1977	Ex Midland Red South, 1992
654	NOE576R	Leyland National 11351A/1R	B49F	1976	Ex Midland Red South, 1992
658	BPT903S	Leyland National 11351A/1R	B49F	1978	Ex Go-Ahead Northern, 1992
660	XVV540S	Leyland National 11351A/1R	B49F	1976	Ex City Line, 1993
661	MFN114R	Leyland National 11351A/1R	B49F	1976	Ex City Line, 1993
663	PHW985S	Leyland National 11351A/1R(DAF)	B52F	1978	Ex Cheltenham & Gloucester, 1995

701-708 — Volvo B6-9.9M — Alexander Dash — B40F — 1994

701	L701FWO	703	L703FWO	705	L705FWO	707	L707FWO	708	L708FWO
702	L702FWO	704	L704FWO	706	L706FWO				

750-770 — Volvo B10M-55 — Alexander PS — DP48F — 1995

750	M750LAX	755	M755LAX	759	M759LAX	763	M763LAX	767	M767LAX
751	M751LAX	756	M756LAX	760	M760LAX	764	M764LAX	768	M768LAX
752	M752LAX	757	M757LAX	761	M761LAX	765	M765LAX	769	M769LAX
753	M753LAX	758	M758LAX	762	M762LAX	766	M766LAX	770	M770LAX
754	M754LAX								

Opposite: **Typifying the standard Stagecoach deliveries are Red & White 356, M356JBO a Mercedes-Benz 709D seen in Cwmbran during June 1995 and Dennis Javelin 942, M942JBO fitted with a Plaxton Interurban body and liveried for the Stagecoach 2000 express service network.** *Richard Godfrey*

New to West Midlands PTE and passing later to London Buses WDA1T is now operating in the Red & White fleet. One of three single-doored Titans it was transferred from Selkent and has been numbered 865. It is seen passing through Much Birch while heading for the English border town of Hereford. *Richard Godfrey*

825	TWS909T	Bristol VRT/SL3/6LXB	Eastern Coach Works	H43/28F	1979	Ex Cheltenham & Gloucester, 1992
827	A541HAC	Leyland Olympian ONLXB/1R	Eastern Coach Works	H43/31F	1983	Ex Midland Red South, 1993
828	A548HAC	Leyland Olympian ONLXB/1R	Eastern Coach Works	H43/31F	1983	Ex Midland Red South, 1993
829	A549HAC	Leyland Olympian ONLXB/1R	Eastern Coach Works	H43/31F	1983	Ex Midland Red South, 1993
830	AET185T	Bristol VRT/SL3/6LXB	Eastern Coach Works	H43/31F	1979	Ex East Midland, 1993
831	DAK201V	Bristol VRT/SL3/501	Eastern Coach Works	H43/31F	1979	Ex East Midland, 1994
832	CBV6S	Bristol VRT/SL3/501(6LXB)	Eastern Coach Works	H43/31F	1977	Ex Ribble, 1994
833	DBV26W	Bristol VRT/SL3/6LXB	Eastern Coach Works	H43/31F	1980	Ex Ribble, 1994

834-844		Bristol VRT/SL3/501	Eastern Coach Works	H43/31F	1980 Ex National Welsh, 1991
					836 is fitted with a 6LXB engine

834	BUH232V	836	GTX738W	840	GTX747W	**843**	GTX750W	**844**	GTX753W
835	BUH237V	838	GTX743W	841	GTX748W		

845	CBV8S	Bristol VRT/SL3/501(6LXB)	Eastern Coach Works	H43/31F	1977	Ex Ribble, 1994
861	OSR206R	Bristol VRT/LL3/501	Alexander AL	H49/38F	1977	Ex National Welsh, 1991
862	OSR207R	Bristol VRT/LL3/501	Alexander AL	H49/38F	1977	Ex National Welsh, 1991
863	OSR208R	Bristol VRT/LL3/501	Alexander AL	H49/38F	1977	Ex National Welsh, 1991
864	OSR209R	Bristol VRT/LL3/501	Alexander AL	H49/38F	1977	Ex National Welsh, 1991
865	WDA1T	Leyland Titan TNLXB1RF	Park Royal	H43/29F	1978	Ex Selkent, 1994
866	WDA2T	Leyland Titan TNLXB1RF	Park Royal	H43/29F	1979	Ex Selkent, 1994
867	WDA5T	Leyland Titan TNLXB1RF	Park Royal	H43/29F	1979	Ex Selkent, 1994
868	AVK163V	Leyland Atlantean AN68A/2R	Alexander AL	H49/37F	1980	Ex Busways, 1995
869	AVK166V	Leyland Atlantean AN68A/2R	Alexander AL	H49/37F	1980	Ex Busways, 1995
870	AVK173V	Leyland Atlantean AN68A/2R	Alexander AL	H49/37F	1980	Ex Busways, 1995

898-915			Leyland Tiger TRCTL11/3R		Plaxton Paramount 3200	C51F*	1983	Ex National Welsh, 1991
								*906-14 are C46F; 915 is C53F

898	AAX450A	901	AAX466A	907	AAL575A	911	AAL516A	914	AAX516A
899	AAX451A	902	AAX488A	909	AAL538A	912	AAX489A	915	AAX529A
900	AAX465A	906	AAL544A	910	AAL518A	913	AAX515A		

916	CYJ492Y	Leyland Tiger TRCTL11/3R	Plaxton Paramount 3200	C50F	1983	Ex Stagecoach South, 1994
917	CYJ493Y	Leyland Tiger TRCTL11/3R	Plaxton Paramount 3200	C50F	1983	Ex Stagecoach South, 1994
925	AKG197A	Leyland Tiger TRCTL11/3R	Duple Laser	C49F	1984	Ex National Welsh, 1991
927	AKG214A	Leyland Tiger TRCTL11/3R	Duple Laser	C49F	1984	Ex National Welsh, 1991
931	AKG271A	Leyland Tiger TRCTL11/3R	Duple Laser	C49F	1984	Ex National Welsh, 1991
934	AKG296A	Leyland Tiger TRCTL11/3R	Duple Laser	C49F	1984	Ex National Welsh, 1991
935	A227MDD	Leyland Tiger TRCTL11/3R	Plaxton Paramount 3200	C51F	1984	Ex Cheltenham & Gloucester, 1994

940-951			Dennis Javelin 11SDA2133		Plaxton Premiére Interurban DP47F		1994	

940	M940JBO	943	M943JBO	946	M946JBO	948	M948JBO	950	M950JBO
941	M941JBO	944	M944JBO	947	M947JBO	949	M949JBO	951	M951JBO
942	M942JBO	945	M945JBO						

952	H159EJU	Dennis Javelin 12SDA1907	Duple 320	C47FT	1991	Ex Whites of Calver, 1995
953	F243OFP	Dennis Javelin 12SDA1907	Duple 320	C47FT	1991	Ex Whites of Calver, 1995
954	HIL8410	Dennis Javelin 12SDA1907	Duple 320	C47FT	1991	Ex Whites of Calver, 1995

Previous Registrations:

A227MDD	A71KDU, 552OHU, A873MRW, YJV806	AAX489A	SDW928Y
AAL516A	SDW927Y	AAX515A	SDW929Y
AAL518A	SDW926Y	AAX516A	SDW930Y
AAL538A	SDW925Y	AAX529A	SDW931Y
AAL544A	SDW922Y	AKG197A	A225VWO
AAL575A	SDW923Y	AKG214A	A227VWO
AAX450A	SDW914Y	AKG271A	A231VWO
AAX451A	SDW915Y	AKG296A	A234VWO
AAX465A	SDW916Y	CYJ492Y	XUF531Y, 401DCD
AAX466A	SDW917Y	CYJ493Y	XUF532Y, 2880CD, 402DCD
AAX488A	SDW918Y	HIL8410	D759JAY

Four Duple Laser-bodied Leyland Tigers from the National Welsh fleet remain. Photographed in Abertillery while heading for Cardiff was 931, AKG271A.
Richard Godfrey

RIBBLE

Stagecoach Ribble, Frenchwood Avenue, Preston, Lancashire, PR1 4LU.

Depots : George Street, Blackburn; Goodwin Street, Bolton; Eaves Lane, Chorley; Pimlico Road, Clitheroe; Sidings Road, Fleetwood; Owen Road, Lancaster; Heysham Road, Morecambe and Selbourne Street, Preston. **Outstations:** Burnley; Garstang and Ingleton.

101-105			Dennis Lance SLF 11SDA3201		Berkhof		B40F	1995		
101	N101...	102	N102...	103	N103...	104	N104...	105	N105...

135	F135SPX	Dennis Javelin 11SDL1914	Duple 300	B63F	1989	Ex Hampshire Bus, 1991
136	F136SPX	Dennis Javelin 11SDL1914	Duple 300	B63F	1989	Ex Hampshire Bus, 1991
137	F137SPX	Dennis Javelin 11SDL1914	Duple 300	B63F	1989	Ex Hampshire Bus, 1991

138-144			Dennis Javelin 11SDL2129		Plaxton Premiére Interurban DP47F		1993		
138	L138BFV	140	L140BFV	142	L142BFV	143	L143BFV	144	L144BFV
139	L139BFV	141	L141BFV						

145-161			Dennis Javelin 11SDL2133		Plaxton Premiére Interurban DP47F		1993		
145	L145BFV	150	L150BFV	153	L153BFV	156	L156BFV	159	L159CCW
146	L146BFV	151	L151BFV	154	L154BFV	157	L157BFV	160	L160CCW
148	L148BFV	152	L152BFV	155	L155BFV	158	L158BFV	161	L161CCW
149	L149BFV								

162-168			Dennis Javelin 11SDL2133		Plaxton Premiére Interurban DP47F		1994	Ex Stagecoach South, 1994	
162	L101SDY	164	L104SDY	166	L102SDY	167	L105SDY	168	L107SDY
163	L103SDY	165	L106SDY						

237-256			Volvo B6-9.9M		Alexander Dash		DP40F	1993		
237	L237CCW	240	L240CCW	251	L251CCK	253	L253CCK	256	L256CCK
239	L239CCW	241	L242CCK	252	L252CCK	255	L255CCK		

257-265			Volvo B6-9.9M		Alexander Dash		DP40F	1993	Ex Fife Scottish, 1994	
257	L667MSF	259	L669MSF	261	L661MSF	263	L663MSF	265	L665MSF
258	L668MSF	260	L660HKS	262	L662MSF	264	L664MSF		

277-283			Volvo B6-9.9M		Alexander Dash		B40F	1993	Ex Cumberland 1994	
277	L277JAO	278	L278JAO	279	L279JAO	281	L281JAO	283	L283JAO

301	CHH214T	Leyland National 10351B/1R	B44F	1978	Ex Cumberland, 1993
311	AHH206T	Leyland National 10351B/1R	B44F	1978	Ex Cumberland, 1993
312	CHH210T	Leyland National 10351B/1R	B44F	1979	Ex Cumberland, 1993
346	NLS986W	Leyland National 2 NL116L11/1R	B52F	1980	Ex Fife Scottish, 1996
348	NLS988W	Leyland National 2 NL116L11/1R	B52F	1980	Ex Fife Scottish, 1996
357	KHH377W	Leyland National 2 NL116L11/1R	B52F	1980	Ex Cumberland, 1993
359	KHH375W	Leyland National 2 NL116L11/1R	B52F	1980	Ex Cumberland, 1993
370	HHH370V	Leyland National 2 NL116L11/1R	B52F	1980	Ex Cumberland, 1993
372	HHH372V	Leyland National 2 NL116L11/1R	B52F	1980	Ex Cumberland, 1993
373	HHH373V	Leyland National 2 NL116L11/1R	B52F	1980	Ex Cumberland, 1993
375	AHH209T	Leyland National 10351B/1R	B44F	1978	Ex Cumberland, 1993
378	KHH378W	Leyland National 2 NL116L11/1R	B52F	1980	Ex Cumberland, 1993
380	NHH380W	Leyland National 2 NL116AL11/1R	B52F	1981	Ex Cumberland, 1993
383	RRM383X	Leyland National 2 NL116AL11/1R	DP52F	1982	Ex Cumberland, 1993
384	CHH211T	Leyland National 10351B/1R	B44F	1978	Ex Cumberland, 1993
385	RRM384X	Leyland National 2 NL116AL11/1R	DP52F	1982	Ex Cumberland, 1993

386-394			Leyland National 2 NL116AL11/1R				B52F	1981-82	Ex Cumberland, 1993	
386	RRM386X	390	SHH390X	391	SHH391X	393	SHH393X	394	SHH394X
387	SHH387X								

The 1996 Stagecoach Bus Handbook

Ribble 277, L277JAO, is one of five Volvo B10Ms to have been transferred from Cumberland during 1994. It is seen at Poulton-le-Fylde while working the Blackpool to Knott End service. *Paul Wigan*

396	WAO396Y	Leyland National 2 NL116HLXB/1R			B52F	1982	Ex Cumberland, 1993		
398	WAO398Y	Leyland National 2 NL116HLXB/1R			B52F	1982	Ex Cumberland, 1993		
399	SHH388X	Leyland National 2 NL116AL11/1R			B52F	1982	Ex Cumberland, 1993		

428-442

		Volvo B10M-55		Alexander PS		DP48F	1994-95		
428	M782PRS	431	M231TBV	434	M234TBV	437	M794PRS	440	M797PRS
429	M783PRS	432	M232TBV	435	M235TBV	438	M795PRS	441	M798PRS
430	M230TBV	433	M233TBV	436	M236TBV	439	M796PRS	442	M799PRS

| 449 | K449YCW | Optare MetroRider | Optare | B31F | 1992 | Ex Lancaster, 1993 |
| 450 | K450YCW | Optare MetroRider | Optare | B31F | 1992 | Ex Lancaster, 1993 |

451-463

		Volvo B10M-55		Alexander PS		B48F	1995		
451	M451VCW	454	M454VCW	457	M457VCW	460	M460VCW	462	M462VCW
452	M452VCW	455	M455VCW	458	M458VCW	461	M461VCW	463	M463VCW
453	M453VCW	456	M456VCW	459	M459VCW				

501-527

| | | Mercedes-Benz L608D | Reeve Burgess | | DP19F* | 1986 | *527 is B20F | | |
							527 ex Cumberland, 1991		
501	D501RCK	507	D507RCK	510	D510RCK	513	D513RCK	521	D521RCK
502	D502RCK	508	D508RCK	512	D512RCK	515	D515RCK	527	D527RCK
505	D505RCK								

| 530 | D672SHH | Mercedes-Benz 609D | Ribble/Cumbria Commercials B20F | 1986 |

536-564

		Mercedes-Benz L608D	Reeve Burgess		B20F	1986	562 ex Cumberland, 1991		
536	D536RCK	545	D545RCK	549	D549RCK	553	D553RCK	556	D556RCK
537	D537RCK	546	D546RCK	551	D551RCK	554	D554RCK	562	D562RCK
541	D541RCK	548	D548RCK	552	D552RCK	555	D555RCK	564	D564RCK
542	D542RCK								

565-592

Mercedes-Benz 709D   Alexander Sprint   B23F*   1990   579/80 ex Magicbus, 1990
*567-572 are DP25F

565	G665PHH	571	G571PRM	577	G577PRM	583	G183PAO	588	G188PAO
566	G566PRM	572	G572PRM	578	G578PRM	584	G184PAO	589	G189PAO
567	G567PRM	573	G573PRM	579	G179PAO	585	G185PAO	590	G190PAO
568	G568PRM	574	G574PRM	580	G180PAO	586	G186PAO	591	G191PAO
569	G569PRM	575	G575PRM	581	G181PAO	587	G187PAO	592	G192PAO
570	G570PRM	576	G576PRM	582	G182PAO				

595-608

Mercedes-Benz 709D   Alexander Sprint   B25F   1993

595	K115XHG	598	K118XHG	600	K120XHG	604	K124XHG	607	L127DRN
596	K116XHG	599	L119DRN	602	L122DRN	605	L125DRN	608	L128DRN
597	K117XHG								

610-628

Mercedes-Benz 709D   Alexander Sprint   B23F   1992-93

610	K610UFR	614	K614UFR	617	K617UFR	620	K620UFR	625	K625UFR
611	K611UFR	615	K615UFR	618	K618UFR	621	K621UFR	627	K627UFR
612	K612UFR	616	K616UFR	619	K619UFR	624	K624UFR	628	K628UFR
613	K613UFR								

629-637

Mercedes-Benz 709D   Alexander Sprint   B25F   1993

629	L629BFV	631	L631BFV	633	L633BFV	635	L635BFV	637	K112XHG
630	L630BFV	632	L632BFV	634	L634BFV	636	L636BFV		

645	WAO645Y	Leyland Tiger TRCTL11/2R	Alexander TE	DP47F	1983	Ex Cumberland, 1991
646	WAO646Y	Leyland Tiger TRCTL11/2R	Alexander TE	DP47F	1983	Ex Cumberland, 1991
802	TRN802V	Leyland National 10351B/1R		B44F	1979	Ex Cumberland, 1993
806	TRN806V	Leyland National 10351B/1R		B44F	1979	Ex Cumberland, 1993
812	TRN812V	Leyland National 10351B/1R		B44F	1979	Ex Cumberland, 1993

813-843

Leyland National 2 NL106L11/1R   B44F   1980   813/4/42 ex Cumberland, 1993

813	YRN813V	819	YRN819V	828	DBV828W	833	DBV833W	839	DBV839W
814	YRN814V	820	YRN820V	829	DBV829W	834	DBV834W	841	DBV841W
815	YRN815V	822	YRN822V	830	DBV830W	835	DBV835W	842	DBV842W
817	YRN817V	825	BCW825V	831	DBV831W	837	DBV837W	843	DBV843W
818	YRN818V	826	BCW826V	832	DBV832W	838	DBV838W		

846-877

Leyland National 2 NL106AL11/1R   B44F   1981   856/7 ex Cumberland, 1993

846	JCK846W	856	LFR856X	859	LFR859X	868	LFR868X	871	LFR871X
847	JCK847W	857	LFR857X	866	LFR866X	870	LFR870X	877	LFR877X
848	JCK848W	858	LFR858X						

878-886

Leyland National 2 NL116AL11/1R   B52F   1982   881 ex Cumberland, 1993

878	RHG878X	879	RHG879X	881	RHG881X	884	RHG884X	886	RHG886X

888	ARN888Y	Leyland National 2 NL116HLXB/1R		B52F	1983	
889	ARN889Y	Leyland National 2 NL116HLXB/1R		B52F	1983	
890	ARN890Y	Leyland National 2 NL116HLXB/1R		B52F	1983	
895	CEO720W	Leyland National 2 NL116L11/1R		B49F	1980	Ex Cumberland, 1993
896	CEO721W	Leyland National 2 NL116L11/1R		B49F	1980	Ex Cumberland, 1993
897	CEO722W	Leyland National 2 NL116L11/1R		B49F	1980	Ex Cumberland, 1993
900	B900WRN	Leyland Tiger TRCTL11/1R		B49F	1984	
1122	J122AHH	Volvo B10M-60	Plaxton Expressliner	C46FT	1992	Ex Cumberland, 1995
1123	J123AHH	Volvo B10M-60	Plaxton Expressliner	C46FT	1992	Ex Cumberland, 1995
1124	J124AHH	Volvo B10M-60	Plaxton Expressliner	C46FT	1992	Ex Cumberland, 1995
1145	PSU775	Leyland Tiger TRCTL11/3RZ	Duple Caribbean 2	C48FT	1985	Ex Cumberland, 1995
1149	PSU788	Leyland Tiger TRCTL11/3RZ	Duple Caribbean 2	C48FT	1985	Ex Cumberland, 1995

Opposite, top: **The remaining 608D minibuses are likely to be replaced during 1996 so that all the minibus fleet is of the 709 type as represented here by one from Fleetwood depot. Once a main depot, the allocation was reduced in the late 1980s. Gradually, Stagecoach are building up the peak vehicle requirement as additional work is obtained and more people travel on the local network.** *Paul Wigan - Opposite, bottom:* **Several East Lancashire-bodied Leyland Atlanteans were acquired from Lancaster City Transport in 1993. Photographed in Lytham on the Preston service is 1215, WCK215Y. All the former Lancaster Atlanteans are now allocated to Preston with the exception of 1205 at Blackburn.** *David Longbottom*

The 1996 Stagecoach Bus Handbook

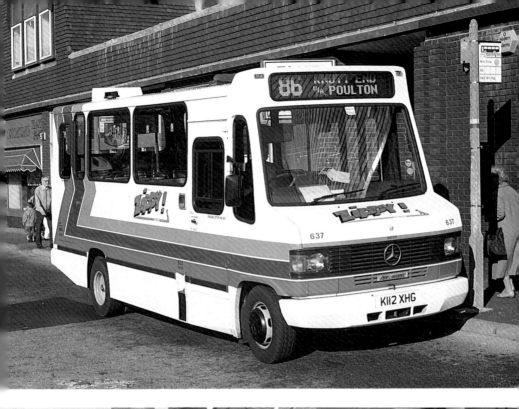

1152	B152WRN	Leyland Tiger TRCTL11/2R	Duple Laser 2	C49F	1985	
1157	927GTA	Leyland Tiger TRCTL11/3R	Duple Laser 2	C53F	1985	
1158	B158WRN	Leyland Tiger TRCTL11/3R	Duple Laser 2	C53F	1985	
1164	M164SCK	Volvo B10M-62	Plaxton Expressliner 2	C46FT	1994	
1165	M165SCK	Volvo B10M-62	Plaxton Expressliner 2	C46FT	1994	
1200	TCK200X	Leyland Atlantean AN68D/2R	East Lancashire	H50/36F	1982	Ex Lancaster, 1993
1205	LFV205X	Leyland Atlantean AN68C/2R	East Lancashire	H50/36F	1981	Ex Lancaster, 1993
1206	LFV206X	Leyland Atlantean AN68C/2R	East Lancashire	H50/36F	1981	Ex Lancaster, 1993
1212	TCK212X	Leyland Atlantean AN68D/2R	East Lancashire	H50/36F	1982	Ex Lancaster, 1993
1213	WCK213Y	Leyland Atlantean AN68D/2R	East Lancashire	H50/36F	1982	Ex Lancaster, 1993
1214	A214MCK	Leyland Atlantean AN68D/2R	East Lancashire	H50/36F	1984	Ex Lancaster, 1993
1215	WCK215Y	Leyland Atlantean AN68D/2R	East Lancashire	H50/36F	1982	Ex Lancaster, 1993
1221	BFV221Y	Leyland Atlantean AN68D/2R	East Lancashire	DPH45/32F	1983	Ex Lancaster, 1993
1222	BFV222Y	Leyland Atlantean AN68D/2R	East Lancashire	DPH45/32F	1983	Ex Lancaster, 1993

1476-1482

		Leyland Atlantean AN68A/1R	Eastern Coach Works	H43/31F	1980	Ex Cumberland, 1992-93

1476	TRN476V	1478	TRN478V	1480	TRN480V	1481	TRN481V	1482	TRN482V

2021	CBV21S	Bristol VRT/SL3/501(6LXB)	Eastern Coach Works	H43/31F	1977	
2030	DBV30W	Bristol VRT/SL3/6LXB	Eastern Coach Works	H43/31F	1980	
2034	URF662S	Bristol VRT/SL3/501(6LXB)	Eastern Coach Works	H43/31F	1977	Ex Potteries, 1982
2040	FDV813V	Bristol VRT/SL3/6LXB	Eastern Coach Works	H43/31F	1980	Ex Magicbus, 1990
2042	RRP858R	Bristol VRT/SL3/501	Eastern Coach Works	H43/31F	1977	Ex United Counties, 1990
2043	FDV817V	Bristol VRT/SL3/6LXB	Eastern Coach Works	H43/31F	1980	Ex Magicbus, 1990
2044	FDV833V	Bristol VRT/SL3/6LXB	Eastern Coach Works	H43/31F	1980	Ex Magicbus, 1990
2045	FDV784V	Bristol VRT/SL3/6LXB	Eastern Coach Works	H43/31F	1980	Ex Magicbus, 1990
2051	LFJ882W	Bristol VRT/SL3/6LXC	Eastern Coach Works	H43/31F	1980	Ex United Counties, 1993
2052	LFJ883W	Bristol VRT/SL3/6LXC	Eastern Coach Works	H43/31F	1980	Ex United Counties, 1993
2053	LFJ858W	Bristol VRT/SL3/6LXB	Eastern Coach Works	H43/31F	1980	Ex United Counties, 1993
2054	LFJ859W	Bristol VRT/SL3/6LXB	Eastern Coach Works	H43/31F	1980	Ex United Counties, 1993
2055	LFJ885W	Bristol VRT/SL3/6LXC	Eastern Coach Works	H43/31F	1980	Ex United Counties, 1993
2056	LFJ866W	Bristol VRT/SL3/6LXB	Eastern Coach Works	H43/31F	1980	Ex United Counties, 1993
2057	LFJ861W	Bristol VRT/SL3/6LXB	Eastern Coach Works	H43/31F	1980	Ex United Counties, 1993
2058	LFJ884W	Bristol VRT/SL3/6LXC	Eastern Coach Works	H43/31F	1980	Ex United Counties, 1993
2076w	UWV622S	Bristol VRT/SL3/6LXB	Eastern Coach Works	O43/31F	1980	Ex East Kent, 1994
2100	DBV100W	Leyland Olympian B45.02	Eastern Coach Works	H45/33F	1980	

2101-2137

		Leyland Olympian ONLXB/1R*	Eastern Coach Works	H45/32F	1981-83	*2124-30 are ONLXBT/1R

2101	GFR101W	2108	JFR8W	2115	OFV15X	2122	OFV22X	2128	VRN828Y
2102	JFR2W	2109	JFR9W	2116	OFV16X	2123	OFV23X	2129	VRN829Y
2103	JFR3W	2110	JFR10W	2117	OFV17X	2124	SCK224X	2130	VRN830Y
2104	JFR4W	2111	JFR11W	2118	OFV18X	2125	SCK225X	2131	DBV131Y
2105	JFR5W	2112	JFR12W	2119	OFV19X	2126	SCK226X	2132	DBV132Y
2106	JFR6W	2113	JFR13W	2120	OFV20X	2127	VRN827Y	2137	DBV137Y
2107	JFR7W	2114	OFV14X	2121	OFV21X				

Ribble have operated several vehicles which have been used as a pool for other companies. Ten Volvo B10Ms were on loan to East London and Hull before being transferred to East Midland while a further ten formed part of the sale of the Stagecoach Manchester operation to Finglands. One of those which remain is 442, M799PRS seen here with dedicated lettering for the M10 operation.
Richard Godfrey

The standard double deck bus for the Ribble fleet is the Leyland Olympian and these range from one of the prototype B45s to many allocated from Stagecoach group orders. The 1990 delivery is represented by 2196, H196WFR seen in Blackpool while working the Preston service. *Paul Wigan*

2138-2152

Leyland Olympian ONLXB/1R   Eastern Coach Works   H45/32F   1984

2138	A138MRN	2142	A142MRN	2143	A143MRN	2145	A145MRN	2152	B152TRN

2156-2179

Leyland Olympian ONLXB/1R   Eastern Coach Works   DPH41/26F 1984-85

2156	A156OFR	2159	A159OFR	2171	C171ECK	2173	C173ECK	2178	C178ECK
2157	A157OFR	2170	C170ECK	2172	C172ECK	2174	C174ECK	2179	C179ECK
2158	A158OFR								

2180-2189

Leyland Olympian ON2R50G16Z4 Alexander RL   DPH51/31F 1989

2180	G180JHG	2182	G182JHG	2184	G184JHG	2186	G186JHG	2188	G188JHG
2181	G181JHG	2183	G183JHG	2185	G185JHG	2187	G187JHG	2189	G189JHG

2191-2197

Leyland Olympian ON2R50G16Z4 Alexander RL   H47/30F   1990

2191	H191WFR	2193	H193WFR	2195	H195WFR	2196	H196WFR	2197	H197WFR
2192	H192WFR	2194	H194WFR						

2198-2210

Leyland Olympian ON2R56G13Z4 Alexander RL   DPH43/27F* 1991   *2204-6/10 are DPH47/27F

2198	J198HFR	2202	J202HFR	2205	J205HFR	2207	J207HFR	2209	J209HFR
2199	J199HFR	2203	J203HFR	2206	J206HFR	2208	J208HFR	2210	J210HFR
2201	J201HFR	2204	J204HFR						

2211-2223

Leyland Olympian ONLXB/1R   Alexander RL   H45/32F   1984-85 Ex Highland Scottish, 1991

2211	A975OST	2214	A979OST	2217	B893UAS	2220	B896UAS	2222	B898UAS
2212	A977OST	2215	B891UAS	2218	B894UAS	2221	B897UAS	2223	B899UAS
2213	A978OST	2216	B892UAS	2219	B895UAS				

Previous Registrations:

927GTA	B157WRN	K450YCW	K200LCT	PSU788	B146ACK
K449YCW	K300LCT	PSU775	B148ACK		

Livery: National Express 1122-4/64/5

SELKENT

South East London and Kent Bus Company, 180 Bromley Road,
Catford, London SE6 2XA

Depots : Hastings Road, Bromley; Bromley Road, Catford and Pettman Crescent, Plumstead.

DT28-55

Dennis Dart 8.5SDL3003   Carlyle Dartline   B28F*   1990   Ex London Buses, 1994
*28/30/1/55 are DP28F

28	49CLT	32	VLT240	35	G35TGW	38	G38TGW	40	G40TGW
30	G30TGW	33	G33TGW	36	G36TGW	39	G39TGW	55	WLT575
31	G31TGW	34	G34TGW	37	G37TGW				

DW59-71

Dennis Dart 8.5SDL3003   Wright Handy-bus   B28F   1991   Ex London Buses, 1994

59	JDZ2359	61	JDZ2361	63	JDZ2363	65	JDZ2365	71	JDZ2371
60	JDZ2360	62	JDZ2362	64	JDZ2364				

601-615

Dennis Dart 9.8SDL3504   Alexander Dash   B40F   1995-96

601	N601KGF	604	N604KGF	607	N607KGF	610	N610KGF	613
602	N602KGF	605	N605KGF	608	N608KGF	611		614
603	N603KGF	606	N606KGF	609	N609KGF	612		615

L7-144

Leyland Olympian ONLXB/1RH   Eastern Coach Works   H42/26D   1986   Ex London Buses, 1994

7	C807BYY	53	C53CHM	76	C76CHM	107	C107CHM	124	D124FYM
9	C809BYY	54	C54CHM	77	C77CHM	108	C108CHM	125	D125FYM
10	C810BYY	55	C55CHM	80	C80CHM	109	C109CHM	126	D126FYM
11	C811BYY	57	C57CHM	81	C81CHM	110	C110CHM	127	D127FYM
12	C812BYY	60	C60CHM	82	C82CHM	111	C111CHM	128	D128FYM
15	C815BYY	61	C61CHM	83	C83CHM	112	C112CHM	129	D129FYM
18	C818BYY	62	C62CHM	86	C86CHM	114	C114CHM	130	D130FYM
19	C819BYY	64	C64CHM	87	C87CHM	115	C115CHM	131	D131FYM
23	C23CHM	67	C67CHM	91	WLT491	116	C116CHM	132	D132FYM
28	C28CHM	68	C68CHM	92	C92CHM	117	C117CHM	133	D133FYM
29	C29CHM	69	C69CHM	94	C94CHM	118	C118CHM	134	D134FYM
30	C30CHM	70	C70CHM	97	C97CHM	119	C119CHM	136	D136FYM
42	C42CHM	71	C71CHM	98	C98CHM	120	C120CHM	137	D137FYM
43	C43CHM	72	C72CHM	103	C103CHM	121	C121CHM	141	D141FYM
44	C44CHM	73	C73CHM	104	C104CHM	122	C122CHM	142	D142FYM
48	C45CHM	74	C74CHM	105	C105CHM	123	D123FYM	144	D144FYM
51	C51CHM	75	C75CHM	106	C106CHM				

L260	VLT20	Leyland Olympian ONLXB/1RH	Eastern Coach Works	DPH42/26D	1986	Ex London Buses, 1994
L262	VLT14	Leyland Olympian ONLXB/1RH	Eastern Coach Works	DPH42/26D	1986	Ex London Buses, 1994
L263	D367JJD	Leyland Olympian ONLXB/1RH	Eastern Coach Works	DPH42/26D	1986	Ex London Buses, 1994

301-352

Volvo Olympian YN2RV18Z4   Northern Counties Palatine II   H45/23D   1995

301	M301DGP	312	M312DGP	323	N323HGK	333	N353HGK	343	N343HGK
302	M302DGP	313	M313DGP	324	N324HGK	334	N334HGK	344	N344HGK
303	M303DGP	314	M314DGP	325	N325HGK	335	N335HGK	345	N345HGK
304	M304DGP	315	M315DGP	326	N326HGK	336	N336HGK	346	N346HGK
305	M305DGP	316	M316DGP	327	N327HGK	337	N337HGK	347	N347HGK
306	M306DGP	317	M317DGP	328	N328HGK	338	N338HGK	348	N348HGK
307	M307DGP	318	M318DGP	329	N329HGK	339	N339HGK	349	N349HGK
308	M308DGP	319	M319DGP	330	N330HGK	340	N340HGK	350	N350HGK
309	M309DGP	320	M320DGP	331	N331HGK	341	N341HGK	351	N351HGK
310	M310DGP	321	N321HGK	332	N332HGK	342	N342HGK	352	N352HGK
311	M311DGP	322	N322HGK					

Selkent received 52 Volvo Olympians during 1995 and will share in an order for further examples during 1996. These have been added to the many inherited from London Buses and have displaced Leyland Titans which have been allocated for further service with Western Scottish and Stagecoach South. Representing the earlier Olympians is L136, D136FYM pictured at East Croydon rail station while the new order is illustrated by 328, N328HGK seen operating the 53 service outside County Hall. *M E Lyons/Tony Wilson*

The 1996 Stagecoach Bus Handbook

Recently Selkent have transferred the FM class to Midland Red while most of the MW class are now with Stagecoach Transit working in Cleveland and Darlington. Of the minibuses still dominating the fleet are 32 Optare MetroRiders which carry Leeds office index marks. Photographed in Bromley during 1995, MRL166, H166WWT is one repainted into all-red livery. *Richard Godfrey*

LV1-12

		Dennis Lance 11SDA3112		Plaxton Verde		B42D	1994	Ex London Buses, 1994		
1	L201YAG	4	L204YAG	7	L207YAG	9	L209YAG	11	L211YAG
2	L202YAG	5	L205YAG	8	L208YAG	10	L210YAG	12	WLT461
3	L203YAG	6	L206YAG						

MA9-41

		Mercedes-Benz 811D		Alexander AM		B28F	1988	Ex London Buses, 1994		
9	F609XMS	16	F616XMS	20	F620XMS	25	F625XMS	31	F631XMS
14	F614XMS	17	F617XMS	21	F621XMS	29	F629XMS	41	F641XMS
15	F615XMS	19	F619XMS	24	F624XMS	30	F630XMS		

MC1-5

		Mercedes-Benz 811D		Carlyle		B28F*	1990	Ex London Buses, 1994 *MC2-5 are B33F		
1	F286KGK	2	H882LOX	3	H883LOX	4	H509AGC	5	H885LOX

MRL141-177

		Optare MetroRider MR03		Optare		B26F	1990-91	Ex London Buses, 1994		
141	H141UUA	148	H148UUA	160	H160WWT	166	H166WWT	172	H172WWT
142	H142UUA	149	H149UUA	161	H161WWT	167	H167WWT	173	H173WWT
143	H143UUA	150	H150UUA	162	H162WWT	168	H168WWT	174	H174WWT
144	H144UUA	151	H151UUA	163	H163WWT	169	H169WWT	175	H175WWT
145	H145UUA	152	H152UUA	164	H564WWR	170	H170WWT	176	H176WWT
146	H146UUA	153	H153UUA	165	H165WWT	171	H171WWT	177	H177WWT
147	H147UUA	154	H154UUA						

MT4	F394DHL	Mercedes-Benz 709D	Reeve Burgess Beaver	B23F	1988	Ex London Buses, 1994

MW2	HDZ2602	Mercedes-Benz 811D	Wright NimBus	B19FL	1989	Ex London Buses, 1994
MW8	HDZ2608	Mercedes-Benz 811D	Wright NimBus	B19FL	1989	Ex London Buses, 1994
MW14	HDZ2614	Mercedes-Benz 811D	Wright NimBus	B19FL	1989	Ex London Buses, 1994

RH1	C501DYM	Iveco Daily 49.10	Robin Hood City Nippy	DP21F	1986	Ex London Buses, 1994
RH5w	C505DYM	Iveco Daily 49.10	Robin Hood City Nippy	B21F	1986	Ex London Buses, 1994
RH22w	D522FYL	Iveco Daily 49.10	Robin Hood City Nippy	B21F	1986	Ex London Buses, 1994
RMC1515	515CLT	AEC Routemaster R2RH	Park Royal	O32/25RD	1962	Ex London Buses, 1994
T130	CUL130V	Leyland Titan TNLXB2RRSp	Park Royal	H44/26D	1979	Ex London Buses, 1994
T267	GYE267W	Leyland Titan TNLXB2RR	Park Royal/Leyland	H44/26D	1981	Ex London Buses, 1994

T368-674

Leyland Titan TNLXB2RR   Leyland   H44/24D   1981-82 Ex London Buses, 1994

368	KYV368X	455	KYV455X	616	NUW616Y	618	NUW618Y	674	NUW674Y
447	KYV447X								

T680-999

Leyland Titan TNLXB2RR   Leyland   H44/24D   1983-84 Ex London Buses, 1994
T877/80 are TNTL112RR; T881/2/3/5 are TNL112RR

680	OHV680Y	797	OHV797Y	822	RYK822Y	848	A848SUL	882	A882SUL
700	OHV700Y	800	OHV800Y	824	A824SUL	850	A850SUL	883	A883SUL
710	OHV710Y	801	OHV801Y	825	A825SUL	854	A854SUL	885	A885SUL
714	OHV714Y	804	OHV804Y	828	A828SUL	855	A855SUL	918	A918SYE
721	OHV721Y	805	OHV805Y	829	A829SUL	856	A856SUL	925	A925SYE
728	OHV728Y	809	OHV809Y	830	A830SUL	857	A857SUL	926	A926SYE
740	OHV740Y	810	OHV810Y	834	A834SUL	858	A858SUL	950	A950SYE
748	OHV748Y	812	OHV812Y	836	A836SUL	859	A859SUL	951	A951SYE
762	OHV762Y	813	OHV813Y	837	A837SUL	866	A866SUL	961	A961SYE
770	OHV770Y	814	OHV814Y	838	A838SUL	868	A868SUL	976	A976SYE
771	OHV771Y	815	RYK815Y	841	A841SUL	874	A874SUL	978	A978SYE
772	OHV772Y	816	RYK816Y	842	A842SUL	877	A877SUL	988	A988SYE
780	OHV780Y	818	RYK818Y	843	A843SUL	880	A880SUL	996	A996SYE
785	OHV785Y	820	RYK820Y	845	A845SUL	881	A881SUL	999	A999SYE
791	OHV791Y	821	RYK821Y	847	A847SUL				

T1003-1077

Leyland Titan TNLXB2RR   Leyland   H44/24D   1984   Ex London Buses, 1994

1003	A603THV	1028	A628THV	1032	A632THV	1045	A645THV	1066	A66THX
1007	A607THV	1029	A629THV	1034	A634THV	1048	A648THV	1067	A67THX
1013	A613THV	1030	A630THV	1035	A635THV	1052	A652THV	1076	A76THX
1025	A625THV	1031	A631THV	1036	A636THV	1065	A65THX	1077	A77THX
1027	A627THV								

T1079-1125

Leyland Titan TNLXB2RR   Leyland   H44/24D   1984   Ex London Buses, 1994

1079	B79WUV	1092	B92WUV	1101	B101WUV	1113	B113WUV	1119	B119WUV
1081	B81WUV	1093	B93WUV	1103	B103WUV	1114	B114WUV	1121	B121WUV
1083	B83WUV	1096	B96WUV	1106	B106WUV	1115	B115WUV	1122	B122WUV
1084	B84WUV	1097	B97WUV	1108	B108WUV	1116	B116WUV	1124	B124WUV
1089	B89WUV	1099	B99WUV	1110	B110WUV	1117	B117WUV	1125	B125WUV
1091	B91WUV	1100	B100WUV	1112	B112WUV	1118	B118WUV		

Previous Registrations:

49CLT	G29TGW	H509AGC	H884LOX, WLT400	WLT461	L212YAG
515CLT	From new	VLT14	D262FYL	WLT491	C91CHM
D367JJD	D263FYL, VLT9	VLT20	D260FYM	WLT575	G41TGW
F286KGK	F430BOP, WLT491	VLT240	G32TGW		

Livery: Red

STAGECOACH SOUTH

Stagecoach (South) Ltd, Lewes Enterprise Centre, 112 Malling Street,
Lewes, East Sussex, BN7 2RB

Depots and outstations:

Hampshire Bus: Mill Lane, Alton; Livingstone Road, Andover; New Market Square, Basingstoke; Abbey Mill, Bishops Waltham; Marlborough; Bedford Road, Petersfield; Hazeldown Farm, Stockbridge, The Broadway, Winchester.

Hants & Surrey: Halimote Road, Aldershot; Mill Lane, Alton; Camberley; Guildford; Haslemere; Lindford; Bedford Road, Petersfield.

Coastline: Southgate, Chichester; Elm Lane, Havant; Henfield; Leigh Park; Littlehampton; Southampton City Bus; Library Place, Worthing.

South Coast Buses: Cavendish Place, Eastbourne; Beaufort Road, Silverhill, Hastings; Eastgate Street, Lewes; Littlestone Road, New Romney; Station Approach, Rye; Claremont Road, Seaford; Uckfield.

East Kent: Brunswick Road, Ashford; St Stephen's Road, Canterbury; South Street, Deal; Russell Street, Dover; Kent Road, Cheriton, Folkestone; High Street, Herne Bay; Littlestone Road, New Romney; Margate Road, Westwood, Thanet.

1	H101EKR	Iveco Daily 49.10	Phoenix	B23F	1991	Ex East Kent, 1993	
2	H102EKR	Iveco Daily 49.10	Phoenix	B23F	1991	Ex East Kent, 1993	
3	H103EKR	Iveco Daily 49.10	Phoenix	B23F	1991	Ex East Kent, 1993	
4	H104EKR	Iveco Daily 49.10	Phoenix	B23F	1991	Ex East Kent, 1993	
5w	D935EBP	Iveco Daily 49.10	Robin Hood City Nippy	B19F	1986	Ex East Kent, 1993	
10	D230VCD	Iveco Daily 49.10	Robin Hood City Nippy	B21F	1986	Ex East Kent, 1993	
11	J121LKO	Iveco Daily 49.10	Dormobile Routemaker	B23F	1991	Ex East Kent, 1993	
12	J112LKO	Iveco Daily 49.10	Carlyle Dailybus	B23F	1991	Ex East Kent, 1993	
13	J113LKO	Iveco Daily 49.10	Carlyle Dailybus	B23F	1991	Ex East Kent, 1993	
14	J114LKO	Iveco Daily 49.10	Carlyle Dailybus	B23F	1991	Ex East Kent, 1993	

15-20

		Iveco Daily 49.10	Dormobile Routemaker	B23F	1991	Ex East Kent, 1993	

15	J115LKO	17	J117LKO	18	J118LKO	19	J119LKO	20	J120LKO
16	J116LKO								

21	F21PSL	Iveco Daily 49.10	Robin Hood City Nippy	B23F	1989	Ex Stagecoach, 1990	
23	F23PSL	Iveco Daily 49.10	Robin Hood City Nippy	B23F	1989	Ex Stagecoach, 1990	
25	F25PSL	Iveco Daily 49.10	Robin Hood City Nippy	B23F	1989	Ex Stagecoach, 1990	
26	F26PSL	Iveco Daily 49.10	Robin Hood City Nippy	B23F	1989	Ex Stagecoach, 1990	
30	G30PSR	Iveco Daily 49.10	Phoenix	B23F	1989	Ex Stagecoach, 1990	
31	F61AVV	Iveco Daily 49.10	Robin Hood City Nippy	B25F	1989	Ex United Counties, 1989	
32	F62AVV	Iveco Daily 49.10	Robin Hood City Nippy	B25F	1989	Ex United Counties, 1989	
33	E233JRF	Iveco Daily 49.10	Phoenix	B25F	1987		

Stagecoach South are currently taking delivery of no less than 59 Volvo Olympians which will oust many of the 144 Bristol VRTs that remain. Early bus-seated examples are allocated to Herne Bay, Basingstoke and Farnborough. Those fitted with high-back seating have also started to enter service. One from the 1990 delivery is 234, G704TCD one of fourteen based at Havant for the Coastline operation.
Richard Godfrey

34-39 Iveco Daily 49.10 Phoenix B23F 1989 Ex Stagecoach, 1990
35 ex East Midland, 1993

34	G34PSR	36	G36SSR	37	G37SSR	38	G38SSR	39	G39SSR
35	G35PSR								

41	D231VCD	Iveco Daily 49.10	Robin Hood City Nippy	B21F	1986	Ex East Kent, 1993
42	G42SSR	Iveco Daily 49.10	Phoenix	B23F	1989	Ex Stagecoach, 1990
43	G43SSR	Iveco Daily 49.10	Phoenix	B23F	1989	Ex Stagecoach, 1990
45	E65BVS	Iveco Daily 49.10	Robin Hood City Nippy	B23F	1988	
46	G446VKK	Iveco Daily 49.10	Carlyle Dailybus	B23F	1990	Ex East Kent, 1993
47	G447VKK	Iveco Daily 49.10	Carlyle Dailybus	B23F	1990	Ex East Kent, 1993

51-70 Iveco Daily 49.10 Robin Hood City Nippy B23F 1987 Ex East Kent, 1993

51	E151UKR	55	E155UKR	59w	E159UKR	63	E163UKR	67	E167UKR
52w	E152UKR	56	E156UKR	60	E160UKR	64	E164UKR	68w	TE168UKR
53w	E153UKR	57	E157UKR	61	E161UKR	65	E165UKR	69	E169UKR
54	E154UKR	58	E158UKR	62	E162UKR	66	E166UKR	70	E170UKR

71-75 Iveco Daily 49.10 Robin Hood City Nippy B23F 1989 Ex East Kent, 1993

71	F71FKK	72	F72FKK	73	F73FKK	74	F74FKK	75	F75FKK

76	J416TGM	Iveco Daily 49.10	Reeve Burgess Beaver	B25F	1991	Ex Alder Valley, 1992

80-87 Iveco Daily 49.10 Robin Hood City Nippy B19F 1987 Ex East Kent, 1993

80	E580TKJ	82w	E582TKJ	84	E584TKJ	86w	E586TKJ	87w	E587TKJ
81w	E581TKJ	83	E583TKJ	85	E585TKJ				

91	G491RKK	Iveco Daily 49.10	Carlyle Dailybus	B23F	1990	Ex East Kent, 1993
93	G493RKK	Iveco Daily 49.10	Carlyle Dailybus	B23F	1990	Ex East Kent, 1993
94	G494RKK	Iveco Daily 49.10	Carlyle Dailybus	B23F	1990	Ex East Kent, 1993
95	G95SKR	Iveco Daily 49.10	Phoenix	B23F	1990	Ex East Kent, 1993
96	G96SKR	Iveco Daily 49.10	Phoenix	B23F	1990	Ex East Kent, 1993
97	G97SKR	Iveco Daily 49.10	Phoenix	B23F	1990	Ex East Kent, 1993
98	G98SKR	Iveco Daily 49.10	Phoenix	B23F	1990	Ex East Kent, 1993

100-118 Leyland National 11351A/1R B52F* 1979 106 ex Hampshire Bus, 1992
*106 is B49F

100	AYJ100T	104	AYJ104T	109	ENJ909V	113	ENJ913V	116	ENJ916V
101	AYJ101T	105	AYJ105T	110	ENJ910V	114	ENJ914V	117	ENJ917V
102	AYJ102T	106	DRU6T	111	ENJ911V	115	ENJ915V	118	ENJ918V
103	AYJ103T	107	AYJ107T	112	ENJ912V				

119-126 Leyland National 2 NL116L11/1R B52F 1980 124 fitted with TL11 engine

119	GYJ919V	121	GYJ921V	123	HFG923V	125	OUF262W	126	SYC852
120	GYJ920V	122	GYJ922V	124	JNJ194V				

127	FDV830V	Leyland National 2 NL116L11/1R	B52F	1980
128	FDV831V	Leyland National 2 NL116L11/1R	B52F	1980

129-138 Leyland National 2 NL116AL11/1R B49F* 1982 *129/32 are B45F
130 is fitted with TL11 engine

129	HUF603X	131	HUF625X	133	HUF639X	135	HUF604X	137	HUF592X
130	HUF579X	132	YLJ332	134	HUF451X	136	HUF593X	138	HUF626X

139	FDV829V	Leyland National 2 NL116L11/1R	B52F	1980	
140	CPO98W	Leyland National 2 NL106L11/1R	B41F	1980	Ex Portsmouth, 1990
141	CPO99W	Leyland National 2 NL106L11/1R	DP40F	1980	Ex Portsmouth, 1990
142	CPO100W	Leyland National 2 NL106L11/1R	DP40F	1980	Ex Portsmouth, 1990
143	ERV115W	Leyland National 2 NL106AL11/1R	B41F	1981	Ex Portsmouth, 1990
144	ERV116W	Leyland National 2 NL106AL11/1R	B41F	1981	Ex Portsmouth, 1990
145	ERV117W	Leyland National 2 NL106AL11/1R	B41F	1981	Ex Portsmouth, 1990
146	ERV118W	Leyland National 2 NL106L11/1R	B41F	1981	Ex Portsmouth, 1990
147	BCW827V	Leyland National 2 NL106L11/1R	B44F	1980	Ex Ribble, 1994
148	UFG48S	Leyland National 11351A/2R	B52F	1977	
149	JCK849W	Leyland National 2 NL106AL11/1R	B44F	1981	Ex Ribble, 1994
152	WPR152S	Leyland National 11351A/1R	B49F	1978	

154	VOD604S	Leyland National 11351A/1R	B52F	1978	Ex Devon General, 1987
155	VOD605S	Leyland National 11351A/1R	B52F	1978	Ex Devon General, 1987
157	UHG757R	Leyland National 11351A/1R	B49F	1977	Ex Ribble, 1986
159	YRN816V	Leyland National 2 NL106L11/1R	B44F	1980	Ex Ribble, 1994
160	YRN821V	Leyland National 2 NL106L11/1R	B44F	1980	Ex Ribble, 1994
162	FPR62V	Leyland National 11351A/1R	B49F	1980	
163	PCD73R	Leyland National 11351A/1R	B49F	1976	
164	VFX984S	Leyland National 11351A/1R	B49F	1978	
165	VOD625S	Leyland National 11351A/1R	B52F	1978	
167	MLJ917P	Leyland National 11351/1R	B49F	1976	
169	WYJ169S	Leyland National 11351A/2R(DAF)	B48F	1978	
173	YCD73T	Leyland National 11351A/2R	B52F	1978	
174	YCD74T	Leyland National 11351A/2R	B48F	1978	
176	YCD76T	Leyland National 11351A/2R	B48F	1978	
177	YCD77T	Leyland National 11351A/2R	B48F	1978	
178	PCD78R	Leyland National 11351A/1R	B49F	1976	
179	PCD79R	Leyland National 11351A/1R	B49F	1977	
180	PCD80R	Leyland National 11351A/1R	B49F	1977	
182	YCD82T	Leyland National 11351A/2R	B48F	1978	
184w	CBV784S	Leyland National 11351A/1R	B49F	1978	Ex Ribble, 1986
186	CBV776S	Leyland National 11351A/1R	B49F	1978	Ex Ribble, 1986
188w	CBV798S	Leyland National 11351A/1R	B49F	1978	Ex Ribble, 1986
189	AYJ89T	Leyland National 11351A/1R	B52F	1979	
190	TEL490R	Leyland National 11351A/1R	DP48F	1977	
191	AYJ91T	Leyland National 11351A/1R	B52F	1979	
192	AYJ92T	Leyland National 11351A/1R	B52F	1979	
195	AYJ95T	Leyland National 11351A/1R	B52F	1979	
196	RJT146R	Leyland National 11351A/1R	B49F	1977	
197	AYJ97T	Leyland National 11351A/1R	B52F	1979	

201-206
Leyland Olympian ON2R56G13Z4 Alexander RL — H51/36F 1988

| 201 | F601MSL | 203 | F603MSL | 204 | F604MSL | 205 | F605MSL | 206 | F606MSL |
| 202 | F602MSL | | | | | | | | |

207-214
Leyland Olympian ON2R56G13Z4 Alexander RL — DPH51/31F 1989

| 207 | G807RTS | 209 | G809RTS | 211 | G211SSL | 213 | G213SSL | 214 | G214SSL |
| 208 | G808RTS | 210 | G210SSL | 212 | G212SSL | | | | |

215-219
Leyland Olympian ON2R56G13Z4 Alexander RL — H51/34F 1990

| 215 | H815CBP | 216 | H816CBP | 217 | H817CBP | 218 | H818CBP | 219 | H819CBP |

220	J720GAP	Leyland Olympian ON2R56G13Z4 Alexander RL	DPH47/27F	1992
221	J721GAP	Leyland Olympian ON2R56G13Z4 Alexander RL	DPH47/27F	1992
222	J722GAP	Leyland Olympian ON2R56G13Z4 Alexander RL	DPH47/27F	1992
223	J623GCR	Leyland Olympian ON2R56G13Z4 Alexander RL	H47/30F	1991
224	J624GCR	Leyland Olympian ON2R56G13Z4 Alexander RL	H47/30F	1991

225-234
Leyland Olympian ON2R56G13Z4 Alexander RL — H51/34F 1990

| 225 | G705TCD | 227 | G707TCD | 229 | G709TCD | 231 | G701TCD | 233 | G703TCD |
| 226 | G706TCD | 228 | G708TCD | 230 | G710TCD | 232 | G702TCD | 234 | G704TCD |

235-240
Leyland Olympian ON2R50G13Z4 Alexander RL — DPH43/27F 1992

| 235 | K235NHC | 237 | K237NHC | 238 | K238NHC | 239 | K239NHC | 240 | K240NHC |
| 236 | K236NHC | | | | | | | | |

241-250
Volvo Olympian YN2RV18Z4 Northern Counties Palatine II DPH43/25F 1993

| 241 | L241SDY | 243 | L243SDY | 245 | L245SDY | 247 | L247SDY | 249 | L249SDY |
| 242 | L242SDY | 244 | L244SDY | 246 | L246SDY | 248 | L248SDY | 250 | L250SDY |

254	K714ASC	Leyland Olympian ON2R50G13Z4 Alexander RL	H47/32F	1992	Ex Fife Scottish, 1994
255	K715ASC	Leyland Olympian ON2R50G13Z4 Alexander RL	H47/32F	1992	Ex Fife Scottish, 1994
256	K716ASC	Leyland Olympian ON2R50G13Z4 Alexander RL	H47/32F	1992	Ex Fife Scottish, 1994
257	K717ASC	Leyland Olympian ON2R50G13Z4 Alexander RL	H47/32F	1992	Ex Fife Scottish, 1994

Four Volvo B6s entered service at Winchester for the Park & Ride service. These are the only B6s in the fleet and are liveried for the service. Each also carry index marks once carried by members of Southdown's open top fleet of Leyland Titan PD3s. *Richard Godfrey*

341-359
Volvo Olympian YN2RC16V3   Alexander RL   DPH47/28F   1996

341	N341MPN	345	N345MPN	349	N349MPN	353	N353MPN	357	N357MPN
342	N342MPN	346	N346MPN	350	N350MPN	354	N354MPN	358	N358MPN
343	N343MPN	347	N347MPN	351	N351MPN	355	N355MPN	359	N359MPN
344	N344MPN	348	N348MPN	352	N352MPN	356	N356MPN		

360-380
Volvo Olympian YN2RC16V3   Alexander RL   H47/32F   1995

360	N360LPN	365	N365LPN	369	N369LPN	373	N373LPN	377	N377LPN
361	N361LPN	366	N366LPN	370	N370LPN	374	N374LPN	378	N378LPN
362	N362LPN	367	N367LPN	371	N371LPN	375	N375LPN	379	N379LPN
363	N363LPN	368	N368LPN	372	N372LPN	376	N376LPN	380	N380LPN
364	N364LPN								

381-399
Volvo Olympian YN2RC16V3   Alexander RL   DPH47/28F   1995-96

381	N381LPN	385	N385LPN	389	N389LPN	393	N393LPN	397	N397LPN
382	N382LPN	386	N386LPN	390	N390LPN	394	N394LPN	398	N398LPN
383	N383LPN	387	N387LPN	391	N391LPN	395	N395LPN	399	N399LPN
384	N384LPN	388	N388LPN	392	N392LPN	396	N396LPN		

400	400DCD	Volvo B6-9.9M	Alexander Dash	B35F	1994
401	401DCD	Volvo B6-9.9M	Alexander Dash	B35F	1994
402	402DCD	Volvo B6-9.9M	Alexander Dash	B35F	1994
403	403DCD	Volvo B6-9.9M	Alexander Dash	B31F	1994

422-450
Bristol VRT/SL3/6LXB   Eastern Coach Works   H43/31F   1979-81

422	FDV818V	435	FDV839V	440	KRU840W	446	LFJ874W	449	LFJ875W
432	ELJ212V	438	KRU838W	441	KRU841W	447	LFJ881W	450	LFJ880W
433	FDV834V	439	KRU839W	444	KRU844W	448	LFJ870W		

460-467 Iveco Daily 49.10 — Reeve Burgess Beaver — B23F* — 1989 — Ex East Midland, 1993
*460 is B25F

460	G910KWF	461	G911KWF	463	G913KWF	464	G914KWF	467	G917KWF

469-476 Iveco Daily 49.10 — Robin Hood City Nippy — B21F — 1986 — Ex Alder Valley, 1992

469	D469WPM	470	D470WPM	471	D471WPM	473	D473WPM	476	D476WPM

477	E201EPB	Iveco Daily 49.10	Robin Hood City Nippy	B25F	1987	Ex Alder Valley, 1992
478w	E202EPB	Iveco Daily 49.10	Robin Hood City Nippy	B25F	1987	Ex Alder Valley, 1992
479w	E203EPB	Iveco Daily 49.10	Robin Hood City Nippy	B25F	1987	Ex Alder Valley, 1992
480	E204EPB	Iveco Daily 49.10	Robin Hood City Nippy	B25F	1987	Ex Alder Valley, 1992
481	G921KWF	Iveco Daily 49.10	Reeve Burgess Beaver	B23F	1989	Ex East Midland, 1993
482	G922KWF	Iveco Daily 49.10	Reeve Burgess Beaver	B23F	1990	Ex East Midland, 1993
483	G923KWF	Iveco Daily 49.10	Reeve Burgess Beaver	B23F	1990	Ex East Midland, 1993
485	F695OPA	Iveco Daily 49.10	Carlyle Dailybus 2	B23F	1988	Ex Alder Valley, 1992

488-492 Iveco Daily 49.10 — Phoenix — B23F — 1990

488	G418RYJ	489	G419RYJ	490	G420RYJ	491	G421RYJ	492	G422RYJ

494	G864BPD	Iveco Daily 49.10	Carlyle Dailybus 2	B23F	1989	Ex Alder Valley, 1992

501-580 Dennis Dart 9.8SDL3017 — Alexander Dash — B41F* — 1991-92 — *535-80 are B40F

501	J501GCD	517	J517GCD	533	J533GCD	549	J549GCD	565	K565NHC
502	J502GCD	518	J518GCD	534	J534GCD	550	J550GCD	566	K566NHC
503	J503GCD	519	J519GCD	535	J535GCD	551	J551GCD	567	K567NHC
504	J504GCD	520	J520GCD	536	J536GCD	552	J552GCD	568	K568NHC
505	J505GCD	521	J521GCD	537	J537GCD	553	K553NHC	569	K569NHC
506	J506GCD	522	J522GCD	538	J538GCD	554	K554NHC	570	K570NHC
507	J507GCD	523	J523GCD	539	J539GCD	555	K655NHC	571	K571NHC
508	J508GCD	524	J524GCD	540	J540GCD	556	K556NHC	572	K572NHC
509	J509GCD	525	J525GCD	541	J541GCD	557	K557NHC	573	K573NHC
510	J510GCD	526	J526GCD	542	J542GCD	558	K558NHC	574	K574NHC
511	J511GCD	527	J527GCD	543	J543GCD	559	K559NHC	575	K575NHC
512	J512GCD	528	J528GCD	544	J544GCD	560	K660NHC	576	K576NHC
513	J513GCD	529	J529GCD	545	J545GCD	561	K561NHC	577	K577NHC
514	J514GCD	530	J530GCD	546	J546GCD	562	K562NHC	578	K578NHC
515	J515GCD	531	J531GCD	547	J547GCD	563	K563NHC	579	K579NHC
516	J516GCD	532	J532GCD	548	J548GCD	564	K564NHC	580	K580NHC

581	J701YRM	Dennis Dart 9.8DL3017	Alexander Dash	B40F	1991	Ex Cumberland, 1992
582	J702YRM	Dennis Dart 9.8DL3017	Alexander Dash	B41F	1991	Ex Cumberland, 1992
583	J703YRM	Dennis Dart 9.8DL3017	Alexander Dash	B41F	1992	Ex Cumberland, 1992

584-588 Dennis Dart 9.8DL3017 — Alexander Dash — B40F* — 1992 — *584 is B41F

584	K584ODY	585	K585ODY	586	K586ODY	587	K587ODY	588	K588ODY

The majority of the midibuses with Stagecoach South are Dennis Darts. Garaged at Winchester is 536, J536GCD, one of thirty currently allocated to the Hampshire Bus operation.
Philip Lamb

601-605

Volvo B10M-55 — Northern Counties Paladin — DP49F — 1994

601	L601VCD	602	L602VCD	603	L603VCD	604	404DCD	605	405DCD

606-635

Volvo B10M-55 — Alexander PS — DP48F — 1994

606	406DCD	612	412DCD	618	L618TDY	624	L624TDY	630	L630TDY
607	407DCD	613	413DCD	619	419DCD	625	L625TDY	631	L631TDY
608	408DCD	614	M614APN	620	420DCD	626	L626TDY	632	L632TDY
609	L609TDY	615	M615APN	621	421DCD	627	L627TDY	633	L633TDY
610	410DCD	616	L616TDY	622	422DCD	628	L628TDY	634	L634TDY
611	411DCD	617	L617TDY	623	L623TDY	629	L629TDY	635	L635TDY

636-652

Volvo B10M-55 — Alexander PS — DP48F — 1995

636	M636BCD	639	M639BCD	642	N642LPN	645	N645LPN	651	M651BCD
637	M637BCD	640	N640LPN	643	N643LPN	650	M650BCD	652	M652BCD
638	M638BCD	641	N641LPN	644	N644LPN				

655	415DCD	Volvo B10M-55	Alexander PS	DP48F	1994	Ex Ribble, 1994
656	416DCD	Volvo B10M-55	Alexander PS	DP48F	1994	Ex Ribble, 1994
657	417DCD	Volvo B10M-55	Alexander PS	DP48F	1994	Ex Ribble, 1994
658	418DCD	Volvo B10M-55	Alexander PS	DP48F	1994	Ex Ribble, 1994
659	K789DAO	Volvo B10M-55	Alexander PS	DP48F	1993	Ex Cumberland, 1994
660	K790DAO	Volvo B10M-55	Alexander PS	DP48F	1993	Ex Cumberland, 1994
661	K791DAO	Volvo B10M-55	Alexander PS	DP48F	1993	Ex Cumberland, 1994

662-670

Volvo B10M-55 — Northern Counties Paladin — DP47F — 1995

662	M662ECD	664	M664ECD	667	M667ECD	669	M669ECD	670	M670ECD
663	M663ECD	665	M665ECD	668	M668ECD				

671	M311YSC	Volvo B10M-55	Alexander PS	DP48F	1995	Ex Fife Scottish, 1995
672	M312YSC	Volvo B10M-55	Alexander PS	DP48F	1995	Ex Fife Scottish, 1995
673	M313YSC	Volvo B10M-55	Alexander PS	DP48F	1995	Ex Fife Scottish, 1995

678-692

Bristol VRT/SL3/6LXB — Eastern Coach Works — H43/31F — 1979-80

678	EAP978V	685	EAP985V	687	EAP987V	690	EAP990V	692	EAP992V
684	EAP984V	686	EAP986V	688	EAP988V	691	EAP991V		

693	ELJ213V	Bristol VRT/SL3/6LXB	Eastern Coach Works	H43/31F	1979	
696	EAP996V	Bristol VRT/SL3/6LXB	Eastern Coach Works	H43/31F	1980	
729w	WKO129S	Bristol VRT/SL3/6LXB	Eastern Coach Works	H43/31F	1978	Ex Hastings & District, 1989
749	BKE849T	Bristol VRT/SL3/6LXB	Eastern Coach Works	H43/31F	1979	Ex Hastings & District, 1989
750	BKE850T	Bristol VRT/SL3/6LXB	Eastern Coach Works	H43/31F	1979	Ex Hastings & District, 1989
751	BKE851T	Bristol VRT/SL3/6LXB	Eastern Coach Works	H43/31F	1979	Ex Hastings & District, 1989

Eastbourne have received an allocation from the latest delivery of B10Ms to Stagecoach South. Shown here working service 712 is 645, N645LPN.
Andrew Jarosz

Fleet	Reg	Chassis	Body	Seating	Year	Notes
758	BKE858T	Bristol VRT/SL3/6LXB	Eastern Coach Works	H43/31F	1979	Ex Hastings & District, 1989
759	BKE859T	Bristol VRT/SL3/6LXB	Eastern Coach Works	H43/31F	1979	Ex Hastings & District, 1989
760	BKE860T	Bristol VRT/SL3/6LXB	Eastern Coach Works	H43/31F	1979	Ex Hastings & District, 1989
761	RJT151R	Bristol VRT/SL3/6LXB	Eastern Coach Works	H43/31F	1977	
768	AAP668T	Bristol VRT/SL3/6LXB	Eastern Coach Works	H43/28F	1979	
780	BAU180T	Bristol VRT/SL3/6LXB	Eastern Coach Works	H43/34F	1978	Ex East Midland, 1993
782	AET182T	Bristol VRT/SL3/6LXB	Eastern Coach Works	H43/34F	1979	Ex East Midland, 1993
787	AET187T	Bristol VRT/SL3/6LXB	Eastern Coach Works	H43/34F	1979	Ex East Midland, 1993
828	D228UHC	Mercedes-Benz L608D	Alexander AM	B20F	1986	Ex Hastings & District, 1989

841-850

Mercedes-Benz 709D   Alexander Sprint   B23F*   1990   *841-3 are DP25F

841	G71APO	843	G73APO	845	G975ARV	847	G977ARV	849	H679BTP
842	G72APO	844	G974ARV	846	G976ARV	848	G978ARV	850	H680BTP

853-888

Mercedes-Benz 709D   Alexander Sprint   B25F   1993

853	K853ODY	861	K861ODY	868	K868ODY	875	K875ODY	882	L882SDY
854	K854ODY	862	K862ODY	869	K869ODY	876	K876ODY	883	L883SDY
855	K855ODY	863	K863ODY	870	K870ODY	877	K877ODY	884	L884SDY
856	K856ODY	864	K864ODY	871	K871ODY	878	K878ODY	885	L885SDY
857	K857ODY	865	K865ODY	872	K872ODY	879	K879ODY	886	L886SDY
858	K858ODY	866	K866ODY	873	K873ODY	880	K880ODY	887	L887SDY
859	K859ODY	867	K867ODY	874	K874ODY	881	L881SDY	888	L188SDY
860	K860ODY								

889-904

Mercedes-Benz 709D   Alexander Sprint   B25F*   1995   *894-904 are B23F

889	M889ECD	892	N192LPN	895	N195LPN	898	N198LPN	902	N202LPN
890	M890ECD	893	N193LPN	896	N196LPN	899	N199LPN	903	N203LPN
891	N191LPN	894	N194LPN	897	N197LPN	901	N201LPN	904	N204LPN

950-995

Bristol VRT/SL3/6LXB   Eastern Coach Works   H43/31F   1978-80   Ex Alder Valley, 1992

950	TPE156S	961	GGM81W	966	WJM826T	972	WJM832T	982	CJH142V
953	VPF283S	962	GGM82W	967	WJM827T	977	CJH117V	985	CJH145V
955	GGM85W	964	WJM824T	968	WJM828T	979	CJH119V	988	KKK888V
956	GGM86W	965	WJM825T	969	WJM829T	980	CJH120V	995	GGM105W
960	GGM80W								

Fleet	Reg	Chassis	Body	Seating	Year	Notes
1003	CYJ531Y	Leyland Tiger TRCTL11/3R	Plaxton Paramount 3200	C50F	1983	
1004	BYJ919Y	Leyland Tiger TRCTL11/3R	Plaxton Paramount 3200	C50F	1983	
1005	UWP105	Leyland Tiger TRCTL11/3R	Plaxton Paramount 3200	C50F	1983	
1017	NFX667	Leyland Leopard PSU5E/4R(TL11)	Plaxton Supreme V	C50F	1982	
1064	VSV564	Leyland Tiger TRCTL11/3R	Plaxton Paramount 3200 E	C49F	1983	Ex Hastings & District, 1989
1066	MSU466	Leyland Tiger TRCTL11/3RH	Duple 340	C53FT	1987	Ex Fife Scottish, 1991
1072	USV672	Leyland Tiger TRCTL11/3R	Plaxton Paramount 3200 E	C49F	1983	Ex Hastings & District, 1989
1084	XDU599	Leyland Tiger TRCTL11/3RZ	Plaxton Paramount 3500 II	C46FT	1986	Ex United Counties, 1993
1094	GPJ894N	Leyland National 11351/1R		B49F	1975	Ex Alder Valley, 1992

1101-1108

Dennis Javelin 11SDL2133   Plaxton Premiere Interurban   DP47F   1994-95

1101	M101CCD	1105	M105CCD	1106	M106CCD	1107	M107CCD	1108	M108CCD

Fleet	Reg	Chassis	Body	Seating	Year	Notes
1115	MFN115R	Leyland National 11351A/1R		B49F	1976	Ex East Kent, 1993
1118	MFN118R	Leyland National 11351A/1R		B49F	1976	Ex East Kent, 1993

1160-1166

Volvo B10M-62   Plaxton Premiére Interurban   DP51F   1994

1160	M160CCD	1162	M162CCD	1164	M164CCD	1165	M165CCD	1166	M166CCD
1161	M161CCD	1163	M163CCD						

Three Dennis Javelins work Stagecoach Express services from the East Kent operation at Herne Bay. Shown at Canterbury is 1105, M105CCD complete with The Dickensian titles used to market this service.

1176	NPJ476R	Leyland National 11351A/1R				B49F	1976	Ex Alder Valley, 1992			
1180	UMO180N	Leyland National 11351/1R				B49F	1974	Ex Alder Valley, 1992			

1181-1189
Leyland National 11351A/1R — DP48F — 1977 — Ex East Kent, 1993

1181	NFN81R	1184	NFN84R	1186	NFN86R	1188	NFN88R	1189	NFN89R

1193	YEL93Y	Leyland Leopard PSU5E/4R	Eastern Coach Works B51	DP55F	1982

1201-1218
Leyland National 11351/1R — B49F — 1975 — Ex Alder Valley, 1992

1201	HPK503N	1203	HPK505N	1214	KPA365P	1215	KPA366P	1218	KPA369P

1223	KPA374P	Leyland National 11351/1R	B49F	1975	Ex Alder Valley, 1992
1228	KPA379P	Leyland National 11351/1R	B49F	1975	Ex Alder Valley, 1992
1232	KPA383P	Leyland National 11351/1R	B49F	1974	Ex Alder Valley, 1992
1236	KPA387P	Leyland National 11351A/1R	B49F	1976	Ex Alder Valley, 1992
1237	KPA388P	Leyland National 11351A/1R	B49F	1976	Ex Alder Valley, 1992
1238	KPA389P	Leyland National 11351A/1R	B49F	1976	Ex Alder Valley, 1992
1247	LPF605P	Leyland National 11351/1R/SC	B49F	1976	Ex Alder Valley, 1992

1253-1272
Leyland National 11351A/1R — B49F — 1976-77 — Ex Alder Valley, 1992

1253	NPJ474R	1259	NPJ480R	1264	NPJ485R	1271	TPE148S	1272	TPE149S
1256	NPJ477R	1261	NPJ482R						

1276	TPE169S	Leyland National 11351A/1R		DP45F	1978	Ex Alder Valley, 1992
1298	SGS504W	Leyland Tiger TRCTL11/3R	Plaxton Supreme IV	C50F	1981	Ex Alder Valley, 1992
1299	XGS762X	Leyland Tiger TRCTL11/3R	Plaxton Supreme IV	C51F	1981	Ex Alder Valley, 1992
1344	PJJ344S	Leyland National 10351A/1R		B41F	1977	Ex East Kent, 1993
1345	PJJ345S	Leyland National 10351A/1R		B41F	1977	Ex East Kent, 1993
1346	PJJ346S	Leyland National 10351A/1R		B41F	1977	Ex East Kent, 1993

1401	J401LKO	DAF SB220LC550	Optare Delta	B49F	1991	Ex East Kent, 1993
1402	J402LKO	DAF SB220LC550	Optare Delta	B49F	1991	Ex East Kent, 1993
1403	J403LKO	DAF SB220LC550	Optare Delta	B49F	1991	Ex East Kent, 1993

1404-1408

		Dennis Lance SLF 11SDA3201	Berkhof 2000	B40F	1994	

1404	M404OKM	1405	M405OKM	1406	M406OKM	1407	M407OKM	1408	M408OKM

1546	GFN546N	Leyland National 10351/1R		B40F	1975	Ex East Kent, 1993
1552	GFN552N	Leyland National 10351/1R		B37F	1975	Ex East Kent, 1993

1890-1900

		Leyland National 11351A/1R		B49F	1976	Ex East Kent, 1993

1890	JJG890P	1893	JJG893P	1895	JJG895P	1898	JJG898P	1900w	JJG900P

2891	G91VMM	Leyland Swift LBM6T/2RA	Wadham Stringer Vanguard	B34FL	1989	On loan from East Sussex CC
2892	G92VMM	Leyland Swift LBM6T/2RA	Wadham Stringer Vanguard	B34FL	1989	On loan from East Sussex CC
2902	F562HPP	MCW MetroRider MF158/9	MCW	B33F	1988	
2903	F563HPP	MCW MetroRider MF158/9	MCW	B33F	1988	
2904	F564HPP	MCW MetroRider MF158/9	MCW	B33F	1988	
2906	F437CJK	MCW MetroRider MF158/10	MCW	B31F	1988	
2907	F438CJK	MCW MetroRider MF154/1	MCW	B31F	1988	
2908	E840HAP	MCW MetroRider MF158/3	MCW	DP33F	1988	
2909	F471CJK	MCW MetroRider MF154/16	MCW	DP28F	1988	
7016	PJJ16S	Bristol VRT/SL3/6LXB	Willowbrook	H43/31F	1977	Ex East Kent, 1993
7021	PJJ21S	Bristol VRT/SL3/6LXB	Willowbrook	H43/31F	1978	Ex East Kent, 1993
7022	PJJ22S	Bristol VRT/SL3/6LXB	Willowbrook	H43/31F	1978	Ex East Kent, 1993
7046	MFN46R	Bristol VRT/SL3/6LXB	Eastern Coach Works	H43/31F	1976	Ex East Kent, 1993
7201	KYV511X	Leyland Titan TNLXB2RR	Leyland	H44/24D	198x	Ex Selkent, 1995
7203	A823SUL	Leyland Titan TNLXB2RR	Leyland	H44/24D	198x	Ex Selkent, 1995
7205	KYN305X	Leyland Titan TNLXB2RR	Leyland	H44/24F	1982	Ex Selkent, 1995
7211	NUW611Y	Leyland Titan TNLXB2RR	Leyland	H44/24D	1982	Ex Selkent, 1995
7215	CUL215V	Leyland Titan TNLXB2RRSp	Park Royal	H44/26D	1980	Ex Selkent, 1995
7220	KYV420X	Leyland Titan TNLXB2RR	Leyland	H44/24D	198x	Ex Selkent, 1995
7223	KYV523X	Leyland Titan TNLXB2RR	Leyland	H44/24F	1982	Ex Selkent, 1995
7225	CUL225V	Leyland Titan TNLXB2RRSp	Park Royal	H44/24D	1980	Ex Selkent, 1995
7229	EYE229V	Leyland Titan TNLXB2RRSp	Park Royal	H44/26F	1980	Ex Selkent, 1995
7233	EYE233V	Leyland Titan TNLXB2RRSp	Park Royal	H44/26D	1980	Ex Selkent, 1995
7237	EYE237V	Leyland Titan TNLXB2RRSp	Park Royal	H44/26F	1980	Ex Selkent, 1995
7240	EYE240V	Leyland Titan TNLXB2RRSp	Park Royal	H44/26F	1980	Ex Selkent, 1995
7242	KYV442X	Leyland Titan TNLXB2RR	Leyland	H44/24F	1982	Ex Selkent, 1995
7244	EYE244V	Leyland Titan TNLXB2RRSp	Park Royal	H44/26D	1980	Ex Selkent, 1995
7245	KYV345X	Leyland Titan TNTL112RR	Leyland	H44/26F	1981	Ex Selkent, 1995
7248	KYV348X	Leyland Titan TNLXB2RR	Leyland	H44/26D	1981	Ex Selkent, 1995
7250	EYE250V	Leyland Titan TNLXB2RRSp	Park Royal	H44/26D	1980	Ex Selkent, 1995
7251	KYV451X	Leyland Titan TNLXB2RR	Leyland	H44/24D	1982	Ex Selkent, 1995
7261	KYV361X	Leyland Titan TNLXB2RR	Leyland	H44/24D	1981	Ex Selkent, 1995
7268	CUL168V	Leyland Titan TNLXB2RRSp	Park Royal	H44/26D	1980	Ex Selkent, 1995
7269	CUL169V	Leyland Titan TNLXB2RRSp	Park Royal	H44/24F	1980	Ex Selkent, 1995
7274	KYV474X	Leyland Titan TNLXB2RR	Leyland	H44/24F	1982	Ex Selkent, 1995
7279	CUL79V	Leyland Titan TNLXB2RRSp	Park Royal	H44/26F	1980	Ex Selkent, 1995
7280	CUL190V	Leyland Titan TNLXB2RRSp	Park Royal	H44/26F	1980	Ex Selkent, 1995
7287	KYN487X	Leyland Titan TNLXB2RR	Leyland	H44/26D	1981	Ex Selkent, 1995
7288	KYN288X	Leyland Titan TNLXB2RR	Leyland	H44/24D	1981	Ex Selkent, 1995
7290	CUL190V	Leyland Titan TNLXB2RRSp	Park Royal	H44/24D	1980	Ex Selkent, 1995
7294	NUW594Y	Leyland Titan TNLXB2RR	Leyland	H44/24D	1982	Ex Selkent, 1995
7296	NUW596Y	Leyland Titan TNLXB2RR	Leyland	H44/24D	1982	Ex Selkent, 1995
7297	KYV397X	Leyland Titan TNLXB2RR	Leyland	H44/24F	1982	Ex Selkent, 1995
7298	CUL198V	Leyland Titan TNLXB2RRSp	Park Royal	H44/26F	1980	Ex Selkent, 1995

7301-7309

		Volvo Citybus B10M-50	Northern Counties	DPH43/33F	1989	

7301	F301MYJ	7303	F303MYJ	7305	F305MYJ	7307	F307MYJ	7309	F309MYJ
7302	F302MYJ	7304	F304MYJ	7306	F306MYJ	7308	F308MYJ		

Opposite: **Stagecoach South are currently receiving a large number of new buses to replace the Leopards, Nationals and VRs inherited with the old NBC fleets. These classics are represented here by Bristol VR 688, EAP988V, seen here working with South Coast Buses at Eastbourne. The village of Bramber is the setting for this picture of 1193, YEL93Y, the sole survivor of a batch of Eastern Coach Works-bodied Leyland Leopards. The service here replaced Sussex Bus route 24 during 1995.** *Richard Godfrey*

7321	VTV171S	Bristol VRT/SL3/6LXB	Eastern Coach Works	H43/31F	1978	Ex East Midland, 1993
7322	VTV172S	Bristol VRT/SL3/CLXD	Eastern Coach Works	H43/31F	1978	Ex East Midland, 1993
7324	XAP644S	Bristol VRT/SL3/6LXB	Eastern Coach Works	H43/31F	1978	
7327	LHG437T	Bristol VRT/SL3/501(6LXB)	Eastern Coach Works	H43/31F	1978	Ex Ribble, 1986
7328w	LHG438T	Bristol VRT/SL3/501(6LXB)	Eastern Coach Works	H43/31F	1978	Ex Ribble, 1986
7347	AAP647T	Bristol VRT/SL3/6LXB	Eastern Coach Works	H43/31F	1978	
7348	AAP648T	Bristol VRT/SL3/6LXB	Eastern Coach Works	H43/31F	1978	

7351-7358

Bristol VRT/SL3/6LXB   Eastern Coach Works   H43/31F*   1980   *7351/3 are DPH43/31F

7351	JWV251W	7353	JWV253W	7355	JWV255W	7356	JWV256W	7358	JWV258W
7352	JWV252W								

7359	DBV29W	Bristol VRT/SL3/6LXB	Eastern Coach Works	DPH43/31F	1980	Ex Ribble, 1986
7360	AAP660T	Bristol VRT/SL3/6LXB	Eastern Coach Works	H43/31F	1978	
7362	AAP662T	Bristol VRT/SL3/6LXB	Eastern Coach Works	H43/31F	1978	
7365	DBV25W	Bristol VRT/SL3/6LXB	Eastern Coach Works	DPH43/31F	1980	Ex Ribble, 1986
7366	JWV266W	Bristol VRT/SL3/680(6LXB)	Eastern Coach Works	H43/31F	1981	
7367	JWV267W	Bristol VRT/SL3/680(6LXB)	Eastern Coach Works	DPH43/27F	1981	
7368	JWV268W	Bristol VRT/SL3/680(6LXB)	Eastern Coach Works	H43/31F	1981	
7369	JWV269W	Bristol VRT/SL3/680(6LXB)	Eastern Coach Works	DPH43/31F	1981	
7370	AAP670T	Bristol VRT/SL3/6LXB	Eastern Coach Works	H43/31F	1979	
7371	AAP671T	Bristol VRT/SL3/6LXB	Eastern Coach Works	H43/31F	1979	
7373	EAP973V	Bristol VRT/SL3/6LXB	Eastern Coach Works	H43/31F	1979	
7374	JWV274W	Bristol VRT/SL3/680(6LXB)	Eastern Coach Works	H43/31F	1981	
7375	JWV275W	Bristol VRT/SL3/680	Eastern Coach Works	H43/31F	1981	
7376	JWV976W	Bristol VRT/SL3/680(6LXB)	Eastern Coach Works	H43/31F	1981	
7377	EAP977V	Bristol VRT/SL3/6LXB	Eastern Coach Works	H43/31F	1979	
7380	EAP980V	Bristol VRT/SL3/6LXB	Eastern Coach Works	H43/31F	1979	
7382	EAP982V	Bristol VRT/SL3/6LXB	Eastern Coach Works	H43/31F	1979	

7391-7397

Bristol VRT/SL3/6LXB   Eastern Coach Works   H43/31F   1978

7391	VPR490S	7394	HFG193T	7395	YEL2T	7396	YEL3T	7397	YEL4T
7392	VPR491S								

7604-7623

Bristol VRT/SL3/6LXB   Eastern Coach Works   CO43/31F   1977-78

7604	UWV604S	7611	UWV611S	7614	UWV614S	7621	UWV621S	7623	UWV623S
7607	UWV607S	7613	UWV613S						

7650-7685

Bristol VRT/SL3/6LXB   Eastern Coach Works   H43/31F   1980-81   Ex East Kent, 1993
7655 was rebodied 1983

7650	XJJ650V	7658	XJJ658V	7665	XJJ665V	7672	BJG672V	7680	SKL680X
7651	XJJ651V	7659	XJJ659V	7666	XJJ666V	7673	BJG673V	7681	SKL681X
7652	XJJ652V	7660	XJJ660V	7667	XJJ667V	7674	BJG674V	7682	SKL682X
7653	XJJ653V	7661	XJJ661V	7668	XJJ668V	7675	BJG675V	7683	SKL683X
7654	XJJ654V	7662	XJJ662V	7669	XJJ669V	7677	CJJ677W	7684	SKL684X
7655	XJJ655V	7663	XJJ663V	7670	XJJ670V	7678	CJJ678W	7685	SKL685X
7657	XJJ657V	7664	XJJ664V	7671	BJG671V	7679	CJJ679W		

7746-7755

MCW Metrobus Mk2 DR132/11   MCW   H46/31F   1988   Ex East Kent, 1993

7746	E746SKR	7748	E748SKR	7750	E750SKR	7752	E752SKR	7754	E754UKR
7747	E747SKR	7749	E749SKR	7751	E751SKR	7753	E753SKR	7755	E755UKR

7761-7767

MCW Metrobus Mk2 DR132/15   MCW   DPH43/27F   1989   Ex East Kent, 1993

7761	F761EKM	7763	F763EKM	7765	F765EKM	7766	F766EKM	7767	F767EKM
7762	F762EKM	7764	F764EKM						

7771-7775

MCW Metrobus Mk2 DR132/14   MCW   H46/31F   1989   Ex East Kent, 1993

7771	F771EKM	7772	F772EKM	7773	F773EKM	7774	F774EKM	7775	F775EKM

7781	F781KKP	Scania N113DRB	Alexander RH	H47/33F	1989	Ex East Kent, 1993
7782	F782KKP	Scania N113DRB	Alexander RH	H47/33F	1989	Ex East Kent, 1993

Chichester received five Mercedes-Benz 709Ds during 1995 for the Coastline Buses operation, their first of the type. Illustrated here is 893, N193LPN. During 1996, some 400 similar minibuses will be delivered to the group displacing older and smaller vehicles. *Philip Lamb*

7801-7810

Leyland Olympian ON2R56C16Z4 Northern Counties   H51/34F   1990   Ex East Kent, 1993

| 7801 | H801BKK | 7803 | H803BKK | 7805 | H805BKK | 7807 | H807BKK | 7809 | H809BKK |
| 7802 | H802BKK | 7804 | H804BKK | 7806 | H806BKK | 7808 | H808BKK | 7810 | H810BKK |

7811	J811NKK	Leyland Olympian ON2R50C13Z4 Northern Counties	H47/30F	1992	Ex East Kent, 1993
7812	J812NKK	Leyland Olympian ON2R50C13Z4 Northern Counties	H47/30F	1992	Ex East Kent, 1993
7813	J813NKK	Leyland Olympian ON2R50C13Z4 Northern Counties	H47/30F	1992	Ex East Kent, 1993
7814	J814NKK	Leyland Olympian ON2R50C13Z4 Northern Counties	H47/30F	1992	Ex East Kent, 1993

7821-7830

Leyland Olympian ON2R50C13Z4 Northern Counties   H47/30F   1993   7821-5 ex East Kent, 1993

| 7821 | K821TKP | 7823 | K823TKP | 7825 | K825TKP | 7827 | L827BKK | 7829 | L829BKK |
| 7822 | K822TKP | 7824 | K824TKP | 7826 | L826BKK | 7828 | L828BKK | 7830 | L830BKK |

7982	TFN982T	Bristol VRT/SL3/6LXB	Willowbrook	H43/31F	1978	Ex East Kent, 1993
7983	EAP983V	Bristol VRT/SL3/6LXB	Eastern Coach Works	H43/31F	1980	
7988	TFN988T	Bristol VRT/SL3/6LXB	Willowbrook	H43/31F	1978	Ex East Kent, 1993
8211	D211VEV	Scania K112CRB	Berkhof Esprite 350	C40DT	1987	Ex East Kent, 1993
8243	SIB8243	Volvo B10M-60	Plaxton Paramount 3500 III	C49F	1990	Ex East Kent, 1993
8399w	A203ODY	MCW Metroliner HR131/1	MCW	C49FT	1983	Ex East Kent, 1993

8404-8410

Volvo B10M-62   Plaxton Premiére 350   C49F*   1995   *8410 is C46FT

| 8404 | M404BFG | 8406 | M406BFG | 8408 | M408BFG | 8409 | M409BFG | 8410 | M410BFG |
| 8405 | M405BFG | 8407 | M407BFG | | | | | | |

8503	IIL3503	Volvo B10M-61	Van Hool Alizée	C49FT	1988	Ex Bluebird Buses, 1995
8505	IIL3505	Volvo B10M-61	Van Hool Alizée	C49FT	1988	Ex Bluebird Buses, 1995
8618	WVT618	Volvo B10M-61	Plaxton Paramount 3500 III	C50F	1987	Ex Bluebird Buses, 1995
8850w	WSU450	MCW Metroliner CR126/8	MCW	C51F	1984	Ex East Kent, 1993
8851w	WSU451	MCW Metroliner CR126/8	MCW	C51F	1984	Ex East Kent, 1993
8852w	WSU452	MCW Metroliner CR126/8	MCW	C51F	1984	Ex East Kent, 1993
8854	E854UKR	MCW Metroliner HR131/12	MCW	C51F	1988	Ex East Kent, 1993
8855	E855UKR	MCW Metroliner HR131/12	MCW	C51F	1988	Ex East Kent, 1993
8856	J856NKK	Scania K93CRB	Plaxton Paramount 3500 III	C49FT	1992	Ex East Kent, 1993

8901	G901PKK	Volvo B10M-60	Plaxton Expressliner	C49FT	1989	Ex East Kent, 1993
8903	G903PKK	Volvo B10M-60	Plaxton Expressliner	C49FT	1989	Ex East Kent, 1993
8909	J909NKP	Volvo B10M-60	Plaxton Expressliner	C46FT	1992	Ex East Kent, 1993
8910	K910TKP	Volvo B10M-60	Plaxton Expressliner 2	C49FT	1993	Ex East Kent, 1993

8911-8918

Volvo B10M-62 — Plaxton Expressliner 2 — C49FT — 1994-95

8911	M911WJK	8913	M913WJK	8915	M915WJK	8917	M917WJK	8918	M918WJK
8912	M912WJK	8914	M914WJK	8916	M916WJK				

8996	PFN873	Bova FHD12.280	Bova Futura	C49FT	1986	Ex East Kent, 1993

Special events vehicles: (traditional liveries)

0135	CD7045	Leyland G7	Short	O27/24R	1922	
0409	409DCD	Leyland Titan PD3/4	Northern Counties	FCO39/30F	1964	
0424	424DCD	Leyland Titan PD3/4	Northern Counties	FCO39/30F	1964	
0770	HKE690L	Bristol VRT/SL2/6LXB	Eastern Coach Works	O43/34F	1973	Ex Hastings & District, 1989
0813	UF4813	Leyland Titan TD1	Brush	O27/24R	1929	
0946	MFN946F	AEC Regent V 3D3RA	Park Royal	H40/32F	1967	Ex Hastings & District, 1989

Operating Companies:

Coastline : 34, 118/20-33/5/9, 209/15-24/8-35/7-40/3-5, 477/88-92, 551-69/74/9, 610-5/21-31/56-8/78/84/6/7/90-2/6, 889-93, 953, 1101/7/60-6/80/93, 1203/36/56/98, 2902/3/6/8, 7229/42/5/51/96-8, 7351/5/6/9/65/7/8/75/6, 7604/7/14,

East Kent North: 1/2/11/3/6/9/35/57/60-2/4/76/91/5/8, 149, 225-7/54-7, 360-5/8-78/81/9/90, 461/4/7/81/3, 632-4/59-61, 899/901-4, 1105/6/8, 1401-8, 7650/1/60-2/6-73/7/9-83/5, 7746-55/63-67/71-5/81/2, 7801-5/7-10/24/5, 7983, 8211/43, 8405-10, 8503/5, 8618, 8856, 8909/11/2.

East Kent South: 3/2/10/2/4/5/7/8/20/6/41/6/7/51/5/6/8/63/5-7/9-75/80/3-6/93/4/6/7, 463/80/2, 639/40, 894-8, 977, 1115/81, 1344, 1546, 1890/5/8, 1900, 7016/21/46, 7652/3/5/7/63-5/74/5/8/84, 7761/2, 7806/11-4/21-3/6-30, 7982, 8246, 8854/5, 8910/3-8/96

Hampshire Bus: 21/5/30/6-9/42/3, 100/4-6/15-7/52/4/64/5/7/86/90-2/6, 201-4/6-8/10-4/36/46-50, 366/7/91-4, 400-3/22/32/3/5/8-41/4/6-50, 522-40/2-50/73/80-2, 606-8/16-7/41-3/51/2/5/62-5/7-70, 787, 841-3/5-50, 950/6/65/6/88, 1003-5/17, 1175, 1214/47/76, 1552, 7269, 7353/8/60/2/6/70/4/7/80/2/91/2/4-7,

Hants & Surrey: 23/31/3/45, 162/89, 207/36, 379/80, 460/9-71/3/6/7, 522/3/70-2/5-8/84-8, 618/35/85, 759/80/2, 853-80, 955/60-2/8/9/72/9/80/2/5/95, 1084/94, 1184/8, 1201/15/8/23/8/32/7/8/58/9/61/4/71/2/99, 2904/7, 7322, 7611

South Coast Buses: 101-3/7/9-14/9/34/6-8/40-7/55/7/9/60/3/9/73/4/6-80/2/95/7, 382-8/95-9, 501-21/41/83, 601-5/9/19/20-36-8/44/5/50/71-3/88/93, 749-51/8/60/1/8, 828/44/81-8, 964/7, 1064/72, 1186, 1345, 2891/2, 2909, 7223/37/40/4/50/68, 7301-9/21/7/8/48/52/69/71/3, 8901/3.

Previous Registrations:

400DCD	M490BFG	F471CJK	F565HPP, 419DCD
401DCD	M401BFG	HUF451X	RUF434X, XLD244
402DCD	M402BFG	HUF579X	RUF430X, 400DCD
403DCD	M403BFG	HUF592X	RUF437X, 407DCD
404DCD	L604VCD	HUF593X	RUF436X, 406DCD
405DCD	L605VCD	HUF603X	RUF429X, 415DCD
406DCD	L606TDY	HUF604X	RUF435X, 405DCD
407DCD	L607TDY	HUF625X	RUF431X, 411DCD
408DCD	L608TDY	HUF626X	RUF438X, 410DCD
409DCD	from new	HUF639X	RUF433X, 420DCD
410DCD	M610APN	IIL3503	E625UNE, TXI2426, E936XSB
411DCD	M611APN	IIL3505	E623UNE, XIA257, E942XSB
412DCD	M612APN	JNJ194V	HFG924V, DSV943
413DCD	M613APN	MSU466	D526ESG
415DCD	L345KCK	NFX667	HHC367Y
416DCD	L346KCK	OUF262W	JWV125W, LYJ145
417DCD	L347KCK	PFN873	C996FKM
418DCD	L348KCK	SIB8243	H826AHS
419DCD	L619TDY	SYC852	JWV126W
420DCD	L620TDY	USV672	FKL172Y
421DCD	L621TDY	UWP105	XUF535Y
422DCD	L622TDY	VSV564	FKL171Y
424DCD	424DCD, AOR158B	WSU448	A848OKK
A203ODY	A543WOB, ABM399A, XDU599	WSU450	B850TKL
BYJ919Y	XUF534V, 404DCD	WSU451	B851TKL
CYJ531Y	XUF533Y, 403DCD	WSU452	B852TKL
E840HAP	E518YWF, 418DCD	WVT618	D202LWX
F437CJK	F816CKJ, 416DCD	XDU599	C84PRP
F438CJK	F817DWG, 417DCD	YLJ332	RUF432X

STAGECOACH TRANSIT

Cleveland Transit Ltd, Hartlepool Transport Ltd, Stagecoach Darlington Ltd,
Church Road, Stockton-on-Tees, Cleveland, TS18 2HW

Depots : Faverdale Industrial Estate, Darlington; Church Street, Hartlepool and Church Road, Stockton.

Cleveland and Darlington:

1-10			Leyland Lynx LX2R11C15Z4R		Leyland Lynx		B49F		1989		
1	F601UVN	3	F603UVN	5	F605UVN	7	F607UVN	9	F609UVN		
2	F602UVN	4	F604UVN	6	F606UVN	8	F608UVN	10	F610UVN		

11-20			Leyland Lynx LX2R1 1C15Z4R		Leyland Lynx 2		B49F		1989		
11	G611CEF	13	G613CEF	15	G615CEF	17	G617CEF	19	G619CEF		
12	G612CEF	14	G614CEF	16	G616CEF	18	G618CEF	20	G620CEF		

21	J901UKV	Leyland Lynx LX2R11V18Z4S	Leyland Lynx 2	B49F	1991	Ex Volvo demonstrator, 1992

22-30			Leyland Lynx LX2R11V18Z4R		Leyland Lynx 2		B49F		1992		
22	K622YVN	24	K624YVN	26	K626YVN	28	K628YVN	30	K630YVN		
23	K623YVN	25	K625YVN	27	K627YVN	29	K629YVN				

31-42			Volvo B10B		Plaxton Verde		B52F		1994		
31	L31HHN	34	L34HHN	37	L37HHN	39	M39PVN	41	M41PVN		
32	L32HHN	35	L35HHN	38	M38PVN	40	M40PVN	42	M42PVN		
33	L33HHN	36	L36HHN								

43-52			Volvo B10M-55		Northern Counties Paladin		B48F		1995		
43	M543SPY	45	M545SPY	47	M547SPY	49	M549SPY	51	M551SPY		
44	M544SPY	46	M546SPY	48	M548SPY	50	M550SPY	52	M552SPY		

101-108			Volvo B6-9.9M		Plaxton Pointer		B41F		1993-94		
101	L101GHN	103	L103GHN	105	M105PVN	107	M107PVN	108	M108PVN		
102	L102GHN	104	M104PVN	106	M106PVN						

The 1995 delivery of Volvo Olympians for the group included five in green, yellow and white livery for the Cleveland unit. These will be the last new buses in the scheme for repainting into corporate livery has now commenced. Pictured in Middlesborough bus station is is 226, M226SVN.
Murdoch Currie

121-157 — Leyland Fleetline FE30AGR — Northern Counties — H43/31F — 1979-83

121	YVN521T	139	JAJ139W	143	JAJ143W	148	PEF148X	153	VEF153Y
129	GAJ129V	139	JAJ139W	144	JAJ144W	149	PEF149X	154	YAJ154Y
130	GAJ130V	140	JAJ140W	145	JAJ145W	150	VEF150Y	155	YAJ155Y
135	GAJ135V	141	JAJ141W	146	JAJ146W	151	VEF151Y	156	YAJ156Y
136	GAJ136V	142	JAJ142W	147	PEF147X	152	VEF152Y	157	YAJ157Y
137	GAJ137V								

189	PES189Y	Leyland Tiger TRCTL11/3R	Duple Goldliner IV	C51F	1983	Ex Busways, 1995
192	PSO179W	Leyland Tiger TRCTL11/3R	Duple Dominant IV	C51F	1981	Ex Busways, 1995
193	CSO389Y	Leyland Tiger TRCTL11/2R	Duple Dominant II Express	C49F	1983	On loan from Busways
194	VSS3X	Leyland Tiger TRCTL11/3R	Duple Goldliner IV	C51F	1982	Ex Busways, 1995

208	A208EHN	Dennis Dominator DDA167	Northern Counties	H43/31F	1984
209	A209EHN	Dennis Dominator DDA167	Northern Counties	H43/31F	1983
211	A211EHN	Dennis Dominator DDA167	Northern Counties	H43/31F	1983
212	A212FVN	Dennis Dominator DDA167	Northern Counties	H43/31F	1984
213	A213FVN	Dennis Dominator DDA172	Northern Counties	H43/31F	1984

214-222 — Dennis Dominator DD906* — Northern Counties — H43/31F — 1985-86 *219-22 are DDA1009

214	B214OAJ	216	B216OAJ	218	B218OAJ	220	C220WAJ	222	C222WAJ
215	B215OAJ	217	B217OAJ	219	C219WAJ	221	C221WAJ		

223-227 — Volvo Olympian YN2RV18Z4 — Northern Counties Palatine — H47/29F — 1995

223	M223SVN	224	M224SVN	225	M225SVN	226	M226SVN	227	M227SVN

301-316 — Mercedes-Benz 811D — Wright NimBus — B26F — 1989 — Ex Selkent, 1995

301	HDZ2601	305	HDZ2605	309	HDZ2609	312	HDZ2612	315	HDZ2615
303	HDZ2603	306	HDZ2606	310	HDZ2610	313	HDZ2613	316	HDZ2616
304	HDZ2604	307	HDZ2607	311	HDZ2611				

324	E324JVN	Renault-Dodge S56	Northern Counties	B20F	1987
333	E333LHN	Renault-Dodge S56	Northern Counties	DP21F	1988
335	F335SPY	Renault-Dodge S56	Northern Counties	DP21F	1988

336-345 — Renault-Dodge S56 — Northern Counties — B23F — 1989

336	F336VEF	338	F338VEF	340	F340VEF	342	F342VEF	344	F344VEF
337	F337VEF	339	F339VEF	341	F341VEF	343	F343VEF	345	F345VEF

353	D607MKH	Iveco Daily 49-10	Robin Hood City Nippy	B25F	1987	Ex Busways, 1995

354-359 — Mercedes-Benz L608D — Reeve Burgess — B20F — 1986 — Ex Busways, 1995

354	D33UAO	356	D526RCK	357	D535RCK	358	D538RCK	359	D543RCK
355	D523RCK								

363	H401DMJ	Renault S75	Reeve Burgess Beaver	B29F	1990	Ex Busways, 1995

364-378 — Renault S75 — Plaxton Beaver — B28F — 1991 — Ex Busways, 1995

364	J553NGS	367	J227JJR	370	J230JJR	373	J233JJR	376	K343PJR
365	J225JJR	368	J228JJR	371	J231JJR	374	K341PJR	377	K344PJR
366	J226JJR	369	J229JJR	372	J232JJR	375	K342PJR	378	K345PJR

500	PRX189B	Leyland Titan PD3/4	Northern Counties	FCO39/30F	1964	Ex Southdown, 1988

511-520 — Volvo B6-9.9M — Alexander Dash — DP40F — 1993 — Ex Ribble, 1995

511	L238CCW	513	L243CCK	515	L245CCK	517	L247CCK	519	L249CCK
512	L242CCK	514	L244CCK	516	L246CCK	518	L250CCK	520	L254CCK

Opposite: **Contrast the style changes over twelve years in the Northern Counties single deck design of 1985 seen on Hartlepool 28, B28PAJ and the latest arrival for Darlington, 552, N552VDC. Three new Alexander PS-bodied B10s were added to the Northern Counties examples delivered earlier in the year, though the latter are worked from the Cleveland depot. Currently, two numbering systems are in use, one covering Hartlepool, the other for vehicles based at Cleveland and Darlington.**
Tony Wilson/Andrew Jarosz

551	N551VDC	Volvo B10M-55	Alexander PS	DP48F	1995	
552	N552VDC	Volvo B10M-55	Alexander PS	DP48F	1995	
553	N553VDC	Volvo B10M-55	Alexander PS	DP48F	1995	
851	NPK236R	Leyland National 10351A/1R(Volvo)		B41F	1976	Ex Mainline, 1995
903	BPY403T	Leyland Leopard PSU3E/4R	Plaxton Supreme IV Express	DP53F	1979	
923	HPY423V	Leyland Leopard PSU3F/4R	Plaxton Supreme IV Express	C53F	1980	

Stagecoach Hartlepool:

1	SHN401R	Leyland National 11351A/2R	B50F	1977	
4	SHN404R	Leyland National 11351A/2R	B52F	1977	
5	SHN405R	Leyland National 11351A/2R	B50F	1977	
7	SHN407R	Leyland National 11351A/2R	B50F	1977	

14-19 Leyland National 2 NL116L11/2R   B50F*   1980   *15/6 are DP48F, 17/8 are B45D

14	KAJ214W	16	KAJ216W	17	KAJ217W	18	KAJ218W	19	KAJ219W
15	KAJ215W								

21-26 Dennis Falcon HC SDA409   Wadham Stringer   B46D   1983

21	YDC21Y	23	YDC23Y	24	YDC24Y	25	YDC25Y	26	YDC26Y

27-32 Dennis Falcon HC SDA409   Northern Counties   B47D   1985

27	B27PAJ	29	B29PAJ	30	B30PAJ	31	B31PAJ	32	B32PAJ
28	B28PAJ								

38	RUF38R	Leyland National 11351A/2R		B50F	1977	Ex Brighton & Hove, 1990
40	RUF40R	Leyland National 11351A/2R		B44D	1977	Ex Brighton & Hove, 1990
49	UFG49S	Leyland National 11351A/2R		B50F	1977	Ex Brighton & Hove, 1990
52	UFG52S	Leyland National 11351A/2R		B50F	1977	Ex Brighton & Hove, 1990
67	MEF67J	Bristol RELL6L	Eastern Coach Works	B46D	1971	
73	OEF73K	Bristol RELL6L	Eastern Coach Works	B46D	1972	
74	OEF74K	Bristol RELL6L	Eastern Coach Works	B46D	1972	
77	OEF77K	Bristol RELL6L	Eastern Coach Works	B46D	1972	
78w	OEF78K	Bristol RELL6L	Eastern Coach Works	B46D	1972	

80-96 Bristol RELL6L   Eastern Coach Works   B46D*   1973-75 *91 is DP47F

80	SEF80L	85	GEF185N	89	GEF189N	93	JAJ293N	95	JAJ295N
81	SEF81L	87	GEF187N	90	GEF190N	94	JAJ294N	96	JAJ296N
84	SEF84L	88w	GEF188N	92	JAJ292N				

101	XCC94V	Leyland Leopard PSU3E/4R	Plaxton Supreme IV Express	C49F	1980	Ex Vale of Llangollen, 1986
102	BTU33W	Leyland Leopard PSU3E/4R	Plaxton Supreme IV Express	C49F	1981	Ex Vale of Llangollen, 1986
103	FSL61W	Leyland Leopard PSU3G/4R	Plaxton Supreme IV Express	C49F	1982	Ex Tayside, 1987
104	FSL62W	Leyland Leopard PSU3G/4R	Plaxton Supreme IV Express	C49F	1982	Ex Tayside, 1987
105	HDZ8683	Volvo B10M-61	Plaxton Paramount 3500	C49F	1984	Ex Allander, Milngavie, 1989
106	837XHW	Volvo B10M-61	Van Hool Alizée	C53F	1987	Ex Streamline, Bath, 1994
131	GAJ131V	Leyland Fleetline FE30AGR	Northern Counties	H43/31F	1980	
132	GAJ132V	Leyland Fleetline FE30AGR	Northern Counties	H43/31F	1980	
133	GAJ133V	Leyland Fleetline FE30AGR	Northern Counties	H43/31F	1980	
134	GAJ134V	Leyland Fleetline FE30AGR	Northern Counties	H43/31F	1980	

401-410 Volvo B10M-55   Northern Counties Paladin   B48F   1995

401	M401SPY	403	M403SPY	405	M405SPY	407	M407SPY	409	M409SPY
402	M402SPY	404	M404SPY	406	M406SPY	408	M408SPY	410	M410SPY

Previous Registrations:

837XHW	D556MVR	HDZ8683	A845UGB, 2367AT, A491WYS
BTU33W	WLG380W, 93FYB	PES189Y	SFS582Y, MSU445
CSO389Y	ASA9Y, TSV779	PRX189B	417DCD
FSL61W	GSL307W, 666TPJ	XCC94V	UMA953V, UAM829
FSL62W	GSL306W, 6689DP		

UNITED COUNTIES

United Counties Omnibus Co Ltd, Rothersthorpe Avenue,
Northampton, NN4 9UT

Depots : St Johns, Bedford; Station Road, Corby; Stukeley Road, Huntingdon; Northampton Road, Kettering and Rothersthorpe Avenue, Northampton. **Outstations** : Biggleswade; Bishops Stortford; Chown's Mill; Daventry; Desborough; Husbands Bosworth; Little Paxton; Mildenhall; Milton Keynes; Somersham; Thrapston; Uppingham; Wellingborough; Wymington and Yardley Hastings.

46	E46MRP	Iveco Daily 49.10	Robin Hood City Nippy	B23F	1988	
47	E47MRP	Iveco Daily 49.10	Robin Hood City Nippy	B23F	1988	
49	E49MRP	Iveco Daily 49.10	Robin Hood City Nippy	B23F	1988	
50	E50MRP	Iveco Daily 49.10	Robin Hood City Nippy	B19F	1988	
51	F494NTR	Iveco Daily 49.10	Robin Hood City Nippy	B19F	1988	Ex Hampshire Bus, 1988
52	F495NTR	Iveco Daily 49.10	Robin Hood City Nippy	B19F	1988	Ex Hampshire Bus, 1988
53	F496NTR	Iveco Daily 49.10	Robin Hood City Nippy	B19F	1988	Ex Hampshire Bus, 1988
54	F491NTR	Iveco Daily 49.10	Robin Hood City Nippy	B25F	1988	Ex Hampshire Bus, 1988
55	F492NTR	Iveco Daily 49.10	Robin Hood City Nippy	B25F	1988	Ex Hampshire Bus, 1988
56	F493NTR	Iveco Daily 49.10	Robin Hood City Nippy	B25F	1988	Ex Hampshire Bus, 1988
57	F57AVV	Iveco Daily 49.10	Robin Hood City Nippy	B23F	1989	
58	F58AVV	Iveco Daily 49.10	Robin Hood City Nippy	B23F	1989	
59	F59AVV	Iveco Daily 49.10	Robin Hood City Nippy	B19F	1989	
60	F60AVV	Iveco Daily 49.10	Robin Hood City Nippy	B19F	1989	

61-75 Iveco Daily 49.10   Phoenix   B19F   1989   68-75 ex Magicbus, 1990
*73 is B23F

61	G61JVV	64	G64JVV	67	G67LVV	70	G27PSR	73	G33SSR
62	G62JVV	65	G65JVV	68	G28PSR	71	G31PSR	74	G40SSR
63	G63JVV	66	G66JVV	69	G29PSR	72	G32PSR	75	G41SSR

81	WLT682	Leyland Tiger TRCTL11/3RZ	Plaxton Paramount 3500 II	C46FT	1986	
82	WLT908	Leyland Tiger TRCTL11/3RZ	Plaxton Paramount 3500 II	C46FT	1986	
83	83CBD	Leyland Tiger TRCTL11/3RZ	Plaxton Paramount 3500	C51F	1983	Ex Stagecoach Malawi, 1994
85	647DYE	Leyland Tiger TRCTL11/3RZ	Plaxton Paramount 3500 II	C46FT	1986	
86	TSU639	Leyland Tiger TRCTL11/3R	Plaxton Paramount 3200 E	C53F	1983	Ex Stagecoach South, 1995
87	TSU640	Leyland Tiger TRCTL11/3R	Plaxton Paramount 3200 E	C53F	1983	Ex Stagecoach South, 1995
88	TSU641	Leyland Tiger TRCTL11/3R	Plaxton Paramount 3200 E	C53F	1983	Ex Stagecoach South, 1995
89	TSU642	Leyland Tiger TRCTL11/3R	Plaxton Paramount 3200 E	C53F	1983	Ex Stagecoach South, 1995

92-96 Volvo B10M-60   Plaxton Premiére 350   C49FT   1992   Ex Park's, 1993
94/5 ex Rainworth Travel, 1993

92	J430HDS	93	J439HDS	94	J445HDS	95	J446HDS	96	J450HDS

102	NBD102Y	Leyland Tiger TRCTL11/3R	Plaxton Paramount 3200 E	C53F	1983	
103	NBD103Y	Leyland Tiger TRCTL11/3R	Plaxton Paramount 3200 E	C53F	1983	
104	NBD104Y	Leyland Tiger TRCTL11/3R	Plaxton Paramount 3200 E	C53F	1983	
105	RBD397Y	Leyland Tiger TRCTL11/3R	Plaxton Paramount 3200 E	C53F	1983	

108-114 Leyland Tiger TRCTL11/3RH   Plaxton Paramount 3200 E   C50FT   1983

108	A108TRP	110	A110TRP	112	A112TRP	113	A113TRP	114	A114TRP
109	A109TRP	111	A111TRP						

115	MSU465	Leyland Tiger TRCTL11/3RH	Duple 340	C53F	1987	Ex Fife Scottish, 1992
116	VLT255	Leyland Tiger TRCTL11/3RZ	Duple Laser 2	C44FT	1985	Ex Stagecoach Malawi, 1993
120	C120PNV	Leyland Tiger TRCTL11/3R7	Plaxton Paramount 3200 IIE	C53F	1986	
121	C121PNV	Leyland Tiger TRCTL11/3RZ	Plaxton Paramount 3200 IIE	C53F	1986	
122	C122PNV	Leyland Tiger TRCTL11/3RZ	Plaxton Paramount 3200 IIE	C53F	1986	
125	A729ANH	Volvo B10M-61	Plaxton Paramount 3200 E	C48FT	1983	Ex Stagecoach, 1988
126	A728ANH	Volvo B10M-61	Plaxton Paramount 3200 E	C48FT	1983	Ex Stagecoach, 1988

130-135 Volvo B10M-61   Plaxton Paramount 3200 III   C53F   1988

130	E130ORP	132	E132ORP	133	E133ORP	134	E134ORP	135	F135URP
131	E131ORP								

Street Shuttle is the name used by United Counties for its minibus operations. Seen here, while heading into Northampton, is 377, L377JBD. It is interesting to compare the roof line of the Alexander Sprint between this 1993 example and a 1995 model illustrated on page 103. *Richard Godfrey*

144-149

Volvo B10M-60 — Plaxton Premiére 350 — C50F — 1992 — Ex Wallace Arnold, 1995

144	J752CWT	146	K758FYG	147	K759FYG	148	K760FYG	149	K761FYG
145	J753CWT								

150-162

Volvo B10M-60 — Plaxton Premiére Interurban — DP53F* — 1993 — *155-162 are DP51F

150	K150DNV	153	K153DNV	156	L156JNH	159	L159JNH	161	L161JNH
151	K151DNV	154	K154DNV	157	L157JNH	160	L160JNH	162	L162JNH
152	K152DNV	155	L155JNH	158	L158JNH				

332-349

Mercedes-Benz 709D — Alexander Sprint — B25F — 1994

332	M332DRP	337	M337DRP	341	M341DRP	344	M344DRP	347	M347DRP
334	M334DRP	338	M338DRP	342	M342DRP	345	M345DRP	348	M348DRP
335	M335DRP	339	M339DRP	343	M343DRP	346	M346DRP	349	M349DRP
336	M336DRP	340	M340DRP						

350-383

Mercedes-Benz 709D — Alexander Sprint — B25F — 1992-93

350	K350ANV	357	K357ANV	364	L364JBD	371	L371JBD	378	L378JBD
351	K351ANV	358	K358ANV	365	L365JBD	372	L372JBD	379	L379JBD
352	K352ANV	359	K359ANV	366	L366JBD	373	L373JBD	380	L380JBD
353	K353ANV	360	L360JBD	367	L367JBD	374	L374JBD	381	L381NBD
354	K354ANV	361	L361JBD	368	L368JBD	375	L375JBD	382	L382NBD
355	K355ANV	362	L362JBD	369	L369JBD	376	L376JBD	383	L383NBD
356	K356ANV	363	L363JBD	370	L370JBD	377	L377JBD		

Thirty Volvo B6s operate with United Counties, illustrated heading for Boston is Northampton-based 422, L422MVV. *Richard Godfrey*

401-422

Volvo B6-9.9M   Alexander Dash   B40F   1993

401	L401JBD	406	L406JBD	411	L411JBD	415	L415JBD	419	L419JBD
402	L402JBD	407	L407JBD	412	L412JBD	416	L416JBD	420	L420JBD
403	L403JBD	408	L408JBD	413	L413JBD	417	L417JBD	421	L421JBD
404	L404JBD	409	L409JBD	414	L414JBD	418	L418JBD	422	L422MVV
405	L405JBD	410	L410JBD						

423-430

Volvo B6-9.9M   Alexander Dash   DP40F   1994

423	L423XVV	425	L425XVV	427	L427XVV	429	M429BNV	430	M430BNV
424	L424XVV	426	L426XVV	428	L428XVV				

500	LFR862X	Leyland National 2 NL106AL11/1R		B44F	1981	Ex Cumberland, 1993
501	LFR864X	Leyland National 2 NL106AL11/1R		B41F	1982	Ex Cumberland, 1993
600	F110NES	Leyland Olympian ON6LXCT/5RZ	Alexander RL	H66/44F	1989	Ex East Midland, 1992

601-611

Leyland Olympian ONLXB/1R   Eastern Coach Works   H45/32F*   1981   *601 is DPH45/27F
*602/5/6 are DPH41/27F

601	ARP601X	604	ARP604X	606	AHP606X	608	ARP608X	610	ARP610X
602	ARP602X	605	ARP605X	607	ARP607X	609	ARP609X	611	ARP611X

612	WLT528	Leyland Olympian ONLXB/1RV	Alexander RL	H43/34F	1987	Ex Bluebird, 1991
613	D383XRS	Leyland Olympian ONLXB/1RV	Alexander RL	H43/34F	1987	Ex Bluebird, 1991
614	WLT512	Leyland Olympian ONLXB/1RV	Alexander RL	H47/34F	1987	Ex Bluebird, 1991
615	685DYE	Leyland Olympian ONLXB/1RV	Alexander RL	H47/34F	1987	Ex Bluebird, 1991
616	GSO6V	Leyland Olympian ONLXB/1RV	Alexander RL	H47/34F	1987	Ex Bluebird, 1991
617	GSO7V	Leyland Olympian ONLXB/1RV	Alexander RL	H47/34F	1987	Ex Bluebird, 1991
618	GSO2V	Leyland Olympian ONLXB/1RV	Alexander RL	H47/34F	1986	Ex Bluebird, 1994

620-649

Leyland Olympian ONLXB/2RZ   Alexander RL   H51/36F*   1988-89   *635-644 are H51/34F
*645-9 are DPH51/31F

620	F620MSL	626	F626MSL	632	F632MSL	638	F638YRP	644	G644EVV
621	F621MSL	627	F627MSL	633	F633MSL	639	G639EVV	645	G645EVV
622	F622MSL	628	F628MSL	634	F634MSP	640	G640EVV	646	G646EVV
623	F623MSL	629	F629MSL	635	F635YRP	641	G641EVV	647	G647EVV
624	F624MSL	630	F630MSL	636	F636YRP	642	G642EVV	648	G648EVV
625	F625MSL	631	F631MSL	637	F637YRP	643	G643EVV	649	G649EVV

650-654

Leyland Olympian ON2R56G13Z4 Alexander RL   H51/34F   1990

650	H650VVV	651	H651VVV	652	H652VVV	653	H653VVV	654	H654VVV

655-670

Leyland Olympian ON2R50G13Z4 Northern Counties Palatine H47/29F   1992

655	K655UNH	658	K658UNH	661	K661UNH	664	K664UNH	668	K668UNH
656	K656UNH	659	K659UNH	662	K662UNH	665	K665UNH	669	K669UNH
657	K657UNH	660	K660UNH	663	K663UNH	667	K667UNH	670	K670UNH

671-685

Volvo Olympian YN2RV18Z4   Alexander RL   H47/29F   1993

671	L671HNV	674	L674HNV	677	L677HNV	680	L680HNV	683	L683HNV
672	L672HNV	675	L675HNV	678	L678HNV	681	L681HNV	684	L684HNV
673	L673HNV	676	L676HNV	679	L679HNV	682	L682HNV	685	L685JBD

708-713

Leyland Olympian ON2R56C13Z4 Alexander RL   H47/32F   1992   Ex Fife Scottish, 1994

708	J808WFS	710	K710ASC	711	K711ASC	712	K712ASC	713	K713ASC
709	K709ASC								

714	J620GCR	Leyland Olympian ON2R56G13Z4 Alexander RL	H51/34F	1991	Ex Bluebird, 1994
715	J621GCR	Leyland Olympian ON2R56G13Z4 Alexander RL	H51/34F	1991	Ex Bluebird, 1994
716	J622GCR	Leyland Olympian ON2R56G13Z4 Alexander RL	H51/34F	1991	Ex Bluebird, 1994

721-740

Bristol VRT/SL3/6LXB   Eastern Coach Works   H43/31F   1980-81 Ex Devon General, 1988-89

721	LFJ862W	725	LFJ854W	732	FDV838V	735	LFJ864W	738	FDV835V
722	LFJ863W	726	LFJ855W	733	LFJ868W	736	LFJ865W	739	LFJ869W
723	LFJ853W	727	LFJ879W	734	FDV812V	737	FDV811V	740	FDV832V
724	LFJ852W	731	FDV809V						

744	LFJ878W	Bristol VRT/SL3/6LXC	Eastern Coach Works	H43/31F	1981	Ex Devon General, 1989
750	FAO417V	Bristol VRT/SL3/6LXB	Eastern Coach Works	H43/31F	1980	Ex Cumberland, 1992
751	FAO418V	Bristol VRT/SL3/6LXB	Eastern Coach Works	H43/31F	1980	Ex Cumberland, 1992
752	FAO419V	Bristol VRT/SL3/6LXB	Eastern Coach Works	H43/31F	1980	Ex Cumberland, 1992
839	LBD839P	Bristol VRT/SL3/6LX	Eastern Coach Works	H43/31F	1975	
840	LEU261P	Bristol VRT/SL3/6LX	Eastern Coach Works	H43/27D	1976	Ex Circle-Line, 1995

849-891

Bristol VRT/SL3/6LXB   Eastern Coach Works   H43/31F   1976-78

849	OVV849R	870	TNH870R	876	WBD876S	885	XNV885S	889	XNV889S
856	OVV856R	871	TNH871R	878	XNV878S	886	XNV886S	890	XNV890S
862	RRP862R	872	TNH872R	879	XNV879S	887	XNV887S	891	XNV891S
863	RRP863R	873	TNH873R	880	XNV880S	888	XNV888S		

900	BAU178T	Bristol VRT/SL3/6LXB	Eastern Coach Works	H43/31F	1978	Ex East Midland, 1993
901	BAU179T	Bristol VRT/SL3/6LXB	Eastern Coach Works	H43/31F	1978	Ex East Midland, 1993

902-967

Bristol VRT/SL3/6LXB   Eastern Coach Works   H43/31F   1978-81 919/61 are DPH41/27F

902	CBD902T	915	HBD915T	930	SNV930W	944	URP944W	954	VVV954W
903	CBD903T	916	HBD916T	931	SNV931W	945	URP945W	961	VVV961W
908	FRP908T	917	HBD917T	935	SNV935W	948	VVV948W	962	VVV962W
909	FRP909T	919	HBD919T	936	SNV936W	949	VVV949W	963	VVV963W
910	FRP910T	920	LBD920V	937	SNV937W	950	VVV950W	965	VVV965W
911	FRP911T	921	LBD921V	939	URP939W	952	VVV952W	966	VVV966W
912	FRP912T	923	LBD923V	940	URP940W	953	VVV953W	967	VVV967W
914	HBD914T	926	ONH926V	941	URP941W				

968	KRN432W	Bristol VRT/SL3/6LXB	Eastern Coach Works	H43/31F	1980	On loan from Cumberland
969	KRN433W	Bristol VRT/SL3/6LXB	Eastern Coach Works	H43/31F	1980	On loan from Cumberland

During 1995 mid-life double deck buses for school contracts have moved to United Counties from other group companies. These have included Fleetlines from Stagecoach Transit, Busways and Midland Red. From the latter's G&G Travel operation has come 992, SDA715S an example with MCW bodywork new to West Midlands PTE. It is seen at the 1995 Showbus rally at Duxford, now considered the premier English event in the rally season, and one where many Stagecoach vehicles gather.
Phillip Stephenson

970-974

970-974		Bristol VRT/SL3/6LXB		Eastern Coach Works		H43/31F	1980	Ex Hampshire Bus, 1988	
970	KRU843W	**971**	KRU845W	**972**	KRU846W	**973**	KRU847W	**974**	KRU852W

980	GAJ125V	Leyland Fleetline FE30AGR	Northern Counties	H43/31F	1980	Ex Cleveland, 1995
981	GAJ126V	Leyland Fleetline FE30AGR	Northern Counties	H43/31F	1980	Ex Cleveland, 1995
982	GAJ127V	Leyland Fleetline FE30AGR	Northern Counties	H43/31F	1980	Ex Cleveland, 1995
983	GAJ128V	Leyland Fleetline FE30AGR	Northern Counties	H43/31F	1980	Ex Cleveland, 1995
984	YVN520T	Leyland Fleetline FE30AGR	Northern Counties	H43/31F	1979	Ex Cleveland, 1995
985	YVN522T	Leyland Fleetline FE30AGR	Northern Counties	H43/31F	1979	Ex Cleveland, 1995
986	YVN524T	Leyland Fleetline FE30AGR	Northern Counties	H43/31F	1979	Ex Cleveland, 1995
987	OCU801R	Leyland Fleetline FE30AGR	Alexander AL	H44/29F	1977	Ex Busways, 1995
988	OCU802R	Leyland Fleetline FE30AGR	Alexander AL	H44/29F	1977	Ex Busways, 1995
989	OCU804R	Leyland Fleetline FE30AGR	Alexander AL	H44/29F	1977	Ex Busways, 1995
990	OCU808R	Leyland Fleetline FE30AGR	Alexander AL	H44/29F	1977	Ex Busways, 1995
991	SDA651S	Leyland Fleetline FE30AGR	Park Royal	H43/32F	1978	Ex G&G Travel, 1995
992	SDA715S	Leyland Fleetline FE30AGR	MCW	H43/33F	1978	Ex G&G Travel, 1995

Previous Registrations:

647DYE	C85PRP	TSU639	FKK839Y
685DYE	D379XRS	TSU640	FKK840Y
83CBD	A294ANH	TSU641	FKK841Y
A728ANH	A800TGG, 4009SC, A332SNH, WLT908	TSU642	FKK842Y
A729ANH	A798TGG, 7878SC, A320SNH, 647DYE	VLT255	B357KNH, Malawi ?,
GSO2V	C472SSO	WLT512	D384XRS
GSO6V	D376XRS	WLT528	D382XRS
GSO7V	D377XRS	WLT682	C81PRP
MSU465	D525ESG	WLT908	C82PRP
RBD397Y	NBD105Y, 83CBD		

Livery variations: National Express: 92-6, 115.

WESTERN SCOTTISH

Western Scottish Buses Ltd, A1 Service Ltd,
Nursery Avenue, Kilmarnock, KA1 3JD

Depots :Ardrossan; Waggon Road, Ayr; Ayr Road, Cumnock; Eastfield Road, Dumfries; Argyll Road, Dunoon; Vicarton Street, Girvan; Nursery Avenue, Kilmarnock; Kirkcudbright; Brodick; Isle of Arran; Pointhouse, Rothesay; Lewis Street, Stranraer; Whithorn.

001-060

Mercedes-Benz 709D — Alexander AM — B25F — 1995-96

001	N601VSS	013	N613VSS	025	N625VSS	037	N637VSS	049	N649VSS
002	N602VSS	014	N614VSS	026	N626VSS	038	N638VSS	050	N650VSS
003	N603VSS	015	N615VSS	027	N627VSS	039	N639VSS	051	N651VSS
004	N604VSS	016	N616VSS	028	N628VSS	040	N640VSS	052	N652VSS
005	N605VSS	017	N617VSS	029	N629VSS	041	N641VSS	053	N653VSS
006	N606VSS	018	N618VSS	030	N630VSS	042	N642VSS	054	N654VSS
007	N607VSS	019	N619VSS	031	N631VSS	043	N643VSS	055	N655VSS
008	N608VSS	020	N620VSS	032	N632VSS	044	N644VSS	056	N656VSS
009	N609VSS	021	N621VSS	033	N633VSS	045	N645VSS	057	N657VSS
010	N610VSS	022	N622VSS	034	N634VSS	046	N646VSS	058	N658VSS
011	N611VSS	023	N623VSS	035	N635VSS	047	N647VSS	059	N659VSS
012	N612VSS	024	N624VSS	036	N636VSS	048	N648VSS	060	N660VSS

037-046

Renault-Dodge S56 — Alexander AM — B25F — 1987

037	D237NCS	039	D239NCS	041	D241NCS	043	D243NCS	046	D246NCS
038	D238NCS								

048	D248NCS	Renault-Dodge S56	Alexander AM	B25F	1987	
051	D251NCS	Renault-Dodge S56	Alexander AM	B25F	1987	
053	D253NCS	Renault-Dodge S56	Alexander AM	B25F	1987	
054	D254NCS	Renault-Dodge S56	Alexander AM	B25F	1987	
101	XSJ656T	Leyland Fleetline FE30AGR	Northern Counties	O44/31F	1978	
102	HDS566H	Daimler Fleetline CRG6LX	Alexander D	O44/31F	1970	Ex Clydeside Scottish, 1989
103	GHV948N	Daimler Fleetline CRG6	Park Royal	O44/27D	1974	Ex Selkent, 1995
104	GHV102N	Daimler Fleetline CRG6	Park Royal	O44/27D	1975	Ex Selkent, 1995
108	J8WSB	Plaxton 425	Lorraine	C51FT	1992	
111	803DYE	Dennis Javelin 12SDA2105	Plaxton Paramount 3200 III	C50F	1990	
113	J13WSB	Dennis Javelin 12SDA1929	Plaxton Paramount 3200 III	C53F	1992	
114	J14WSB	Dennis Javelin 12SDA1919	Plaxton Paramount 3200 III	C53F	1992	
115	J15WSB	Dennis Javelin 12SDA2102	Plaxton Premiére 320	C53F	1992	

116-121

Dennis Dorchester SDA811 — Alexander TC — C55F — 1987

116	WLT526	118	WLT415	119	VLT73	120	WLT447	121	WLT501
117	FSU737								

135	G386PNV	Volvo B10M-60	Plaxton Expressliner	C46FT	1990	Ex Bluebird Buses, 1995
136	G387PNV	Volvo B10M-60	Plaxton Expressliner	C46FT	1990	Ex Bluebird Buses, 1995
137	G344FFX	Volvo B10M-60	Plaxton Expressliner	C46FT	1990	Ex Dorset Travel, 1995
138	G345FFX	Volvo B10M-60	Plaxton Expressliner	C46FT	1990	Ex Dorset Travel, 1995
139	H149CVU	Volvo B10M-60	Plaxton Expressliner	C49F	1990	Ex Ribble, 1995
140	H150CVU	Volvo B10M-60	Plaxton Expressliner	C49F	1990	Ex Ribble, 1995
141	IIL3507	Volvo B10M-60	Plaxton Paramount 3500 III	C50F	1989	Ex Ribble, 1995
170	VLT54	DAF SB2305DHTD585	Plaxton Paramount 3200 III	C57F	1989	Ex Arran Coaches, 1994
171	TSU638	Leyland Tiger TRCTL11/3R	Plaxton Paramount 3200 E	C53F	1983	Ex East Midland, 1995
172	13CLT	Leyland Tiger TRCTL11/3RH	Duple 340	C48FT	1987	Ex Kelvin Central, 1990
173	WLT546	Leyland Tiger TRCTL11/3RH	Duple 340	C48FT	1987	Ex Kelvin Central, 1990
174	PSO177W	Leyland Tiger TRCTL11/3R	Duple Dominant IV	C53F	1981	Ex Bluebird Buses, 1995
175	PSO178W	Leyland Tiger TRCTL11/3R	Duple Dominant IV	C51F	1981	Ex Bluebird Buses, 1995
176	RRS225X	Leyland Tiger TRCTL11/3R	Duple Goldliner IV	C53F	1982	Ex Bluebird Buses, 1995
177	CSO390Y	Leyland Tiger TRCTL11/2R	Duple Dominant II Express	C49F	1983	Ex Bluebird Buses, 1995
178	CSO386Y	Leyland Tiger TRCTL11/2R	Duple Dominant II Express	C47F	1983	Ex Bluebird Buses, 1995
179	UM7681	Leyland Tiger TRCTL11/3R	Plaxton Paramount 3200	C57F	1984	Ex East Midland, 1995
180	439UG	Leyland Tiger TRCTL11/3R	Plaxton Paramount 3200	C57F	1985	Ex East Midland, 1995
181	5796MX	Leyland Tiger TRCTL11/3RH	Plaxton Paramount 3500	C51F	1985	Ex East Midland, 1995
182	295UB	Leyland Tiger TRCTL11/3RH	Plaxton Paramount 3500	C53F	1985	Ex East Midland, 1995

Much investment has been made in the Western Scottish fleet during 1995. The geography of the operating area, with large distances between centres of population was a particular problem for the inherited ageing fleet. No less than 92 'M' registered buses entered service with a similar number receiving 'N' registrations. Here is one of 20 Mercedes 709Ds, 262, M662FYS. *Phillip Stephenson*

183	283URB	Volvo B10M-60	Plaxton Paramount 3500 III	C53F	1987	Ex East Midland, 1995
184	K574DFS	Volvo B10M-60	Plaxton Premiére 320	C53F	1993	Ex Fife Scottish, 1995
185	K575DFS	Volvo B10M-60	Plaxton Premiére 320	C53F	1993	Ex Fife Scottish, 1995
186	896HOD	Volvo B10M-61	Plaxton Paramount 3500 II	C46F	1985	Ex Stagecoach South, 1995
187	495FFJ	Volvo B10M-61	Plaxton Paramount 3500 II	C52F	1985	Ex Stagecoach South, 1995
188	L582JSA	Volvo B10M-60	Plaxton Premiére Interurban	DP51F	1993	
189	L583JSA	Volvo B10M-60	Plaxton Premiére Interurban	DP51F	1993	
190	L584JSA	Volvo B10M-60	Plaxton Premiére Interurban	DP51F	1993	

191-197

		Volvo B10M-61	Plaxton Paramount 3500	C49FT*	1985	*196/7 are C51FT

191	VCS391	**194**	VLT37	**195**	WLT978	**196**	WLT465	**197**	WLT697

198	WLT720	Volvo B10M-61	Berkhof Emperor 395	C53F	1985	

200	D230UHC	Mercedes-Benz L608D	Alexander AM	B20F	1986	Ex Stagecoach South, 1995
201	C101KDS	Mercedes-Benz L608D	Alexander AM	B21F	1986	Ex Kelvin Scottish, 1987
202	D40UAO	Mercedes-Benz L608D	Reeve Burgess	B20F	1987	Ex Cumberland, 1995
203	D41UAO	Mercedes-Benz L608D	Reeve Burgess	B20F	1987	Ex Cumberland, 1995

204-218

		Mercedes-Benz L608D	Alexander AM	B21F	1986	Ex Kelvin Scottish, 1987

204	C104KDS	**207**	D107NUS	**210**	D110NUS	**213**	D113NUS	**216**	D116NUS
205	C105KDS	**208**	D108NUS	**211**	D111NUS	**214**	D114NUS	**217**	D117NUS
206	C106KDS	**209**	D109NUS	**212**	D112NUS	**215**	D115NUS	**218**	D118NUS

219	L882LFS	Mercedes-Benz 709D	Alexander AM Sprint	B25F	1994	
220	L883LFS	Mercedes-Benz 709D	Alexander AM Sprint	B25F	1994	
221	G574FSD	Mercedes-Benz 709D	Reeve Burgess Beaver	B25F	1990	Ex Arran Coaches, 1994
222	D122NUS	Mercedes-Benz L608D	Alexander AM	B21F	1986	Ex Kelvin Scottish, 1987
223	D123NUS	Mercedes-Benz L608D	Alexander AM	B21F	1986	Ex Kelvin Scottish, 1987
224	D124NUS	Mercedes-Benz L608D	Alexander AM	B21F	1986	Ex Kelvin Scottish, 1987
225	L262VSU	Mercedes-Benz 709D	Dormobile Routemaker	B29F	1994	Ex William Hamilton, Maybole, 1995
226	D136NUS	Mercedes-Benz L608D	Alexander AM	B21F	1986	Ex Kelvin Scottish, 1987
227	G461SGB	Mercedes-Benz 609D	North West CS	C24F	1990	Ex Clyde Coast, 1995
228	D128NUS	Mercedes-Benz L608D	Alexander AM	B21F	1986	Ex Kelvin Scottish, 1987

229	D129NUS	Mercedes-Benz L608D	Alexander AM	B21F	1986	Ex Kelvin Scottish, 1987
230	D130NUS	Mercedes-Benz L608D	Alexander AM	B21F	1986	Ex Kelvin Scottish, 1987
231	D121NUS	Mercedes-Benz L608D	Alexander AM	B21F	1986	Ex Kelvin Scottish, 1987
232	E638YUS	Mercedes-Benz 609D	Reeve Burgess	C19F	1988	Ex Arran Coaches, 1994
233	C594SHC	Mercedes-Benz L608D	PMT Hanbridge	B20F	1986	Ex Cheltenham & Gloucester, 1995
234	C591SHC	Mercedes-Benz L608D	PMT Hanbridge	B20F	1986	Ex Cheltenham & Gloucester, 1995

235-244

			MCW MetroRider MF158/1	MCW	B30F	1988	Ex East London, 1995
							*239-244 are MF158/16 and B28F

235	E643KYW	237	E645KYW	239	F114YVP	241	F119YVP	243	F121YVP
236	E644KYW	238	E647KYW	240	F118YVP	242	F120YVP	244	F128YVP

248-265

			Mercedes-Benz 709D	Alexander Sprint	B25F	1995

248	M648FYS	252	M652FYS	256	M656FYS	260	M660FYS	263	M663FYS
249	M649FYS	253	M653FYS	257	M657FYS	261	M661FYS	264	M664FYS
250	M650FYS	254	M654FYS	258	M658FYS	262	M662FYS	265	M665FYS
251	M651FYS	255	M655FYS	259	M659FYS				

266	L916UGA	Mercedes-Benz 709D	Dormobile Routemaker	B29F	1993	Ex Clyde Coast, 1995
267	M667FYS	Mercedes-Benz 709D	Alexander Sprint	B25F	1995	
268	M668FYS	Mercedes-Benz 709D	Alexander Sprint	B25F	1995	
269	K208OHS	Mercedes-Benz 709D	Dormobile Routemaker	B29F	1993	Ex Clyde Coast, 1995
270	G575YTR	Iveco Daily 49.10	Phoenix	B25F	1990	Ex A1 Service (Docherty), 1995
271	G576YTR	Iveco Daily 49.10	Phoenix	B25F	1990	Ex A1 Service (Docherty), 1995
272	K209OHS	Mercedes-Benz 709D	Dormobile Routemaker	B29F	1993	Ex Clyde Coast, 1995
273	D94EKV	Peugeot-Talbot Freeway	Talbot	DP12FL	1987	Ex Sochulbus, Ashford, 1992

274-278

			Peugeot-Talbot Freeway	Talbot	DP12FL	1989-90

274	F334JHS	275	F335JHS	276	F336JHS	277	G825VGA	278	G831VGA

279	L577NSB	Mercedes-Benz 709D	Dormobile Routemaker	B21FL	1993	Ex Arran Coaches, 1994
280	L578NSB	Mercedes-Benz 709D	Dormobile Routemaker	B21FL	1993	Ex Arran Coaches, 1994
281	D301SDS	Renault-Dodge S56	Alexander AM	DP25F	1987	Ex Clydeside Scottish, 1989
283	D303SDS	Renault-Dodge S56	Alexander AM	B25F	1987	Ex Clydeside Scottish, 1989
284	F51RFS	MCW MetroRider MF150/98	MCW	B25F	1988	Ex Bluebird, 1995
285	F52RFS	MCW MetroRider MF150/98	MCW	B25F	1988	Ex Bluebird, 1995
286	F63RFS	MCW MetroRider MF150/100	MCW	B25F	1988	Ex Bluebird, 1995
287	F64RFS	MCW MetroRider MF150/99	MCW	B25F	1988	Ex Bluebird, 1995
288	F65RFS	MCW MetroRider MF150/101	MCW	B25F	1988	Ex Bluebird, 1995

290-296

			Renault-Dodge S46	Dormobile	B25F	1987	Ex Fife Scottish, 1994

290	E634DCK	292	E637DCK	294	E643DCK	295	E644DCK	296	E646DCK
291	E636DCK	293	E640DCK						

Type prefix letters showing depot code and vehicle type previously applied to the Western Scottish fleet are now considered to serve little practical use and have been discontinued though some will remain on the vehicles until repaint, as shown in this picture of Volvo B6 324, M724BCS.
Phillip Stephenson

| 298 | E402TBS | Renault-Dodge S56 | Alexander AM | B25F | 1988 | Ex A1 Service (Docherty), 1995 |
| 299 | E403TBS | Renault-Dodge S56 | Alexander AM | B25F | 1988 | Ex A1 Service (Docherty), 1995 |

301-310
Dennis Dart 9.8SDL3017 — Alexander Dash — B40F — 1992

| 301 | J301BRM | 303 | J303BRM | 305 | J305BRM | 307 | J307BRM | 309 | J309BRM |
| 302 | J302BRM | 304 | J304BRM | 306 | J306BRM | 308 | J308BRM | 310 | J310BRM |

312-341
Volvo B6-9.9M — Alexander Dash — DP40F — 1994

312	M772BCS	321	M721BCS	326	M726BCS	334	M734BSJ	338	M738BSJ
313	M773BCS	322	M722BCS	327	M727BCS	335	M735BSJ	339	M739BSJ
318	M718BCS	323	M723BCS	332	M732BSJ	336	M736BSJ	340	M740BSJ
319	M719BCS	324	M724BCS	333	M733BSJ	337	M737BSJ	341	M741BSJ
320	M720BCS	325	M725BCS						

351-358
Volvo B6-9.9M — Alexander Dash — B40F — 1994

| 351 | M674SSX | 353 | M676SSX | 355 | M678SSX | 357 | M680SSX | 358 | M681SSX |
| 352 | M675SSX | 354 | M677SSX | 356 | M679SSX | | | | |

| 399 | L208PSB | Dennis Dart 9SDL3031 | Marshall C36 | B39F | 1994 | Ex Arran Coaches, 1994 |

403-410
Dennis Dorchester SDA801 — Plaxton Paramount 3200E — C49F — 1983 — 404/5/7-10 ex Clydeside, 1989

| 403 | 703DYE | 405 | WLT727 | 407 | WLT830 | 409 | WLT444 | 410 | WLT874 |
| 404 | VLT104 | 406 | WLT794 | 408 | VCS376 | | | | |

427	ESU435	Volvo B10M-61	East Lancashire (1994)	DP51F	1982
428	FSU739	Volvo B10M-61	Duple Dominant IV	C46FT	1982
431	VLT154	Volvo B10M-61	East Lancashire (1994)	DP51F	1981

434-481
Seddon Pennine 7 — Alexander AT — C49F* — 1979-80 *470 is DP53F
436/40/57/70 are ex Clydeside Scottish, 1988-89

434w	DSD934V	443	DSD943V	448	DSD948V	456w	DSD956V	475w	DSD975V
436	DSD936V	444w	DSD944V	449w	DSD949V	457w	DSD957V	476w	DSD976V
440	DSD940V	445	DSD945V	451w	DSD951V	470w	DSD970V	480	DSD980V
442	DSD942V	447	DSD947V	454	DSD954V	473	DSD973V	481	DSD981V

| 490 | WLT809 | Volvo B10M-61 | Duple Goldliner IV | C46FT | 1983 | |
| 501 | M151FGB | Volvo B10B | Wright Endurance | B51F | 1994 | Ex A1 Service, 1994 |

505-512
Volvo B10M-56 — Alexander PS — DP48F — 1995

| 505 | M488ASW | 507 | M871ASW | 509 | M469ASW | 511 | M483ASW | 512 | M468ASW |
| 506 | M869ASW | 508 | M485ASW | 510 | M481ASW | | | | |

Most of the modern vehicles purchased with A1 Service have now received corporate livery. Photographed at Saltcoats is 597, WLT774, a Volvo B10M with Duple 300 bus bodywork. One of a pair new to A1 in 1988, only five of this body style feature in the Stagecoach group, the other three being on Dennis Javelins now working with Ribble. *Paul Wigan*

519-546   Seddon Pennine 7   Alexander AY   B53F   1978-79

519	YSD819T	526w	ASD826T	529	ASD829T	537w	ASD037T	543	ASD843T
520	YSD820T	527	ASD827T	534w	ASD834T	542	ASD842T	544	ASD844T

560w	BSD860T	Seddon Pennine 7	Alexander AY	DP49F	1979
562w	BSD862T	Seddon Pennine 7	Alexander AY	DP49F	1979
563w	BSD863T	Seddon Pennine 7	Alexander AY	DP49F	1979
564w	BSD864T	Seddon Pennine 7	Alexander AY	DP49F	1979

565-594   Volvo B10M-55   Alexander PS   DP48F   1995

565	M480ASW	571	M471ASW	577	M477ASW	583	M466ASW	589	M789PRS
566	M486ASW	572	M472ASW	578	M478ASW	584	M784PRS	590	M790PRS
567	M487ASW	573	M473ASW	579	M479ASW	585	M785PRS	591	M791PRS
568	M489ASW	574	M474ASW	580	M870ASW	586	M786PRS	592	M792PRS
569	M482ASW	575	M475ASW	581	M484ASW	587	M787PRS	593	M793PRS
570	M470ASW	576	M476ASW	582	M872ASW	588	M788PRS	594	M467ASW

597	WLT774	Volvo B10M-56	Duple 300	B53F	1988	Ex A1 Service, 1995
598	WLT538	Volvo B10M-56	Duple 300	B53F	1988	Ex A1 Service, 1995
599	WLT439	Volvo B10M-55	Plaxton Derwent	B55F	1990	Ex A1 Service, 1995
600	C802KBT	Leyland Cub CU435	Optare	DP33F	1986	Ex Arran Coaches, 1994
616	N616USS	Volvo B10M-62	Plaxton Expressliner 2	C44FT	1995	
617	N617USS	Volvo B10M-62	Plaxton Expressliner 2	C44FT	1995	
624	WFS136W	Leyland Leopard PSU3F/4R	Alexander AYS	B53F	1980	Ex Bluebird Buses, 1995
625	YSF98S	Leyland Leopard PSU3D/4R	Alexander AYS	B53F	1977	Ex Bluebird Buses, 1995
626	YSF100S	Leyland Leopard PSU3E/4R	Alexander AYS	B53F	1977	Ex Bluebird Buses, 1995
627	NPA229W	Leyland Leopard PSU3E/4R	Plaxton Supreme IV Express	C53F	1981	Ex Bluebird Buses, 1995
629	GMS285S	Leyland Leopard PSU3E/4R	Alexander AYS	B53F	1978	Ex Kelvin Scottish, 1987
630	GMS292S	Leyland Leopard PSU3E/4R	Alexander AYS	B53F	1978	Ex Kelvin Scottish, 1987

633-699   Leyland Leopard PSU3E/4R*   Alexander AY   B53F*   1977-80   *637 is DP49F

*667/70/1/6/8-80/5/91-3 are PSU3D/4R; 633/95-7 ex Clydeside Scottish, 1989

633	GCS33V	649	GCS49V	662	GCS62V	678	TSJ78S	693	TSJ33S
637	GCS37V	651	GCS51V	665	GCS65V	679	TSJ79S	695	BSJ895T
638	GCS38V	653	GCS53V	667	TSJ67S	680	TSJ80S	696	BSJ896T
641	GCS41V	657	GCS57V	669	GCS69V	685	TSJ85S	697	BSJ917T
645	GCS45V	658	GCS58V	670	TSJ70S	691	TSJ31S	698	BSJ930T
647	GCS47V	660	GCS60V	671	TSJ71S	692	TSJ32S	699	BSJ931T
648	GCS48V	661	GCS61V	676	TSJ76S				

701	UIB3541	Leyland National 11351A/1R	B48F	1979	Ex Kelvin Central, 1989

702-706   Leyland National 11351A/3R   B48F   1978-79 Ex British Airways, Heathrow, 1993

702	UIB3542	703	UIB3543	704	OIW7024	705	OIW7025	706	UIB3076

710	KMA399T	Leyland National 11351A/1R(Gardner)		B51F	1979	Ex A1 Service, 1994
721	MCS138W	Bedford YMT	Duple Dominant II Express	C53F	1981	Ex Arran Coaches, 1994
725	D167TRA	Bedford YMT	Duple Dominant	B53F	1986	Ex Arran Coaches, 1994
726	D917GRU	Bedford YMT	Plaxton Derwent	B53F	1987	Ex Arran Coaches, 1994
727	D799USB	Bedford YMT	Duple Dominant	B55F	1987	Ex Arran Coaches, 1994
728	D918GRU	Bedford YMT	Plaxton Derwent	B53F	1987	Ex Arran Coaches, 1994
729	E849AAO	Bedford YNV	Plaxton Paramount 3200 III	C57F	1987	Ex Arran Coaches, 1994

771-791   Leyland National 2 NL116L11/1R   B52F*   1980-81 Ex Kelvin Scottish, 1988

*774-7/85/7-91 are B48F

771	WAS771V	776	MDS866V	780	YFS308W	784	RFS584V	788	WAS768V
773	RFS583V	777	MDS859V	781	MSO18W	785	NLS985W	789	NLS989W
774	YFS304W	778	MDS858V	782	RFS582V	786	SNS826W	790	YFS310W
775	MDS865V	779	RFS579V	783	NLS983W	787	MSO17W	791	YFS309W

Opposite, top: **One of the last new vehicles for the A1 Services fleet is now numbered 501 Western, its original registration M1ABO, having been replaced with M151FGB on sale to Stagecoach. Currently the only Wright Endurance body in the group this bus is also one of only three Volvo B10B chassis with the group. The bus is seen at Ardrossan during a driver change over.** *Tony Wilson*
Opposite, bottom: **A1 Service had gathered a number of Volvo double-deck buses during its operation, most constructed in the near-by Volvo plant at Irvine. Two of the B10M-based vehicles have joined four already with Western. Pictured leaving Saltcoats for Ardrossan is 893, B24CGA.** *Paul Wigan*

792	KRS540V	Leyland National 2 NL106L11/1R		B41F	1980	Ex Bluebird, 1993
793	KRS542V	Leyland National 2 NL106L11/1R		B41F	1980	Ex Bluebird, 1993
795	MSO10W	Leyland National 2 NL106L11/1R		B41F	1980	Ex Bluebird, 1993
796	NLP388V	Leyland National 2 NL116L11/3R		B48F	1980	Ex British Airways, Heathrow, 1993
797	JTF971W	Leyland National 2 NL116AL11/1R		B48F	1981	Ex Mitchell, Plean, 1994
800	UNA853S	Leyland Atlantean AN68A/1R	Park Royal	H43/32F	1977	Ex GM Buses, 1991
801	UNA863S	Leyland Atlantean AN68A/1R	Park Royal	H43/32F	1978	Ex GM Buses, 1991
802	WVM884S	Leyland Atlantean AN68A/1R	Park Royal	H43/32F	1978	Ex GM Buses, 1991
804	ANA211T	Leyland Atlantean AN68A/1R	Northern Counties	H43/32F	1978	Ex GM Buses, 1991
805	BNC936T	Leyland Atlantean AN68A/1R	Park Royal	H43/32F	1979	Ex GM Buses, 1991
806	RJA702R	Leyland Atlantean AN68A/1R	Northern Counties	H43/32F	1977	Ex GM Buses, 1991
807	UNA772S	Leyland Atlantean AN68A/1R	Northern Counties	H43/32F	1977	Ex GM Buses, 1991
808	RJA801R	Leyland Atlantean AN68A/1R	Park Royal	H43/32F	1977	Ex GM Buses, 1992
809	VBA161S	Leyland Atlantean AN68A/1R	Northern Counties	H43/32F	1978	Ex GM Buses, 1992
810	UNA824S	Leyland Atlantean AN68A/1R	Park Royal	H43/32F	1977	Ex GM Buses, 1992
811	UNA840S	Leyland Atlantean AN68A/1R	Park Royal	H43/32F	1977	Ex GM Buses, 1992
812	WVM888S	Leyland Atlantean AN68A/1R	Park Royal	H43/32F	1978	Ex GM Buses, 1992
813	JHK500N	Leyland Atlantean AN68/1R	Eastern Coach Works	H43/31F	1975	Ex A1 Service, 1995
814	NCS15P	Leyland Atlantean AN68/1R	Alexander AL	H43/31F	1976	Ex A1 Service, 1995
817	HGD213T	Leyland Atlantean AN68A/1R	Alexander AL	H45/33F	1979	Ex A1 Service, 1995
819	KSD62W	Leyland Atlantean AN68B/1R	Alexander AL	H45/33F	1980	Ex A1 Service, 1995
840	ULS660T	Leyland Fleetline FE30AGR	Eastern Coach Works	H43/32F	1979	Ex Kelvin Central, 1989
842	ASA22T	Leyland Fleetline FE30AGR	Eastern Coach Works	H43/32F	1978	Ex Northern Scottish, 1987
843	ASA23T	Leyland Fleetline FE30AGR	Eastern Coach Works	H43/32F	1978	Ex Northern Scottish, 1987
847	ASA27T	Leyland Fleetline FE30AGR	Eastern Coach Works	H43/32F	1978	Ex Northern Scottish, 1987

851-889

	Leyland Fleetline FE30AGR	Northern Counties	H44/31F	1978-79
		859-6/9/80/5/9 ex Clydeside Scottish, 1988-89		

851	XSJ651T	859	XSJ659T	867	XSJ667T	876	ECS876V	882	ECS882V
853	XSJ653T	860	XSJ660T	868	XSJ668T	877	ECS877V	883	ECS883V
854	XSJ654T	861	XSJ661T	869	XSJ669T	878	ECS878V	885	ECS885V
855	XSJ655T	862	XSJ662T	870	BCS870T	879	ECS879V	888	BCS865T
857	XSJ657T	865	XSJ665T	871	BCS871T	880	ECS880V	889	BCS869T
858	XSJ658T	866	XSJ666T						

892	A308RSU	Volvo Citybus B10M-50	East Lancashire	H47/36F	1983	Ex A1 Service, 1995
893	B24CGA	Volvo Citybus B10M-50	Alexander RV	H47/37F	1985	Ex A1 Service, 1995
894	E864RCS	Volvo Citybus B10M-50	Alexander RV	DPH41/29F	1987	
895	E865RCS	Volvo Citybus B10M-50	Alexander RV	DPH45/33F	1987	
896	E866RCS	Volvo Citybus B10M-50	Alexander RV	DPH45/33F	1987	
897	E867RCS	Volvo Citybus B10M-50	Alexander RV	DPH43/33F	1987	

During the year no less than 21 new Volvo Olympians and many modern mid-life vehicles were placed with this operation to replace elderly vehicles in the A1 fleet which had been the subject of a Traffic Commissioners hearing and warning shortly prior to the sale to Stagecoach. Seen entering Kilmarnock bus station is 924, N858VHH. Interestingly, Carlisle marks were obtained for this batch.
Paul Wigan

901-906 — Leyland Olympian ONLXB/1R — Roe — H47/29F 1982-83 Ex A1 Service, 1995

901	HSB698Y	903	CUB73Y	904	EWY74Y	905	EWY75Y	906	EWY76Y
902	CUB72Y								

907	C800HCS	Leyland Olympian ONLXB/1R	Eastern Coach Works	H45/32F	1986	Ex A1 Service, 1995
908	F41XCS	Leyland Olympian ONCL10/1RZ	Leyland	H47/31F	1989	Ex A1 Service, 1995
909	F524WSJ	Leyland Olympian ONCL10/1RZ	Leyland	H47/31F	1989	Ex A1 Service, 1995
910	F149XCS	Leyland Olympian ONCL10/1RZ	Leyland	H47/31F	1989	Ex A1 Service, 1995
911	PJI4983	Leyland Olympian ONTL11/2RSp	Eastern Coach Works	CH45/24F	1985	Ex Cleveland Transit, 1995

912-932 — Volvo Olympian YN2RV18Z4 — Alexander RH — H47/32F 1995

912	M490ASW	917	N851VHH	921	N855VHH	925	N859VHH	929	N863VHH
913	M491ASW	918	N852VHH	922	N856VHH	926	N860VHH	930	N864VHH
914	M492ASW	919	N853VHH	923	N857VHH	927	N861VHH	931	N865VHH
915	N849VHH	920	N854VHH	924	N858VHH	928	N862VHH	932	N866VHH
916	N850VHH								

933-942 — Leyland Titan TNLXB2RRSp — Park Royal — H44/26D 1978-80 Ex East London, 1995

933	EYE236V	935	CUL179V	937	WYV5T	939	WYV29T	941	EYE246V
934	CUL189V	936	CUL209V	938	WYV27T	940	CUL197V	942	EYE248V

943-949 — Leyland Titan TNLXB2RRSp — Leyland — H44/26D 1981-83 Ex East London, 1995

943	GYE252W	945	GYE273W	947	OHV684Y	948	A833SUL	949	A876SUL
944	GYE254W	946	GYE281W						

955	NSP336R	Ailsa B55-10	Alexander AV	H44/31D	1976	Ex A1 Service, 1995
964	WYV49T	Leyland Titan TNLXB2RRSp	Park Royal	H44/22D	1979	Ex Selkent, 1995
965	WYV56T	Leyland Titan TNLXB2RRSp	Park Royal	H44/22D	1979	Ex Selkent, 1995
966	CUL208V	Leyland Titan TNLXB2RRSp	Park Royal	H44/26D	1980	Ex Selkent, 1995
967	KYV410X	Leyland Titan TNLXB2RRSp	Leyland	H44/24D	1982	Ex Selkent, 1995

Special event vehicles - traditional liveries

L1059	YSD350L	Leyland Leopard PSU3/3R	Alexander AY	B41F	1972	
W1074	YYS174	Bedford C5Z1	Duple Vista	C21FM	1960	Ex David MacBrayne, 1970
D1684	RCS382	Leyland Titan PD3A/3	Alexander AM	L35/32RD	1961	
N1795	UCS659	Albion Lowlander LR3	Alexander AM	H40/31F	1963	

Previous Registrations:

13CLT	D317SGB	UIB3541	EGB89T
283URB	E551UHS	UIB3542	EGT451T
295UB	B421CMC	UIB3543	WGY589S
439UG	B422CMC	UM7681	A317ONE
495FFJ	B193CGA	VCS376	TSD158Y, WLT652
5796MX	B106REL	VCS391	B191CGA
703DYE	TSD153Y	VLT37	B194CGA
803DYE	H661UWR	VLT54	G262EHD
896HOD	B192CGA	VLT73	D219NCS
CSO386Y	ASA10Y, TSV780	VLT104	TSD154Y
CSO390Y	ASA9Y, TSV779	VLT154	NCS121W, WLT415, WGB646W
ESU435	GGE127X, FSU737, TOS530X	WLT415	D218NCS
F149XCS	F523WSJ	WLT439	G569ESD
FSU737	D217NCS	WLT444	TSD159Y
FSU739	GGE128X	WLT447	D220NCS
HDS566H	SMS402H, 703DYE	WLT465	B196CGA
HSB698Y	CUB50Y	WLT501	D221NCS
IIL3507	F410DUG	WLT526	D216NCS
KRS540V	GSO6V	WLT538	E159XHS
KRS542V	GSO8V	WLT546	D318SGB
M151FGB	M1ABO	WLT697	B197CGA
OIW7024	GLP433T	WLT720	B198CGA
OIW7025	GLP427T	WLT727	TSD155Y
PJI4983	B577LPE	WLT774	E158XHS
PSO177W	BSG549W, 630DYE, WGB175W, CSU920	WLT794	TSD156Y
PSO178W	BSG547W, WLT741, WGB176W, CSU921	WLT809	TSD150Y
RRS225X	MSC556X, CSU923	WLT830	TSD157Y
TSU638	FKK838Y	WLT874	TSD152Y
UIB3076	EGT458T, WGY598S	WLT978	B195CGA

HONG KONG

Stagecoach Hong Kong Ltd, Suite 1606, 16/F, Sha Tin Galleria Building
18-24 Shan Mei Street, Fo Tan, New Territories, Hong Kong.

1	FW6766	Volvo B10M-56	Alexander PS	DP50F	1994
2	FW6555	Volvo B10M-56	Alexander PS	DP50F	1994
3L	FW6832	Volvo B10M-56	Alexander PS	DP50F	1994
4L	FW8231	Volvo B10M-56	Alexander PS	DP50F	1994
5L	FW7894	Volvo B10M-56	Alexander PS	DP50F	1994
6	GK7584	Volvo Olympian YN3RV18Z4	Alexander RH	H68/42D	1995
7	GK2009	Volvo Olympian YN3RV18Z4	Alexander RH	H68/42D	1995
8	GK3194	Volvo Olympian YN3RV18Z4	Alexander RH	H68/42D	1995
9	GK3895	Volvo Olympian YN3RV18Z4	Alexander RH	H68/42D	1995
10	GK3188	Volvo Olympian YN3RV18Z4	Alexander RH	H68/42D	1995
11	GK3250	Volvo Olympian YN3RV18Z4	Alexander RH	H68/42D	1995

After operating a residents service using Volvo B10Ms, additional journeys commenced during 1995 with six tri-axle Olympians. These handsome vehicles carry both Chinese and English lettering as displayed on 8, GK3194 shown here behind one of the saloons. *Stagecoach International*

KENYA BUS

Kenya Bus Services Ltd, General Waruingi Street, Eastleigh,
P O Box 41001, Nairobi, Kenya.

Depots : Mombasa and Nairobi.

301-320   ERF Trailblazer 6LXB   Suleman   B47D   1983-85

301	KUW565	305	KUY829	309	KWE549	313	KWP182	317	KWQ651
302	KUW634	306	KUZ807	310	KWE764	314	KWP609	318	KWQ673
303	KUY279	307	KUZ834	311	KWG808	315	KWP640	319	KWQ732
304	KUY289	308	KWC094	312	KWH535	316	KWQ159	320	KWT363

321-331   ERF Trailblazer 6LXB   Labh Singh   B49D*   1986-88   *330 is B43D, 331 is B46D 334-8 are B47D, 325 is B51F

321	KXQ484	324	KXR388	326	KYD117	328	KYV458	330	KYY078
322	KXR065	325	KYD116	327	KYW205	329	KYV457	331	KYW206
323	KXR282								

332-340   ERF Trailblazer 6LXB   Suleman   B53D*   1986-87

332	KYE173	334	KYH176	336	KYM857	338	KYS305	340	KYU693
333	KYE579	335	KYH535	337	KYN019	339	KYU264		

341-399   ERF Trailblazer 6LXB MkII   Labh Singh   B45D*   1993-94   *347 is B46D, 378 is B48D

341	KAC649X	353	KAD535A	365	KAD743D	377	KAD117G	389	KAD822K
342	KAC929X	354	KAD619A	366	KAD737D	378	KAD194G	390	KAD889Y
343	KAC023Y	355	KAD841A	367	KAD779D	379	KAD233G	391	KAD902Y
344	KAC022Y	356	KAD902A	368	KAD826D	380	KAD589H	392	KAD932Y
345	KAC021Y	357	KAD535A	369	KAD899D	381	KAD641H	393	KAD938Y
346	KAC287Y	358	KAD126C	370	KAD994D	382	KAD846H	394	KAD105Z
347	KAC290Y	359	KAD127C	371	KAD021E	383	KAD947H	395	KAD135Z
348	KAC289Y	360	KAD158C	372	KAD261E	384	KAD075J	396	KAD688A
349	KAC288Y	361	KAD225C	373	KAD360E	385	KAD199J	397	KAE689Y
350	KAD527A	362	KAD368C	374	KAD407E	386	KAD386J	398	KAE918A
351	KAD521A	363	KAD447C	375	KAD860F	387	KAD378J	399	KAE919A
352	KAD528A	364	KAD553C	376	KAD147G	388	KAD659K		

400-449   ERF Trailblazer 6LXB MkII   Labh Singh   B52D   1994-95

400	KAE660C	410		420		430		440	
401	KAE	411		421		431		441	
402	KAE	412		422		432		442	
403	KAE	413		423		433		443	
404	KAE	414		424		434		444	
405	KAE	415		425		435		445	
406	KAE	416		426		436		446	
407	KAE	417		427		437		447	
408	KAE	418		428		438		448	
409	KAE	419		429		439		449	

601	KAA128N	DAF TB2100DHT	Labh Singh	B47D	1990
602	KAA351N	DAF TB2100DHT	Labh Singh	B47D	1990
603	KAA330N	DAF TB2100DHT	Labh Singh	B47D	1990
604	KAA313Q	DAF TB2100DHT	Labh Singh	B47D	1990

605-616   DAF TB2100DHT   Labh Singh   B43D   1992

605	KAC145H	608	KAC253H	611	KAC592J	613	KAC865J	615	KAC519L
606	KAC146H	609	KAC447H	612	KAC672J	614	KAC887J	616	KAC243K
607	KAC252H	610	KAC485J						

Second from the 12-metre batch of ERF Trailblazers is 401, seen here at Eastleigh depot in Nairobi immediately after the corporate stripes were applied. The buses are delivered from Labh Singh in all white, the final livery details being applied by Kenya Bus. Interestingly, this batch were the first to have a door forward of the front axle and at peak times two conductors are carried, one for each of the manual doors. Following a period of experimenting with destination blinds, the company have reverted to using boards in the nearside front window. *Andrew Jarosz*

701-720

Leyland Victory J MkII — Labh Singh — B49D* — 1979-80 — *710 is B47D, *711 is B56D, 713 is B48D

701	KVR629	705	KVR866	709	KVS307	713	KVT703	717	KVU018
702	KVR652	706	KVR952	710	KVS284	714	KVT857	718	KVU079
703	KVR787	707	KVR995	711	KVS328	715	KVT909	719	KVU211
704	KVR818	708	KVS025	712	KVT664	716	KVT973	720	KVU156

721-736

Leyland Victory J MkII — Labh Singh — B49D* — 1980-82 — *722 is B44D, *730 is B42D, 731 is B41D,

721	KVU237	725	KVW013	728	KVY046	731	KVY237	734	KVZ919
722	KVU369	726	KVX651	729	KVY074	732	KVZ671	735	KSJ158
723	KVV809	727	KVX664	730	KVY316	733	KVZ703	736	KSJ265
724	KVV957								

737-745

Leyland Victory J MkII — Suleman — B49D — 1979-80

737	KVU147	739	KTE936	741	KTE554	743	KSH120	745	KSP840
738	KTE826	740	KTE447	742	KSH004	744	KSH443		

Opposite, top: **Over a hundred ERF Trailblazer chassis feature in the 1996 Stagecoach orders for the Kenya and Malawi fleets and these will be fitted with local bodywork for short haul useage. These chassis will be fitted with Gardner engines and delivery is to commence shortly. Shown working along Nyali Beach Road heading for Mombasa is 317, KWO651, which carries Suleman bodywork.**
Opposite, bottom: **A later version of the ERF Trailblazer is 369, KAD899D seen about to depart from the main Kenya Bus terminal in Nairobi. The bodywork shown is Labh Singh.** *Andrew Jarosz*

Sixteen DAF TB2100 rugged chassis were the last vehicles supplied new to the Kenya Bus operation before its sale to Stagecoach. The fleet in Nairobi is divided into three management units A,B and C, all garaged together but with different teams of drivers and managers. The allocation of the buses to teams is indicated as a suffix to the fleet number, the teams competing for aspects of performance measurement. Seen shortly after unloading at the bus station is 602, KAA351N. *Andrew Jarosz*

746-779

Leyland Victory J MkII   Labh Singh   B49D*   1980-82   *747 are B48D, *755 is B59D, 767 is B47D, 778 is B46D

746	KSP338	753	KSW895	760	KTG376	767	KTP917	774	KTR553
747	KSP339	754	KSW879	761	KTJ159	768	KTQ004	775	KTR630
748	KSP337	755	KTF528	762	KTJ235	769	KTQ164	776	KTR678
749	KSW894	756	KTF527	763	KTK846	770	KTQ249	777	KTT617
750	KSW877	757	KTF834	764	KTM915	771	KTQ287	778	KTT881
751	KSW876	758	KTF809	765	KTM946	772	KTQ398	779	KTV814
752	KSW875	759	KTG230	766	KTN216	773	KTR405		

780-796

Leyland Victory J MkII   Suleman   B53D*   1981-82   *Seating varies

780	KSW663	784	KTN321	788	KTU010	791	KTY066	794	KUE168
781	KSZ136	785	KTN339	789	KTU064	792	KUD378	795	KUF305
782	KSY974	786	KTR094	790	KTW693	793	KUE121	796	KUF366
783	KTN313	787	KTR124						

797-824

Leyland Victory J MkII   Labh Singh   B49D*   1980-82   *Seating varies

797	KTW268	803	KUG560	809	KUG938	815	KUJ874	820	KUJ890
798	KTW190	804	KUH104	810	KUG978	816	KUJ638	821	KUM688
799	KTY110	805	KUG585	811	KUH141	817	KUJ998	822	KUM870
800	KUF144	806	KUJ641	812	KUH254	818	KUJ889	823	KUM534
801	KUG599	807	KUG850	813	KUH275	819	KUK083	824	KUK271
802	KUG474	808	KUG860	814	KUJ561				

825-830

Leyland Victory J MkII   Suleman   B53D*   1982   *Seating varies

825	KUF947	827	KUK402	828	KUK427	829	KUK494	830	KUK979
826	KUK401								

831-850

								Leyland Victory J MkII	Labh Singh	B49D*	1983-84	*Seating varies
831	KUY105	835	KWA577	839	KWB295	843	KWK134	847	KWM059
832	KWA562	836	KWA574	840	KWC826	844	KWK144	848	KWM145
833	KWA575	837	KWB994	841	KWE920	845	KWL823	849	KWM189
834	KWA576	838	KWB286	842	KWE971	846	KWL923	850	KWN536

851-874

Leyland Victory J MkII — Labh Singh — B49D* — 1984-85 — *870 is B45D

851	KWP262	856	KWR077	861	KWS725	866	KWT169	871	KWX948
852	KWQ584	857	KWR105	862	KWS971	867	KWT337	872	KWY155
853	KWQ808	858	KWR140	863	KWS985	868	KWV976	873	KWY371
854	KWQ914	859	KWS524	864	KWT030	869	KWX587	874	KXA037
855	KWQ946	860	KWS690	865	KWT146	870	KWX892		

875	KXD749	Leyland Victory J MkIII	Suleman	B48D	1986

876-900

Leyland Victory J MkII — Labh Singh — B49D* — 1985-86 — *Seating varies

876	KXD797	881	KXG262	886	KXH624	891	KXJ173	896	KXM065
877	KXK017	882	KXG278	887	KXH875	892	KXJ369	897	KXN855
878	KXK503	883	KXH320	888	KXH896	893	KXJ474	898	KXN982
879	KXD761	884	KXH321	889	KXH993	894	KXK610	899	KXP038
880	KXD781	885	KXH623	890	KXJ010	895	KXK708	900	KXP187

906-924

Leyland Victory J — Labh Singh — B48D* — 1974-75 — *921/4 are B47D

906	KPW130	920	KQC946	921	KQD110	922	KQD302	924	KQF075
915	KQB978								

931-942

Leyland Victory J — Labh Singh — B47D* — 1976-78 — *935 is B41D, 936 B50D, 940 B46D

931	KQV346	934	KQW802	937	KQX875	939	KRP967	941	KRQ083
932	KQW687	935	KQW958	938	KRP893	940	KRP995	942	KRQ125
933	KQW743	936	KQW994						

946-959

Leyland Victory J — Labh Singh — B49D — 1979

946	KVK649	949	KVK823	952	KVL108	954	KVL266	957	KVN055
947	KVK708	950	KVK941	953	KVL232	956	KVM733	959	KVN137
948	KVK751	951	KVK993						

961	KUF067	Leyland Victory J	Labh Singh	B49D	1982 Rebuild
962	KUG695	Leyland Victory J	Labh Singh	B45D	1982 Rebuild
963	KUT967	Leyland Victory J	Labh Singh	B49D	1983 Rebuild
964	KNY401	Leyland Victory J	Labh Singh	B47D	1985 Rebuild
965	KUT615	Leyland Victory J	Labh Singh	B47D	1985 Rebuild
966	KZF894	Leyland Victory J	Labh Singh	B49D	1988 Rebuild
967	KQB925	Leyland Victory J	Labh Singh	B48D	1974 Rebuild
968	KQD250	Leyland Victory J	Labh Singh	B48D	1975 Rebuild
969	KPW753	Leyland Victory J	Labh Singh	B48D	1974 Rebuild
970	KPW294	Leyland Victory J	Labh Singh	B45D	1974 Rebuild
971	KUR801	Leyland Victory J MkII	Labh Singh	B45D	1983
972	KUR811	Guy Victory J MkII	Labh Singh	B42D	1983
973	KUS386	Leyland Victory J MkII	Labh Singh	B50D	1983
974	KUT208	Leyland Victory J MkII	Labh Singh	B35D	1983
981	KWY053	ERF Trailblazer 6LX	Suleman	B47F	1985
982	KWY095	ERF Trailblazer 6LX	Suleman	B47F	1985
983	KWY472	ERF Trailblazer 6LX	Suleman	B47F	1985
984	KXA410	ERF Trailblazer 6LX	Suleman	B47F	1985

991-997

Leyland Victory J MkII — Labh Singh — B49D* — 1979 — *991 is B43D

991	KZC129	993	KZA013	995	KYZ546	996	KZD894	997	KZB481
992	KZC481	994	KZF416						

Operating Companies:
Kenya Bus Services (Mombasa): 302/6-9/11-8, 332/3/5/9/40/92/3/5/7, 737-45/80-96, 825-30/75, 965/73/4/81-4.
KBS Companies A+B+C (Nairobi): Remainder.

MALAWI

Stagecoach Malawi, P O Box 176, Blantyre, Malawi.

Depots : Chichiri, Lilongwe, Makata and Mzuzu.

1	BH9601	Volvo B10M-61		Plaxton Paramount 3500 III	C46FT	1988	Ex Travellers, London, 1991
2w	BH9602	Volvo B10M-61		Plaxton Paramount 3500 III	C46FT	1988	Ex Travellers, London, 1991
3	BH9603	Volvo B10M-61		Plaxton Paramount 3500 III	C46FT	1988	Ex Travellers, London, 1991
4	BH9604	Volvo B10M-61		Plaxton Paramount 3500 III	C46FT	1988	Ex Travellers, London, 1991
5	BJ4981	Volvo B10M-61		Plaxton Paramount 3500 III	C46FT	1988	Ex Wallace Arnold, 1993
6	BJ8256	Volvo B10M-61		Plaxton Paramount 3500 III	C46FT	1988	Ex ??, 1994
7	BJ8257	Volvo B10M-61		Plaxton Paramount 3500 III	C46FT	1988	Ex ??, 1994

204-233

ERF Trailblazer 6LXB   PEW   B61F   1993

204	BJ6020	210	BJ6112	216	BJ6255	222	BJ6414	228	BJ6512
205	BJ6021	211	BJ6137	217	BJ6258	223	BJ6419	229	BJ6521
206	BJ6066	212	BJ6147	218	BJ6313	224	BJ6439	230	BJ6525
207	BJ6070	213	BJ6157	219	BJ6341	225	BJ6450	231	BJ6542
208	BJ6080	214	BJ6205	220	BJ6353	226	BJ6460	232	BJ6594
209	BJ6079	215	BJ6245	221	BJ6405	227	BJ6471	233	BJ6595

307   BC6557   Guy Victory J   AUT(1983)   B51F   1971

311-330

Leyland Victory J   AUT*   B54D   1975   *309-12 rebuilt 1984-85

311	BD2508	325	BD6253	328	BD6256	329	BD6257	330	BD6258
314	BD2514	322	BD2522						

338-345

Leyland Victory J   AUT   B55D   1978

338	BE3166	340	BE3168	343	BE5105	344	BE5106	345	BE5107
339	BE3167	341	BE5103						

346	BF363	Leyland Victory J MkII	AUT	B53D	1980
347	BF364	Leyland Victory J MkII	AUT	B55D	1981
348	BF365	Leyland Victory J MkII	AUT(1986)	B53D	1981

Not many Stagecoach buses operate with trailers, but working the Blantyre to Lilongwe service is Leyland Victory 902, BJ1755, complete with freight trailer.
Stagecoach Malawi

350-371   Leyland Victory J MkII   AUT   B57D   1985-87

350	BG150	355	BG1255	360	BG1260	364	BG7364	368	BG7368
351	BG151	356	BG1256	361	BG149	365	BG7365	369	BG7369
352	BG152	357	BG1257	362	BG7362	366	BG7366	370	BG7370
353	BG153	358	BG1258	363	BG7363	367	BG7367	371	BG7371
354	BG154	359	BG1259						

422	BG2422	Leyland Victory J MkII	AUT(1989)	B59F	1985
423	BG2423	Leyland Victory J MkII	AUT(1988)	B59F	1985
424	BG2434	Leyland Victory J MkII	AUT(1989)	B49D	1985
425	BG2435	Leyland Victory J MkII	AUT(1989)	B49D	1985

426-437   AVM Dahmer DH825   AUT   B59F   1989

426	BH1886	429	BH1889	432	BH1892	434	BH1894	436	BH1896
427	BH1887	430	BH1890	433	BH1893	435	BH1895	437	BH1897
428	BH1888	431	BH1891						

438-443   DAF TB2105   AUT   B59F   1989

438	BH1808	440	BH1910	441	BH1911	442	BH1912	443	BH1913
439	BH1909							

447-465   ERF Trailblazer   PEW   B59F   1990-92

447	BH5747	453	BH2380	456	BH2577	458	BH2451	464	BJ2713
451	BH5751	454	BH2381	457	BH2450	459	BJ2711	465	BJ3095
452	BH9333	455	BH2576						

447-489   Volvo B10M-55   Alexander PS   B53F   1993

470	BJ5558	474	BJ5554	478	BJ5753	482	BJ5967	486	BJ6195
471	BJ5551	475	BJ5643	479	BJ5779	483	BJ6075	487	BJ6249
472	BJ5552	476	BJ5604	480	BJ5960	485	BJ6114	489	BJ6764
473	BJ5553	477	BJ5752	481	BJ5966				

500	BJ7150	ERF SuperTrailblazer	PEW	B??F	1994

501-510   ERF SuperTrailblazer   PEW   B??F   1996

501	503	505	507	509
502	504	506	508	510

720-798   Leyland Victory J MkII   AUT   B57D   1981-85   *720/1 are B59F, 773 is B56F

720	BG2420	783	BF8810	787	BF8814	791	BF8978	797	BF8984
721	BG2421	784	BF8811	788	BF8815	792	BF8979	798	BF8985
773	BF2232	785	BF8812	790	BF8977	793	BF8980		

ERF Trailblazers have been added to the Malawi fleet in recent years, including 205, BJ6021 in 1993. Promoting Lipton's Tea, and carrying a respectable load, it features a PEW locally-built body. *Stagecoach Malawi*

800-819
Leyland Victory J MkII AUT B53F 1985

800	BF8987	804	BG134	808	BG138	812	BG142	815	BG145
801	BG131	805	BG135	809	BG139	813	BG143	816	BG146
802	BG132	806	BG136	811	BG141	814	BG144	819	BG691
803	BG133	807	BG137						

826-861
Leyland Victory J MkII AUT B53F 1986-87

826	BG3826	834	BG3834	842	BG3842	849	BG3849	856	BG3856
827	BG3827	835	BG3835	843	BG3843	850	BG3850	857	BG3857
828	BG3828	836	BG3836	844	BG3844	851	BG3851	858	BG3858
829	BG3829	837	BG3837	845	BG3845	852	BG3852	859	BG3859
830	BG3830	838	BG3838	846	BG3846	854	BG3854	860	BG3860
832	BG3832	839	BG3839	847	BG3847	855	BG3855	861	BG3861
833	BG3833	841	BG3841	848	BG3848				

862-897
ERF Trailblazer PEW B61F 1991-92

862	BH5862	870	BH5870	877	BH5877	884	BH9599	891	BJ1191
863	BH5863	871	BH5871	878	BH8178	885	BJ445	892	BJ1192
864	BH5864	872	BH5872	879	BH8179	886	BJ446	893	BJ1283
865	BH5865	873	BH5873	880	BH5752	887	BJ447	894	BJ1284
866	BH5866	874	BH5874	881	BH9596	888	BJ448	895	BJ1285
867	BH5867	875	BH5875	882	BH9597	889	BJ1193	896	BJ1286
868	BH5868	876	BH5876	883	BH9598	890	BJ1194	897	BJ1287
869	BH5869								

898-949
ERF Trailblazer PEW B61F 1992

898	BJ1604	909	BJ2063	920	BJ3247	930	BJ3600	940	BJ4044
899	BJ1605	910	BJ2064	921	BJ3246	931	BJ3604	941	BJ4064
900	BJ1606	911	BJ2065	922	BJ3354	932	BJ3673	942	BJ4151
901	BJ1754	912	BJ2331	923	BJ3373	933	BJ3674	943	BJ4161
902	BJ1755	913	BJ2332	924	BJ3387	934	BJ3675	944	BJ4212
903	BJ1756	914	BJ2333	925	BJ3402	935	BJ3857	945	BJ4213
904	BJ1974	915	BJ3095	926	BJ3403	936	BJ3858	946	BJ4301
905	BJ1975	916	BJ3136	927	BJ3461	937	BJ3872	947	BJ4358
906	BJ1976	917	BJ3203	928	BJ3519	938	BJ3971	948	BJ4394
907	BJ2061	918	BJ3244	929	BJ3521	939	BJ3997	949	BJ4438
908	BJ2062	919	BJ3245						

950	BJ5517	ERF Trailblazer	PEW	B47F	1993

951-960
ERF Trailblazer PEW B59F 1990-92

951	BH5748	953	BF5750	955	BJ2715	957	BJ3094	959	BH5745
952	BH5749	954	BJ2712	956	BJ2710	958	BH5744	960	BH5746

970-979
ERF Trailblazer PEW B59F 1994-95

970	BJ9093	972	BJ9140	974	BJ9558	976	BJ9123	978	BJ9122
971	BJ9138	973	BJ9592	975	BJ9516	977	BJ9517	979	BJ9130

970-979
ERF Trailblazer PEW B59F 1996

980	984	988	992	996
981	985	989	993	997
982	986	990	994	998
983	987	991	995	999

1013-1056
Daimler CVG6LX-34 Metsec H52/33D 1971-72 Ex KMB, Hong Kong, 1989-90

1013	BH2639	1034	BH5134	1048	BH5848	1054	BH6754	1056	BH6756
1015	BH2641	1045	BH5845	1049	BH5849				

2001-2010
Dennis Dragon DDA1811 Duple-Metsec H67/41F 1992

2001	BJ3701	2003	BJ4302	2005	BJ4397	2007	BJ4575	2009	BJ4618
2002	BJ4153	2004	BJ4370	2006	BJ4505	2008	BJ4590	2010	BJ4915

STAGECOACH PORTUGAL

Stagecoach Portugal, Av do Brasil, 45-1 - 1700 Lisboa, Portugal

Depots : Queluz de Baixo and Cascais

166	CG-74-44	UTIC-AEC Reliance U2045	Caetano(1987)	B42D	1972	Ex Rodoviária del Lisboa, 1996
183	EL-44-91	UTIC-AEC Reliance U2055	Caetano(1987)	B42D	1972	Ex Rodoviária del Lisboa, 1996
188	DE-62-72	UTIC-AEC Reliance U2055	Caetano(1990)	B42D	1972	Ex Rodoviária del Lisboa, 1996
191	CG-62-04	UTIC-AEC Reliance U2055	Caetano(1988)	B42D	1972	Ex Rodoviária del Lisboa, 1996
219	IM-97-87	UTIC-AEC Reliance U2055	UTIC(1990)	B42D	1974	Ex Rodoviária del Lisboa, 1996
473	GT-83-73	Volvo B58-60	Caetano	DP47D	1979	Ex Rodoviária del Lisboa, 1996
482	GT-83-64	Volvo B58-60	Caetano	DP47D	1980	Ex Rodoviária del Lisboa, 1996
490	GT-83-70	Volvo B58-60	Caetano	DP47D	1980	Ex Rodoviária del Lisboa, 1996
491	IS-72-66	Volvo B58-60	Caetano	DP47D	1980	Ex Rodoviária del Lisboa, 1996

534-551

		Volvo B10R		Camo		DP47D	1979	Ex Rodoviária del Lisboa, 1996

534	IS-98-38	**535**	NP-75-76	**536**	HS-59-99	**537**	HS-70-33	**551**	ES-83-85

555-575

		Volvo B10R		Camo		DP34D	1980	Ex Rodoviária del Lisboa, 1996

555	EU-37-45	**572**	FU-30-97	**573**	FU-31-00	**574**	CT-68-99	.	**575**	CT-69-01
571	FU-30-95									

584-628

		Volvo B10R		Camo		DP40D	1981	Ex Rodoviária del Lisboa, 1996

584	FS-09-56	**593**	FS-09-77	**595**	FS-09-60	**597**	FS-09-58	**625**	FS-09-73
591	FS-09-80	**594**	FS-09-55	**596**	FS-09-54	**622**	IV-72-52	**628**	FS-09-57
592	FS-09-79								

665	RP-69-35	Volvo B10MA	Camo U90	AB49T	1987	Ex Rodoviária del Lisboa, 1996
783	AL-47-83	UTIC-AEC Reliance U2035	UTIC(1989)	B42D	1969	Ex Rodoviária del Lisboa, 1996
785	IL-88-36	UTIC-AEC Reliance U2035	UTIC(1985)	B42D	1969	Ex Rodoviária del Lisboa, 1996
790	FB-76-06	UTIC-AEC Reliance U2035	UTIC(1989)	B42D	1970	Ex Rodoviária del Lisboa, 1996
791	BH-42-09	UTIC-AEC Reliance U2035	Camo(198?)	B42D	1970	Ex Rodoviária del Lisboa, 1996
792	BH-42-08	UTIC-AEC Reliance U2035	Eurobus(1989)	B42D	1970	Ex Rodoviária del Lisboa, 1996
794	FA-55-45	UTIC-AEC Reliance U2045	UTIC(1986)	B42D	1971	Ex Rodoviária del Lisboa, 1996
797	EB-67-53	UTIC-AEC Reliance U2045	Caetano(1987)	B42D	1971	Ex Rodoviária del Lisboa, 1996
798	GC-70-23	UTIC-AEC Reliance U2055	UTIC	B39D	1972	Ex Rodoviária del Lisboa, 1996
799	GC-76-76	UTIC-AEC Reliance U2055	UTIC	B37D	1972	Ex Rodoviária del Lisboa, 1996
800	CG-32-08	UTIC-AEC Reliance U2055	UTIC	B36D	1972	Ex Rodoviária del Lisboa, 1996
801	CG-32-09	UTIC-AEC Reliance U2055	UTIC	B36D	1972	Ex Rodoviária del Lisboa, 1996
802	GC-70-20	UTIC-AEC Reliance U2055	UTIC	B52D	1972	Ex Rodoviária del Lisboa, 1996
806	GO-54-92	UTIC-AEC Reliance U2055	UTIC	B39D	1975	Ex Rodoviária del Lisboa, 1996
807	GO-54-93	UTIC-AEC Reliance U2055	UTIC	B39D	1975	Ex Rodoviária del Lisboa, 1996
808	AT-91-50	UTIC-AEC Reliance U2055	UTIC	B39D	1975	Ex Rodoviária del Lisboa, 1996
809	AT-91-52	UTIC-AEC Reliance U2055	UTIC	B39D	1975	Ex Rodoviária del Lisboa, 1996
820	GG-70-11	UTIC-AEC Reliance U2055	UTIC	B47D	1972	Ex Rodoviária del Lisboa, 1996
821	GG-32-07	UTIC-AEC Reliance U2055	UTIC	B38D	1972	Ex Rodoviária del Lisboa, 1996
824	EH-63-39	UTIC-AEC Reliance U2055	UTIC	B48D	1973	Ex Rodoviária del Lisboa, 1996
826	DN-45-88	UTIC-AEC Reliance U2055	UTIC	B47D	1973	Ex Rodoviária del Lisboa, 1996
830	EH-83-23	UTIC-AEC Reliance U2041	UTIC	C41D	1973	Ex Rodoviária del Lisboa, 1996
833	ER-60-86	UTIC-AEC Reliance U2055	UTIC	B39D	1974	Ex Rodoviária del Lisboa, 1996
834	ER-60-87	UTIC-AEC Reliance U2055	UTIC	B39D	1974	Ex Rodoviária del Lisboa, 1996
836	DO-89-76	UTIC-AEC Reliance U2055	UTIC	B39D	1975	Ex Rodoviária del Lisboa, 1996
839	DO-89-74	UTIC-AEC Reliance U2055	UTIC	B39D	1975	Ex Rodoviária del Lisboa, 1996
845	BP-45-14	UTIC-AEC Reliance U2075	UTIC	B39D	1976	Ex Rodoviária del Lisboa, 1996
847	BP-45-15	UTIC-AEC Reliance U2075	UTIC	B39D	1976	Ex Rodoviária del Lisboa, 1996
848	EN-67-93	UTIC-AEC Reliance U2075	UTIC	B39D	1976	Ex Rodoviária del Lisboa, 1996
849	IM-97-84	UTIC-AEC Reliance U2055	UTIC(1990)	B42D	1974	Ex Rodoviária del Lisboa, 1996
850	CO-48-73	UTIC-AEC Reliance U2055	UTIC(1990)	B42D	1974	Ex Rodoviária del Lisboa, 1996
856	FV-68-50	UTIC-AEC Reliance U2075	UTIC	B42D	1976	Ex Rodoviária del Lisboa, 1996
859	IU-81-04	UTIC-AEC Reliance U2075	UTIC	DP55D	1976	Ex Rodoviária del Lisboa, 1996
860	IU-81-04	UTIC-AEC Reliance U2075	UTIC	DP55D	1976	Ex Rodoviária del Lisboa, 1996
863	GP-32-77	UTIC-AEC Reliance U2077	UTIC	DP55D	1977	Ex Rodoviária del Lisboa, 1996
866	BZ-73-12	UTIC-AEC Reliance U2077	UTIC	DP47D	1979	Ex Rodoviária del Lisboa, 1996
867	BZ-73-13	UTIC-AEC Reliance U2077	UTIC	DP47D	1979	Ex Rodoviária del Lisboa, 1996
868	BZ-73-24	UTIC-AEC Reliance U2077	UTIC	DP47D	1979	Ex Rodoviária del Lisboa, 1996
869	BZ-73-22	UTIC-AEC Reliance U2077	UTIC	DP47D	1979	Ex Rodoviária del Lisboa, 1996

The Stagecoach Portugal management commences in January 1996 with the transfer of two bus depots and the Sintra tram system to Stagecoach. The inherited fleet includes seven Volvo B10M bendibuses. Illustrated here is 982, RM-54-78. The current livery scheme is white and orange, though corporate livery is expected to be introduced soon. *Stagecoach*

During 1994 seven DAF FA45150 minibuses entered service. These carry Camo Olympus bodywork which is used in dual-door configuration. Pictured on service 416 to Urbana Cascans is 997, 87-41-EI with European-standard index marks. The 1996 intake will be fifty Scania L113 single deck buses with bodywork by Marco Polo of Porto. *Stagecoach*

870	BZ-73-10	UTIC-AEC Reliance U2077	UTIC	DP48D	1979	Ex Rodoviária del Lisboa, 1996
871	BZ-73-11	UTIC-AEC Reliance U2077	UTIC	DP47D	1979	Ex Rodoviária del Lisboa, 1996
872	BZ-73-23	UTIC-AEC Reliance U2077	UTIC	DP47D	1979	Ex Rodoviária del Lisboa, 1996

885-898

		UITC-Leyland MTL11R		UTIC Europa	DP53D*	1982	Ex Rodoviária del Lisboa, 1996
							*885/7/9 are DP57D

885	CF-08-63	888	CU-20-01	890	CF-08-66	892	DG-05-43	894	HC-09-88
886	EA-08-86	889	FF-09-76	891	DG-05-44	893	EF-06-24	898	CL-08-58
887	EA-08-87								

900-917

Volvo B58-60   Caetano   DP47D   1979   Ex Rodoviária del Lisboa, 1996

900	IS-12-02	906	IS-49-12	909	GT-83-71	912	CV-70-85	915	CV-70-82
901	CV-70-94	907	GT-83-72	910	CV-70-93	913	CV-70-88	916	GT-83-74
904	CV-70-91	908	GT-83-68	911	CV-70-89	914	GT-83-65	917	IS-72-65
905	IS-12-01								

918	IS-72-67	Volvo B58-60	Camo	DP47D	1979	Ex Rodoviária del Lisboa, 1996
920	SS-47-77	Magirus-Deutz 230E	Caetano	C53D	1980	Ex Rodoviária del Lisboa, 1996
922	TM-98-25	Magirus-Deutz 230E	Caetano	C53D	1980	Ex Rodoviária del Lisboa, 1996

930-937

Volvo B10R   Camo   DP47D   1979-80   Ex Rodoviária del Lisboa, 1996

| 930 | HS-59-93 | 932 | ES-83-88 | 934 | ES-83-79 | 936 | ES-83-84 | 937 | EU-51-03 |
| 931 | HS-59-97 | 933 | HS-59-94 | 935 | ES-83-82 | | | | |

938-967

Volvo B10R   Camo   DP34D   1979-81   Ex Rodoviária del Lisboa, 1996

938	EU-37-35	943	EU-37-37	948	IS-98-43	955	IV-72-53	963	FS-09-67
939	EU-37-36	944	EU-37-40	949	EU-37-55	959	FS-09-62	964	FS-09-68
940	EU-37-38	945	EU-37-43	950	EU-37-56	960	DV-03-13	965	GO-08-85
941	EU-37-39	946	EU-37-54	951	IV-72-51	961	FS-09-78	967	FS-09-57
942	EU-37-44	947	EU-37-57	954	BS-64-71	962	FS-09-74		

| 970 | TX-14-72 | Scania K113CRB | Caetano | C49F | 1991 | Ex Rodoviária del Lisboa, 1996 |
| 971 | VX-75-26 | Scania K113CRB | Caetano | C49F | 1991 | Ex Rodoviária del Lisboa, 1996 |

980-984

Volvo B10MA   Camo U90   AB49T   1987-88   Ex Rodoviária del Lisboa, 1996

| 980 | RP-95-43 | 981 | RP-95-44 | 982 | RM-54-78 | 983 | QM-54-94 | 984 | QM-89-83 |

| 986 | OQ-79-80 | Volvo B10MA | Caetano | AB52T | 1991 | Ex Rodoviária del Lisboa, 1996 |

991-999

DAF FA45150   Camo Olympus   DP19D   1994   Ex Rodoviária del Lisboa, 1996

| 991 | 87-40-EI | 994 | 87-33-EI | 997 | 87-41-EI | 998 | 87-36-EI | 999 | 87-42-EI |
| 992 | 87-34-EI | 996 | 87-38-EI | | | | | | |

Livery: White and orange or white and green (minibuses)

Photographed at Lyall Bay is Stagecoach Wellington's 160, NL9566, a dual doored MAN with Coachwork International bodywork. Seating over the front axle is arranged with two facing rearwards, similar to that used in Great Britain over the rear axle. *Stagecoach New Zealand*

As transport systems throughout the world look for better means of propulsion, Stagecoach is gaining experience in Wellington with electric power by way of the trolleybus system. Over fifty trolleybuses are operated, all based on the Volvo B58 chassis. Pictured outside the rail station while heading for Seatoun is 233, KJ8244. *Stagecoach New Zealand*

STAGECOACH WELLINGTON

Wellington City Transport Ltd, 45 Onepu Road, Kilbirnie, P O Box 14 070,

1	FL4297	Ford R1114	New Zealand Motor Bodies	DP48F	1976	
2	NA4281	Isuzu MR113	Coachwork International	B28F	1987	
3	FL4281	Ford R1014	New Zealand Motor Bodies	DP40F	1973	
4	NA4279	Isuzu MR113	Coachwork International	B28F	1987	
5	NA3943	Isuzu MR113	Coachwork International	B28F	1987	
6	SK700	Isuzu ECR570	Demac	C45F	1986	
7	FL4279	Ford R192	New Zealand Motor Bodies	DP41F	1972	
8	NY58	Isuzu ECR570	Coachwork International	DP45F	1988	
9	MQ8716	Isuzu ECR570	Coachwork International	DP49F	1986	
10	JR48	Ford R1114	New Zealand Motor Bodies	DP48F	1980	
11	ON223	Isuzu ECR570	Austral	B45F	1989	
12	PT2685	Hino RG197	Coachwork International	B37D	1991	
13	JR47	Ford R1114	New Zealand Motor Bodies	DP48F	1980	
14	IN2551	Ford R1114	New Zealand Motor Bodies	DP48F	1977	
15	JZ7041	Ford R1114	New Zealand Motor Bodies	DP48F	1981	
16	OB1552	Isuzu ECR570	Coachwork International	DP49F	1988	
17	JR2616	Mercedes-Benz 0303	New Zealand Motor Bodies	B41D	1980	
18	JW8024	Mercedes-Benz 0303	New Zealand Motor Bodies	B41D	1980	
19	LE4641	Hino BX341	New Zealand Motor Bodies	DP48F	1983	
21	MC609	Isuzu ECR570	Coachwork International	DP49F	1985	

141-170

MAN SL202 Coachwork International B40D 1986-89

141	NF2109	147	NH2755	153	NL9414	159	NL9540	165	NZ8003
142	NF2117	148	NH5642	154	NL9420	160	NL9566	166	NZ8266
143	NH2634	149	NI5704	155	NL9466	161	OB1550	167	OG8397
144	NH2652	150	NL5718	156	NL9460	162	NT9387	168	OG8398
145	NH2754	151	NL9377	157	NL9461	163	PA6879	169	OG8399
146	NH2756	152	NL9393	158	NL9531	164	NZ8004	170	OG8551

171-180

MAN 16.200 UOCL Coachwork International B39D 1989-91

171	ON525	173	PL5272	175	PL5274	177	PL5823	179	PP5206
172	PL5003	174	PL5273	176	PL5822	178	PL5824	180	PP5205

181 PP5219 MAN 16.240 UOCL Coachwork International B41D 1991

201-233

Volvo B58 Trolleybus Hawke Coachwork B40D 1981-83

201	KA9102	207	JY5832	213	KA9184	220	KA7235	226	KD7487
202u	KA9108	208	JY5831	214	KA9185	221	KD7490	227	KH4274
203u	PE8106	209	KA9103	216	KA9192	222	KD7488	229	KH4358
204	JM7127	210	KA9109	217	NA87	223	KD7485	232	KJ8245
205u	JM7125	211	KA9110	218	KA7233	224	KD7486	233	KJ8244
206	JY6549	212	KA9111	219	KA7234	225	KH4273		

235-254

Volvo B58 Trolleybus International Coachwork B40D 1984-85

235	LW6465	239	MB7635	243	ME9235	247	MJ2016	251	MJ2168
236	MA8821	240	MB7638	244	ME9236	248	MJ2015	252	MJ2169
237	MA5210	241	MB7636	245	ME2504	249	MJ2014	253	MJ2171
238	MA5209	242	MB7637	246	MJ2012	250	MJ2013	254	MJ2172

255-268

Volvo B58 Trolleybus International Coachwork B40D 1986

255	MO1322	258	SC2911	261	MS1706	264	MS1703	267	MS1812
256	MO1321	259	MO1397	262	MS1705	265	MS1814	268	MS1815
257	MO1391	260	MS1707	263	MS1704	266	MS1813		

270	MC6399	Hino AC140	Micanta	C23F	1985	
290	PD1036	Renault S75	Coachwork International	B23F	1990	
291	PD1037	Renault S75	Coachwork International	B23F	1990	
292	PD1038	Renault S75	Coachwork International	B23F	1990	
293	PE5096	Renault S75	Coachwork International	B23F	1990	
294	RM4511	Toyota Hiace	Toyota	M15	1992	Ex Wellington, 1993

The latest deliveries to Wellington are the first low floor MAN 11.190 chassis for the fleet. These buses, like last years' delivery, feature the standard Stagecoach moquette pattern which is visible in this view of 602, TJ2542, taken on the banks of Lyall Bay. *Stagecoach New Zealand*

401-416

		Leyland Leopard PSU3C/2R		Hawke Coachwork		B40D	1976-77				
401	HZ2712	404u	FL349	407	HE2657	411u	HQ3939	414	TIK7802		
402	HI1974	405u	FL350	408u	HQ3899	412	IL4519	415u	IL4461		
403	GA6806	406	HE2656	409u	HQ3907	413	IL4518	416u	IK7801		

417-480

		Leyland Leopard PSU3E/2R		Hawke Coachwork		B40D	1978-79 479/80 ex Goldstar, Frankton, 1992		
417	IU9434	430	IX3808	443	JC2506	455	JF1910	467	JA1188
418	IU9433	431	IX3817	444	JC2568	456	JF1911	468	LH1322
419	IU9432	432	PA6877	445	JC2569	457	JF1913	469	JA1184
420	IU9431	433	IX7765	446	JC2570	458	JF1914	470	JA1197
421	IX7733	434	IX7763	447	JD184	459	IX3806	471	JA2261
422	IX7732	435	IU9931	448	JD183	460	IX3814	472	JC2505
423	IX3304	436	IU9932	449	JD182	461	IX3815	473	NR3918
424	IX3302	437	IU9929	450	JD196	462	IX7767	474	JD181
425	IX3781	438	JC2431	451	JD197	463	IX7766	475	JC2520
426	IX3660	439	JC2430	452	JF1903	464	TD5442	476	JD199
427	IX3783	440	JA1187	453	JF1909	465	IU9928	477	JF1902
428	IX3782	441	JA1185	454	JF1908	466	KP7998	478	JF1912
429	IX3807	442	JA1198						

479	IX3303	Leyland Leopard PSU3E/2R	Hawke Coachwork	B45D	1979	Ex Goldstar, Frankton, 1992
480	IX7734	Leyland Leopard PSU3E/2R	Hawke Coachwork	B45D	1979	Ex Goldstar, Frankton, 1992
481	LA5234	Leyland Leopard PSU3E/2R	Hawke Coachwork	B44D	1983	Ex Invercargill, 1992
482	JT684	Leyland Leopard PSU3E/2R	Hawke Coachwork	B40D	1982	Ex Cesta Travel, 1993
483	NA6947	Hino RK176	Coachwork International	B45D	1987	Ex Cityline HV, 1993

501-520

		MAN 11.190 HOCL		Designline		B39D	1994-95		
501	SS5537	505	SX7725	509	SY1641	513	TA2667	517	TB6042
502	SS5538	506	SW4400	510	SY1631	514	TA2691	518	TB6050
503	ST7109	507	SW4435	511	SY5917	515	TA2714	519	TB6056
504	SX7724	508	SW4436	512	SZ5918	516	TB6023	520	TB6057

The 1996 Stagecoach Bus Handbook

During 1995 vehicles have been re-allocated between fleets with some of the MAN saloons moving to Auckland where they operate under the Cityline name. Allocated to Auckland and Hutt valley are the Hino buses supplied in the late 1980s. illustrated here is one of the Cityline examples.
Stagecoach New Zealand

521-554

MAN 11.190 HOCL   Designline   B39D   1995

521	TB6106	**528**	TE2325	**535**	TG5856	**542**	TG5895	**549**	TJ2515
522	TB6107	**529**	TE2326	**536**	TG5857	**543**	TG5896	**550**	TJ2516
523	TD2564	**530**	TE2327	**537**	TG5871	**544**	TG5897	**551**	TR1643
524	TD2593	**531**	TF6235	**538**	TG5872	**545**	TG5898	**552**	TR1644
525	TD2594	**532**	TF6236	**539**	TG5876	**546**	TG5899	**553**	TR1645
526	TD2630	**533**	TF6237	**540**	TG5877	**547**	TH5837	**554**	TR1646
527	TD2631	**534**	TG5855	**541**	TG5878	**548**	TH5838		

601-626

MAN 11.190 HOCL   Designline   B39D   1995-96

601	TJ2541	**607**		**612**		**617**		**622**	
602	TJ2542	**608**		**613**		**618**		**623**	
603		**609**		**614**		**619**		**624**	
604		**610**		**615**		**620**		**625**	
605		**611**		**616**		**621**		**626**	
606									

5907	1055IC	Hino BG300	Emslie	C41F	1980
6009	JZ6948	Bedford NFM/6BD1	NZ Motor Bodies	B37D	1981
6890	MI8415	Hino RK176	Coachwork International	B45D	1987

7193-7253

Hino RK176   Coachwork International   B47D*   1987-88   *6890/7193/7-7200 are B45D

7193	NA6078	**7231**	NA7352	**7238**	NA7359	**7246**	NL7827	**7250**	NL7831
7197	NA6060	**7232**	NA7350	**7239**	NA7361	**7247**	NL7828	**7251**	NA7832
7198	NA6947	**7233**	NA7351	**7242**	NL7824	**7248**	NL7829	**7252**	NA7833
7200	NA6945	**7236**	NA7357	**7244**	NL7825	**7249**	NL7830	**7253**	NL7834
7201	NK8507	**7237**	NA7358	**7245**	NL7826				

7255-7556
Hino RK177 · Coachwork International · B47D · 1988-89

7255	NL7823	7266	NL8272	7278	NX9487	7538	OB4297	7547	OB7912
7256	NL7790	7267	NL7793	7279	NX9488	7539	OB4208	7548	OE7917
7258	NL7796	7268	NL8264	7532	NX9510	7540	OB4215	7549	OG5328
7259	NL7797	7269	NL8265	7533	NX9509	7542	OB4213	7551	OG5327
7260	NL7799	7270	NL8266	7534	NX9507	7543	OE4212	7553	OG5341
7261	NL7794	7271	NL8273	7535	NX9508	7544	OB4214	7554	OG5342
7263	NL7791	7273	NL8267	7536	NX9516	7545	OE7913	7555	OG5343
7264	NL7792	7274	NL8268	7537	NX9517	7546	OE7916	7556	OG5344
7265	NL7798	7276	NX9485						

7601-7620
Mercedes-Benz L608D · Alexander · B19F* · 1986 · Ex Stagecoach South, 1994
*7601 is DP19F

7601	SN7492	7605	SX6698	7609	TD7288	7613	TA7462	7617	TD8460
7602	ST9425	7606	SX6699	7610	TE3787	7614	TA7468	7618	TJ4753
7603	ST9430	7607	SZ205	7611	SZ8591	7615	SZ8598	7619	TE4794
7604	SW6560	7608	TA7124	7612	SZ8592	7616	TD8481	7620	TK9266

Kelburn Cable Car

1		Habegger		Habegger		S28D	1979
2		Habegger		Habegger		S28D	1979

Previous Registrations:

MQ9796	SK700	SZ205	D225UHC	TD7288	C809SDY
SN7492	D949UDY	SZ8591	C813SDY	TD8460	C801SDY
ST9425	C811SDY	SZ8592	C807SDY	TD8481	C799SDY
ST9430	C818SDY	SZ8598	D947UDY	TE3787	C815SDY
SW6560	C804SDY	TA7124	C814SDY	TE4794	C810SDY
SX6698	C816SDY	TA7462	D952UDY	TJ4753	C803SDY
SX6699	D231UHC	TA7468	D951UDY	TK9266	C800SDY

Operations:

Cityline Auckland:	5, 413/25/64, 501-15, 6890, 7193/231-3/9/42/53/5/6/9/63/4/7/71/8/9, 7532-5/40/2-6/8/9/51/5/6, 7612/3/9/20
Cityline Hutt Valley:	290-4/407/10/2/7/9/20/4/8/9/42/58, 7197/8/200/1/236-8/44-52/8/60/1/5/6/8-70/3/4/6, 7536-9/47/53/4, 7601-11/4/5/8
Eastbourne Buses:	2/4/6/8-19/21;
Newlands:	414/65;
Runcimans:	1/3/7, 401/3/6/21/3/7/33/8/48/51/2/7/69, 5907, 6009.
Stagecoach Wellington:	Remainder

Minibus operation was introduced to the New Zealand operation with the import of twenty Mercedes-Benz L609Ds from Stagecoach South. These have been allocated to Hutt Valley, Wellington and Auckland. Parked at the Strathmore Shops timing point is 7617, TD8460, which was previously C801SDY. *Stagecoach New Zealand*

142

UK Vehicle Index

Reg	Operator	Reg	Operator	Reg	Operator	Reg	Operator
1JVK	Busways	4012VC	Midland Red	A214MCK	Ribble	A840SUL	East London
2JVK	Busways	4585SC	Bluebird Buses	A227MDD	Red & White	A841SUL	Selkent
13CLT	Western Scottish	4828VC	Midland Red	A243YGF	East Midland	A842SUL	Selkent
49CLT	Selkent	5796MX	Western Scottish	A305DCU	Busways	A843SUL	Selkent
83CBD	United Counties	6253VC	Midland Red	A308RSU	Western Scottish	A845SUL	Selkent
109DRM	Cumberland	6267AC	Midland Red	A314XWG	East Midland	A846SUL	East London
126ASV	Bluebird Buses	6804VC	Midland Red	A315XWG	East Midland	A847SUL	Selkent
127ASV	Bluebird Buses	9258VC	Midland Red	A316XWG	East Midland	A848SUL	Selkent
128ASV	Bluebird Buses	9492SC	Bluebird Buses	A317XWG	East Midland	A848VML	Midland Red
145CLT	Bluebird Buses	9737VC	Midland Red	A318XWG	East Midland	A849SUL	East London
147YFM	Bluebird Buses	9984PG	Midland Red	A319YWJ	East Midland	A850SUL	Selkent
283URB	Western Scottish	A7GGT	Midland Red	A320YWJ	East Midland	A854SUL	Selkent
295UB	Western Scottish	A8GGT	Midland Red	A321YWJ	East Midland	A855SUL	Selkent
331HWD	Midland Red	A39XHE	East Midland	A322AKU	East Midland	A856SUL	Selkent
400DCD	Stagecoach South	A40XHE	Bluebird Buses	A323AKU	East Midland	A857SUL	Selkent
401DCD	Stagecoach South	A41XHE	East Midland	A324AKU	East Midland	A858SUL	Selkent
402DCD	Stagecoach South	A42XHE	East Midland	A325AKU	East Midland	A859SUL	Selkent
403DCD	Stagecoach South	A43XHE	East Midland	A469TUV	Cheltenham & G	A866SUL	Selkent
404DCD	Stagecoach South	A44FRS	Bluebird Buses	A541HAC	Red & White	A867SUL	East London
405DCD	Stagecoach South	A44XHE	East Midland	A542HAC	Midland Red	A868SUL	Selkent
406DCD	Stagecoach South	A45FRS	Bluebird Buses	A543HAC	Midland Red	A873SUL	East London
407DCD	Stagecoach South	A46FRS	Bluebird Buses	A544HAC	Midland Red	A874SUL	Selkent
408DCD	Stagecoach South	A47FRS	Bluebird Buses	A545HAC	Midland Red	A876SUL	Western Scottish
409DCD	Stagecoach South	A65THX	Selkent	A546HAC	Midland Red	A877SUL	Selkent
410DCD	Stagecoach South	A66THX	Selkent	A547HAC	Midland Red	A880SUL	Selkent
411DCD	Stagecoach South	A67THX	Selkent	A548HAC	Red & White	A881SUL	Selkent
412DCD	Stagecoach South	A71GEE	East Midland	A549HAC	Red & White	A882SUL	Selkent
413DCD	Stagecoach South	A72GEE	East Midland	A561KWY	Cambus	A883SUL	Selkent
415DCD	Stagecoach South	A73GEE	East Midland	A603THV	Selkent	A885SUL	Selkent
416DCD	Stagecoach South	A74GEE	East Midland	A607THV	Selkent	A902SYE	East London
417DCD	Stagecoach South	A75NAC	Midland Red	A613THV	Selkent	A905SYE	East London
418DCD	Stagecoach South	A76NAC	Midland Red	A622THV	East London	A918SYE	Selkent
419DCD	Stagecoach South	A76THX	Selkent	A625THV	Selkent	A921SYE	East London
420DCD	Stagecoach South	A77THX	Selkent	A626THV	East London	A922SYE	East London
420GAC	Midland Red	A102DAO	Cumberland	A627THV	Selkent	A925SYE	Selkent
421DCD	Stagecoach South	A108TRP	United Counties	A628THV	Selkent	A926SYE	Selkent
422DCD	Stagecoach South	A109TRP	United Counties	A629THV	Selkent	A935SYE	East London
424DCD	Stagecoach South	A110TRP	United Counties	A630THV	Selkent	A940XGG	Bluebird Buses
439UG	Western Scottish	A111TRP	United Counties	A631THV	Selkent	A941XGG	Bluebird Buses
461CLT	East London	A112TRP	United Counties	A632THV	Selkent	A942XGG	Bluebird Buses
467WYA	Cheltenham & G	A113TRP	United Counties	A634THV	Selkent	A944SYE	East London
485CLT	East London	A114TRP	United Counties	A635THV	Selkent	A945SYE	East London
486CLT	East London	A116ESA	Bluebird Buses	A636THV	Selkent	A949SYE	East London
491GAC	Midland Red	A117ESA	Bluebird Buses	A645THV	Selkent	A950SYE	Selkent
491JVX	Busways	A118ESA	Bluebird Buses	A648THV	Selkent	A951SYE	Selkent
495FFJ	Western Scottish	A121GSA	Bluebird Buses	A650THV	East London	A953SYE	East London
498FYB	Midland Red	A122GSA	Bluebird Buses	A652THV	Selkent	A960SYE	East London
511OHU	Cheltenham & G	A123GSA	Bluebird Buses	A663WSU	Bluebird Buses	A961SYE	Selkent
515CLT	Selkent	A124GSA	Bluebird Buses	A681KDV	Cambus	A965SYE	East London
527CLT	East London	A125GSA	Bluebird Buses	A683KDV	Cambus	A967YSX	Fife Scottish
552OHU	Midland Red	A126GSA	Bluebird Buses	A728ANH	United Counties	A968YSX	Fife Scottish
552UTE	Busways	A127GSA	Bluebird Buses	A729ANH	United Counties	A969YSX	Fife Scottish
644HKX	Busways	A138MRN	Ribble	A823SUL	Stagecoach South	A970YSX	Fife Scottish
647DYE	United Counties	A142MRN	Ribble	A824SUL	Selkent	A971SYE	East London
685DYE	United Counties	A143MRN	Ribble	A825SUL	Selkent	A971YSX	Fife Scottish
703DYE	Western Scottish	A145MRN	Ribble	A826SUL	East London	A972YSX	Fife Scottish
803DYE	Western Scottish	A156OFR	Ribble	A827SUL	East London	A973YSX	Fife Scottish
813VPU	Busways	A157OFR	Ribble	A828SUL	Selkent	A974YSX	Fife Scottish
837XHW	Stagecoach Transit	A158OFR	Ribble	A829SUL	Selkent	A975OST	Ribble
866NHT	Bluebird Buses	A159OFR	Ribble	A830SUL	Selkent	A976SYE	Selkent
896HOD	Western Scottish	A203ODY	Stagecoach South	A832SUL	East London	A977OST	Ribble
927GTA	Ribble	A208EHN	Stagecoach Transit	A833SUL	Western Scottish	A978OST	Ribble
1412NE	Bluebird Buses	A209EHN	Stagecoach Transit	A834SUL	Selkent	A978SYE	Selkent
3063VC	Midland Red	A211EHN	Stagecoach Transit	A836SUL	Selkent	A979OST	Ribble
3273AC	Midland Red	A212FVN	Stagecoach Transit	A837SUL	Selkent	A988SYE	Selkent
3669DG	Midland Red	A213FVN	Stagecoach Transit	A838SUL	Selkent	A996SYE	Selkent

Reg	Operator	Reg	Operator	Reg	Operator	Reg	Operator
A999SYE	Selkent	ASA23T	Western Scottish	B28PAJ	Stagecoach Transit	B215OAJ	Stagecoach Transit
AAE644V	Cheltenham & G	ASA27T	Western Scottish	B29PAJ	Stagecoach Transit	B216OAJ	Stagecoach Transit
AAE648V	Cheltenham & G	ASD826T	Western Scottish	B30PAJ	Stagecoach Transit	B217OAJ	Stagecoach Transit
AAE649V	Cheltenham & G	ASD827T	Western Scottish	B31PAJ	Stagecoach Transit	B218OAJ	Stagecoach Transit
AAE650V	Cheltenham & G	ASD829T	Western Scottish	B32PAJ	Stagecoach Transit	B348LSO	Bluebird Buses
AAE651V	Cheltenham & G	ASD834T	Western Scottish	B43MAO	Cumberland	B349LSO	Bluebird Buses
AAE659V	Cheltenham & G	ASD837T	Western Scottish	B49DWE	East Midland	B350LSO	Bluebird Buses
AAE660V	Cheltenham & G	ASD841T	Cheltenham & G	B52DWE	East Midland	B351LSO	Bluebird Buses
AAE665V	Cheltenham & G	ASD842T	Western Scottish	B53DWJ	East Midland	B352LSO	Bluebird Buses
AAL516A	Red & White	ASD843T	Western Scottish	B54DWJ	East Midland	B353LSO	Bluebird Buses
AAL518A	Red & White	ASD844T	Western Scottish	B60WKH	Kingston-u-Hull	B354LSO	Bluebird Buses
AAL538A	Red & White	AVK134V	Busways	B79WUV	Selkent	B355LSO	Bluebird Buses
AAL544A	Red & White	AVK135V	Busways	B81WUV	Selkent	B356LSO	Bluebird Buses
AAL575A	Red & White	AVK136V	Busways	B83WUV	Selkent	B357LSO	Bluebird Buses
AAP647T	Stagecoach South	AVK137V	Busways	B84WUV	Selkent	B358LSO	Bluebird Buses
AAP648T	Stagecoach South	AVK138V	Busways	B89WUV	Selkent	B359LSO	Bluebird Buses
AAP660T	Stagecoach South	AVK139V	Busways	B91WUV	Selkent	B360LSO	Bluebird Buses
AAP662T	Stagecoach South	AVK140V	Busways	B92WUV	Selkent	B439WTC	Cheltenham & G
AAP668T	Stagecoach South	AVK141V	Busways	B93WUV	Selkent	B443WTC	Cheltenhåm & G
AAP670T	Stagecoach South	AVK142V	Busways	B96WUV	Selkent	B625DWF	East Midland
AAP671T	Stagecoach South	AVK143V	Busways	B97WUV	Selkent	B626DWF	East Midland
AAX450A	Red & White	AVK144V	Busways	B99WUV	Selkent	B627DWF	East Midland
AAX451A	Red & White	AVK145V	Busways	B100WUV	Selkent	B628DWF	East Midland
AAX465A	Red & White	AVK146V	Busways	B101WUV	Selkent	B629DWF	East Midland
AAX466A	Red & White	AVK147V	Busways	B103HAO	Cumberland	B630DWF	East Midland
AAX488A	Red & White	AVK148V	Busways	B103WUV	Selkent	B631DWF	East Midland
AAX489A	Red & White	AVK149V	Busways	B105HAO	Cumberland	B632DWF	East Midland
AAX515A	Red & White	AVK150V	Busways	B106HAO	Cumberland	B633DWF	East Midland
AAX516A	Red & White	AVK151V	Busways	B106UAT	Kingston-u-Hull	B707FWA	East Midland
AAX529A	Red & White	AVK153V	Busways	B106WUV	Selkent	B875GSG	Bluebird Buses
AAX589A	Bluebird Buses	AVK154V	Busways	B107UAT	Kingston-u-Hull	B891UAS	Ribble
AAX600A	Bluebird Buses	AVK156V	Busways	B108CCS	Fife Scottish	B892UAS	Ribble
AAX601A	Bluebird Buses	AVK157V	Busways	B108UAT	Kingston-u-Hull	B893UAS	Ribble
AAX631A	Bluebird Buses	AVK158V	Busways	B108WUV	Selkent	B894UAS	Ribble
ABA13T	East Midland	AVK159V	Busways	B109UAT	Kingston-u-Hull	B895UAS	Ribble
ABA18T	East Midland	AVK160V	Busways	B110UAT	Kingston-u-Hull	B896UAS	Ribble
ABA25T	East Midland	AVK161V	Busways	B110WUV	Selkent	B897UAS	Ribble
ABV669A	Fife Scottish	AVK162V	Busways	B112WUV	Selkent	B898UAS	Ribble
AET181T	Midland Red	AVK163V	Red & White	B113WUV	Selkent	B899UAS	Ribble
AET182T	Stagecoach South	AVK164V	Busways	B114WUV	Selkent	B900WRN	Ribble
AET185T	Red & White	AVK166V	Red & White	B115WUV	Selkent	B910ODU	Midland Red
AET187T	Stagecoach South	AVK167V	Busways	B116WUV	Selkent	B911ODU	Midland Red
AHH206T	Ribble	AVK168V	Busways	B117WUV	Selkent	B912ODU	Midland Red
AHH209T	Ribble	AVK169V	Busways	B118WUV	Selkent	B960ODU	Midland Red
AHN388T	Busways	AVK170V	Busways	B119WUV	Selkent	B961ODU	Midland Red
AHN389T	Busways	AVK171V	Busways	B121WUV	Selkent	BAU178T	United Counties
AHN390T	Busways	AVK172V	Busways	B122WUV	Selkent	BAU179T	United Counties
AIB4053	Midland Red	AVK173V	Red & White	B124WUV	Selkent	BAU180T	Stagecoach South
AKG162A	Bluebird Buses	AVK174V	Busways	B125WUV	Selkent	BCL213T	Cambus
AKG197A	Red & White	AVK176V	Busways	B150DHL	East Midland	BCS865T	Western Scottish
AKG214A	Red & White	AVK177V	Busways	B151DHL	East Midland	BCS869T	Western Scottish
AKG232A	Bluebird Buses	AVK178V	Busways	B151WRN	Cumberland	BCS870T	Western Scottish
AKG271A	Red & White	AVK179V	Busways	B152DHL	East Midland	BCS871T	Western Scottish
AKG296A	Bluebird Buses	AVK180V	Busways	B152TRN	Ribble	BCW825V	Ribble
ALD968B	Bluebird Buses	AVK181V	Busways	B152WRN	Ribble	BCW826V	Ribble
ANA211T	Western Scottish	AVK182V	Busways	B153DHL	East Midland	BCW827V	Stagecoach South
ANA435Y	Midland Red	AVK183V	Busways	B153WRN	Cumberland	BFV221Y	Ribble
ARB528T	East Midland	AYJ89T	Stagecoach South	B154DHL	East Midland	BFV222Y	Ribble
ARN888Y	Ribble	AYJ91T	Stagecoach South	B154WRN	Cumberland	BFW136W	East Midland
ARN889Y	Ribble	AYJ92T	Stagecoach South	B155DHL	East Midland	BFX570T	Cambus
ARN890Y	Ribble	AYJ95T	Stagecoach South	B158WRN	Ribble	BHO441V	East Midland
ARN892Y	Cheltenham & G	AYJ97T	Stagecoach South	B162WRN	Cumberland	BHY996V	Cheltenham & G
ARP601X	United Counties	AYJ100T	Stagecoach South	B177FFS	Fife Scottish	BHY997V	Cheltenham & G
ARP602X	United Counties	AYJ101T	Stagecoach South	B178FFS	Fife Scottish	BHY998V	Cheltenham & G
ARP604X	United Counties	AYJ102T	Stagecoach South	B179FFS	Fife Scottish	BIW4977	Midland Red
ARP605X	United Counties	AYJ103T	Stagecoach South	B180FFS	Fife Scottish	BJG671V	Stagecoach South
ARP606X	United Counties	AYJ104T	Stagecoach South	B181FFS	Fife Scottish	BJG672V	Stagecoach South
ARP607X	United Counties	AYJ105T	Stagecoach South	B182FFS	Fife Scottish	BJG673V	Stagecoach South
ARP608X	United Counties	AYJ107T	Stagecoach South	B183FFS	Fife Scottish	BJG674V	Stagecoach South
ARP609X	United Counties	AYR322T	East Midland	B184FFS	Fife Scottish	BJG675V	Stagecoach South
ARP610X	United Counties	B21AUS	Midland Red	B185FFS	Fife Scottish	BJV103L	East Midland
ARP611X	United Counties	B24CGA	Western Scottish	B186FFS	Fife Scottish	BKE849T	Stagecoach South
ASA22T	Western Scottish	B27PAJ	Stagecoach Transit	B214OAJ	Stagecoach Transit	BKE850T	Stagecoach South

Reg	Operator	Reg	Operator	Reg	Operator	Reg	Operator
BKE851T	Stagecoach South	C98CHM	Selkent	C462SSO	Bluebird Buses	C639LFT	Busways
BKE858T	Stagecoach South	C101KDS	Western Scottish	C463SSO	Bluebird Buses	C639SFH	Cheltenham & G
BKE859T	Stagecoach South	C102HKG	Midland Red	C466SSO	Bluebird Buses	C640LFT	Busways
BKE860T	Stagecoach South	C103CHM	Selkent	C467SSO	Bluebird Buses	C640SFH	Cheltenham & G
BNC936T	Western Scottish	C104CHM	Selkent	C468SSO	Bluebird Buses	C641LFT	Busways
BOU6V	Cheltenham & G	C104KDS	Western Scottish	C469SSO	Bluebird Buses	C641SFH	Cheltenham & G
BPT903S	Red & White	C105CHM	Selkent	C470SSO	Bluebird Buses	C642LFT	Busways
BPY403T	Stagecoach Transit	C105KDS	Western Scottish	C480BFB	Cheltenham & G	C642SFH	Cheltenham & G
BSD848T	Cheltenham & G	C106CHM	Selkent	C499BFB	Cheltenham & G	C643LFT	Busways
BSD860T	Western Scottish	C106KDS	Western Scottish	C501DYM	Selkent	C643SFH	Cheltenham & G
BSD862T	Western Scottish	C107CHM	Selkent	C505DYM	Selkent	C644LFT	Busways
BSD863T	Western Scottish	C108CHM	Selkent	C544RAO	Cumberland	C644SFH	Cheltenham & G
BSD864T	Western Scottish	C109CHM	Selkent	C591SHC	Western Scottish	C645LFT	Busways
BSJ895T	Western Scottish	C110CHM	Selkent	C593SHC	Red & White	C645SFH	Cheltenham & G
BSJ896T	Western Scottish	C111CAT	Kingston-u-Hull	C594SHC	Western Scottish	C646LFT	Busways
BSJ917T	Western Scottish	C111CHM	Selkent	C596SHC	Red & White	C647LFT	Busways
BSJ930T	Western Scottish	C111JCS	Bluebird Buses	C601LFT	Busways	C648LFT	Busways
BSJ931T	Western Scottish	C112CAT	Kingston-u-Hull	C602LFT	Busways	C649LFT	Busways
BSK756	Bluebird Buses	C112CHM	Selkent	C603LFT	Busways	C649XDF	Cheltenham & G
BTU33W	Stagecoach Transit	C113CAT	Kingston-u-Hull	C604LFT	Busways	C650LFT	Busways
BUH210V	Red & White	C114CHM	Selkent	C605LFT	Busways	C650XDF	Cheltenham & G
BUH211V	Red & White	C115CHM	Selkent	C606LFT	Busways	C651LFT	Busways
BUH212V	Red & White	C116CHM	Selkent	C608LFT	Busways	C651XDF	Cheltenham & G
BUH214V	Red & White	C117CHM	Selkent	C609LFT	Busways	C652LFT	Busways
BUH232V	Red & White	C118CHM	Selkent	C610LFT	Busways	C652XDF	Cheltenham & G
BUH237V	Red & White	C119CHM	Selkent	C611LFT	Busways	C653LFT	Busways
BUT24Y	Kingston-u-Hull	C120CHM	Selkent	C612LFT	Busways	C653XDF	Cheltenham & G
BUT25Y	Kingston-u-Hull	C120PNV	United Counties	C613LFT	Busways	C654LFT	Busways
BVP771V	Midland Red	C121CHM	Selkent	C614LFT	Busways	C654XDF	Cheltenham & G
BVP772V	Midland Red	C121PNV	United Counties	C615LFT	Busways	C655LFT	Busways
BVP791V	Midland Red	C122CAT	Kingston-u-Hull	C616LFT	Busways	C655XDF	Cheltenham & G
BVP808V	Midland Red	C122CHM	Selkent	C617LFT	Busways	C656LFT	Busways
BVP816V	Midland Red	C122PNV	United Counties	C617SFH	Cheltenham & G	C656XDF	Cheltenham & G
BVP817V	Midland Red	C123CAT	Kingston-u-Hull	C618LFT	Busways	C657LFT	Busways
BVP818V	Midland Red	C124CAT	Kingston-u-Hull	C618SFH	Midland Red	C657XDF	Cheltenham & G
BYJ919Y	Stagecoach South	C125CAT	Kingston-u-Hull	C619LFT	Busways	C658LFT	Busways
C23CHM	Selkent	C126CAT	Kingston-u-Hull	C619SFH	Midland Red	C658XDF	Cheltenham & G
C28CHM	Selkent	C127CAT	Kingston-u-Hull	C620LFT	Busways	C659LFT	Busways
C29CHM	Selkent	C128CAT	Kingston-u-Hull	C620SFH	Midland Red	C659XDF	Cheltenham & G
C30CHM	Selkent	C129CAT	Kingston-u-Hull	C621LFT	Busways	C660LFT	Busways
C42CHM	Selkent	C131CAT	Kingston-u-Hull	C621SFH	Cheltenham & G	C660XDF	Cheltenham & G
C43CHM	Selkent	C170ECK	Ribble	C622LFT	Busways	C661LFT	Busways
C44CHM	Selkent	C171ECK	Ribble	C622SFH	Midland Red	C661XDF	Cheltenham & G
C45CHM	Selkent	C172ECK	Ribble	C623LFT	Busways	C662LFT	Busways
C51CHM	Selkent	C173ECK	Ribble	C623SFH	Midland Red	C662XDF	Cheltenham & G
C53CHM	Selkent	C174ECK	Ribble	C624LFT	Busways	C663LFT	Busways
C54CHM	Selkent	C175ECK	Cumberland	C625LFT	Busways	C664LFT	Busways
C55CHM	Selkent	C176ECK	Cumberland	C626LFT	Busways	C665LFT	Busways
C57CHM	Selkent	C177ECK	Cumberland	C626SFH	Cheltenham & G	C693VAD	Cheltenham & G
C60CHM	Selkent	C178ECK	Ribble	C627LFT	Busways	C694VAD	Cheltenham & G
C61CHM	Selkent	C179ECK	Ribble	C627SFH	Midland Red	C696VAD	Cheltenham & G
C62CHM	Selkent	C219WAJ	Stagecoach Transit	C628LFT	Busways	C697VAD	Cheltenham & G
C64CHM	Selkent	C220WAJ	Stagecoach Transit	C628SFH	Midland Red	C702FKE	Midland Red
C67CHM	Selkent	C221WAJ	Stagecoach Transit	C629LFT	Busways	C703FKE	Midland Red
C68CHM	Selkent	C222WAJ	Stagecoach Transit	C629SFH	Midland Red	C705FKE	Midland Red
C69CHM	Selkent	C326HWJ	East Midland	C630LFT	Busways	C712LWE	East Midland
C70CHM	Selkent	C327HWJ	East Midland	C630SFH	Cheltenham & G	C714FKE	Midland Red
C71CHM	Selkent	C328DND	Midland Red	C631LFT	Busways	C715FKE	Midland Red
C72CHM	Selkent	C328HWJ	East Midland	C631SFH	Cheltenham & G	C716FKE	Midland Red
C73CHM	Selkent	C329HWJ	East Midland	C632LFT	Busways	C718FKE	Midland Red
C74CHM	Selkent	C330HWJ	East Midland	C632SFH	Cheltenham & G	C724FKE	Midland Red
C75CHM	Selkent	C331HWJ	East Midland	C633LFT	Busways	C729JJO	Midland Red
C76CHM	Selkent	C332HWJ	East Midland	C633SFH	Cheltenham & G	C738CUC	Cheltenham & G
C77CHM	Selkent	C333HWJ	East Midland	C634LFT	Busways	C787USG	Fife Scottish
C80CHM	Selkent	C334HWJ	East Midland	C634SFH	Midland Red	C788USG	Fife Scottish
C81CHM	Selkent	C335HWJ	East Midland	C635LFT	Busways	C789USG	Fife Scottish
C82CHM	Selkent	C336HWJ	East Midland	C635SFH	Midland Red	C790USG	Fife Scottish
C83CHM	Selkent	C336SFL	Cambus	C636LFT	Busways	C791USG	Fife Scottish
C86CHM	Selkent	C382SAO	Cumberland	C636SFH	Cheltenham & G	C792USG	Fife Scottish
C87CHM	Selkent	C383SAO	Cumberland	C637LFT	Busways	C793USG	Fife Scottish
C92CHM	Selkent	C447NNV	Cambus	C637SFH	Cheltenham & G	C794USG	Fife Scottish
C94CHM	Selkent	C448NNV	Cambus	C638LFT	Busways	C795USG	Fife Scottish
C97CHM	Selkent	C461SSO	Bluebird Buses	C638SFH	Midland Red	C796USG	Fife Scottish

Reg	Operator	Reg	Operator	Reg	Operator	Reg	Operator
C797USG	Fife Scottish	CRS71T	Bluebird Buses	D94EKV	Western Scottish	D138VRP	Cambus
C798USG	Fife Scottish	CRS73T	Bluebird Buses	D101VRP	Cambus	D139VRP	Cambus
C799USG	Fife Scottish	CRS74T	Bluebird Buses	D102VRP	Cambus	D140VRP	Cambus
C800HCS	Western Scottish	CSF158W	Fife Scottish	D103VRP	Cambus	D141FYM	Selkent
C800USG	Fife Scottish	CSF159W	Fife Scottish	D104VRP	Cambus	D141VRP	Cambus
C801USG	Fife Scottish	CSF160W	Fife Scottish	D105VRP	Cambus	D142FYM	Selkent
C802KBT	Western Scottish	CSF161W	Fife Scottish	D106VRP	Cambus	D142VRP	Cambus
C802USG	Fife Scottish	CSF162W	Fife Scottish	D107NUS	Western Scottish	D143VRP	Cambus
C803USG	Fife Scottish	CSF163W	Fife Scottish	D107VRP	Cambus	D144FYM	Selkent
C804USG	Fife Scottish	CSF164W	Fife Scottish	D108NUS	Western Scottish	D144VRP	Cambus
C805USG	Fife Scottish	CSF165W	Fife Scottish	D108VRP	Cambus	D145VRP	Cambus
C806USG	Fife Scottish	CSF166W	Fife Scottish	D109NDW	Red & White	D147VRP	Cambus
C807BYY	Selkent	CSF167W	Fife Scottish	D109NUS	Western Scottish	D148VRP	Cambus
C807USG	Fife Scottish	CSF168W	Fife Scottish	D109VRP	Cambus	D155VRP	Cambus
C808SDY	Red & White	CSF169W	Fife Scottish	D110NUS	Western Scottish	D156VRP	Cambus
C809BYY	Selkent	CSO386Y	Western Scottish	D110VRP	Cambus	D164VRP	Cambus
C810BYY	Selkent	CSO389Y	Stagecoach Transit	D111NUS	Western Scottish	D167TRA	Western Scottish
C811BYY	Selkent	CSO390Y	Western Scottish	D111VRP	Cambus	D177VRP	Cambus
C812BYY	Selkent	CSU920	Bluebird Buses	D112NUS	Western Scottish	D181VRP	Cambus
C815BYY	Selkent	CSU921	Bluebird Buses	D112VRP	Cambus	D183VRP	Cambus
C818BYY	Selkent	CSU922	Bluebird Buses	D113NUS	Western Scottish	D192VRP	Cambus
C819BYY	Selkent	CSU923	Bluebird Buses	D113VRP	Cambus	D211VEV	Stagecoach South
C820SDY	Red & White	CSV219	Midland Red	D114NUS	Western Scottish	D228UHC	Stagecoach South
C901HWF	Bluebird Buses	CUB72Y	Western Scottish	D114VRP	Cambus	D230UHC	Western Scottish
C902HWF	Red & White	CUB73Y	Western Scottish	D115NUS	Western Scottish	D230VCD	Stagecoach South
C962XVC	Midland Red	CUL79V	Stagecoach South	D115VRP	Cambus	D231VCD	Stagecoach South
C963XVC	Midland Red	CUL80V	East London	D116NUS	Western Scottish	D237NCS	Western Scottish
C964XVC	Midland Red	CUL130V	Selkent	D116VRP	Cambus	D238NCS	Western Scottish
CBB476V	Busways	CUL140V	East London	D117NUS	Western Scottish	D239NCS	Western Scottish
CBB477V	Busways	CUL163V	East London	D117VRP	Cambus	D241NCS	Western Scottish
CBD902T	United Counties	CUL168V	Stagecoach South	D118NUS	Western Scottish	D243NCS	Western Scottish
CBD903T	United Counties	CUL169V	Stagecoach South	D118VRP	Cambus	D246NCS	Western Scottish
CBV2S	Cumberland	CUL175V	East London	D119VRP	Cambus	D248NCS	Western Scottish
CBV6S	Red & White	CUL179V	Western Scottish	D120VRP	Cambus	D251NCS	Western Scottish
CBV8S	Red & White	CUL189V	Western Scottish	D121NUS	Western Scottish	D253NCS	Western Scottish
CBV9S	Cambus	CUL190V	Stagecoach South	D121VRP	Cambus	D254NCS	Western Scottish
CBV11S	Midland Red	CUL190V	Stagecoach South	D122NUS	Western Scottish	D271OOJ	Midland Red
CBV16S	Midland Red	CUL193V	East London	D122VRP	Cambus	D273OOJ	Midland Red
CBV19S	Cambus	CUL197V	Western Scottish	D123FYM	Selkent	D277FAS	Fife Scottish
CBV20S	Midland Red	CUL198V	Stagecoach South	D123NUS	Western Scottish	D278FAS	Fife Scottish
CBV21S	Ribble	CUL208V	Western Scottish	D123VRP	Cambus	D279FAS	Fife Scottish
CBV776S	Stagecoach South	CUL209V	Western Scottish	D124FYM	Selkent	D301SDS	Western Scottish
CBV780S	Midland Red	CUL214V	East London	D124NUS	Western Scottish	D303SDS	Western Scottish
CBV784S	Stagecoach South	CUL215V	Stagecoach South	D124VRP	Cambus	D313WPE	Midland Red
CBV798S	Stagecoach South	CUL222V	East London	D125FYM	Selkent	D314WPE	Midland Red
CD7045	Stagecoach South	CUL223V	East London	D125VRP	Cambus	D315WPE	Midland Red
CEO720W	Ribble	CUL225V	Stagecoach South	D126FYM	Selkent	D320WPE	Midland Red
CEO721W	Ribble	CUV272C	East London	D126VRP	Cambus	D322MNC	Bluebird Buses
CEO722W	Ribble	CUV286C	East London	D127FYM	Selkent	D367JJD	Selkent
CHH210T	Ribble	CUV300C	East London	D127VRP	Cambus	D380XRS	Cumberland
CHH211T	Ribble	CUV303C	East London	D128FYM	Selkent	D381XRS	Cumberland
CHH214T	Ribble	CUV311C	East London	D128NUS	Western Scottish	D383XRS	United Counties
CJH117V	Stagecoach South	CYJ492Y	Red & White	D128VRP	Cambus	D384XAO	Cumberland
CJH119V	Stagecoach South	CYJ493Y	Red & White	D129FYM	Selkent	D385XRS	Bluebird Buses
CJH120V	Stagecoach South	CYJ531Y	Stagecoach South	D129NUS	Western Scottish	D386XRS	Bluebird Buses
CJH142V	Stagecoach South	D33UAO	Stagecoach Transit	D129VRP	Cambus	D387XRS	Bluebird Buses
CJH145V	Stagecoach South	D34KAX	Midland Red	D130FYM	Selkent	D388XRS	Bluebird Buses
CJJ677W	Stagecoach South	D34UAO	East Midland	D130NUS	Western Scottish	D389XRS	Bluebird Buses
CJJ678W	Stagecoach South	D35UAO	Cumberland	D130VRP	Cambus	D401TFT	Busways
CJJ679W	Stagecoach South	D36UAO	Cumberland	D131FYM	Selkent	D402TFT	Busways
CMJ447T	Busways	D37UAO	Cumberland	D131VRP	Cambus	D403TFT	Busways
CMJ450T	Busways	D38UAO	Cumberland	D132FYM	Selkent	D404TFT	Busways
CPO98W	Stagecoach South	D39UAO	Cumberland	D132VRP	Cambus	D405TFT	Busways
CPO99W	Stagecoach South	D40UAO	Western Scottish	D133FYM	Selkent	D406TFT	Busways
CPO100W	Stagecoach South	D41UAO	Western Scottish	D133VRP	Cambus	D407TFT	Busways
CPY704T	East Midland	D42UAO	Cumberland	D134FYM	Selkent	D408TFT	Busways
CRS60T	Bluebird Buses	D43KAX	Midland Red	D134VRP	Cambus	D409TFT	Busways
CRS61T	Bluebird Buses	D43UAO	Cumberland	D135VRP	Cambus	D410TFT	Busways
CRS62T	Bluebird Buses	D44UAO	Cumberland	D136FYM	Selkent	D411TFT	Busways
CRS63T	Bluebird Buses	D45KAX	Midland Red	D136NUS	Western Scottish	D412TFT	Busways
CRS68T	Bluebird Buses	D45UAO	Cumberland	D136VRP	Cambus	D413TFT	Busways
CRS69T	Bluebird Buses	D46UAO	Cumberland	D137FYM	Selkent	D414TFT	Busways
CRS70T	Bluebird Buses	D47KAX	Midland Red	D137VRP	Cambus	D415TFT	Busways

The 1996 Stagecoach Bus Handbook

Reg	Operator	Reg	Operator	Reg	Operator	Reg	Operator
D416TFT	Busways	D558RCK	Cumberland	DBV831W	Ribble	E47HFE	East Midland
D417TFT	Busways	D559RCK	Cumberland	DBV832W	Ribble	E47MRP	United Counties
D418TFT	Busways	D560RCK	Cumberland	DBV833W	Ribble	E48CHH	Cumberland
D419TFT	Busways	D561RCK	East Midland	DBV834W	Ribble	E48HFE	East Midland
D420TFT	Busways	D562RCK	Ribble	DBV835W	Ribble	E49CHH	Cumberland
D435RYS	Bluebird Buses	D564RCK	Ribble	DBV837W	Ribble	E49HFE	East Midland
D436RYS	Bluebird Buses	D581VBV	Cheltenham & G	DBV838W	Ribble	E49MRP	United Counties
D469WPM	Stagecoach South	D601MKH	Kingston-u-Hull	DBV839W	Ribble	E50CHH	Cumberland
D470WPM	Stagecoach South	D602MKH	Kingston-u-Hull	DBV841W	Ribble	E50HFE	East Midland
D471WPM	Stagecoach South	D603MKH	Kingston-u-Hull	DBV842W	Ribble	E50MRP	United Counties
D473WPM	Stagecoach South	D603NOE	Cambus	DBV843W	Ribble	E51HFE	East Midland
D476PON	East London	D604HTC	Cheltenham & G	DDW433V	Red & White	E52WAG	Kingston-u-Hull
D476WPM	Stagecoach South	D604MKH	Kingston-u-Hull	DDW434V	Red & White	E56HFE	East Midland
D501RCK	Ribble	D604NOE	Cambus	DDZ8844	Bluebird Buses	E57HFE	East Midland
D502RCK	Ribble	D605HTC	Cheltenham & G	DEX227T	Cambus	E58HFE	East Midland
D503RCK	East Midland	D605MKH	Kingston-u-Hull	DEX228T	Cambus	E60WDT	East Midland
D504RCK	East Midland	D605NOE	Cambus	DEX231T	Cambus	E61WDT	East Midland
D505RCK	Ribble	D606MKH	Kingston-u-Hull	DHW350W	Cheltenham & G	E65BVS	Stagecoach South
D507RCK	Ribble	D607MKH	Stagecoach Transit	DHW352W	Cheltenham & G	E66MVV	Cambus
D508RCK	Ribble	D608MKH	Kingston-u-Hull	DMS20V	Red & White	E67MVV	Cambus
D510RCK	Ribble	D609MKH	Kingston-u-Hull	DMS22V	Red & White	E68MVV	Cambus
D511RCK	East Midland	D611MKH	Kingston-u-Hull	DNE545Y	Cheltenham & G	E69MVV	Cambus
D512CSF	Fife Scottish	D612MKH	Kingston-u-Hull	DNG232T	Cambus	E70MVV	Cambus
D512RCK	Ribble	D613MKH	Kingston-u-Hull	DNG233T	Cambus	E71MVV	Cambus
D513RCK	Ribble	D614ASG	Fife Scottish	DNG234T	Cambus	E71XKW	East Midland
D515RCK	Ribble	D614MKH	Kingston-u-Hull	DRU6T	Stagecoach South	E72MVV	Cambus
D516DSX	Fife Scottish	D615ASG	Fife Scottish	DSD934V	Western Scottish	E73MVV	Cambus
D517DSX	Fife Scottish	D615MKH	Kingston-u-Hull	DSD936V	Western Scottish	E77PUH	Midland Red
D518DSX	Fife Scottish	D631NOE	Cambus	DSD940V	Western Scottish	E90YWB	East Midland
D518RCK	East Midland	D632NOE	Cambus	DSD942V	Western Scottish	E91YWB	East Midland
D519DSX	Fife Scottish	D640NOE	Cambus	DSD943V	Western Scottish	E92YWB	East Midland
D519RCK	East Midland	D642NOE	Cambus	DSD944V	Western Scottish	E93YWB	East Midland
D520DSX	Fife Scottish	D645NOE	Cambus	DSD945V	Western Scottish	E94YWB	East Midland
D520RCK	Cumberland	D647NOE	Cambus	DSD947V	Western Scottish	E95OUH	Midland Red
D521DSX	Fife Scottish	D648NOE	Cambus	DSD948V	Western Scottish	E95YWB	East Midland
D521RCK	Ribble	D672SHH	Ribble	DSD949V	Western Scottish	E96YWB	East Midland
D522DSX	Fife Scottish	D713CSC	Fife Scottish	DSD951V	Western Scottish	E97YWB	East Midland
D522FYL	Selkent	D735OOG	Midland Red	DSD954V	Western Scottish	E98YWB	East Midland
D522RCK	East Midland	D736OOG	Midland Red	DSD956V	Western Scottish	E99OUH	Midland Red
D523DSX	Fife Scottish	D744BRS	Bluebird Buses	DSD957V	Western Scottish	E102OUH	Cheltenham & G
D523KSE	Bluebird Buses	D799USB	Western Scottish	DSD970V	Western Scottish	E113RBO	Red & White
D523RCK	Stagecoach Transit	D851CKV	Midland Red	DSD973V	Western Scottish	E114SDW	Red & White
D524DSX	Fife Scottish	D852CKV	Midland Red	DSD975V	Western Scottish	E115SDW	Red & White
D525RCK	Cumberland	D853CKV	Midland Red	DSD976V	Western Scottish	E127KYW	Busways
D526RCK	Stagecoach Transit	D854CKV	Midland Red	DSD977V	Cheltenham & G	E130ORP	United Counties
D527RCK	Ribble	D856CKV	Midland Red	DSD980V	Western Scottish	E131ORP	United Counties
D528RCK	Cumberland	D857CKV	Midland Red	DSD981V	Western Scottish	E132ORP	United Counties
D529RCK	Cumberland	D858CKV	Midland Red	DSV943	Cumberland	E132SAT	Kingston-u-Hull
D530RCK	Cumberland	D859CKV	Midland Red	DWF22V	East Midland	E133ORP	United Counties
D531RCK	Cumberland	D862CKV	Midland Red	DWF23V	East Midland	E133SAT	Kingston-u-Hull
D533RCK	Cumberland	D885CKV	Midland Red	DWF24V	East Midland	E134ORP	United Counties
D534RCK	Cumberland	D888CKV	Midland Red	DWF25V	East Midland	E134SAT	Kingston-u-Hull
D535RCK	Stagecoach Transit	D917GRU	Western Scottish	DWF26V	East Midland	E135SAT	Kingston-u-Hull
D536RCK	Ribble	D918GRU	Western Scottish	DWF188V	Bluebird Buses	E136SAT	Kingston-u-Hull
D537RCK	Ribble	D935EBP	Stagecoach South	DWF189V	Midland Red	E137SAT	Kingston-u-Hull
D538RCK	Stagecoach Transit	D950UDY	Red & White	DWF190V	Bluebird Buses	E138SAT	Kingston-u-Hull
D539RCK	East Midland	DAK201V	Red & White	DWF191V	Bluebird Buses	E139SAT	Kingston-u-Hull
D540RCK	Red & White	DBV24W	Cumberland	DWF193V	Bluebird Buses	E140SAT	Kingston-u-Hull
D541RCK	Ribble	DBV25W	Stagecoach South	DWF194V	Midland Red	E141SAT	Kingston-u-Hull
D542RCK	Ribble	DBV26W	Red & White	DWF195V	Midland Red	E142BKH	Kingston-u-Hull
D543RCK	Stagecoach Transit	DBV28W	Cambus	DWF197V	Midland Red	E143BKH	Kingston-u-Hull
D544RCK	Red & White	DBV29W	Stagecoach South	DWF198V	Fife Scottish	E144BKH	Kingston-u-Hull
D545RCK	Ribble	DBV30W	Ribble	DWF199V	Fife Scottish	E145BKH	Kingston-u-Hull
D546RCK	Ribble	DBV31W	Midland Red	DWF200V	Fife Scottish	E146BKH	Kingston-u-Hull
D547RCK	East Midland	DBV32W	Cumberland	E42RDW	Cambus	E146KYW	Busways
D548RCK	Ribble	DBV100W	Ribble	E43RDW	Cambus	E147BKH	Kingston-u-Hull
D549RCK	Ribble	DBV131Y	Ribble	E44RDW	Cambus	E148BKH	Kingston-u-Hull
D551RCK	Ribble	DBV132Y	Cumberland	E45HFE	East Midland	E149BKH	Kingston-u-Hull
D552RCK	Ribble	DBV134Y	Ribble	E45RDW	Cambus	E150BKH	Kingston-u-Hull
D553RCK	Ribble	DBV137Y	Ribble	E46HFE	East Midland	E151BKH	Kingston-u-Hull
D554RCK	Ribble	DBV828W	Ribble	E46MRP	United Counties	E151UKR	Stagecoach South
D555RCK	Ribble	DBV829W	Ribble	E46RDW	Cambus	E152UKR	Stagecoach South
D556RCK	Ribble	DBV830W	Ribble	E47CHH	Cumberland	E153UKR	Stagecoach South

Reg	Operator	Reg	Operator	Reg	Operator	Reg	Operator
E154UKR	Stagecoach South	E501LFL	Cambus	E855UKR	Stagecoach South	EJR114W	Busways
E155CGJ	East London	E502LFL	Cambus	E864RCS	Western Scottish	EJR115W	Busways
E155UKR	Stagecoach South	E510PVV	Cumberland	E865RCS	Western Scottish	EJR117W	Busways
E156UKR	Stagecoach South	E511PVV	Cumberland	E866RCS	Western Scottish	EJR118W	Busways
E157UKR	Stagecoach South	E512PVV	Cumberland	E867RCS	Western Scottish	EJR119W	Busways
E158UKR	Stagecoach South	E580TKJ	Stagecoach South	E880DRA	East Midland	EJR122W	Busways
E159UKR	Stagecoach South	E581TKJ	Stagecoach South	E901KYR	Busways	EJR123W	Busways
E160UKR	Stagecoach South	E582TKJ	Stagecoach South	E905KYR	Busways	EJV31Y	East Midland
E161UKR	Stagecoach South	E583TKJ	Stagecoach South	E906KYR	Busways	EJV32Y	East Midland
E162UKR	Stagecoach South	E584TKJ	Stagecoach South	E907KYR	Busways	EJV33Y	East Midland
E163UKR	Stagecoach South	E585TKJ	Stagecoach South	E908KYR	Busways	EJV34Y	East Midland
E164UKR	Stagecoach South	E586TKJ	Stagecoach South	E909KSG	Fife Scottish	EKW614V	East Midland
E165UKR	Stagecoach South	E587TKJ	Stagecoach South	E909KYR	Busways	EKW615V	East Midland
E166UKR	Stagecoach South	E621BVK	Busways	E910KSG	Fife Scottish	EKW616V	East Midland
E167UKR	Stagecoach South	E622BVK	Busways	E910KYR	Busways	EKY21V	East Midland
E168UKR	Stagecoach South	E623BVK	Busways	E911KYR	Busways	EKY22V	East Midland
E169UKR	Stagecoach South	E624BVK	Busways	E911LVE	Cambus	EKY23V	East Midland
E170UKR	Stagecoach South	E625BVK	Busways	E912KYR	Busways	EKY24V	East Midland
E201EPB	Stagecoach South	E626BVK	Busways	E912LVE	Cambus	EKY25V	East Midland
E202EPB	Stagecoach South	E627BVK	Busways	E913NEW	Cambus	EKY26V	East Midland
E203EPB	Stagecoach South	E628BVK	Busways	E914KYR	Busways	EKY27V	East Midland
E204EPB	Stagecoach South	E629BVK	Busways	E915KYR	Busways	EKY28V	East Midland
E233JRF	Stagecoach South	E630BVK	Busways	E917KYR	Busways	EKY29V	East Midland
E317BRM	Busways	E630KCX	Midland Red	E918KYR	Busways	ELJ209V	Midland Red
E324JVN	Stagecoach Transit	E631BVK	Busways	E919KYR	Busways	ELJ212V	Stagecoach South
E333LHN	Stagecoach Transit	E632BVK	Busways	E920KYR	Busways	ELJ213V	Stagecoach South
E364YGB	Bluebird Buses	E633BVK	Busways	E921KYR	Busways	ENJ909V	Stagecoach South
E402TBS	Western Scottish	E634BVK	Busways	E922KYR	Busways	ENJ910V	Stagecoach South
E403TBS	Western Scottish	E634DCK	Western Scottish	E923KYR	Busways	ENJ911V	Stagecoach South
E421AFT	Busways	E635BVK	Busways	E924KYR	Busways	ENJ912V	Stagecoach South
E422AFT	Busways	E636BVK	Busways	E925KYR	Busways	ENJ913V	Stagecoach South
E423AFT	Busways	E636DCK	Western Scottish	E927KYR	Busways	ENJ914V	Stagecoach South
E424AFT	Busways	E637BVK	Busways	E927PBE	East Midland	ENJ915V	Stagecoach South
E425AFT	Busways	E637DCK	Western Scottish	E928PBE	East Midland	ENJ916V	Stagecoach South
E426AFT	Busways	E638BVK	Busways	E929PBE	East Midland	ENJ917V	Stagecoach South
E427AFT	Busways	E638YUS	Western Scottish	E930PBE	East Midland	ENJ918V	Stagecoach South
E428AFT	Busways	E639BVK	Busways	E947BHS	Bluebird Buses	ENU93H	East Midland
E429AFT	Busways	E640BVK	Busways	EAP973V	Stagecoach South	EPW516K	Busways
E430AFT	Busways	E640DCK	Western Scottish	EAP977V	Stagecoach South	ERV115W	Stagecoach South
E431AFT	Busways	E643DCK	Western Scottish	EAP978V	Stagecoach South	ERV116W	Stagecoach South
E432AFT	Busways	E643KYW	Western Scottish	EAP980V	Stagecoach South	ERV117W	Stagecoach South
E433AFT	Busways	E644DCK	Western Scottish	EAP982V	Stagecoach South	ERV118W	Stagecoach South
E433YHL	Midland Red	E644KYW	Western Scottish	EAP983V	Stagecoach South	ERV251D	Cumberland
E434AFT	Busways	E645KYW	Western Scottish	EAP984V	Stagecoach South	ESU263	Busways
E435AFT	Busways	E646DCK	Western Scottish	EAP985V	Stagecoach South	ESU435	Western Scottish
E436AFT	Busways	E647KYW	Western Scottish	EAP986V	Stagecoach South	ESU913	Cambus
E437AFT	Busways	E657RVP	Cambus	EAP987V	Stagecoach South	ESU920	Cambus
E438AFT	Busways	E663JAD	Cheltenham & G	EAP988V	Stagecoach South	EWE202V	Bluebird Buses
E439AFT	Busways	E664RVP	Cambus	EAP990V	Stagecoach South	EWE203V	East Midland
E440AFT	Busways	E665JAD	Cheltenham & G	EAP991V	Stagecoach South	EWE204V	Fife Scottish
E441AFT	Busways	E667JAD	Cheltenham & G	EAP992V	Stagecoach South	EWE205V	Bluebird Buses
E442AFT	Busways	E674KDG	Cheltenham & G	EAP996V	Stagecoach South	EWE206V	East Midland
E443AFT	Busways	E676KDG	Cheltenham & G	ECS876V	Western Scottish	EWS740W	Cheltenham & G
E444AFT	Busways	E709MFV	Cumberland	ECS877V	Western Scottish	EWS743W	Cheltenham & G
E445AFT	Busways	E712LYU	East London	ECS878V	Western Scottish	EWS746W	Cheltenham & G
E446AFT	Busways	E713LYU	Bluebird Buses	ECS879V	Western Scottish	EWS748W	Cheltenham & G
E447AFT	Busways	E714LYU	Bluebird Buses	ECS880V	Western Scottish	EWS751W	Cheltenham & G
E448AFT	Busways	E721BVO	East Midland	ECS882V	Western Scottish	EWY74Y	Western Scottish
E449AFT	Busways	E746SKR	Stagecoach South	ECS883V	Western Scottish	EWY75Y	Western Scottish
E450AFT	Busways	E747SKR	Stagecoach South	ECS885V	Western Scottish	EWY76Y	Western Scottish
E451AFT	Busways	E748SKR	Stagecoach South	ECU201E	Busways	EYE229V	Stagecoach South
E452AFT	Busways	E749SKR	Stagecoach South	EDS50A	Bluebird Buses	EYE230V	East London
E453AFT	Busways	E750SKR	Stagecoach South	EFU935Y	East Midland	EYE233V	Stagecoach South
E454AFT	Busways	E750VWT	Cambus	EHU383K	Busways	EYE236V	Western Scottish
E455AFT	Busways	E751SKR	Stagecoach South	EJR104W	Busways	EYE237V	Stagecoach South
E456AFT	Busways	E752SKR	Stagecoach South	EJR105W	Busways	EYE240V	Stagecoach South
E457AFT	Busways	E753SKR	Stagecoach South	EJR107W	Busways	EYE244V	Stagecoach South
E458AFT	Busways	E754UKR	Stagecoach South	EJR108W	Busways	EYE246V	Western Scottish
E459AFT	Busways	E755UKR	Stagecoach South	EJR109W	Busways	EYE248V	Western Scottish
E460AFT	Busways	E840HAP	Stagecoach South	EJR110W	Busways	EYE250V	Western Scottish
E461TEW	Cambus	E842KAS	Bluebird Buses	EJR111W	Busways	F21PSL	Stagecoach South
E481DAU	East Midland	E849AAO	Western Scottish	EJR112W	Busways	F23PSL	Stagecoach South
E500LFL	Cambus	E854UKR	Stagecoach South	EJR113W	Busways	F25PSL	Stagecoach South

Reg	Operator	Reg	Operator	Reg	Operator	Reg	Operator
F26PSL	Stagecoach South	F124HVK	Busways	F438CJK	Stagecoach South	F653KNL	Busways
F32CWY	East London	F125HVK	Busways	F471CJK	Stagecoach South	F658KNL	Busways
F41XCS	Western Scottish	F128YVP	Western Scottish	F491NTR	United Counties	F659KNL	Busways
F50CWY	East London	F135SPX	Ribble	F492NTR	United Counties	F660PWK	Midland Red
F51RFS	Western Scottish	F135URP	United Counties	F493NTR	United Counties	F661KNL	Busways
F52RFS	Western Scottish	F136SPX	Ribble	F494NTR	United Counties	F661PWK	Midland Red
F53EAT	Kingston-u-Hull	F137SPX	Ribble	F495NTR	United Counties	F677PDF	Cheltenham & G
F53RFS	Cheltenham & G	F149XCS	Western Scottish	F496NTR	United Counties	F695OPA	Stagecoach South
F54RFS	Cheltenham & G	F152HAT	Kingston-u-Hull	F506NJE	Cambus	F701BAT	Kingston-u-Hull
F55EAT	Kingston-u-Hull	F153HAT	Kingston-u-Hull	F507NJE	Cambus	F702BAT	Kingston-u-Hull
F55RFS	Fife Scottish	F154HAT	Kingston-u-Hull	F508NJE	Cambus	F703BAT	Kingston-u-Hull
F56RFS	Fife Scottish	F155HAT	Kingston-u-Hull	F509NJE	Cambus	F704BAT	Kingston-u-Hull
F57AVV	United Counties	F156FWY	East London	F510NJE	Cambus	F705BAT	Kingston-u-Hull
F57RFS	Fife Scottish	F156HAT	Kingston-u-Hull	F511NJE	Cambus	F706CAG	Kingston-u-Hull
F58AVV	United Counties	F157HAT	Kingston-u-Hull	F512NJE	Cambus	F761EKM	Stagecoach South
F58RFS	Fife Scottish	F160FWY	East London	F513NJE	Cambus	F762EKM	Stagecoach South
F59AVV	United Counties	F164XCS	Bluebird Buses	F514NJE	Cambus	F763EKM	Stagecoach South
F60AVV	United Counties	F165FWY	East London	F515NJE	Cambus	F764EKM	Stagecoach South
F60RFS	Fife Scottish	F166FWY	East London	F516NJE	Cambus	F765EKM	Stagecoach South
F61AVV	Stagecoach South	F167SMT	Cambus	F517NJE	Cambus	F766EKM	Stagecoach South
F61RFS	Fife Scottish	F168SMT	Cambus	F524WSJ	Western Scottish	F767EKM	Stagecoach South
F62AVV	Stagecoach South	F169FWY	Bluebird Buses	F562HPP	Stagecoach South	F771EKM	Stagecoach South
F62RFS	Fife Scottish	F170FWY	East London	F563HPP	Stagecoach South	F772EKM	Stagecoach South
F63RFS	Western Scottish	F171FWY	East London	F564HPP	Stagecoach South	F773EKM	Stagecoach South
F64RFS	Western Scottish	F171SMT	Cambus	F601MSL	Stagecoach South	F774EKM	Stagecoach South
F65RFS	Western Scottish	F172FWY	East London	F601UVN	Stagecoach Transit	F775EKM	Stagecoach South
F66RFS	Fife Scottish	F173FWY	East London	F602MSL	Stagecoach South	F781KKP	Stagecoach South
F67RFS	Fife Scottish	F174FWY	East London	F602UVN	Stagecoach Transit	F782KKP	Stagecoach South
F68RFS	Fife Scottish	F175FWY	East London	F603MSL	Stagecoach South	F790PSN	Fife Scottish
F69RFS	Fife Scottish	F176FWY	East London	F603UVN	Stagecoach Transit	F803FAO	Cumberland
F71FKK	Stagecoach South	F177FWY	Bluebird Buses	F604MSL	Stagecoach South	F804FAO	Cumberland
F71LAL	Midland Red	F178FWY	East London	F604UVN	Stagecoach Transit	F805FAO	Cumberland
F72FKK	Stagecoach South	F179FWY	East London	F605MSL	Stagecoach South	F806FAO	Cumberland
F73FKK	Stagecoach South	F180FWY	Bluebird Buses	F605UVN	Stagecoach Transit	F807FAO	Cumberland
F74DCW	Red & White	F201FHH	Cumberland	F606MSL	Stagecoach South	F808FAO	Cumberland
F74FKK	Stagecoach South	F202FHH	Cumberland	F606UVN	Stagecoach Transit	F809FAO	Cumberland
F75FKK	Stagecoach South	F243OFP	Red & White	F607UVN	Stagecoach Transit	F810FAO	Cumberland
F75TFU	East Midland	F251JRM	Cumberland	F608UVN	Stagecoach Transit	F811FAO	Cumberland
F76TFU	East Midland	F252JRM	Cumberland	F609UVN	Stagecoach Transit	F862FWB	Bluebird Buses
F77HAU	Bluebird Buses	F252OFP	Cambus	F609XMS	Selkent	F864PAC	Midland Red
F77TFU	East Midland	F253KAO	Cumberland	F610UVN	Stagecoach Transit	F865PAC	Midland Red
F78TFU	East Midland	F277WAF	Bluebird Buses	F614XMS	Selkent	F866PAC	Midland Red
F101HVK	Busways	F286KGK	Selkent	F615XMS	Selkent	F867PAC	Midland Red
F102HVK	Busways	F301MYJ	Stagecoach South	F616XMS	Selkent	F868PAC	Midland Red
F103HVK	Busways	F302MYJ	Stagecoach South	F617XMS	Selkent	F871UAC	Midland Red
F104HVK	Busways	F303MYJ	Stagecoach South	F619XMS	Selkent	F872UAC	Midland Red
F105HVK	Busways	F304MYJ	Stagecoach South	F620MSL	United Counties	F901JRG	Busways
F106HVK	Busways	F305MYJ	Stagecoach South	F620XMS	Selkent	F902JRG	Busways
F107HVK	Busways	F306MYJ	Stagecoach South	F621MSL	United Counties	F903JRG	Busways
F107NRT	Cambus	F307MYJ	Stagecoach South	F621XMS	Selkent	F904JRG	Busways
F108HVK	Busways	F308MYJ	Stagecoach South	F622MSL	United Counties	F905JRG	Busways
F108NRT	Cambus	F309MYJ	Stagecoach South	F623MSL	United Counties	F906JRG	Busways
F109HVK	Busways	F310MYJ	Fife Scottish	F624MSL	United Counties	F907JRG	Busways
F110HVK	Busways	F311DET	Cheltenham & G	F624XMS	Selkent	F908JRG	Busways
F110NES	United Counties	F311MYJ	Fife Scottish	F625MSL	United Counties	F909JRG	Busways
F111HVK	Busways	F312MYJ	Fife Scottish	F625XMS	Selkent	F910JRG	Busways
F112HVK	Busways	F334JHS	Western Scottish	F626MSL	United Counties	F911JRG	Busways
F113HVK	Busways	F335JHS	Western Scottish	F627MSL	United Counties	F912JRG	Busways
F114HVK	Busways	F335SPY	Stagecoach Transit	F628MSL	United Counties	F912YWY	East London
F114YVP	Western Scottish	F336JHS	Western Scottish	F629MSL	United Counties	F913JRG	Busways
F115HVK	Busways	F336VEF	Stagecoach Transit	F629XMS	Selkent	F913YWY	East London
F116HVK	Busways	F337VEF	Stagecoach Transit	F630MSL	United Counties	F914JRG	Busways
F117HVK	Busways	F338VEF	Stagecoach Transit	F630XMS	Selkent	F915JRG	Busways
F118HVK	Busways	F339VEF	Stagecoach Transit	F631MSL	United Counties	F916JRG	Busways
F118YVP	Western Scottish	F340VEF	Stagecoach Transit	F631XMS	Selkent	F917JRG	Busways
F119HVK	Busways	F341VEF	Stagecoach Transit	F632MSL	United Counties	F918JRG	Busways
F119YVP	Western Scottish	F342VEF	Stagecoach Transit	F633MSL	United Counties	F919JRG	Busways
F120HVK	Busways	F343VEF	Stagecoach Transit	F634MSP	United Counties	F920JRG	Busways
F120YVP	Western Scottish	F344VEF	Stagecoach Transit	F635YRP	United Counties	F947NER	Cambus
F121HVK	Busways	F345VEF	Stagecoach Transit	F636YRP	United Counties	F948NER	Cambus
F121YVP	Western Scottish	F359GKN	Cambus	F637YRP	United Counties	F958HTO	Red & White
F122HVK	Busways	F394DHL	Selkent	F638YRP	United Counties	FAO417V	United Counties
F123HVK	Busways	F437CJK	Stagecoach South	F641XMS	Selkent	FAO418V	United Counties

Reg	Operator	Reg	Operator	Reg	Operator	Reg	Operator
FAO419V	United Counties	G38SSR	Stagecoach South	G190PAO	Ribble	G337KKW	Fife Scottish
FAO420V	Cumberland	G38TGW	Selkent	G191PAO	Ribble	G338KKW	Fife Scottish
FAO421V	Cumberland	G39SSR	Stagecoach South	G192PAO	Ribble	G339KKW	East Midland
FAO422V	Cumberland	G39TGW	Selkent	G193PAO	Bluebird Buses	G340KKW	East Midland
FAO423V	Cumberland	G40SSR	United Counties	G194PAO	Bluebird Buses	G341KKW	East Midland
FAO424V	Cumberland	G40TGW	Selkent	G195PAO	Bluebird Buses	G342KKW	East Midland
FAO425V	Cumberland	G41SSR	United Counties	G196PAO	Bluebird Buses	G343KKW	East Midland
FAO426V	Cumberland	G42SSR	Stagecoach South	G197PAO	Bluebird Buses	G344FFX	Western Scottish
FAO427V	Cumberland	G43SSR	Stagecoach South	G198PAO	Bluebird Buses	G345FFX	Western Scottish
FAO428V	Cumberland	G56SAG	Kingston-u-Hull	G199PAO	Bluebird Buses	G386PNV	Western Scottish
FAO429V	Bluebird Buses	G61JVV	United Counties	G200PAO	Bluebird Buses	G387PNV	Western Scottish
FCY286W	Western Scottish	G62JVV	United Counties	G201PAO	Bluebird Buses	G418RYJ	Stagecoach South
FDC408V	East Midland	G63JVV	United Counties	G202PAO	Bluebird Buses	G419RYJ	Stagecoach South
FDC413V	East Midland	G64JVV	United Counties	G203PAO	Bluebird Buses	G420RYJ	Stagecoach South
FDV784V	Ribble	G65JVV	United Counties	G210SSL	Stagecoach South	G421RYJ	Stagecoach South
FDV799V	Cumberland	G66JVV	United Counties	G211SSL	Stagecoach South	G422RYJ	Stagecoach South
FDV809V	United Counties	G67LVV	United Counties	G212SSL	Stagecoach South	G446VKK	Stagecoach South
FDV810V	Bluebird Buses	G71APO	Stagecoach South	G213SSL	Stagecoach South	G447VKK	Stagecoach South
FDV811V	United Counties	G72APO	Stagecoach South	G214SSL	Stagecoach South	G461SGB	Western Scottish
FDV812V	United Counties	G73APO	Stagecoach South	G251TSL	Bluebird Buses	G491RKK	Stagecoach South
FDV813V	Ribble	G79VFW	East Midland	G252TSL	Bluebird Buses	G493RKK	Stagecoach South
FDV816V	Bluebird Buses	G80VFW	East Midland	G253TSL	Bluebird Buses	G494RKK	Stagecoach South
FDV817V	Ribble	G81VFW	East Midland	G254TSL	Bluebird Buses	G520LWU	Cambus
FDV818V	Stagecoach South	G86KUB	Bluebird Buses	G255TSL	Bluebird Buses	G525LWU	Cambus
FDV819V	Bluebird Buses	G91KUB	East London	G256TSL	Bluebird Buses	G526LWU	Cambus
FDV829V	Stagecoach South	G91VMM	Stagecoach South	G257TSL	Bluebird Buses	G527LWU	Cambus
FDV830V	Stagecoach South	G92VMM	Stagecoach South	G258TSL	Bluebird Buses	G528LWU	Midland Red
FDV831V	Stagecoach South	G93ERP	Cambus	G259TSL	Bluebird Buses	G529LWU	Midland Red
FDV832V	United Counties	G94ERP	Cambus	G260TSL	Bluebird Buses	G530LWU	Midland Red
FDV833V	Ribble	G95SKR	Stagecoach South	G261TSL	Bluebird Buses	G531LWU	Midland Red
FDV834V	Stagecoach South	G96ERP	Cambus	G262TSL	Bluebird Buses	G532LWU	Midland Red
FDV835V	United Counties	G96SKR	Stagecoach South	G263TSL	Cumberland	G533LWU	Cheltenham & G
FDV838V	United Counties	G97ERP	Cambus	G264TSL	Cumberland	G534LWU	Cheltenham & G
FDV839V	Stagecoach South	G97SKR	Stagecoach South	G265TSL	Cumberland	G535LWU	Midland Red
FDV840V	Bluebird Buses	G98NBD	Cambus	G266TSL	Cumberland	G546LWU	Cheltenham & G
FPR62V	Stagecoach South	G98SKR	Stagecoach South	G267TSL	Cumberland	G547LWU	Cheltenham & G
FRP905T	Cambus	G99NBD	Cambus	G268TSL	Cumberland	G548LWU	Cheltenham & G
FRP908T	United Counties	G100NBD	Cambus	G269TSL	Cumberland	G566PRM	Ribble
FRP909T	United Counties	G101AAD	Cheltenham & G	G270TSL	Bluebird Buses	G567PRM	Ribble
FRP910T	United Counties	G102AAD	Cheltenham & G	G271TSL	Bluebird Buses	G568PRM	Ribble
FRP911T	United Counties	G103AAD	Cheltenham & G	G272TSL	Bluebird Buses	G568UAS	Bluebird Buses
FRP912T	United Counties	G104AAD	Cheltenham & G	G273TSL	Bluebird Buses	G569PRM	Ribble
FSL61W	Stagecoach Transit	G105AAD	Cheltenham & G	G274TSL	Bluebird Buses	G570PRM	Ribble
FSL62W	Stagecoach Transit	G105KUB	East London	G275TSL	Bluebird Buses	G571PRM	Ribble
FSU737	Western Scottish	G106KUB	East London	G276TSL	Bluebird Buses	G572PRM	Ribble
FSU739	Western Scottish	G107KUB	East London	G277TSL	Bluebird Buses	G573PRM	Ribble
FWR216T	Cambus	G108CEH	Busways	G278TSL	Bluebird Buses	G574FSD	Western Scottish
FWR217T	Cambus	G113SKX	Busways	G279TSL	Bluebird Buses	G574PRM	Ribble
FWR218T	Cambus	G115OGA	Midland Red	G280TSL	Fife Scottish	G575PRM	Ribble
FWR219T	Cambus	G119KUB	East London	G281TSL	Fife Scottish	G575YTR	Western Scottish
FYX824W	Busways	G133USE	Bluebird Buses	G282TSL	Bluebird Buses	G576PRM	Ribble
G21CSG	Red & White	G178PAO	Cumberland	G283TSL	Bluebird Buses	G576YTR	Western Scottish
G22CSG	Busways	G179PAO	Ribble	G284TSL	Bluebird Buses	G577PRM	Ribble
G23CSG	Busways	G180JHG	Ribble	G285TSL	Bluebird Buses	G578PRM	Ribble
G24CSG	Red & White	G180PAO	Ribble	G286TSL	Bluebird Buses	G611CEF	Stagecoach Transit
G26XBK	Midland Red	G181JHG	Ribble	G287TSL	Bluebird Buses	G612CEF	Stagecoach Transit
G27PSR	United Counties	G181PAO	Ribble	G288TSL	Bluebird Buses	G613CEF	Stagecoach Transit
G28PSR	United Counties	G182JHG	Ribble	G289TSL	Bluebird Buses	G614CEF	Stagecoach Transit
G30PSR	Stagecoach South	G182PAO	Ribble	G290TSL	Bluebird Buses	G615CEF	Stagecoach Transit
G30TGW	Selkent	G183JHG	Ribble	G291TSL	Bluebird Buses	G616CEF	Stagecoach Transit
G31PSR	United Counties	G183PAO	Ribble	G292TSL	Bluebird Buses	G617CEF	Stagecoach Transit
G31TGW	Selkent	G184JHG	Ribble	G293TSL	Cumberland	G618CEF	Stagecoach Transit
G32PSR	United Counties	G184PAO	Ribble	G294TSL	Cumberland	G619CEF	Stagecoach Transit
G33SSR	United Counties	G185JHG	Ribble	G295TSL	Cumberland	G620CEF	Stagecoach Transit
G33TGW	Selkent	G185PAO	Ribble	G296TSL	Cumberland	G639EVV	United Counties
G34PSR	Stagecoach South	G186JHG	Ribble	G297TSL	Cumberland	G640EVV	United Counties
G34TGW	Selkent	G186PAO	Ribble	G298TSL	Cumberland	G641EVV	United Counties
G35PSR	Stagecoach South	G187JHG	Ribble	G299TSL	Cumberland	G642EVV	United Counties
G35TGW	Selkent	G187PAO	Ribble	G29PSR	United Counties	G643EVV	United Counties
G36SSR	Stagecoach South	G188JHG	Ribble	G300TSL	Cumberland	G644EVV	United Counties
G36TGW	Selkent	G188PAO	Ribble	G301WHP	Midland Red	G645EVV	United Counties
G37SSR	Stagecoach South	G189JHG	Ribble	G302WHP	Midland Red	G646EVV	United Counties
G37TGW	Selkent	G189PAO	Ribble	G303WHP	Midland Red	G647EVV	United Counties

The 1996 Stagecoach Bus Handbook

Reg	Operator	Reg	Operator	Reg	Operator	Reg	Operator
G648EVV	United Counties	GAJ129V	Stagecoach Transit	GSO92V	Bluebird Buses	H163WWT	Selkent
G649EVV	United Counties	GAJ130V	Stagecoach Transit	GSO93V	Bluebird Buses	H165WWT	Selkent
G665PHH	Ribble	GAJ131V	Stagecoach Transit	GSO94V	Bluebird Buses	H166WWT	Selkent
G679AAD	Cheltenham & G	GAJ132V	Stagecoach Transit	GSO95V	Bluebird Buses	H167WWT	Selkent
G680AAD	Cheltenham & G	GAJ133V	Stagecoach Transit	GSU341	Fife Scottish	H168WWT	Selkent
G681AAD	Cheltenham & G	GAJ134V	Stagecoach Transit	GSU342	Fife Scottish	H169WWT	Selkent
G682AAD	Cheltenham & G	GAJ135V	Stagecoach Transit	GSU343	Fife Scottish	H170WWT	Selkent
G683AAD	Cheltenham & G	GAJ136V	Stagecoach Transit	GSU344	Fife Scottish	H171WWT	Selkent
G684AAD	Cheltenham & G	GAJ137V	Stagecoach Transit	GTO798V	Bluebird Buses	H172WWT	Selkent
G684KNW	East London	GCS33V	Western Scottish	GTX738W	Red & White	H173WWT	Selkent
G701TCD	Stagecoach South	GCS37V	Western Scottish	GTX743W	Red & White	H174WWT	Selkent
G702TCD	Stagecoach South	GCS38V	Western Scottish	GTX746W	Midland Red	H175WWT	Selkent
G703TCD	Stagecoach South	GCS41V	Western Scottish	GTX747W	Red & White	H176WWT	Selkent
G704TCD	Stagecoach South	GCS45V	Western Scottish	GTX748W	Red & White	H177WWT	Selkent
G705TCD	Stagecoach South	GCS47V	Western Scottish	GTX750W	Red & White	H191WFR	Ribble
G706TCD	Stagecoach South	GCS48V	Western Scottish	GTX753W	Red & White	H192WFR	Ribble
G707TCD	Stagecoach South	GCS49V	Western Scottish	GTX754W	Midland Red	H193WFR	Ribble
G708TCD	Stagecoach South	GCS51V	Western Scottish	GWE617V	East Midland	H194WFR	Ribble
G709TCD	Stagecoach South	GCS53V	Western Scottish	GWE618V	East Midland	H195WFR	Ribble
G710TCD	Stagecoach South	GCS57V	Western Scottish	GWE619V	East Midland	H196WFR	Ribble
G801JRH	Kingston-u-Hull	GCS58V	Western Scottish	GYE252W	Western Scottish	H197WFR	Ribble
G802JRH	Kingston-u-Hull	GCS60V	Western Scottish	GYE254W	Western Scottish	H257THL	East Midland
G803JRH	Kingston-u-Hull	GCS61V	Western Scottish	GYE260W	East London	H301PAX	Red & White
G804JRH	Kingston-u-Hull	GCS62V	Western Scottish	GYE261W	East London	H344SWA	East Midland
G805JRH	Kingston-u-Hull	GCS65V	Western Scottish	GYE262W	East London	H345SWA	East Midland
G806JRH	Kingston-u-Hull	GCS69V	Western Scottish	GYE263W	East London	H346SWA	East Midland
G807LAG	Kingston-u-Hull	GEF185N	Stagecoach Transit	GYE264W	East London	H347SWA	East Midland
G807RTS	Stagecoach South	GEF187N	Stagecoach Transit	GYE266W	East London	H348SWA	East Midland
G808LAG	Kingston-u-Hull	GEF188N	Stagecoach Transit	GYE267W	Selkent	H370PNY	Red & White
G808RTS	Stagecoach South	GEF189N	Stagecoach Transit	GYE268W	East London	H401DMJ	Stagecoach Transit
G809RTS	Stagecoach South	GEF190N	Stagecoach Transit	GYE270W	East London	H401MRW	Midland Red
G820KWF	East Midland	GFJ665N	East Midland	GYE273W	East London	H402DEG	Cambus
G821KWF	East Midland	GFN546N	Stagecoach South	GYE273W	Western Scottish	H402MRW	Midland Red
G822KWF	East Midland	GFN552N	Stagecoach South	GYE281W	Western Scottish	H403DEG	Cambus
G823KWF	East Midland	GFR101W	Ribble	GYJ919V	Stagecoach South	H403MRW	Midland Red
G824KWF	East Midland	GGM80W	Stagecoach South	GYJ920V	Stagecoach South	H404MRW	Midland Red
G825KWF	East Midland	GGM81W	Stagecoach South	GYJ921V	Stagecoach South	H406GAV	Cambus
G825VGA	Western Scottish	GGM82W	Stagecoach South	GYJ922V	Stagecoach South	H406MRW	Midland Red
G826KWF	East Midland	GGM85W	Stagecoach South	H71XKH	Kingston-u-Hull	H407GAV	Cambus
G827KWF	East Midland	GGM86W	Stagecoach South	H101EKR	Stagecoach South	H421BNL	Busways
G831VGA	Western Scottish	GGM105W	Stagecoach South	H102EKR	Stagecoach South	H422BNL	Busways
G864BPD	Stagecoach South	GHB146N	Red & White	H103EKR	Stagecoach South	H423BNL	Busways
G901PKK	Stagecoach South	GHB148N	Red & White	H104EKR	Stagecoach South	H424BNL	Busways
G903PKK	Stagecoach South	GHV102N	Western Scottish	H112SAO	Cumberland	H425BNL	Busways
G910KWF	Stagecoach South	GHV948N	Western Scottish	H113SAO	Cumberland	H426BNL	Busways
G911KWF	Stagecoach South	GMS285S	Western Scottish	H114SAO	Cumberland	H427BNL	Busways
G912KWF	Red & White	GMS292S	Western Scottish	H115SAO	Cumberland	H428BNL	Busways
G913KWF	Stagecoach South	GNF6V	Cheltenham & G	H116SAO	Cumberland	H428EFT	Busways
G914KWF	Stagecoach South	GNF8V	Cheltenham & G	H117SAO	Cumberland	H429BNL	Busways
G915KWF	East Midland	GNF9V	Cheltenham & G	H118SAO	Cumberland	H429EFT	Busways
G916KWF	East Midland	GNF10V	Cheltenham & G	H120SAO	Cumberland	H430BNL	Busways
G917KWF	Stagecoach South	GNF11V	Cheltenham & G	H126ACU	Busways	H430EFT	Busways
G919KWF	Red & White	GNG711N	Cambus	H127ACU	Busways	H431EFT	Busways
G920KWF	Red & White	GNJ575N	Cambus	H141UUA	Selkent	H432EFT	Busways
G921KWF	Stagecoach South	GOL398N	East Midland	H142UUA	Selkent	H433EFT	Busways
G921TCU	Busways	GOL406N	Cheltenham & G	H143UUA	Selkent	H434EFT	Busways
G922KWF	Stagecoach South	GOL413N	Midland Red	H144UUA	Selkent	H435EFT	Busways
G922TCU	Busways	GOL420N	East Midland	H145UUA	Selkent	H436EFT	Busways
G923KWF	Stagecoach South	GOL426N	Midland Red	H146UUA	Selkent	H437EFT	Busways
G923TCU	Busways	GOL436N	East Midland	H147UUA	Selkent	H473CEG	Cambus
G924KWF	Red & White	GPJ894N	Stagecoach South	H148UUA	Selkent	H474CEG	Cambus
G924TCU	Busways	GRM625V	Cumberland	H149CVU	Western Scottish	H475CEG	Cambus
G925TCU	Busways	GSO1V	Bluebird Buses	H149UUA	Selkent	H482BEE	East Midland
G926TCU	Busways	GSO2V	United Counties	H150CVU	Western Scottish	H483BEE	East Midland
G974ARV	Stagecoach South	GSO6V	United Counties	H150UUA	Selkent	H484BEE	East Midland
G975ARV	Stagecoach South	GSO7V	United Counties	H151UUA	Selkent	H485BEE	East Midland
G976ARV	Stagecoach South	GSO8V	East Midland	H152UUA	Selkent	H495MRW	Midland Red
G977ARV	Stagecoach South	GSO82V	Fife Scottish	H153UUA	Selkent	H509AGC	Selkent
G978ARV	Stagecoach South	GSO83V	Fife Scottish	H154UUA	Selkent	H556TUG	Red & White
GAJ125V	United Counties	GSO84V	Fife Scottish	H159EJU	Red & White	H564WWR	Selkent
GAJ126V	United Counties	GSO89V	Bluebird Buses	H160WWT	Selkent	H642UWR	Cambus
GAJ127V	United Counties	GSO90V	Bluebird Buses	H161WWT	Selkent	H643UWR	Cambus
GAJ128V	United Counties	GSO91V	Bluebird Buses	H162WWT	Selkent	H649UWR	Cambus

Reg	Operator	Reg	Operator	Reg	Operator
H650VVV	United Counties	HDZ2616	Stagecoach Transit	J112WSC	East London	J225JJR	Stagecoach Transit
H651VVV	United Counties	HDZ8683	Stagecoach Transit	J113LKO	Stagecoach South	J226JJR	Stagecoach Transit
H652UWR	Cambus	HEU120N	Cheltenham & G	J113WSC	East London	J227JJR	Stagecoach Transit
H652VVV	United Counties	HEU122N	Midland Red	J114LKO	Stagecoach South	J228JJR	Stagecoach Transit
H653UWR	Cambus	HFG193T	Stagecoach South	J114WSC	East London	J229JJR	Stagecoach Transit
H653VVV	United Counties	HFG923V	Stagecoach South	J115LKO	Stagecoach South	J230JJR	Stagecoach Transit
H654UWR	East London	HGD213T	Western Scottish	J115WSC	East London	J230XKY	East London
H654VVV	United Counties	HHH370V	Ribble	J116LKO	Stagecoach South	J231JJR	Stagecoach Transit
H655UWR	East London	HHH372V	Ribble	J116WSC	East London	J231XKY	East London
H657UWR	East London	HHH373V	Ribble	J117LKO	Stagecoach South	J232JJR	Stagecoach Transit
H658UWR	East Midland	HIL6075	Cheltenham & G	J118LKO	Stagecoach South	J233JJR	Stagecoach Transit
H659UWR	East Midland	HIL8410	Red & White	J119LKO	Stagecoach South	J301BRM	Western Scottish
H667BNL	Busways	HIL8426	Busways	J120AAO	Cumberland	J302BRM	Western Scottish
H668BNL	Busways	HIL8427	Busways	J120AHH	Cumberland	J302TUH	Red & White
H669BNL	Busways	HKE690L	Stagecoach South	J120LKO	Stagecoach South	J303BRM	Western Scottish
H670BNL	Busways	HNE252V	Bluebird Buses	J120XHH	Bluebird Buses	J303TUH	Red & White
H671BNL	Busways	HNE253V	Cumberland	J121AAO	Cumberland	J304BRM	Western Scottish
H672BNL	Busways	HNE254V	Bluebird Buses	J121AHH	Cumberland	J304THP	Midland Red
H673BNL	Busways	HPK503N	Stagecoach South	J121LKO	Stagecoach South	J304UKG	Red & White
H674BNL	Busways	HPK505N	Stagecoach South	J121XHH	Bluebird Buses	J305BRM	Western Scottish
H675BNL	Busways	HPW522L	Busways	J122AAO	Cumberland	J305THP	Midland Red
H676BNL	Busways	HPY423V	Stagecoach Transit	J122AHH	Ribble	J305UKG	Red & White
H679BTP	Stagecoach South	HSB698Y	Western Scottish	J122XHH	Bluebird Buses	J306BRM	Western Scottish
H680BTP	Stagecoach South	HSK760	Bluebird Buses	J123AHH	Ribble	J306UKG	Red & White
H801BKK	Stagecoach South	HSV194	Cambus	J123XHH	Cumberland	J307BRM	Western Scottish
H802BKK	Stagecoach South	HSV195	Cambus	J124AHH	Ribble	J307UKG	Red & White
H803BKK	Stagecoach South	HSV196	Cambus	J124XHH	Cumberland	J308BRM	Western Scottish
H804BKK	Stagecoach South	HTG354N	Red & White	J125XHH	Cumberland	J309BRM	Western Scottish
H805BKK	Stagecoach South	HTY137W	Busways	J126XHH	Cumberland	J310BRM	Western Scottish
H806BKK	Stagecoach South	HTY138W	Busways	J127XHH	Cumberland	J349XET	East Midland
H807BKK	Stagecoach South	HTY139W	Busways	J132HMT	East London	J350XET	East Midland
H808BKK	Stagecoach South	HUD475S	Midland Red	J133HMT	East London	J351XET	East Midland
H809BKK	Stagecoach South	HUD479S	Midland Red	J134HMT	East London	J352XET	East Midland
H809WKH	Kingston-u-Hull	HUD480S	Midland Red	J135HMT	East London	J353XET	East Midland
H810BKK	Stagecoach South	HUF451X	Stagecoach South	J136HMT	East London	J371BNW	Busways
H810WKH	Kingston-u-Hull	HUF579X	Stagecoach South	J137HMT	East London	J372BNW	Busways
H811WKH	Kingston-u-Hull	HUF592X	Stagecoach South	J138HMT	East London	J373BNW	Busways
H812WKH	Kingston-u-Hull	HUF593X	Stagecoach South	J139HMT	East London	J374BNW	Busways
H813WKH	Kingston-u-Hull	HUF603X	Stagecoach South	J140HMT	East London	J375BNW	Busways
H814WKH	Kingston-u-Hull	HUF604X	Stagecoach South	J141HMT	East London	J376BNW	Busways
H815CBP	Stagecoach South	HUF625X	Stagecoach South	J142HMT	East London	J377BNW	Busways
H815WKH	Kingston-u-Hull	HUF626X	Stagecoach South	J143HMT	East London	J378BNW	Busways
H816CBP	Stagecoach South	HUF639X	Stagecoach South	J144HMT	East London	J379BNW	Busways
H816WKH	Kingston-u-Hull	HWG207W	Bluebird Buses	J145HMT	East London	J380BNW	Busways
H817CBP	Stagecoach South	HWG208W	Fife Scottish	J196YSS	Bluebird Buses	J401LKO	Stagecoach South
H818CBP	Stagecoach South	HWJ620W	East Midland	J197YSS	Bluebird Buses	J402LKO	Stagecoach South
H819CBP	Stagecoach South	HWJ621W	East Midland	J198HFR	Ribble	J403LKO	Stagecoach South
H882LOX	Selkent	IIL1319	Kingston-u-Hull	J198YSS	Bluebird Buses	J407PRW	Midland Red
H883LOX	Selkent	IIL1321	Kingston-u-Hull	J199HFR	Ribble	J408PRW	Midland Red
H885LOX	Selkent	IIL3503	Stagecoach South	J199YSS	Bluebird Buses	J408TEW	Cambus
H912XGA	Midland Red	IIL3504	Fife Scottish	J201HFR	Ribble	J409PRW	Midland Red
HAH237V	Cambus	IIL3505	Stagecoach South	J201JRP	Cambus	J409TEW	Cambus
HBD914T	United Counties	IIL3506	Fife Scottish	J202HFR	Ribble	J410PRW	Midland Red
HBD915T	United Counties	IIL3507	Western Scottish	J202JRP	Cambus	J411PRW	Midland Red
HBD916T	United Counties	J8WSB	Western Scottish	J203HFR	Ribble	J411WSC	East London
HBD917T	United Counties	J13WSB	Western Scottish	J203JRP	Cambus	J412PRW	Midland Red
HBD919T	United Counties	J14WSB	Western Scottish	J204HFR	Ribble	J413PRW	Midland Red
HDS566H	Western Scottish	J15WSB	Western Scottish	J204JKH	Kingston-u-Hull	J414PRW	Midland Red
HDZ2601	Stagecoach Transit	J91DJV	East Midland	J204JRP	Cambus	J415PRW	Midland Red
HDZ2602	Selkent	J92DJV	East Midland	J205HFR	Ribble	J416PRW	Midland Red
HDZ2603	Stagecoach Transit	J93DJV	East Midland	J205JKH	Kingston-u-Hull	J416TGM	Stagecoach South
HDZ2604	Stagecoach Transit	J94DJV	East Midland	J206HFR	Ribble	J417PRW	Midland Red
HDZ2605	Stagecoach Transit	J101WSC	East London	J207HFR	Ribble	J418PRW	Midland Red
HDZ2606	Stagecoach Transit	J102WSC	East London	J208HFR	Ribble	J430HDS	United Counties
HDZ2607	Stagecoach Transit	J103WSC	East London	J209HFR	Ribble	J439HDS	United Counties
HDZ2608	Selkent	J104WSC	East London	J210HFR	Ribble	J445HDS	United Counties
HDZ2609	Stagecoach Transit	J105WSC	East London	J213AET	East Midland	J446HDS	United Counties
HDZ2610	Stagecoach Transit	J106WSC	East London	J214AET	East Midland	J447HDS	Cambus
HDZ2611	Stagecoach Transit	J107WSC	East London	J215AET	East Midland	J448HDS	Cambus
HDZ2612	Stagecoach Transit	J108WSC	East London	J216AET	East Midland	J450HDS	United Counties
HDZ2613	Stagecoach Transit	J109WSC	East London	J217AET	East Midland	J455FSR	Bluebird Buses
HDZ2614	Selkent	J110WSC	East London	J218AET	East Midland	J456FSR	Bluebird Buses
HDZ2615	Stagecoach Transit	J112LKO	Stagecoach South	J219AET	East Midland	J501FPS	Bluebird Buses

Reg	Operator	Reg	Operator	Reg	Operator	Reg	Operator
J501GCD	Stagecoach South	J702YRM	Stagecoach South	JAJ142W	Stagecoach Transit	JKJ277V	East Midland
J502FPS	Bluebird Buses	J703YRM	Stagecoach South	JAJ143W	Stagecoach Transit	JMW166P	Busways
J502GCD	Stagecoach South	J706CWT	Cambus	JAJ144W	Stagecoach Transit	JMW167P	Busways
J503FPS	Bluebird Buses	J711CYG	East London	JAJ145W	Stagecoach Transit	JMW168P	Busways
J503GCD	Stagecoach South	J712CYG	East London	JAJ146W	Stagecoach Transit	JMW169P	Busways
J504FPS	Bluebird Buses	J713CYG	East London	JAJ292N	Stagecoach Transit	JMW170P	Busways
J504GCD	Stagecoach South	J714CYG	East London	JAJ293N	Stagecoach Transit	JND260V	Bluebird Buses
J505FPS	Bluebird Buses	J715CYG	East London	JAJ294N	Stagecoach Transit	JNJ194V	Stagecoach South
J505GCD	Stagecoach South	J716CYG	East London	JAJ295N	Stagecoach Transit	JOU160P	Cheltenham & G
J506FPS	Bluebird Buses	J717CYG	East London	JAJ296N	Stagecoach Transit	JOX502P	Midland Red
J506GCD	Stagecoach South	J718CYG	East London	JAK209W	Bluebird Buses	JOX503P	Midland Red
J507FPS	Bluebird Buses	J719CYG	East London	JAK210W	Bluebird Buses	JOX504P	Midland Red
J507GCD	Stagecoach South	J720CYG	East London	JAK211W	East Midland	JOX505P	Cheltenham & G
J508FPS	Bluebird Buses	J720GAP	Stagecoach South	JAK212W	Bluebird Buses	JPU817	Cumberland
J508GCD	Stagecoach South	J721CYG	East London	JAO477V	East Midland	JSA101V	Bluebird Buses
J509FPS	Bluebird Buses	J721GAP	Stagecoach South	JCK846W	Ribble	JSA102V	Bluebird Buses
J509GCD	Stagecoach South	J722CYG	East London	JCK847W	Ribble	JSA103V	Bluebird Buses
J510FPS	Bluebird Buses	J722GAP	Stagecoach South	JCK848W	Ribble	JSA104V	Bluebird Buses
J510GCD	Stagecoach South	J723CYG	East London	JCK849W	Stagecoach South	JTF971W	Western Scottish
J511FPS	Bluebird Buses	J724CYG	East London	JDZ2359	Selkent	JUB650V	Cambus
J511GCD	Stagecoach South	J725CYG	East London	JDZ2360	Selkent	JWA27W	Midland Red
J512FPS	Bluebird Buses	J726CYG	East London	JDZ2361	Selkent	JWV251W	Stagecoach South
J512GCD	Stagecoach South	J727CYG	East London	JDZ2362	Selkent	JWV252W	Stagecoach South
J513GCD	Stagecoach South	J728CYG	East London	JDZ2363	Selkent	JWV253W	Stagecoach South
J514GCD	Stagecoach South	J729CYG	East London	JDZ2364	Selkent	JWV255W	Stagecoach South
J515GCD	Stagecoach South	J739CWT	Cambus	JDZ2365	Selkent	JWV256W	Stagecoach South
J516GCD	Stagecoach South	J740CWT	Cambus	JDZ2371	Selkent	JWV258W	Stagecoach South
J517GCD	Stagecoach South	J741CWT	Cambus	JFR2W	Ribble	JWV266W	Stagecoach South
J518GCD	Stagecoach South	J742CWT	Cambus	JFR3W	Ribble	JWV267W	Stagecoach South
J519GCD	Stagecoach South	J743CWT	Cambus	JFR4W	Ribble	JWV268W	Stagecoach South
J520GCD	Stagecoach South	J744CWT	Cambus	JFR5W	Ribble	JWV269W	Stagecoach South
J521GCD	Stagecoach South	J746CWT	East Midland	JFR6W	Ribble	JWV274W	Stagecoach South
J522GCD	Stagecoach South	J748CWT	East Midland	JFR7W	Ribble	JWV275W	Stagecoach South
J523GCD	Stagecoach South	J749CWT	Kingston-u-Hull	JFR8W	Ribble	JWV976W	Stagecoach South
J524GCD	Stagecoach South	J752CWT	United Counties	JFR9W	Ribble	K96OGA	Cambus
J525GCD	Stagecoach South	J753CWT	United Counties	JFR10W	Ribble	K101JWJ	East Midland
J526GCD	Stagecoach South	J801WFS	Fife Scottish	JFR11W	Ribble	K101XHG	Bluebird Buses
J527GCD	Stagecoach South	J802WFS	Fife Scottish	JFR12W	Ribble	K102JWJ	East Midland
J528GCD	Stagecoach South	J803WFS	Fife Scottish	JFR13W	Ribble	K102XHG	Bluebird Buses
J529GCD	Stagecoach South	J804WFS	Fife Scottish	JHK500N	Western Scottish	K103JWJ	East Midland
J530GCD	Stagecoach South	J805DWW	Cambus	JHU899X	Cheltenham & G	K103XHG	Bluebird Buses
J531GCD	Stagecoach South	J805WFS	Fife Scottish	JHU912X	Cheltenham & G	K104JWJ	East Midland
J532GCD	Stagecoach South	J806DWW	Cambus	JJD392D	East London	K104XHG	Bluebird Buses
J533GCD	Stagecoach South	J806WFS	Fife Scottish	JJD399D	East London	K105JWJ	East Midland
J534GCD	Stagecoach South	J807DWW	Cambus	JJD402D	East London	K105XHG	Bluebird Buses
J535GCD	Stagecoach South	J807WFS	Fife Scottish	JJD415D	East London	K106JWJ	East Midland
J536GCD	Stagecoach South	J808WFS	United Counties	JJD429D	East London	K106XHG	Bluebird Buses
J537GCD	Stagecoach South	J811NKK	Stagecoach South	JJD435D	East London	K107JWJ	East Midland
J538GCD	Stagecoach South	J812NKK	Stagecoach South	JJD437D	East London	K107XHG	Bluebird Buses
J539GCD	Stagecoach South	J813NKK	Stagecoach South	JJD444D	East London	K108XHG	Bluebird Buses
J540GCD	Stagecoach South	J814NKK	Stagecoach South	JJD445D	East London	K109SRH	East London
J541GCD	Stagecoach South	J822HMC	East London	JJD450D	East London	K109XHG	Bluebird Buses
J542GCD	Stagecoach South	J823HMC	East London	JJD451D	East London	K110SRH	East London
J543GCD	Stagecoach South	J824HMC	East London	JJD456D	East London	K110XHG	Bluebird Buses
J544GCD	Stagecoach South	J825HMC	East London	JJD462D	East London	K112SRH	East London
J545GCD	Stagecoach South	J826HMC	East London	JJD470D	East London	K112XHG	Ribble
J546GCD	Stagecoach South	J827HMC	East London	JJD481D	East London	K113SRH	East London
J547GCD	Stagecoach South	J828HMC	East London	JJD488D	East London	K113XHG	Cumberland
J548GCD	Stagecoach South	J829HMC	East London	JJD493D	East London	K114SRH	East London
J549GCD	Stagecoach South	J856NKK	Stagecoach South	JJD495D	East London	K114XHG	Cumberland
J550GCD	Stagecoach South	J901UKV	Stagecoach Transit	JJD496D	East London	K115SRH	East London
J551GCD	Stagecoach South	J909NKP	Stagecoach South	JJD497D	East London	K115XHG	Ribble
J552GCD	Stagecoach South	J917LEM	Bluebird Buses	JJD541D	East London	K116SRH	East London
J553NGS	Stagecoach Transit	J919LEM	Bluebird Buses	JJD550D	East London	K116XHG	Ribble
J620GCR	United Counties	J960DWX	Cambus	JJD565D	East London	K117SRH	East London
J621GCR	United Counties	J961DWX	Cambus	JJD581D	East London	K117XHG	Ribble
J622GCR	United Counties	J962DWX	Cambus	JJD592D	East London	K118SRH	East London
J623GCR	Stagecoach South	JAH552D	Cambus	JJG890P	Stagecoach South	K118XHG	Ribble
J624GCR	Stagecoach South	JAH553D	Cambus	JJG893P	Stagecoach South	K119SRH	East London
J701KCU	Busways	JAJ139W	Stagecoach Transit	JJG895P	Stagecoach South	K120SRH	East London
J701YRM	Stagecoach South	JAJ139W	Stagecoach Transit	JJG898P	Stagecoach South	K120XHG	Ribble
J702CWT	Cambus	JAJ140W	Stagecoach Transit	JJG900P	Stagecoach South	K121SRH	East London
J702KCU	Busways	JAJ141W	Stagecoach Transit	JJT441N	Cambus	K121XHG	Cumberland

Reg	Operator	Reg	Operator	Reg	Operator	Reg	Operator
K122SRH	East London	K334RCN	Busways	K553NHC	Stagecoach South	K622UFR	Cumberland
K123SRH	East London	K335RCN	Busways	K554NHC	Stagecoach South	K622YVN	Stagecoach Transit
K124SRH	East London	K336RCN	Busways	K556NHC	Stagecoach South	K623UFR	Cumberland
K124XHG	Ribble	K337RCN	Busways	K557NHC	Stagecoach South	K623YVN	Stagecoach Transit
K125SRH	East London	K341PJR	Stagecoach Transit	K558NHC	Stagecoach South	K624UFR	Ribble
K126SRH	East London	K342PJR	Stagecoach Transit	K559NHC	Stagecoach South	K624YVN	Stagecoach Transit
K127SRH	East London	K343PJR	Stagecoach Transit	K561GSA	Bluebird Buses	K625UFR	Ribble
K128DAO	Cumberland	K344PJR	Stagecoach Transit	K561NHC	Stagecoach South	K625YVN	Stagecoach Transit
K128SRH	East London	K345PJR	Stagecoach Transit	K562GSA	Bluebird Buses	K626UFR	Cumberland
K129DAO	Cumberland	K350ANV	United Counties	K562NHC	Stagecoach South	K626YVN	Stagecoach Transit
K129SRH	East London	K351ANV	United Counties	K563GSA	Bluebird Buses	K627UFR	Ribble
K130DAO	Cumberland	K352ANV	United Counties	K563NHC	Stagecoach South	K627YVN	Stagecoach Transit
K130SRH	East London	K353ANV	United Counties	K564GSA	Bluebird Buses	K628UFR	Ribble
K131DAO	Cumberland	K354ANV	United Counties	K564NHC	Stagecoach South	K628YVN	Stagecoach Transit
K131SRH	East London	K354DWJ	East Midland	K565GSA	Bluebird Buses	K629YVN	Stagecoach Transit
K132DAO	Cumberland	K355ANV	United Counties	K565NHC	Stagecoach South	K630HWX	East London
K132SRH	East London	K355DWJ	East Midland	K566GSA	Bluebird Buses	K630YVN	Stagecoach Transit
K133DAO	Cumberland	K356ANV	United Counties	K566NHC	Stagecoach South	K631HWX	East London
K133SRH	East London	K356DWJ	East Midland	K567GSA	Bluebird Buses	K632HWX	East London
K134DAO	Cumberland	K357ANV	United Counties	K567NHC	Stagecoach South	K633HWX	East London
K134SRH	East London	K357DWJ	East Midland	K568GSA	Bluebird Buses	K634HWX	East London
K135DAO	Cumberland	K358ANV	United Counties	K568NHC	Stagecoach South	K635HWX	East London
K135SRH	East London	K358DWJ	East Midland	K569GSA	Bluebird Buses	K655NHC	Stagecoach South
K150DNV	United Counties	K359ANV	United Counties	K569NHC	Stagecoach South	K655UNH	United Counties
K151DNV	United Counties	K359DWJ	East Midland	K570GSA	Bluebird Buses	K656UNH	United Counties
K152DNV	United Counties	K360DWJ	East Midland	K570NHC	Stagecoach South	K657UNH	United Counties
K153DNV	United Counties	K361DWJ	East Midland	K571DFS	Kingston-u-Hull	K658UNH	United Counties
K154DNV	United Counties	K362DWJ	East Midland	K571LTS	Bluebird Buses	K659UNH	United Counties
K162FYG	Busways	K363DWJ	East Midland	K571NHC	Stagecoach South	K660NHC	Stagecoach South
K163FYG	Busways	K390TCE	Cambus	K572DFS	Kingston-u-Hull	K660UNH	United Counties
K164FYG	Busways	K391KUA	Cambus	K572LTS	Bluebird Buses	K661UNH	United Counties
K165FYG	Busways	K392KUA	Cambus	K572NHC	Stagecoach South	K662UNH	United Counties
K166FYG	Busways	K393KUA	Cambus	K573DFS	Kingston-u-Hull	K663UNH	United Counties
K171CAV	Cambus	K419FAV	Cambus	K573LTS	Bluebird Buses	K664UNH	United Counties
K172CAV	Cambus	K420ARW	Midland Red	K573NHC	Stagecoach South	K665UNH	United Counties
K173CAV	Cambus	K421ARW	Midland Red	K574DFS	Western Scottish	K667UNH	United Counties
K174CAV	Cambus	K422ARW	Midland Red	K574LTS	Bluebird Buses	K668UNH	United Counties
K175CAV	Cambus	K423ARW	Midland Red	K574NHC	Stagecoach South	K669UNH	United Counties
K176CAV	Cambus	K424ARW	Midland Red	K575DFS	Western Scottish	K670UNH	United Counties
K177CAV	Cambus	K425ARW	Midland Red	K575LTS	Bluebird Buses	K699ERM	Cumberland
K208OHS	Western Scottish	K426FAV	Cambus	K575NHC	Stagecoach South	K700DAO	Cumberland
K209OHS	Western Scottish	K428FAV	Cambus	K576DFS	Fife Scottish	K701DAO	Cumberland
K211SRH	East London	K449YCW	Ribble	K576LTS	Bluebird Buses	K701NDO	East Midland
K235NHC	Stagecoach South	K450YCW	Ribble	K576NHC	Stagecoach South	K702DAO	Cumberland
K236NHC	Stagecoach South	K457PNR	Cambus	K577DFS	Fife Scottish	K702NDO	East Midland
K237NHC	Stagecoach South	K458PNR	Cambus	K577LTS	Bluebird Buses	K703DAO	Cumberland
K238NHC	Stagecoach South	K485FFS	Fife Scottish	K577NHC	Stagecoach South	K703NDO	East Midland
K239NHC	Stagecoach South	K486FFS	Fife Scottish	K578LTS	Bluebird Buses	K703PCN	Busways
K240NHC	Stagecoach South	K487FFS	Fife Scottish	K578NHC	Stagecoach South	K704ERM	Cumberland
K302FYG	East London	K488FFS	Fife Scottish	K579NHC	Stagecoach South	K704NDO	East Midland
K306ARW	Midland Red	K489FFS	Fife Scottish	K580NHC	Stagecoach South	K704PCN	Busways
K308YKG	Cheltenham & G	K490FFS	Fife Scottish	K584ODY	Stagecoach South	K705DAO	Cumberland
K308YKG	Red & White	K491FFS	Fife Scottish	K585ODY	Stagecoach South	K705PCN	Busways
K309YKG	Red & White	K492FFS	Fife Scottish	K586ODY	Stagecoach South	K706DAO	Cumberland
K310YKG	Red & White	K493FFS	Fife Scottish	K587ODY	Stagecoach South	K706PCN	Busways
K311YKG	Red & White	K494FFS	Fife Scottish	K588ODY	Stagecoach South	K707DAO	Cumberland
K312YKG	Red & White	K508ESS	Bluebird Buses	K601ESH	Fife Scottish	K707PCN	Busways
K313YKG	Red & White	K509ESS	Bluebird Buses	K602ESH	Fife Scottish	K708DAO	Cumberland
K314YKG	Red & White	K510ESS	Bluebird Buses	K603ESH	Fife Scottish	K708PCN	Busways
K315YKG	Red & White	K511ESS	Bluebird Buses	K604ESH	Fife Scottish	K709ASC	United Counties
K316YKG	Red & White	K515ESS	Bluebird Buses	K605ESH	Fife Scottish	K709DAO	Cumberland
K317YKG	Red & White	K518ESS	Bluebird Buses	K610UFR	Ribble	K709PCN	Busways
K318YKG	Red & White	K521EFL	Midland Red	K611UFR	Ribble	K710ASC	United Counties
K319YKG	Red & White	K522EFL	Midland Red	K612UFR	Ribble	K710DAO	Cumberland
K320YKG	Red & White	K523EFL	Midland Red	K613UFR	Ribble	K710PCN	Busways
K321YKG	Red & White	K524EFL	Midland Red	K614UFR	Ribble	K711ASC	United Counties
K322YKG	Red & White	K525EFL	Midland Red	K615UFR	Ribble	K711DAO	Cumberland
K323YKG	Red & White	K526EFL	Midland Red	K616UFR	Ribble	K711PCN	Busways
K324YKG	Red & White	K527EFL	Midland Red	K617UFR	Ribble	K712ASC	United Counties
K325YKG	Red & White	K528EFL	Midland Red	K618UFR	Ribble	K712DAO	Cumberland
K330RCN	Busways	K529EFL	Midland Red	K619UFR	Ribble	K712PCN	Busways
K331RCN	Busways	K530EFL	Midland Red	K620UFR	Ribble	K713ASC	United Counties
K332RCN	Busways	K546RJX	East Midland	K621UFR	Ribble	K713DAO	Cumberland

The 1996 Stagecoach Bus Handbook

Reg	Operator	Reg	Operator	Reg	Operator	Reg	Operator
K713PCN	Busways	K759DAO	Cumberland	K865LMK	East London	KPA387P	Stagecoach South
K714ASC	Stagecoach South	K759FYG	United Counties	K865ODY	Stagecoach South	KPA388P	Stagecoach South
K714DAO	Cumberland	K760DAO	Cumberland	K866LMK	East London	KPA389P	Stagecoach South
K714PCN	Busways	K760FYG	United Counties	K866ODY	Stagecoach South	KRM430W	Bluebird Buses
K715ASC	Stagecoach South	K761DAO	Cumberland	K867LMK	East London	KRM431W	Cumberland
K715DAO	Cumberland	K761FYG	United Counties	K867ODY	Stagecoach South	KRM432W	Cumberland
K715PCN	Busways	K762DAO	Cumberland	K868LMK	East London	KRM433W	Cumberland
K716ASC	Stagecoach South	K763DAO	Cumberland	K868ODY	Stagecoach South	KRM434W	Cumberland
K716DAO	Cumberland	K764DAO	Cumberland	K869LMK	East London	KRM435W	Cumberland
K716PCN	Busways	K765DAO	Cumberland	K869ODY	Stagecoach South	KRM436W	Cumberland
K717ASC	Stagecoach South	K766DAO	Cumberland	K870LMK	East London	KRM437W	Cumberland
K717DAO	Cumberland	K767DAO	Cumberland	K870ODY	Stagecoach South	KRN103T	Cumberland
K717PCN	Busways	K768DAO	Cumberland	K871GHH	Cumberland	KRN105T	Cumberland
K718ASC	Fife Scottish	K769DAO	Cumberland	K871LMK	East London	KRN113T	Cumberland
K718DAO	Cumberland	K770DAO	Cumberland	K871ODY	Stagecoach South	KRN119T	Cumberland
K718PCN	Busways	K771DAO	Cumberland	K872GHH	Cumberland	KRN432W	United Counties
K719ASC	Fife Scottish	K772DAO	Cumberland	K872ODY	Stagecoach South	KRN433W	United Counties
K719DAO	Cumberland	K773DAO	Cumberland	K873GHH	Cumberland	KRS529V	Bluebird Buses
K719PCN	Busways	K774DAO	Cumberland	K873ODY	Stagecoach South	KRS531V	Bluebird Buses
K720ASC	Fife Scottish	K775DAO	Cumberland	K874GHH	Cumberland	KRS532V	Bluebird Buses
K720DAO	Cumberland	K776DAO	Cumberland	K874ODY	Stagecoach South	KRS540V	Western Scottish
K720PCN	Busways	K777DAO	Cumberland	K875GHH	Cumberland	KRS542V	Western Scottish
K721ASC	Fife Scottish	K778DAO	Cumberland	K875ODY	Stagecoach South	KRU838W	Stagecoach South
K721DAO	Cumberland	K779DAO	Cumberland	K876GHH	Cumberland	KRU839W	Stagecoach South
K721PCN	Busways	K780DAO	Cumberland	K876ODY	Stagecoach South	KRU840W	Stagecoach South
K722ASC	Fife Scottish	K781DAO	Cumberland	K877GHH	Cumberland	KRU841W	Stagecoach South
K722DAO	Cumberland	K783DAO	Cumberland	K877ODY	Stagecoach South	KRU843W	United Counties
K722PCN	Busways	K784DAO	Cumberland	K878GHH	Cumberland	KRU844W	Stagecoach South
K723ASC	Fife Scottish	K785DAO	Cumberland	K878ODY	Stagecoach South	KRU845W	United Counties
K723DAO	Cumberland	K786DAO	Cumberland	K879ODY	Stagecoach South	KRU846W	United Counties
K723PNL	Busways	K787DAO	Cumberland	K880ODY	Stagecoach South	KRU847W	United Counties
K724ASC	Fife Scottish	K788DAO	Cumberland	K910TKP	Stagecoach South	KRU852W	United Counties
K724DAO	Cumberland	K789DAO	Stagecoach South	K911RGE	Cambus	KRW532V	Cheltenham & G
K724PNL	Busways	K790DAO	Stagecoach South	K912RGE	Cambus	KSD62W	Western Scottish
K725ASC	Fife Scottish	K791DAO	Stagecoach South	K963HUB	Cambus	KSF6N	Fife Scottish
K725DAO	Cumberland	K801OMW	Cheltenham & G	K964HUB	Cambus	KSU454	Busways
K725PNL	Busways	K802OMW	Cheltenham & G	K965HUB	Cambus	KSU455	Busways
K726DAO	Cumberland	K821TKP	Stagecoach South	K966HUB	Cambus	KSU456	Busways
K726PNL	Busways	K822TKP	Stagecoach South	K967HUB	Cambus	KSU457	Busways
K727DAO	Cumberland	K823TKP	Stagecoach South	K968HUB	Cambus	KSU458	Busways
K727PNL	Busways	K823TKP	Stagecoach South	K969HUB	Cambus	KSU459	Busways
K728DAO	Cumberland	K824TKP	Stagecoach South	K970HUB	Cambus	KSU460	Busways
K728PNL	Busways	K846LMK	East London	K971HUB	Cambus	KSU462	Busways
K729DAO	Cumberland	K847LMK	East London	K972HUB	Cambus	KSU463	Busways
K730DAO	Cumberland	K848LMK	East London	K973HUB	Cambus	KSU464	Busways
K731DAO	Cumberland	K849LMK	East London	K974HUB	Cambus	KTX242L	Busways
K732DAO	Cumberland	K850LMK	East London	K975HUB	Cambus	KUC968P	Midland Red
K733DAO	Cumberland	K851LMK	East London	KAJ214W	Stagecoach Transit	KVF245V	Cambus
K734DAO	Cumberland	K852LMK	East London	KAJ215W	Stagecoach Transit	KVF246V	Cambus
K735DAO	Cumberland	K853LMK	East London	KAJ216W	Stagecoach Transit	KVF247V	Cambus
K736DAO	Cumberland	K853ODY	Stagecoach South	KAJ217W	Stagecoach Transit	KVF248V	Cambus
K737DAO	Cumberland	K854LMK	East London	KAJ218W	Stagecoach Transit	KVF249V	Cambus
K738DAO	Cumberland	K854ODY	Stagecoach South	KAJ219W	Stagecoach Transit	KVF250V	Cambus
K739DAO	Cumberland	K855LMK	East London	KBB118D	Busways	KWA213W	Bluebird Buses
K740DAO	Cumberland	K855ODY	Stagecoach South	KHH375W	Ribble	KWA214W	East Midland
K741DAO	Cumberland	K856LMK	East London	KHH376W	Cheltenham & G	KWA215W	Bluebird Buses
K742DAO	Cumberland	K856ODY	Stagecoach South	KHH377W	Ribble	KWA216W	Bluebird Buses
K743DAO	Cumberland	K857LMK	East London	KHH378W	Ribble	KWA217W	Fife Scottish
K744DAO	Cumberland	K857ODY	Stagecoach South	KHT121P	East Midland	KWA218W	East Midland
K745DAO	Cumberland	K858I MK	East London	KHT122P	Midland Red	KWA219W	Bluebird Buses
K746DAO	Cumberland	K858ODY	Stagecoach South	KHT124P	Midland Red	KWA221W	East Midland
K748DAO	Cumberland	K859LMK	East London	KIB8140	Midland Red	KWA223W	East Midland
K749DAO	Cumberland	K859ODY	Stagecoach South	KKK888V	Stagecoach South	KWA224W	East Midland
K750DAO	Cumberland	K860LMK	East London	KKW65P	Cheltenham & G	KWJ130P	East Midland
K751DAO	Cumberland	K860ODY	Stagecoach South	KKY220W	Fife Scottish	KYN282X	East London
K752DAO	Cumberland	K861LMK	East London	KKY222W	Bluebird Buses	KYN285X	East London
K753DAO	Cumberland	K861ODY	Stagecoach South	KMA399T	Western Scottish	KYN286X	East London
K754DAO	Cumberland	K862LMK	East London	KPA365P	Stagecoach South	KYN288X	Stagecoach South
K755DAO	Cumberland	K862ODY	Stagecoach South	KPA366P	Stagecoach South	KYN298X	East London
K756DAO	Cumberland	K863LMK	East London	KPA369P	Stagecoach South	KYN305X	Stagecoach South
K757DAO	Cumberland	K863ODY	Stagecoach South	KPA374P	Stagecoach South	KYN306X	East London
K758DAO	Cumberland	K864LMK	East London	KPA379P	Stagecoach South	KYN487X	Stagecoach South
K758FYG	United Counties	K864ODY	Stagecoach South	KPA383P	Stagecoach South	KYV311X	East London

Reg	Operator	Reg	Operator	Reg	Operator	Reg	Operator
KYV318X	East London	KYV513X	East London	L140VRH	East London	L252CCK	Ribble
KYV320X	East London	KYV514X	East London	L141BFV	Ribble	L253CCK	Ribble
KYV326X	East London	KYV515X	East London	L141VRH	East London	L254CCK	Stagecoach Transit
KYV331X	East London	KYV517X	East London	L142BFV	Ribble	L255CCK	Ribble
KYV334X	East London	KYV521X	East London	L142VRH	East London	L256CCK	Ribble
KYV340X	East London	KYV522X	East London	L143BFV	Ribble	L262VSU	Western Scottish
KYV345X	Stagecoach South	KYV523X	Stagecoach South	L143VRH	East London	L267CCK	Fife Scottish
KYV348X	Stagecoach South	KYV525X	East London	L144BFV	Ribble	L268CCK	Fife Scottish
KYV360X	East London	KYV526X	East London	L144VRH	East London	L269CCK	Fife Scottish
KYV361X	Stagecoach South	KYV527X	East London	L145BFV	Ribble	L270LHH	Cumberland
KYV366X	East London	KYV529X	East London	L145VRH	East London	L271LHH	Cumberland
KYV368X	Selkent	KYV531X	East London	L146BFV	Ribble	L272LHH	Cumberland
KYV378X	East London	KYV532X	East London	L146VRH	East London	L273LHH	Cumberland
KYV379X	East London	KYV533X	East London	L148BFV	Ribble	L274LHH	Cumberland
KYV380X	East London	KYV535X	East London	L149BFV	Ribble	L275JAO	Cumberland
KYV386X	East London	KYV536X	East London	L150BFV	Ribble	L276JAO	Cumberland
KYV387X	East London	KYV537X	East London	L151BFV	Ribble	L277JAO	Ribble
KYV394X	East London	KYV539X	East London	L152BFV	Ribble	L278JAO	Ribble
KYV395X	East London	KYV540X	East London	L153BFV	Ribble	L279JAO	Ribble
KYV397X	Stagecoach South	KYV541X	East London	L154BFV	Ribble	L281JAO	Ribble
KYV403X	East London	KYV542X	East London	L155BFV	Ribble	L282JAO	Cumberland
KYV404X	East London	KYV543X	East London	L155JNH	United Counties	L283JAO	Ribble
KYV406X	East London	KYV544X	East London	L156BFV	Ribble	L301JSA	Bluebird Buses
KYV410X	Western Scottish	KYV545X	East London	L156JNH	United Counties	L301PSC	Fife Scottish
KYV420X	Stagecoach South	KYV546X	East London	L157BFV	Ribble	L302JSA	Bluebird Buses
KYV428X	East London	KYV548X	East London	L157JNH	United Counties	L302PSC	Fife Scottish
KYV434X	East London	KYV549X	East London	L158BFV	Ribble	L303JSA	Bluebird Buses
KYV437X	East London	L26JSA	Bluebird Buses	L158JNH	United Counties	L303PSC	Fife Scottish
KYV439X	East London	L27JSA	Bluebird Buses	L159CCW	Ribble	L304PSC	Fife Scottish
KYV441X	East London	L28JSA	Bluebird Buses	L159JNH	United Counties	L305PSC	Fife Scottish
KYV442X	Stagecoach South	L31HHN	Stagecoach Transit	L160CCW	Ribble	L306PSC	Fife Scottish
KYV444X	East London	L32HHN	Stagecoach Transit	L160JNH	United Counties	L307PSC	Fife Scottish
KYV445X	East London	L33HHN	Stagecoach Transit	L161CCW	Ribble	L307SKV	Midland Red
KYV446X	East London	L34HHN	Stagecoach Transit	L161JNH	United Counties	L308PSC	Fife Scottish
KYV447X	Selkent	L35HHN	Stagecoach Transit	L162JNH	United Counties	L308YDU	Midland Red
KYV448X	East London	L36HHN	Stagecoach Transit	L188SDY	Stagecoach South	L309PSC	Fife Scottish
KYV451X	Stagecoach South	L37HHN	Stagecoach Transit	L201YAG	Selkent	L309YDU	Midland Red
KYV453X	East London	L81YBB	Busways	L202YAG	Selkent	L310PSC	Fife Scottish
KYV454X	East London	L82YBB	Busways	L203YAG	Selkent	L310YDU	Midland Red
KYV455X	Selkent	L83YBB	Busways	L204YAG	Selkent	L311YDU	Midland Red
KYV456X	East London	L84YBB	Busways	L205YAG	Selkent	L312YDU	Midland Red
KYV458X	East London	L100JLB	Bluebird Buses	L206YAG	Selkent	L313YDU	Midland Red
KYV460X	East London	L101GHN	Stagecoach Transit	L207YAG	Selkent	L314YDU	Midland Red
KYV461X	East London	L101JSA	Bluebird Buses	L208PSB	Western Scottish	L315JSA	Bluebird Buses
KYV462X	East London	L101SDY	Ribble	L208YAG	Selkent	L315YDU	Midland Red
KYV465X	East London	L102GHN	Stagecoach Transit	L209YAG	Selkent	L316JSA	Bluebird Buses
KYV466X	East London	L102JSA	Bluebird Buses	L210YAG	Selkent	L316YDU	Midland Red
KYV467X	East London	L102SDY	Ribble	L211YAG	Selkent	L317YDU	Midland Red
KYV469X	East London	L103GHN	Stagecoach Transit	L237CCW	Ribble	L318YDU	Midland Red
KYV470X	East London	L103SDY	Ribble	L238CCW	Stagecoach Transit	L319YDU	Midland Red
KYV471X	East London	L104SDY	Ribble	L239CCW	Ribble	L320YDU	Midland Red
KYV473X	East London	L105SDY	Ribble	L240CCW	Ribble	L321YDU	Midland Red
KYV474X	Stagecoach South	L106SDY	Ribble	L241SDY	Stagecoach South	L322YDU	Midland Red
KYV476X	East London	L107SDY	Ribble	L242CCK	Ribble	L323YDU	Midland Red
KYV480X	East London	L108LHH	East Midland	L242CCK	Stagecoach Transit	L324YDU	Midland Red
KYV486X	East London	L109LHH	East Midland	L242SDY	Stagecoach South	L325YDU	Midland Red
KYV488X	East London	L119DRN	Ribble	L243CCK	Stagecoach Transit	L326CHB	Red & White
KYV490X	East London	L122DRN	Ribble	L243SDY	Stagecoach South	L326YKV	Midland Red
KYV492X	East London	L123DRN	Cumberland	L244CCK	Stagecoach South	L327CHB	Red & White
KYV495X	East London	L125DRN	Ribble	L244SDY	Stagecoach South	L327YKV	Midland Red
KYV496X	East London	L125NAO	Cumberland	L245CCK	Stagecoach Transit	L328CHB	Red & White
KYV497X	East London	L126DRN	Cumberland	L245SDY	Stagecoach South	L328YKV	Midland Red
KYV498X	East London	L126NAO	Cumberland	L246CCK	Stagecoach Transit	L329CHB	Red & White
KYV500X	East London	L127DRN	Ribble	L246SDY	Stagecoach South	L329YKV	Midland Red
KYV501X	East London	L127NAO	Cumberland	L247CCK	Stagecoach Transit	L330CHB	Cheltenham & G
KYV502X	East London	L128DRN	Ribble	L247SDY	Stagecoach South	L330YKV	Midland Red
KYV503X	East London	L136VRH	East London	L248CCK	Cheltenham & G	L331CHB	Red & White
KYV504X	East London	L137VRH	East London	L248SDY	Stagecoach South	L334FWO	Red & White
KYV505X	East London	L138BFV	Ribble	L249CCK	Stagecoach Transit	L335FWO	Red & White
KYV506X	East London	L138VRH	East London	L249SDY	Stagecoach South	L336FWO	Red & White
KYV508X	East London	L139BFV	Ribble	L250CCK	Stagecoach Transit	L337FWO	Red & White
KYV511X	Stagecoach South	L139VRH	East London	L250SDY	Stagecoach South	L338FWO	Red & White
KYV512X	East London	L140BFV	Ribble	L251CCK	Ribble	L339FWO	Red & White

Reg	Operator	Reg	Operator	Reg	Operator	Reg	Operator
L339KCK	East Midland	L440LWA	East Midland	L637LDT	East Midland	L706HFU	East Midland
L340FWO	Red & White	L441LWA	East Midland	L638LDT	East Midland	L707FWO	Red & White
L340KCK	East Midland	L442LWA	East Midland	L639LDT	East Midland	L707HFU	East Midland
L341FWO	Red & White	L443LWA	East Midland	L640LDT	East Midland	L708FWO	Red & White
L341KCK	East Midland	L445LWA	East Midland	L641LDT	East Midland	L708HFU	East Midland
L342FWO	Red & White	L446LWA	East Midland	L642LDT	East Midland	L709FWO	Cheltenham & G
L342KCK	East Midland	L447LWA	East Midland	L643LDT	East Midland	L709HFU	East Midland
L343FWO	Red & White	L448LWA	East Midland	L651HKS	Fife Scottish	L710FWO	Cheltenham & G
L343KCK	East Midland	L449LWA	East Midland	L652HKS	Fife Scottish	L711FWO	Cheltenham & G
L344KCK	East Midland	L450LWA	East Midland	L653HKS	Fife Scottish	L712FWO	Cheltenham & G
L360JBD	United Counties	L451LWA	East Midland	L654HKS	Fife Scottish	L729VNL	Busways
L361JBD	United Counties	L451YAC	Midland Red	L655HKS	Fife Scottish	L730VNL	Busways
L362JBD	United Counties	L452LWA	East Midland	L655MFL	Cambus	L731LWA	East Midland
L363JBD	United Counties	L452YAC	Midland Red	L656HKS	Fife Scottish	L731VNL	Busways
L364JBD	United Counties	L453LHL	East Midland	L656MFL	Cambus	L732LWA	East Midland
L365JBD	United Counties	L453YAC	Midland Red	L657HKS	Fife Scottish	L732VNL	Busways
L366JBD	United Counties	L454YAC	Midland Red	L657MFL	Cambus	L733LWA	East Midland
L367JBD	United Counties	L455YAC	Midland Red	L658HKS	Fife Scottish	L733VNL	Busways
L368JBD	United Counties	L456YAC	Midland Red	L658MFL	Cambus	L734LWA	East Midland
L369JBD	United Counties	L557EHD	East Midland	L659HKS	Fife Scottish	L734VNL	Busways
L370JBD	United Counties	L577NSB	Western Scottish	L659MFL	Cambus	L735LWA	East Midland
L371JBD	United Counties	L578HSG	Fife Scottish	L660HKS	Ribble	L735VNL	Busways
L372JBD	United Counties	L578NSB	Western Scottish	L660MFL	Cambus	L736LWA	East Midland
L373JBD	United Counties	L579HSG	Fife Scottish	L661MFL	Cambus	L736VNL	Busways
L374JBD	United Counties	L579JSA	Bluebird Buses	L661MSF	Ribble	L737LWA	East Midland
L375JBD	United Counties	L580HSG	Fife Scottish	L662MFL	Cambus	L737VNL	Busways
L376JBD	United Counties	L580JSA	Bluebird Buses	L662MSF	Ribble	L738LWA	East Midland
L377JBD	United Counties	L581HSG	Fife Scottish	L663MFL	Cambus	L738VNL	Busways
L378JBD	United Counties	L581JSA	Bluebird Buses	L663MSF	Ribble	L739LWA	East Midland
L379JBD	United Counties	L582HSG	Fife Scottish	L664MFL	Cambus	L739VNL	Busways
L380JBD	United Counties	L582JSA	Western Scottish	L664MSF	Ribble	L740LWA	East Midland
L381NBD	United Counties	L583HSG	Fife Scottish	L665MFL	Cambus	L740VNL	Busways
L382NBD	United Counties	L583JSA	Western Scottish	L665MSF	Ribble	L741LWA	East Midland
L383NBD	United Counties	L584HSG	Fife Scottish	L667MFL	Cambus	L741VNL	Busways
L401JBD	United Counties	L584JSA	Western Scottish	L667MSF	Ribble	L742LWA	East Midland
L402JBD	United Counties	L585HSG	Fife Scottish	L668MFL	Cambus	L742VNL	Busways
L403JBD	United Counties	L585JSA	Bluebird Buses	L668MSF	Ribble	L743LWA	East Midland
L404JBD	United Counties	L586HSG	Fife Scottish	L669MFL	Cambus	L743VNL	Busways
L405JBD	United Counties	L586JSA	Bluebird Buses	L669MSF	Ribble	L744LWA	East Midland
L406JBD	United Counties	L587HSG	Fife Scottish	L671HNV	United Counties	L744VNL	Busways
L407JBD	United Counties	L587JSA	Bluebird Buses	L672HNV	United Counties	L745LWA	East Midland
L408JBD	United Counties	L588HSG	Fife Scottish	L673HNV	United Counties	L745VNL	Busways
L409JBD	United Counties	L588JSA	Bluebird Buses	L674HNV	United Counties	L746LWA	East Midland
L410JBD	United Counties	L589HSG	Fife Scottish	L675HNV	United Counties	L746VNL	Busways
L411JBD	United Counties	L590HSG	Fife Scottish	L676HNV	United Counties	L748LWA	East Midland
L412JBD	United Counties	L601VCD	Stagecoach South	L677HNV	United Counties	L748VNL	Busways
L413JBD	United Counties	L602VCD	Stagecoach South	L678HNV	United Counties	L749LWA	East Midland
L414JBD	United Counties	L603VCD	Stagecoach South	L679HNV	United Counties	L749VNL	Busways
L415JBD	United Counties	L609TDY	Stagecoach South	L680HNV	United Counties	L750LWA	East Midland
L416JBD	United Counties	L616TDY	Stagecoach South	L681HNV	United Counties	L750VNL	Busways
L417JBD	United Counties	L617TDY	Stagecoach South	L682HNV	United Counties	L751LHL	East Midland
L418JBD	United Counties	L618TDY	Stagecoach South	L683HNV	United Counties	L751VNL	Busways
L419JBD	United Counties	L623TDY	Stagecoach South	L684HNV	United Counties	L752VNL	Busways
L420JBD	United Counties	L624TDY	Stagecoach South	L685CDD	Red & White	L753VNL	Busways
L421JBD	United Counties	L625TDY	Stagecoach South	L685JBD	United Counties	L754VNL	Busways
L422MVV	United Counties	L626TDY	Stagecoach South	L686CDD	Cheltenham & G	L755VNL	Busways
L423MVV	Fife Scottish	L627TDY	Stagecoach South	L687CDD	Cheltenham & G	L756VNL	Busways
L423XVV	United Counties	L628TDY	Stagecoach South	L688CDD	Cheltenham & G	L757VNL	Busways
L424MVV	Fife Scottish	L629BFV	Ribble	L689CDD	Cheltenham & G	L758VNL	Busways
L424XVV	United Counties	L629TDY	Stagecoach South	L690CDD	Cheltenham & G	L759VNL	Busways
L425MVV	Fife Scottish	L630BFV	Ribble	L691CDD	Cheltenham & G	L760ARG	Busways
L425XVV	United Counties	L630TDY	Stagecoach South	L692CDD	Cheltenham & G	L761ARG	Busways
L426MVV	Fife Scottish	L631BFV	Ribble	L693CDD	Cheltenham & G	L762ARG	Busways
L426XVV	United Counties	L631TDY	Stagecoach South	L694CDD	Cheltenham & G	L763ARG	Busways
L427MVV	Fife Scottish	L632BFV	Ribble	L695CDD	Cheltenham & G	L764ARG	Busways
L427XVV	United Counties	L632TDY	Stagecoach South	L696CDD	Cheltenham & G	L765ARG	Busways
L428MVV	Fife Scottish	L633BFV	Ribble	L701FWO	Red & White	L803XDG	Cheltenham & G
L428XVV	United Counties	L633TDY	Stagecoach South	L702FWO	Red & White	L804XDG	Cheltenham & G
L435LWA	East Midland	L634BFV	Ribble	L703FWO	Red & White	L805XDG	Cheltenham & G
L436LWA	East Midland	L634TDY	Stagecoach South	L704FWO	Red & White	L806XDG	Cheltenham & G
L437LWA	East Midland	L635BFV	Ribble	L705FWO	Red & White	L826BKK	Stagecoach South
L438LWA	East Midland	L635TDY	Stagecoach South	L705HFU	East Midland	L827BKK	Stagecoach South
L438LWA	East Midland	L636BFV	Ribble	L706FWO	Red & White	L828BKK	Stagecoach South

Reg	Operator	Reg	Operator	Reg	Operator	Reg	Operator
L829BKK	Stagecoach South	LFR870X	Ribble	M201DRG	Busways	M342LHP	Midland Red
L830BKK	Stagecoach South	LFR871X	Ribble	M201LHP	Midland Red	M343DRP	United Counties
L831CDG	Cheltenham & G	LFR873X	Cheltenham & G	M202DRG	Busways	M343LHP	Midland Red
L832CDG	Cheltenham & G	LFR877X	Ribble	M202LHP	Midland Red	M344DRP	United Counties
L833CDG	Cheltenham & G	LFV205X	Ribble	M203DRG	Busways	M344JBO	Red & White
L834CDG	Cheltenham & G	LFV206X	Ribble	M203LHP	Midland Red	M344LHP	Midland Red
L835CDG	Cheltenham & G	LHG437T	Stagecoach South	M204DRG	Busways	M345DRP	United Counties
L836CDG	Cheltenham & G	LHG438T	Stagecoach South	M204LHP	Midland Red	M345JBO	Red & White
L837CDG	Cheltenham & G	LHT724P	Midland Red	M205LHP	Midland Red	M345LHP	Midland Red
L838CDG	Cheltenham & G	LHT725P	Midland Red	M209LHP	Midland Red	M346DRP	United Counties
L839CDG	Cheltenham & G	LHT726P	Cheltenham & G	M210LHP	Midland Red	M346JBO	Red & White
L840CDG	Cheltenham & G	LJC800	Cumberland	M223SVN	Stagecoach Transit	M346LHP	Midland Red
L841CDG	Cheltenham & G	LJY145	Cumberland	M224SVN	Stagecoach Transit	M347DRP	United Counties
L842CDG	Cheltenham & G	LOA838X	Cheltenham & G	M225SVN	Stagecoach Transit	M347JBO	Red & White
L881SDY	Stagecoach South	LOD724P	Cambus	M226SVN	Stagecoach Transit	M348DRP	United Counties
L882LFS	Western Scottish	LOD725P	Cambus	M227SVN	Stagecoach Transit	M348JBO	Red & White
L882SDY	Stagecoach South	LPF605P	Stagecoach South	M230TBV	Ribble	M349DRP	United Counties
L883LFS	Western Scottish	LPU452J	Busways	M231TBV	Ribble	M349JBO	Red & White
L883SDY	Stagecoach South	LSK528	Bluebird Buses	M232TBV	Ribble	M350JBO	Red & White
L884SDY	Stagecoach South	LSK547	Bluebird Buses	M233TBV	Ribble	M351JBO	Red & White
L885SDY	Stagecoach South	LSK548	Bluebird Buses	M234TBV	Ribble	M352JBO	Red & White
L886SDY	Stagecoach South	LSX10P	Fife Scottish	M235TBV	Ribble	M353JBO	Red & White
L887SDY	Stagecoach South	LSX16P	Fife Scottish	M236TBV	Ribble	M354JBO	Red & White
L916UGA	Western Scottish	LSX17P	Fife Scottish	M301DGP	Selkent	M355JBO	Red & White
LAG188V	East Midland	LSX33P	Fife Scottish	M302DGP	Selkent	M356JBO	Red & White
LAG189V	East Midland	LSX38P	Fife Scottish	M303DGP	Selkent	M357JBO	Red & White
LBD839P	United Counties	LUA273V	Cumberland	M304DGP	Selkent	M358JBO	Red & White
LBD920V	United Counties	LUA275V	Cumberland	M305DGP	Selkent	M359JBO	Red & White
LBD921V	United Counties	LUG96P	East Midland	M306DGP	Selkent	M360JBO	Red & White
LBD923V	United Counties	LUG98P	East Midland	M307DGP	Selkent	M361LAX	Red & White
LBN201P	Busways	LUG104P	East Midland	M308DGP	Selkent	M362LAX	Red & White
LBN202P	Busways	LUL511X	Cheltenham & G	M309DGP	Selkent	M363LAX	Red & White
LDS210A	Bluebird Buses	LWS33Y	Cheltenham & G	M310DGP	Selkent	M364LAX	Red & White
LEO736Y	Fife Scottish	LWS34Y	Cheltenham & G	M311DGP	Selkent	M365LAX	Red & White
LEU261P	United Counties	LWS35Y	Cheltenham & G	M311YSC	Stagecoach South	M366LAX	Red & White
LEU266P	Cheltenham & G	LWS36Y	Cheltenham & G	M312DGP	Selkent	M367LAX	Red & White
LEU267P	Cheltenham & G	LWS37Y	Cheltenham & G	M312YSC	Stagecoach South	M368LAX	Red & White
LFF875	East London	LWS38Y	Cheltenham & G	M313DGP	Selkent	M369LAX	Red & White
LFJ852W	United Counties	LWS39Y	Cheltenham & G	M313YSC	Stagecoach South	M370LAX	Red & White
LFJ853W	United Counties	LWS40Y	Cheltenham & G	M314DGP	Selkent	M371LAX	Red & White
LFJ854W	United Counties	LWS41Y	Cheltenham & G	M314PKS	Fife Scottish	M401SPY	Stagecoach Transit
LFJ855W	United Counties	LWU466V	Cambus	M315DGP	Selkent	M402SPY	Stagecoach Transit
LFJ858W	Ribble	LWU467V	Cambus	M315PKS	Fife Scottish	M403SPY	Stagecoach Transit
LFJ859W	Ribble	LWU468V	Cambus	M316DGP	Selkent	M404BFG	Stagecoach South
LFJ861W	Ribble	LWU470V	Cambus	M317DGP	Selkent	M404OKM	Stagecoach South
LFJ862W	United Counties	M38PVN	Stagecoach Transit	M317RSO	Bluebird Buses	M404SPY	Stagecoach Transit
LFJ863W	United Counties	M39PVN	Stagecoach Transit	M318DGP	Selkent	M405BFG	Stagecoach South
LFJ864W	United Counties	M40PVN	Stagecoach Transit	M318RSO	Bluebird Buses	M405OKM	Stagecoach South
LFJ865W	United Counties	M41PVN	Stagecoach Transit	M319DGP	Selkent	M405SPY	Stagecoach Transit
LFJ866W	Ribble	M42PVN	Stagecoach Transit	M319RSO	Bluebird Buses	M406BFG	Stagecoach South
LFJ868W	United Counties	M101CCD	Stagecoach South	M320DGP	Selkent	M406OKM	Stagecoach South
LFJ869W	United Counties	M102CDD	Fife Scottish	M320RSO	Bluebird Buses	M406SPY	Stagecoach Transit
LFJ870W	Stagecoach South	M103CDD	Fife Scottish	M321RSO	Bluebird Buses	M407BFG	Stagecoach South
LFJ874W	Stagecoach South	M104CDD	Fife Scottish	M331LHP	Midland Red	M407OKM	Stagecoach South
LFJ875W	Stagecoach South	M104PVN	Stagecoach Transit	M332DRP	United Counties	M407SPY	Stagecoach Transit
LFJ878W	United Counties	M105CCD	Stagecoach South	M332LHP	Midland Red	M408BFG	Stagecoach South
LFJ879W	United Counties	M105PVN	Stagecoach Transit	M334DRP	United Counties	M408OKM	Stagecoach South
LFJ880W	Stagecoach South	M106CCD	Stagecoach South	M334LHP	Midland Red	M408SPY	Stagecoach Transit
LFJ881W	Stagecoach South	M106PVN	Stagecoach South	M335DRP	United Counties	M409BFG	Stagecoach South
LFJ882W	Ribble	M107CCD	Stagecoach South	M335LHP	Midland Red	M409SPY	Stagecoach Transit
LFJ883W	Ribble	M107PVN	Stagecoach Transit	M336DRP	United Counties	M410BFG	Stagecoach South
LFJ884W	Ribble	M108CCD	Stagecoach South	M336LHP	Midland Red	M410SPY	Stagecoach Transit
LFJ885W	Ribble	M108PVN	Stagecoach Transit	M337DRP	United Counties	M411RRN	East Midland
LFR856X	Ribble	M151FGB	Western Scottish	M337LHP	Midland Red	M412RRN	East Midland
LFR857X	Ribble	M160CCD	Stagecoach South	M338DRP	United Counties	M413RRN	East Midland
LFR858X	Ribble	M161CCD	Stagecoach South	M338LHP	Midland Red	M414RRN	East Midland
LFR859X	Ribble	M162CCD	Stagecoach South	M339DRP	United Counties	M429BNV	United Counties
LFR860X	Cheltenham & G	M163CCD	Stagecoach South	M339LHP	Midland Red	M430BNV	United Counties
LFR861X	Cheltenham & G	M164CCD	Stagecoach South	M340DRP	United Counties	M451VCW	Ribble
LFR862X	United Counties	M164SCK	Ribble	M340LHP	Midland Red	M452VCW	Ribble
LFR864X	United Counties	M165CCD	Stagecoach South	M341DRP	United Counties	M453VCW	Ribble
LFR866X	Ribble	M165SCK	Ribble	M341LHP	Midland Red	M454VCW	Ribble
LFR868X	Ribble	M166CCD	Stagecoach South	M342DRP	United Counties	M455VCW	Ribble

The 1996 Stagecoach Bus Handbook

M456VCW	Ribble	M601VHE	East Midland	M710JDG	Cheltenham & G	M780TFS	Fife Scottish
M457VCW	Ribble	M602VHE	East Midland	M710KRH	Kingston-u-Hull	M782PRS	Ribble
M458VCW	Ribble	M603VHE	East Midland	M711FMR	Cheltenham & G	M783PRS	Ribble
M459VCW	Ribble	M604VHE	East Midland	M711KRH	Kingston-u-Hull	M784PRS	Western Scottish
M460VCW	Ribble	M605VHE	East Midland	M712FMR	Cheltenham & G	M785PRS	Western Scottish
M461VCW	Ribble	M606VHE	East Midland	M712KRH	Kingston-u-Hull	M786PRS	Western Scottish
M462VCW	Ribble	M607VHE	East Midland	M713FMR	Cheltenham & G	M787PRS	Western Scottish
M463VCW	Ribble	M608WET	East Midland	M713KRH	Kingston-u-Hull	M788PRS	Western Scottish
M466ASW	Western Scottish	M609WET	East Midland	M714FMR	Cheltenham & G	M789PRS	Western Scottish
M467ASW	Western Scottish	M614APN	Stagecoach South	M714KRH	Kingston-u-Hull	M790PRS	Western Scottish
M468ASW	Western Scottish	M615APN	Stagecoach South	M715FMR	Cheltenham & G	M791PRS	Western Scottish
M469ASW	Western Scottish	M636BCD	Stagecoach South	M715KRH	Kingston-u-Hull	M792PRS	Western Scottish
M470ASW	Western Scottish	M637BCD	Stagecoach South	M716KRH	Kingston-u-Hull	M793PRS	Western Scottish
M471ASW	Western Scottish	M638BCD	Stagecoach South	M717KRH	Kingston-u-Hull	M794PRS	Ribble
M472ASW	Western Scottish	M639BCD	Stagecoach South	M718BCS	Western Scottish	M795PRS	Ribble
M473ASW	Western Scottish	M648FYS	Western Scottish	M718KRH	Kingston-u-Hull	M796PRS	Ribble
M474ASW	Western Scottish	M649FYS	Western Scottish	M719BCS	Western Scottish	M797PRS	Ribble
M475ASW	Western Scottish	M650BCD	Stagecoach South	M720BCS	Western Scottish	M798PRS	Ribble
M476ASW	Western Scottish	M650FYS	Western Scottish	M721BCS	Western Scottish	M799PRS	Ribble
M477ASW	Western Scottish	M651BCD	Stagecoach South	M722BCS	Western Scottish	M808JTY	Busways
M478ASW	Western Scottish	M651FYS	Western Scottish	M723BCS	Western Scottish	M808WWR	Cambus
M479ASW	Western Scottish	M652BCD	Stagecoach South	M724BCS	Western Scottish	M809WWR	Cambus
M480ASW	Western Scottish	M652FYS	Western Scottish	M725BCS	Western Scottish	M810WWR	Cambus
M481ASW	Western Scottish	M653FYS	Western Scottish	M726BCS	Western Scottish	M817KRH	Kingston-u-Hull
M482ASW	Western Scottish	M654FYS	Western Scottish	M727BCS	Western Scottish	M818KRH	Kingston-u-Hull
M483ASW	Western Scottish	M655FYS	Western Scottish	M732BSJ	Western Scottish	M819KRH	Kingston-u-Hull
M484ASW	Western Scottish	M656FYS	Western Scottish	M733BSJ	Western Scottish	M843EMW	Cheltenham & G
M485ASW	Western Scottish	M657FYS	Western Scottish	M734BSJ	Western Scottish	M844EMW	Cheltenham & G
M486ASW	Western Scottish	M658FYS	Western Scottish	M735BSJ	Western Scottish	M845EMW	Cheltenham & G
M487ASW	Western Scottish	M659FYS	Western Scottish	M736BSJ	Western Scottish	M847HDF	Cheltenham & G
M488ASW	Western Scottish	M660FYS	Western Scottish	M737BSJ	Western Scottish	M869ASW	Western Scottish
M489ASW	Western Scottish	M661FYS	Western Scottish	M738BSJ	Western Scottish	M870ASW	Western Scottish
M490ASW	Western Scottish	M662ECD	Stagecoach South	M739BSJ	Western Scottish	M871ASW	Western Scottish
M491ASW	Western Scottish	M662FYS	Stagecoach South	M740BSJ	Western Scottish	M872ASW	Western Scottish
M492ASW	Western Scottish	M663ECD	Stagecoach South	M741BSJ	Western Scottish	M889ECD	Stagecoach South
M527RSO	Bluebird Buses	M663FYS	Western Scottish	M750LAX	Red & White	M890ECD	Stagecoach South
M528RSO	Bluebird Buses	M664ECD	Stagecoach South	M751LAX	Red & White	M901DRG	Busways
M529RSO	Bluebird Buses	M664FYS	Western Scottish	M752LAX	Red & White	M902DRG	Busways
M530RSO	Bluebird Buses	M665ECD	Stagecoach South	M753LAX	Red & White	M911WJK	Stagecoach South
M531RSO	Bluebird Buses	M665FYS	Western Scottish	M754LAX	Red & White	M912WJK	Stagecoach South
M532RSO	Bluebird Buses	M667ECD	Stagecoach South	M755LAX	Red & White	M913WJK	Stagecoach South
M533RSO	Bluebird Buses	M667FYS	Western Scottish	M756LAX	Red & White	M914WJK	Stagecoach South
M534RSO	Bluebird Buses	M668ECD	Stagecoach South	M757LAX	Red & White	M915WJK	Stagecoach South
M535RSO	Bluebird Buses	M668FYS	Western Scottish	M758LAX	Red & White	M916WJK	Stagecoach South
M536RSO	Bluebird Buses	M669ECD	Stagecoach South	M759LAX	Red & White	M917WJK	Stagecoach South
M537RSO	Bluebird Buses	M670ECD	Stagecoach South	M760LAX	Red & White	M918WJK	Stagecoach South
M538RSO	Bluebird Buses	M670SSX	Fife Scottish	M761LAX	Red & White	M940JBO	Red & White
M539RSO	Bluebird Buses	M671SSX	Fife Scottish	M762LAX	Red & White	M941JBO	Red & White
M540RSO	Bluebird Buses	M672SSX	Fife Scottish	M763LAX	Red & White	M942JBO	Red & White
M541RSO	Bluebird Buses	M673SSX	Fife Scottish	M764LAX	Red & White	M942TSX	Fife Scottish
M542RSO	Bluebird Buses	M674SSX	Western Scottish	M765LAX	Red & White	M943JBO	Red & White
M543RSO	Bluebird Buses	M675SSX	Western Scottish	M766DRG	Busways	M943TSX	Fife Scottish
M543SPY	Stagecoach Transit	M676SSX	Western Scottish	M766LAX	Busways	M944JBO	Red & White
M544RSO	Bluebird Buses	M677SSX	Western Scottish	M767DRG	Busways	M944TSX	Fife Scottish
M544SPY	Stagecoach Transit	M678SSX	Western Scottish	M767LAX	Red & White	M945JBO	Red & White
M545SPY	Stagecoach Transit	M679SSX	Western Scottish	M768DRG	Busways	M945TSX	Fife Scottish
M546SPY	Stagecoach Transit	M680SSX	Western Scottish	M768LAX	Red & White	M946JBO	Red & White
M547SPY	Stagecoach Transit	M681SSX	Western Scottish	M769DRG	Busways	M946TSX	Fife Scottish
M548SPY	Stagecoach Transit	M697EDD	Cheltenham & G	M769LAX	Red & White	M947JBO	Red & White
M549SPY	Stagecoach Transit	M698EDD	Cheltenham & G	M770DRG	Busways	M947TSX	Fife Scottish
M550SPY	Stagecoach Transit	M699EDD	Cheltenham & G	M770LAX	Red & White	M948JBO	Red & White
M551SPY	Stagecoach Transit	M701EDD	Cheltenham & G	M770TFS	Fife Scottish	M948TSX	Fife Scottish
M552SPY	Stagecoach Transit	M702EDD	Cheltenham & G	M771DRG	Busways	M949JBO	Red & White
M589OSO	Bluebird Buses	M703EDD	Cheltenham & G	M771TFS	Fife Scottish	M949TSX	Fife Scottish
M590OSO	Bluebird Buses	M704JDG	Cheltenham & G	M772BCS	Western Scottish	M950JBO	Red & White
M591OSO	Bluebird Buses	M705JDG	Cheltenham & G	M772TFS	Fife Scottish	M950TSX	Fife Scottish
M592OSO	Bluebird Buses	M706JDG	Cheltenham & G	M773BCS	Western Scottish	M951DRG	Busways
M593OSO	Bluebird Buses	M707JDG	Cheltenham & G	M773TFS	Fife Scottish	M951JBO	Red & White
M594OSO	Bluebird Buses	M707KRH	Kingston-u-Hull	M774TFS	Fife Scottish	M951TSX	Fife Scottish
M595OSO	Bluebird Buses	M708JDG	Cheltenham & G	M775TFS	Fife Scottish	M952DRG	Busways
M596OSO	Bluebird Buses	M708KRH	Kingston-u-Hull	M776TFS	Fife Scottish	M952TSX	Fife Scottish
M597OSO	Bluebird Buses	M709JDG	Cheltenham & G	M778TFS	Fife Scottish	M953DRG	Busways
M598OSO	Bluebird Buses	M709KRH	Kingston-u-Hull	M779TFS	Fife Scottish		

Reg	Operator	Reg	Operator	Reg	Operator	Reg	Operator
M953TSX	Fife Scottish	N131AET	East Midland	N305AMC	East London	N349HGK	Selkent
M954DRG	Busways	N131VAO	Cumberland	N306AMC	East London	N349MPN	Stagecoach South
M954TSX	Fife Scottish	N132AET	East Midland	N307AMC	East London	N350HGK	Selkent
M955TSX	Fife Scottish	N132VAO	Cumberland	N308AMC	East London	N350MPN	Stagecoach South
M956TSX	Fife Scottish	N133AET	East Midland	N309AMC	East London	N351HGK	Selkent
M975WWR	Cambus	N134AET	East Midland	N310AMC	East London	N351MPN	Stagecoach South
M976WWR	Cambus	N135AET	East Midland	N311AMC	East London	N352HGK	Selkent
M977WWR	Cambus	N136AET	East Midland	N312AMC	East London	N352MPN	Stagecoach South
M978WWR	Cambus	N137AET	East Midland	N313AMC	East London	N353HGK	Selkent
M979VWY	Cambus	N138AET	East Midland	N314AMC	East London	N353MPN	Stagecoach South
MAU145P	Midland Red	N139AET	East Midland	N315AMC	East London	N354MPN	Stagecoach South
MAU146P	Bluebird Buses	N140AET	East Midland	N316AMC	East London	N355MPN	Stagecoach South
MBE613R	East Midland	N141AET	East Midland	N316VMS	Fife Scottish	N356MPN	Stagecoach South
MCL937P	Cambus	N141VDU	Fife Scottish	N317AMC	East London	N357MPN	Stagecoach South
MCS138W	Western Scottish	N142AET	East Midland	N317VMS	Fife Scottish	N358MPN	Stagecoach South
MDM282P	Cambus	N143AET	East Midland	N318AMC	East London	N359MPN	Stagecoach South
MDS858V	Western Scottish	N144AET	East Midland	N318VMS	Fife Scottish	N360LPN	Stagecoach South
MDS859V	Western Scottish	N191LPN	Stagecoach South	N319AMC	East London	N361LPN	Stagecoach South
MDS865V	Western Scottish	N192LPN	Stagecoach South	N319VMS	Fife Scottish	N362LPN	Stagecoach South
MDS866V	Western Scottish	N193LPN	Stagecoach South	N320AMC	East London	N363LPN	Stagecoach South
MEF67J	Stagecoach Transit	N194LPN	Stagecoach South	N320VMS	Fife Scottish	N364LPN	Stagecoach South
MEL556P	Cambus	N195LPN	Stagecoach South	N321AMC	East London	N365LPN	Stagecoach South
MEL559P	Cambus	N196LPN	Stagecoach South	N321HGK	Selkent	N366LPN	Stagecoach South
MFN114R	Red & White	N197LPN	Stagecoach South	N321VMS	Fife Scottish	N367LPN	Stagecoach South
MFN115R	Stagecoach South	N198LPN	Stagecoach South	N322AMC	East London	N368LPN	Stagecoach South
MFN118R	Stagecoach South	N199LPN	Stagecoach South	N322HGK	Selkent	N369LPN	Stagecoach South
MFN46R	Stagecoach South	N201LPN	Stagecoach South	N322VMS	Fife Scottish	N370LPN	Stagecoach South
MFN946F	Stagecoach South	N201LTN	Busways	N323AMC	East London	N371LPN	Stagecoach South
MHS4P	Bluebird Buses	N201UHH	Cumberland	N323HGK	Selkent	N372LPN	Stagecoach South
MHS5P	Bluebird Buses	N202LPN	Stagecoach South	N323VMS	Fife Scottish	N373LPN	Stagecoach South
MKV86V	Midland Red	N202LTN	Busways	N324AMC	East London	N374LPN	Stagecoach South
MKV87V	Midland Red	N202UHH	Cumberland	N324HGK	Selkent	N375LPN	Stagecoach South
MLJ917P	Stagecoach South	N203LPN	Stagecoach South	N324VMS	Fife Scottish	N376LPN	Stagecoach South
MNS6Y	Fife Scottish	N203LTN	Busways	N325AMC	East London	N377LPN	Stagecoach South
MNS7Y	Fife Scottish	N203UHH	Cumberland	N325HGK	Selkent	N378LPN	Stagecoach South
MNS8Y	Fife Scottish	N204LPN	Stagecoach South	N325VMS	Fife Scottish	N379LPN	Stagecoach South
MNS9Y	Fife Scottish	N204UHH	Cumberland	N326AMC	East London	N380LPN	Stagecoach South
MNS10Y	Fife Scottish	N205LTN	Busways	N326HGK	Selkent	N381LPN	Stagecoach South
MOU739R	Cheltenham & G	N205UHH	Cumberland	N326VMS	Fife Scottish	N382LPN	Stagecoach South
MOU740R	Cheltenham & G	N206LTN	Busways	N327AMC	East London	N383LPN	Stagecoach South
MRJ270W	East Midland	N206TDU	Midland Red	N327HGK	Selkent	N384LPN	Stagecoach South
MRJ275W	Cumberland	N206UHH	Cumberland	N327VMS	Fife Scottish	N385LPN	Stagecoach South
MSO10W	Western Scottish	N207LTN	Busways	N328HGK	Selkent	N386LPN	Stagecoach South
MSO13W	Red & White	N207TDU	Midland Red	N328VMS	Fife Scottish	N387LPN	Stagecoach South
MSO14W	Red & White	N207UHH	Cumberland	N329HGK	Selkent	N388LPN	Stagecoach South
MSO17W	Western Scottish	N208TDU	Midland Red	N329VMS	Fife Scottish	N389LPN	Stagecoach South
MSO18W	Western Scottish	N208UHH	Cumberland	N330HGK	Selkent	N390LPN	Stagecoach South
MSU445	Fife Scottish	N209LTN	Busways	N330VMS	Fife Scottish	N391LPN	Stagecoach South
MSU465	United Counties	N209UHH	Cumberland	N331HGK	Selkent	N392LPN	Stagecoach South
MSU466	Stagecoach South	N210LTN	Busways	N332HGK	Selkent	N393LPN	Stagecoach South
MSU499	Fife Scottish	N210UHH	Cumberland	N334HGK	Selkent	N394LPN	Stagecoach South
MTE16R	Busways	N211LTN	Busways	N335HGK	Selkent	N395LPN	Stagecoach South
MTV754P	East Midland	N211TDU	Midland Red	N336HGK	Selkent	N396LPN	Stagecoach South
MUA872P	Cheltenham & G	N211UHH	Cumberland	N337HGK	Selkent	N397LPN	Stagecoach South
MVK500R	Busways	N212LTN	Busways	N338HGK	Selkent	N398LPN	Stagecoach South
MVK521R	Busways	N212TDU	Midland Red	N339HGK	Selkent	N399LPN	Stagecoach South
MVK532R	Busways	N212UHH	Cumberland	N340HGK	Selkent	N401LDF	Cheltenham & G
MVK540R	Busways	N213LTN	Busways	N341HGK	Selkent	N402LDF	Cheltenham & G
MVK541R	Busways	N213TDU	Midland Red	N341MPN	Stagecoach South	N403LDF	Cheltenham & G
MVK543R	Busways	N213UHH	Cumberland	N342HGK	Selkent	N404LDF	Cheltenham & G
MVK544R	Busways	N214LTN	Busways	N342MPN	Stagecoach South	N405LDF	Cheltenham & G
MVK551R	Busways	N214TDU	Midland Red	N343HGK	Selkent	N406LDF	Cheltenham & G
MVK558R	Busways	N214UHH	Cumberland	N343MPN	Stagecoach South	N407LDF	Cheltenham & G
MVK561R	Busways	N215LTN	Busways	N344HGK	Selkent	N408LDF	Cheltenham & G
MVK563R	Busways	N215TDU	Midland Red	N344MPN	Stagecoach South	N409LDF	Cheltenham & G
MVK564R	Busways	N215UHH	Cumberland	N345HGK	Selkent	N445XVA	Cambus
MWG622X	East Midland	N216LTN	Busways	N345MPN	Stagecoach South	N446XVA	Cambus
MWG623X	East Midland	N216TDU	Midland Red	N346HGK	Selkent	N447XVA	Cambus
MWG624X	East Midland	N217LTN	Busways	N346MPN	Stagecoach South	N448XVA	Cambus
N128VAO	Cumberland	N301AMC	East London	N347HGK	Selkent	N449XVA	Cambus
N129VAO	Cumberland	N302AMC	East London	N347MPN	Stagecoach South	N450XVA	Cambus
N130AET	East Midland	N303AMC	East London	N348HGK	Selkent	N451XVA	Cambus
N130VAO	Cumberland	N304AMC	East London	N348MPN	Stagecoach South	N452XVA	Cambus

The 1996 Stagecoach Bus Handbook

After a period working with Stagecoach Manchester, ten of Ribble's Volvo B10Ms were lent first to East London, while they awaited their Darts, and then to Hull until their Northern Counties-bodied B10s were delivered. These have now been transferred from Ribble to East Midland where they operate on Chesterfield services. Seen in Vicar Lane, Chesterfield is 600, M414RRN. *Tony Wilson*

Reg	Operator	Reg	Operator	Reg	Operator	Reg	Operator
N518XER	Cambus	N617VSS	Western Scottish	N644LPN	Stagecoach South	N716KAM	Cheltenham & G
N519XER	Cambus	N618USS	Bluebird Buses	N644VSS	Western Scottish	N716LTN	Busways
N520XER	Cambus	N618VSS	Western Scottish	N645LPN	Stagecoach South	N717KAM	Cheltenham & G
N551VDC	Stagecoach Transit	N619USS	Bluebird Buses	N645VSS	Western Scottish	N717LTN	Busways
N552VDC	Stagecoach Transit	N619VSS	Western Scottish	N646VSS	Western Scottish	N718LTN	Busways
N553VDC	Stagecoach Transit	N620USS	Bluebird Buses	N647VSS	Western Scottish	N719LTN	Busways
N601KGF	Selkent	N620VSS	Western Scottish	N648VSS	Western Scottish	N720LTN	Busways
N601VSS	Western Scottish	N621VSS	Western Scottish	N649VSS	Western Scottish	N721LTN	Busways
N602KGF	Selkent	N622VSS	Western Scottish	N650VSS	Western Scottish	N722LTN	Busways
N602VSS	Western Scottish	N623VSS	Western Scottish	N651VSS	Western Scottish	N723LTN	Busways
N603KGF	Selkent	N624VSS	Western Scottish	N652VSS	Western Scottish	N724LTN	Busways
N603VSS	Western Scottish	N625VSS	Western Scottish	N653VSS	Western Scottish	N725LTN	Busways
N604KGF	Selkent	N626VSS	Western Scottish	N654VSS	Western Scottish	N726LTN	Busways
N604VSS	Western Scottish	N627VSS	Western Scottish	N655VSS	Western Scottish	N727LTN	Busways
N605KGF	Selkent	N628VSS	Western Scottish	N656VSS	Western Scottish	N728LTN	Busways
N605VSS	Western Scottish	N629VSS	Western Scottish	N657VSS	Western Scottish	N729LTN	Busways
N606KGF	Selkent	N630VSS	Western Scottish	N658VSS	Western Scottish	N730LTN	Busways
N606VSS	Western Scottish	N631VSS	Western Scottish	N659VSS	Western Scottish	N731LTN	Busways
N607KGF	Selkent	N632VSS	Western Scottish	N660VSS	Western Scottish	N732LTN	Busways
N607VSS	Western Scottish	N633VSS	Western Scottish	N701LTN	Busways	N733LTN	Busways
N608KGF	Selkent	N634VSS	Western Scottish	N702LTN	Busways	N734LTN	Busways
N608VSS	Western Scottish	N635VSS	Western Scottish	N703LTN	Busways	N735LTN	Busways
N609KGF	Selkent	N636VSS	Western Scottish	N704LTN	Busways	N736LTN	Busways
N609VSS	Western Scottish	N637VSS	Western Scottish	N705LTN	Busways	N737LTN	Busways
N610KGF	Selkent	N638VSS	Western Scottish	N706LTN	Busways	N738LTN	Busways
N610VSS	Western Scottish	N639VSS	Western Scottish	N707LTN	Busways	N739LTN	Busways
N611VSS	Western Scottish	N640LPN	Stagecoach South	N708LTN	Busways	N740LTN	Busways
N612VSS	Western Scottish	N640VSS	Western Scottish	N709LTN	Busways	N752CKU	East Midland
N613VSS	Western Scottish	N641LPN	Stagecoach South	N710LTN	Busways	N753CKU	East Midland
N614VSS	Western Scottish	N641VSS	Western Scottish	N711LTN	Busways	N754CKU	East Midland
N615VSS	Western Scottish	N642LPN	Stagecoach South	N712LTN	Busways	N755CKU	East Midland
N616USS	Western Scottish	N642VSS	Western Scottish	N713LTN	Busways	N756CKU	East Midland
N616VSS	Western Scottish	N643LPN	Stagecoach South	N714LTN	Busways	N757CKU	East Midland
N617USS	Western Scottish	N643VSS	Western Scottish	N715LTN	Busways	N758CKU	East Midland

Reg	Operator	Reg	Operator	Reg	Operator	Reg	Operator
N759CKU	East Midland	NFB603R	Cheltenham & G	NOE603R	Midland Red	NUW605Y	East London
N760CKU	East Midland	NFN81R	Stagecoach South	NOE604R	Midland Red	NUW606Y	East London
N761CKU	East Midland	NFN84R	Stagecoach South	NOE605R	Midland Red	NUW608Y	East London
N789NRM	Cumberland	NFN86R	Stagecoach South	NOE606R	Midland Red	NUW609Y	East London
N790NRM	Cumberland	NFN88R	Stagecoach South	NPA229W	Western Scottish	NUW610Y	East London
N804LTN	Busways	NFN89R	Stagecoach South	NPA230W	Midland Red	NUW611Y	Stagecoach South
N808LTN	Busways	NFS170Y	Fife Scottish	NPJ474R	Stagecoach South	NUW613Y	East London
N849VHH	Western Scottish	NFS171Y	Fife Scottish	NPJ476R	Stagecoach South	NUW614Y	East London
N850VHH	Western Scottish	NFS172Y	Fife Scottish	NPJ477R	Stagecoach South	NUW615Y	East London
N851VHH	Western Scottish	NFS173Y	Fife Scottish	NPJ480R	Stagecoach South	NUW616Y	Selkent
N852VHH	Western Scottish	NFS174Y	Fife Scottish	NPJ482R	Stagecoach South	NUW617Y	East London
N853VHH	Western Scottish	NFS175Y	Fife Scottish	NPJ485R	Stagecoach South	NUW618Y	Selkent
N854VHH	Western Scottish	NFS176Y	Fife Scottish	NPK236R	Stagecoach Transit	NUW619Y	East London
N855VHH	Western Scottish	NFS177Y	Fife Scottish	NRP580V	East Midland	NUW621Y	East London
N856VHH	Western Scottish	NFS178Y	Fife Scottish	NRU307M	Cambus	NUW622Y	East London
N857VHH	Western Scottish	NFS179Y	Fife Scottish	NRU310M	Cambus	NUW623Y	East London
N858VHH	Western Scottish	NFX667	Stagecoach South	NRU311M	Cambus	NUW624Y	East London
N859VHH	Western Scottish	NHH380W	Ribble	NSG636A	Bluebird Buses	NUW625Y	East London
N860VHH	Western Scottish	NHH382W	Cheltenham & G	NSP334R	Fife Scottish	NUW626Y	East London
N861VHH	Western Scottish	NHL301X	East Midland	NSP336R	Western Scottish	NUW627Y	East London
N862VHH	Western Scottish	NHL302X	East Midland	NTC132Y	Cheltenham & G	NUW629Y	East London
N863VHH	Western Scottish	NHL303X	East Midland	NUM341V	Cambus	NUW630Y	East London
N864VHH	Western Scottish	NHL304X	East Midland	NUW550Y	East London	NUW631Y	East London
N865VHH	Western Scottish	NHL305X	East Midland	NUW551Y	East London	NUW632Y	East London
N866VHH	Western Scottish	NHU670R	Cheltenham & G	NUW552Y	East London	NUW633Y	East London
NAH136P	Cambus	NHU671R	Midland Red	NUW553Y	East London	NUW634Y	East London
NAH137P	Cambus	NHU672R	Midland Red	NUW554Y	East London	NUW636Y	East London
NAH138P	Cambus	NIB4138	Bluebird Buses	NUW555Y	East London	NUW637Y	East London
NAK29X	Midland Red	NIB5232	Bluebird Buses	NUW556Y	East London	NUW639Y	East London
NBD102Y	United Counties	NIB5233	Bluebird Buses	NUW557Y	East London	NUW640Y	East London
NBD103Y	United Counties	NIB5455	Bluebird Buses	NUW558Y	East London	NUW641Y	East London
NBD104Y	United Counties	NJT34P	Cambus	NUW559Y	East London	NUW642Y	East London
NCS15P	Western Scottish	NKG246M	Busways	NUW560Y	East London	NUW643Y	East London
NDZ3015	East London	NKY143R	East Midland	NUW562Y	East London	NUW644Y	East London
NDZ3016	East London	NKY146R	East Midland	NUW563Y	East London	NUW645Y	East London
NDZ3017	East London	NKY148R	East Midland	NUW564Y	East London	NUW646Y	East London
NDZ3018	East London	NKY149R	East Midland	NUW565Y	East London	NUW647Y	East London
NDZ3019	East London	NLP388V	Western Scottish	NUW566Y	East London	NUW648Y	East London
NDZ3020	East London	NLS983W	Western Scottish	NUW568Y	East London	NUW649Y	East London
NDZ3021	East London	NLS985W	Western Scottish	NUW569Y	East London	NUW650Y	East London
NDZ3022	East London	NLS986W	Ribble	NUW571Y	East London	NUW651Y	East London
NDZ3023	East London	NLS987W	Red & White	NUW572Y	East London	NUW652Y	East London
NDZ3024	East London	NLS988W	Ribble	NUW573Y	East London	NUW653Y	East London
NDZ3025	East London	NLS989W	Western Scottish	NUW574Y	East London	NUW654Y	East London
NDZ3026	East London	NML607E	East London	NUW575Y	East London	NUW657Y	East London
NDZ3133	East London	NML610E	East London	NUW576Y	East London	NUW658Y	East London
NDZ3134	East London	NML616E	East London	NUW577Y	East London	NUW659Y	East London
NDZ3135	East London	NML624E	East London	NUW578Y	East London	NUW660Y	East London
NDZ3136	East London	NML639E	East London	NUW579Y	East London	NUW662Y	East London
NDZ3137	East London	NML641E	East London	NUW580Y	East London	NUW663Y	East London
NDZ3138	East London	NML642E	East London	NUW581Y	East London	NUW664Y	East London
NDZ3139	East London	NML657E	East London	NUW582Y	East London	NUW665Y	East London
NDZ3140	East London	NMY635E	East London	NUW583Y	East London	NUW666Y	East London
NDZ3141	East London	NMY640E	East London	NUW584Y	East London	NUW668Y	East London
NDZ3142	East London	NMY643E	Bluebird Buses	NUW585Y	East London	NUW669Y	East London
NDZ3143	East London	NNU123M	East Midland	NUW586Y	East London	NUW670Y	East London
NDZ3144	East London	NOE551R	Midland Red	NUW587Y	East London	NUW671Y	East London
NDZ3145	East London	NOE552R	Red & White	NUW588Y	East London	NUW672Y	East London
NDZ3146	East London	NOE553R	Midland Red	NUW589Y	East London	NUW673Y	East London
NDZ3147	East London	NOE554R	Midland Red	NUW590Y	East London	NUW674Y	Selkent
NDZ3148	East London	NOE571R	Midland Red	NUW591Y	East London	NUW675Y	East London
NDZ3149	East London	NOE572R	Red & White	NUW592Y	East London	NWO454R	Red & White
NDZ3150	East London	NOE573R	Red & White	NUW593Y	East London	NWO457R	Red & White
NDZ3151	East London	NOE576R	Red & White	NUW594Y	Stagecoach South	NWO461R	Red & White
NDZ3152	East London	NOE577R	Midland Red	NUW595Y	East London	NWO468R	Red & White
NDZ3153	East London	NOE578R	Midland Red	NUW596Y	Stagecoach South	NWS288R	Cheltenham & G
NDZ3154	East London	NOE581R	Midland Red	NUW597Y	East London	NWS289R	Cheltenham & G
NDZ3155	East London	NOE582R	Midland Red	NUW598Y	East London	OAH552M	East Midland
NDZ3156	East London	NOE586R	Midland Red	NUW600Y	East London	OBD842P	Cheltenham & G
NDZ3157	East London	NOE587R	Midland Red	NUW601Y	East London	OCK363K	Busways
NDZ3158	East London	NOE589R	Midland Red	NUW602Y	East London	OCK369K	Busways
NDZ3159	East London	NOE590R	Midland Red	NUW603Y	East London	OCU801R	United Counties
NFB114R	Cheltenham & G	NOE602R	Midland Red	NUW604Y	East London	OCU802R	United Counties

OCU803R	Busways	OHV810Y	Selkent	PCK335	Cumberland	PWY37W	Cambus
OCU804R	United Counties	OHV812Y	Selkent	PEF147X	Stagecoach Transit	PWY39W	Cambus
OCU807R	Busways	OHV813Y	Selkent	PEF148X	Stagecoach Transit	PWY40W	Cambus
OCU808R	United Counties	OHV814Y	Selkent	PEF149X	Stagecoach Transit	PWY45W	Cambus
OCU814R	Busways	OIW7024	Western Scottish	PES189Y	Stagecoach Transit	PWY46W	Cambus
OCU815R	Busways	OIW7025	Western Scottish	PES190Y	Bluebird Buses	PWY47W	Cambus
OCU816R	Busways	OJD136R	Midland Red	PEU511R	Midland Red	PWY48W	Cambus
OCU817R	Busways	OJD241R	Midland Red	PEU515R	Cheltenham & G	PWY49W	Cambus
OCU818R	Busways	OJL822Y	East Midland	PEU516R	Midland Red	PWY50W	Cambus
OCU819R	Busways	OJL823Y	East Midland	PEX386R	Cambus	PYE841Y	East Midland
OCU820R	Busways	OJV120S	East Midland	PEX618W	Cambus	PYE842Y	East Midland
OCU821R	Busways	OJV121S	East Midland	PEX619W	Cambus	RAH260W	Cambus
OCU822R	Busways	OJV122S	East Midland	PEX620W	Cambus	RAH264W	Cambus
OCU824R	Busways	OJV123S	East Midland	PEX621W	Cambus	RAH265W	Cambus
OCU825R	Busways	OJV124S	East Midland	PEX622W	Cambus	RAH268W	Cambus
OCY910R	Bluebird Buses	OMS910W	Bluebird Buses	PFN873	Stagecoach South	RAH681F	Busways
OEF73K	Stagecoach Transit	ONH846P	Midland Red	PHW985S	Red & White	RAU597R	East Midland
OEF74K	Stagecoach Transit	ONH926V	United Counties	PHW988S	Cheltenham & G	RBD397Y	United Counties
OEF77K	Stagecoach Transit	ONH927V	Cambus	PHW989S	Cheltenham & G	RBU180R	East Midland
OEF78K	Stagecoach Transit	ONL645X	Busways	PHY693S	Cheltenham & G	RCS382	Western Scottish
OFV14X	Ribble	OPW179P	Cambus	PIB8019	Midland Red	RCU826S	Busways
OFV15X	Ribble	OPW180P	Cambus	PJI4314	East Midland	RCU827S	Busways
OFV16X	Ribble	OPW182P	Cambus	PJI4316	East Midland	RCU828S	Busways
OFV17X	Ribble	ORY640	Cumberland	PJI4317	East Midland	RCU829S	Busways
OFV18X	Ribble	OSC47V	Fife Scottish	PJI4983	Western Scottish	RCU830S	Busways
OFV19X	Ribble	OSC48V	Fife Scottish	PJJ16S	Stagecoach South	RCU831S	Busways
OFV20X	Ribble	OSC49V	Fife Scottish	PJJ21S	Stagecoach South	RCU832S	Busways
OFV21X	Ribble	OSC50V	Fife Scottish	PJJ22S	Stagecoach South	RCU833S	Busways
OFV22X	Ribble	OSC51V	Fife Scottish	PJJ344S	Stagecoach South	RCU834S	Busways
OFV23X	Ribble	OSC52V	Fife Scottish	PJJ345S	Stagecoach South	RCU835S	Busways
OHV680Y	Selkent	OSC53V	Fife Scottish	PJJ346S	Stagecoach South	RCU837S	Busways
OHV684Y	Western Scottish	OSC54V	Fife Scottish	PPH468R	Cheltenham & G	RCU838S	Busways
OHV686Y	East London	OSC55V	Fife Scottish	PRA109R	Bluebird Buses	RDZ6115	East London
OHV688Y	East London	OSC56V	Fife Scottish	PRA110R	Bluebird Buses	RDZ6116	East London
OHV691Y	East London	OSC57V	Fife Scottish	PRA112R	Bluebird Buses	RDZ6117	East London
OHV697Y	East London	OSC60V	Fife Scottish	PRU917R	Fife Scottish	RDZ6118	East London
OHV699Y	East London	OSC61V	Fife Scottish	PRX189B	Stagecoach Transit	RDZ6119	East London
OHV700Y	Selkent	OSC62V	Fife Scottish	PS2743	East Midland	RDZ6120	East London
OHV702Y	East London	OSC63V	Fife Scottish	PS3696	East Midland	RDZ6121	East London
OHV710Y	Selkent	OSC64V	Fife Scottish	PSO177W	Bluebird Buses	RDZ6122	East London
OHV714Y	Selkent	OSC65V	Fife Scottish	PSO178W	Western Scottish	RDZ6123	East London
OHV719Y	East London	OSC66V	Fife Scottish	PSO179W	Kingston-u-Hull	RDZ6124	East London
OHV721Y	Selkent	OSJ634R	Bluebird Buses	PSU443	East Midland	RDZ6125	East London
OHV724Y	East London	OSJ635R	Bluebird Buses	PSU764	East Midland	RDZ6126	East London
OHV728Y	Selkent	OSJ636R	Bluebird Buses	PSU775	Ribble	RDZ6127	East London
OHV729Y	East London	OSJ643R	Bluebird Buses	PSU787	Cumberland	RDZ6128	East London
OHV731Y	East London	OSJ644R	Bluebird Buses	PSU788	Ribble	RDZ6129	East London
OHV738Y	East London	OSR206R	Red & White	PSX180Y	Fife Scottish	RDZ6130	East London
OHV740Y	Selkent	OSR207R	Red & White	PSX181Y	Fife Scottish	REU309S	Cheltenham & G
OHV743Y	East London	OSR208R	Red & White	PSX182Y	Fife Scottish	REU310S	Cheltenham & G
OHV744Y	East London	OSR209R	Red & White	PSX183Y	Fife Scottish	REU311S	Cheltenham & G
OHV748Y	Selkent	OTD824R	Busways	PSX184Y	Fife Scottish	RFB617S	Cheltenham & G
OHV749Y	East London	OTD825R	Busways	PSX185Y	Fife Scottish	RFS579V	Western Scottish
OHV751Y	East London	OUC42R	Midland Red	PSX186Y	Fife Scottish	RFS582V	Western Scottish
OHV759Y	East London	OUC44R	Midland Red	PSX187Y	Fife Scottish	RFS583V	Western Scottish
OHV761Y	East London	OUD436M	Cambus	PSX188Y	Fife Scottish	RFS584V	Western Scottish
OHV762Y	Selkent	OUF262W	Stagecoach South	PSX189Y	Fife Scottish	RHG878X	Ribble
OHV769Y	East London	OVL473	Bluebird Buses	PTD641S	East Midland	RHG879X	Ribble
OHV770Y	Selkent	OVV849R	United Counties	PTD652S	East Midland	RHG880X	Cheltenham & G
OHV771Y	Selkent	OVV850R	Fife Scottish	PTD668S	East Midland	RHG881X	Ribble
OHV772Y	Selkent	OVV856R	United Counties	PTF762L	East Midland	RHG884X	Ribble
OHV780Y	Selkent	OWB30X	East Midland	PTT92R	Cambus	RHG886X	Ribble
OHV784Y	East London	OWB31X	East Midland	PUK621R	Midland Red	RHL174X	East Midland
OHV785Y	East London	OWB32X	East Midland	PUK622R	Midland Red	RJA702R	Western Scottish
OHV789Y	East London	OWB33X	East Midland	PUK623R	Midland Red	RJA801R	Western Scottish
OHV791Y	Selkent	OWB34X	East Midland	PUK624R	Midland Red	RJT146R	Stagecoach South
OHV797Y	Selkent	OWC720M	Busways	PUK625R	Midland Red	RJT151R	Stagecoach South
OHV800Y	Selkent	OWC722M	Busways	PUK626R	Midland Red	RJT153R	Fife Scottish
OHV801Y	Selkent	OWC723M	Busways	PUK627R	Midland Red	RJT155R	Bluebird Buses
OHV802Y	East London	PCD73R	Stagecoach South	PUK628R	Midland Red	RPR716R	Fife Scottish
OHV804Y	Selkent	PCD78R	Stagecoach South	PUK629R	Midland Red	RRM383X	Ribble
OHV805Y	Selkent	PCD79R	Stagecoach South	PVF353R	Cambus	RRM384X	Ribble
OHV809Y	Selkent	PCD80R	Stagecoach South	PVT221L	Busways	RRM385X	Cheltenham & G

RRM386X	Ribble	SAG527W	Kingston-u-Hull	SGS504W	Stagecoach South	SNS828W	Busways
RRP858R	Ribble	SAG528W	Kingston-u-Hull	SHE306Y	East Midland	SNV930W	United Counties
RRP862R	United Counties	SAG529W	Kingston-u-Hull	SHE307Y	East Midland	SNV931W	United Counties
RRP863R	United Counties	SAG530W	Kingston-u-Hull	SHE308Y	East Midland	SNV935W	United Counties
RRS46R	Bluebird Buses	SAO410R	Bluebird Buses	SHE309Y	East Midland	SNV936W	United Counties
RRS47R	Bluebird Buses	SAO412R	Bluebird Buses	SHE310Y	East Midland	SNV937W	United Counties
RRS48R	Bluebird Buses	SCK224X	Ribble	SHE311Y	East Midland	SOA664S	Midland Red
RRS50R	Bluebird Buses	SCK225X	Ribble	SHH387X	Ribble	SSA2X	Bluebird Buses
RRS53R	Bluebird Buses	SCK226X	Ribble	SHH388X	Ribble	SSA3X	Bluebird Buses
RRS225X	Western Scottish	SCN244S	Fife Scottish	SHH389X	Cheltenham & G	SSA4X	Bluebird Buses
RSC190Y	Fife Scottish	SCN247S	Busways	SHH390X	Ribble	SSA5X	Bluebird Buses
RSC191Y	Fife Scottish	SCN248S	Busways	SHH391X	Ribble	SSA6X	Bluebird Buses
RSC192Y	Fife Scottish	SCN249S	Busways	SHH392X	Midland Red	SSA7X	Bluebird Buses
RSC193Y	Fife Scottish	SCN250S	Busways	SHH393X	Ribble	STW24W	Cambus
RSC194Y	Fife Scottish	SCN251S	Busways	SHH394X	Ribble	STW30W	Cambus
RSG814V	Red & White	SCN252S	Busways	SHN401R	Stagecoach Transit	SUA123R	East Midland
RSG815V	Red & White	SCN254S	Busways	SHN404R	Stagecoach Transit	SUB790W	Cambus
RSG823V	Red & White	SCN255S	Busways	SHN405R	Stagecoach Transit	SUB791W	Cambus
RSG824V	Red & White	SCN256S	Busways	SHN407R	Stagecoach Transit	SUB792W	Cambus
RSG825V	Red & White	SCN257S	Fife Scottish	SIB8243	Stagecoach South	SUB793W	Cambus
RTH924S	Fife Scottish	SCN258S	Busways	SKG908S	Red & White	SUB794W	Cambus
RUF38R	Stagecoach Transit	SCN259S	Busways	SKG915S	Red & White	SUB795W	Cambus
RUF40R	Stagecoach Transit	SCN261S	Fife Scottish	SKG923S	Red & White	SVK627G	Busways
RVB973S	Fife Scottish	SCN262S	Busways	SKL680X	Stagecoach South	SVV586W	East Midland
RVB974S	Fife Scottish	SCN263S	Busways	SKL681X	Stagecoach South	SVV589W	Midland Red
RVB978S	Fife Scottish	SCN264S	Busways	SKL682X	Stagecoach South	SWC25K	Busways
RYK815Y	Selkent	SCN266S	Busways	SKL683X	Stagecoach South	SWC26K	Busways
RYK816Y	Selkent	SCN267S	Busways	SKL684X	Stagecoach South	SYC852	Stagecoach South
RYK818Y	Selkent	SCN268S	Busways	SKL685X	Stagecoach South	TAE639S	Midland Red
RYK819Y	East London	SCN270S	Busways	SKY31Y	East Midland	TAE641S	Cheltenham & G
RYK820Y	Selkent	SCN271S	Busways	SKY32Y	East Midland	TAE642S	Cheltenham & G
RYK821Y	Selkent	SCN273S	Busways	SMK661F	East London	TAE644S	Cheltenham & G
RYK822Y	Selkent	SCN275S	Busways	SMK665F	East London	TBC1X .	Busways
SAE752S	Cheltenham & G	SCN276S	Busways	SMK670F	East London	TBC2X	Busways
SAE753S	Midland Red	SCN277S	Busways	SMK671F	East London	TCK200X	Ribble
SAE754S	Cheltenham & G	SCN278S	Busways	SMK696F	East London	TCK212X	Ribble
SAE756S	Cheltenham & G	SCN279S	Busways	SMK705F	East London	TCK841	Cumberland
SAG516W	Kingston-u-Hull	SCN280S	Busways	SMK709F	East London	TDL567K	Busways
SAG517W	Kingston-u-Hull	SCN281S	Busways	SMK723F	East London	TEL490R	Stagecoach South
SAG518W	Kingston-u-Hull	SCN282S	Busways	SMK738F	East London	TEX405R	Cambus
SAG519W	Kingston-u-Hull	SCN283S	Busways	SMK743F	East London	TFN982T	Stagecoach South
SAG520W	Kingston-u-Hull	SCN285S	Busways	SMK748F	East London	TFN988T	Stagecoach South
SAG521W	Kingston-u-Hull	SCN286S	Busways	SMK749F	East London	TFN990T	Fife Scottish
SAG522W	Kingston-u-Hull	SDA651S	United Counties	SMK760F	East London	TFU59T	East Midland
SAG523W	Kingston-u-Hull	SDA715S	United Counties	SND710X	Cheltenham & G	TFU60T	East Midland
SAG524W	Kingston-u-Hull	SEF80L	Stagecoach Transit	SNS822W	Busways	TFU61T	East Midland
SAG525W	Kingston-u-Hull	SEF81L	Stagecoach Transit	SNS825W	Cheltenham & G	TFU62T	East Midland
SAG526W	Kingston-u-Hull	SEF84L	Stagecoach Transit	SNS826W	Western Scottish	TFU63T	East Midland

Cherished marks have been used to good advantage by several operations, Stagecoach South preserving those which were new to the open-top fleet by placing them on modern buses. Illustrating the point is 656, 416DCD.
Richard Godfrey

TFU64T	East Midland	TWS903T	Midland Red	UWV609S	Bluebird Buses	VOD596S	Cheltenham & G
THX179S	East Midland	TWS906T	Cheltenham & G	UWV610S	Cumberland	VOD597S	Cheltenham & G
THX231S	Midland Red	TWS909T	Red & White	UWV611S	Stagecoach South	VOD598S	Cheltenham & G
THX401S	East London	TWS913T	Cheltenham & G	UWV612S	Cumberland	VOD604S	Stagecoach South
THX402S	East London	TWS914T	Cheltenham & G	UWV613S	Stagecoach South	VOD605S	Stagecoach South
TMS404X	Fife Scottish	UCS659	Western Scottish	UWV614S	Stagecoach South	VOD625S	Stagecoach South
TMS405X	Fife Scottish	UDT312Y	East Midland	UWV617S	Fife Scottish	VPF283S	Stagecoach South
TMS406X	Fife Scottish	UDT313Y	East Midland	UWV618S	Cumberland	VPR487S	Fife Scottish
TMS407X	Fife Scottish	UF4813	Stagecoach South	UWV620S	Cumberland	VPR490S	Stagecoach South
TNH870R	United Counties	UFG48S	Stagecoach South	UWV621S	Stagecoach South	VPR491S	Stagecoach South
TNH871R	United Counties	UFG49S	Stagecoach Transit	UWV622S	Cumberland	VPW85S	Cambus
TNH872R	United Counties	UFG52S	Stagecoach Transit	UWV622S	Ribble	VRN827Y	Ribble
TNH873R	United Counties	UFS875R	Fife Scottish	UWV623S	Stagecoach South	VRN828Y	Ribble
TOF707S	Midland Red	UFS876R	Fife Scottish	UWW3X	Cambus	VRN829Y	Ribble
TOF708S	Midland Red	UFS877R	Fife Scottish	UWW4X	Cambus	VRN830Y	Ribble
TOF709S	Midland Red	UFS878R	Fife Scottish	UWW7X	Cheltenham & G	VRR447	Cumberland
TOF710S	Midland Red	UHG741R	East Midland	UWW8X	Cambus	VSS3X	Stagecoach Transit
TPE148S	Stagecoach South	UHG757R	Stagecoach South	UYJ654	Bluebird Buses	VSV564	Stagecoach South
TPE149S	Stagecoach South	UIB3076	Western Scottish	VAE499T	Cheltenham & G	VTV167S	Fife Scottish
TPE156S	Stagecoach South	UIB3541	Western Scottish	VAE501T	Cheltenham & G	VTV170S	Midland Red
TPE169S	Stagecoach South	UIB3542	Western Scottish	VAE502T	Midland Red	VTV171S	Stagecoach South
TRN476V	Ribble	UIB3543	Western Scottish	VAE507T	Cheltenham & G	VTV172S	Stagecoach South
TRN478V	Ribble	ULS660T	Western Scottish	VAH278X	Cambus	VVV948W	United Counties
TRN480V	Ribble	UM7681	Western Scottish	VAH279X	Cambus	VVV949W	United Counties
TRN481V	Ribble	UMO180N	Stagecoach South	VAH280X	Cambus	VVV950W	United Counties
TRN482V	Ribble	UNA772S	Western Scottish	VBA161S	Western Scottish	VVV952W	United Counties
TRN802V	Ribble	UNA824S	Western Scottish	VCS376	Western Scottish	VVV953W	United Counties
TRN806V	Ribble	UNA840S	Western Scottish	VCS391	Western Scottish	VVV954W	United Counties
TRN810V	Cumberland	UNA853S	Western Scottish	VCU302T	Busways	VVV961W	United Counties
TRN812V	Ribble	UNA863S	Western Scottish	VCU303T	Busways	VVV962W	United Counties
TRY118H	Busways	URA605S	East Midland	VCU304T	Busways	VVV963W	United Counties
TSJ31S	Western Scottish	URB826S	Cambus	VCU309T	Busways	VVV965W	United Counties
TSJ32S	Western Scottish	URF661S	Midland Red	VCU310T	Busways	VVV966W	United Counties
TSJ33S	Western Scottish	URF662S	Ribble	VCU312T	Busways	VVV967W	United Counties
TSJ67S	Western Scottish	URM801Y	Cumberland	VEF150Y	Stagecoach Transit	VWA34Y	East Midland
TSJ70S	Western Scottish	URM802Y	Cumberland	VEF151Y	Stagecoach Transit	VWA35Y	East Midland
TSJ71S	Western Scottish	URP939W	United Counties	VEF152Y	Stagecoach Transit	VWA36Y	East Midland
TSJ76S	Western Scottish	URP940W	United Counties	VEF153Y	Stagecoach Transit	WAO396Y	Ribble
TSJ78S	Western Scottish	URP941W	United Counties	VEU231T	Cheltenham & G	WAO397Y	Busways
TSJ79S	Western Scottish	URP942W	Cambus	VEX289X	Cambus	WAO398Y	Ribble
TSJ80S	Western Scottish	URP943W	Cambus	VEX291X	Cambus	WAO643Y	Bluebird Buses
TSJ85S	Western Scottish	URP944W	United Counties	VEX293X	Cambus	WAO645Y	Ribble
TSO12X	Bluebird Buses	URP945W	United Counties	VEX295X	Cambus	WAO646Y	Ribble
TSO13X	Bluebird Buses	USK625	Bluebird Buses	VEX296X	Cambus	WAS765V	Red & White
TSO14X	Bluebird Buses	USV672	Stagecoach South	VEX298X	Cambus	WAS767V	Red & White
TSO15X	Bluebird Buses	UTX726S	Red & White	VEX299X	Cambus	WAS768V	Western Scottish
TSO16X	Bluebird Buses	UVF623X	Cambus	VEX300X	Cambus	WAS771V	Western Scottish
TSO17X	Bluebird Buses	UVK287T	Busways	VEX301X	Cambus	WBD875S	Cheltenham & G
TSO20X	Bluebird Buses	UVK288T	Busways	VEX303X	Cambus	WBD876S	United Counties
TSO21X	Bluebird Buses	UVK289T	Busways	VEX304X	Cambus	WBN468T	East Midland
TSO23X	Bluebird Buses	UVK290T	Busways	VFX984S	Stagecoach South	WBN469T	East Midland
TSO24X	Bluebird Buses	UVK291T	Busways	VKE566S	East Midland	WBN470T	East Midland
TSO29X	Bluebird Buses	UVK292T	Busways	VKU71S	East Midland	WBN473T	East Midland
TSO30X	Bluebird Buses	UVK294T	Busways	VKU72S	East Midland	WBN477T	East Midland
TSO31X	Bluebird Buses	UVK295T	Busways	VKU73S	East Midland	WBN479T	East Midland
TSO32X	Bluebird Buses	UVK297T	Busways	VKU74S	East Midland	WBN480T	East Midland
TSU638	Western Scottish	UVK298T	Busways	VKU75S	East Midland	WBN482T	East Midland
TSU639	United Counties	UVK299T	Busways	VKU76S	East Midland	WBN484T	East Midland
TSU640	United Counties	UVK300T	Busways	VKU77S	East Midland	WCK213Y	Ribble
TSU641	United Counties	UWA150S	East Midland	VKU78S	East Midland	WCK215Y	Ribble
TSU642	United Counties	UWA151S	East Midland	VKU79S	East Midland	WDA1T	Red & White
TSV718	Bluebird Buses	UWA152S	East Midland	VKU80S	East Midland	WDA2T	Red & White
TSV719	Bluebird Buses	UWA153S	East Midland	VLT14	Selkent	WDA5T	Red & White
TSV720	Bluebird Buses	UWA154S	East Midland	VLT20	Selkent	WDA994T	Midland Red
TSV721	Bluebird Buses	UWA155S	East Midland	VLT37	Western Scottish	WFR392V	Midland Red
TSV722	Bluebird Buses	UWA157S	East Midland	VLT54	Western Scottish	WFS135W	Bluebird Buses
TSV778	Bluebird Buses	UWA158S	East Midland	VLT73	Western Scottish	WFS136W	Western Scottish
TSV779	Bluebird Buses	UWA159S	East Midland	VLT77	Fife Scottish	WFS137W	Bluebird Buses
TSV780	Bluebird Buses	UWP105	Stagecoach South	VLT104	Western Scottish	WFS138W	Fife Scottish
TSV781	Bluebird Buses	UWV604S	Stagecoach South	VLT154	Western Scottish	WFS139W	Fife Scottish
TVC504W	Midland Red	UWV605S	Bluebird Buses	VLT240	Selkent	WFS140W	Fife Scottish
TWF201Y	East Midland	UWV607S	Stagecoach South	VLT255	United Counties	WFS141W	Fife Scottish
TWF202Y	East Midland	UWV608S	Bluebird Buses	VOD593S	Cheltenham & G	WFS142W	Fife Scottish

The 1996 Stagecoach Bus Handbook

Reg	Operator	Reg	Operator	Reg	Operator	Reg	Operator
WFS147W	Fife Scottish	WYV4T	East London	XJJ660V	Stagecoach South	YDC26Y	Stagecoach Transit
WFS148W	Fife Scottish	WYV5T	Western Scottish	XJJ661V	Stagecoach South	YDG616	Cumberland
WFS149W	Fife Scottish	WYV6T	East London	XJJ662V	Stagecoach South	YEL2T	Stagecoach South
WFS150W	Fife Scottish	WYV7T	East London	XJJ663V	Stagecoach South	YEL3T	Stagecoach South
WFU465V	East Midland	WYV8T	East London	XJJ664V	Stagecoach South	YEL4T	Stagecoach South
WFU466V	East Midland	WYV9T	East London	XJJ665V	Stagecoach South	YEL93Y	Stagecoach South
WFU467V	East Midland	WYV10T	East London	XJJ666V	Stagecoach South	YEU446V	Midland Red
WFU468V	East Midland	WYV11T	East London	XJJ667V	Stagecoach South	YFB972V	Cheltenham & G
WFU469V	East Midland	WYV12T	East London	XJJ668V	Stagecoach South	YFB973V	Cheltenham & G
WFU470V	East Midland	WYV13T	East London	XJJ669V	Stagecoach South	YFS304W	Western Scottish
WHH415S	Fife Scottish	WYV14T	East London	XJJ670V	Stagecoach South	YFS308W	Western Scottish
WJM824T	Stagecoach South	WYV15T	East London	XMS420Y	Fife Scottish	YFS309W	Western Scottish
WJM825T	Stagecoach South	WYV16T	East London	XMS422Y	Fife Scottish	YFS310W	Western Scottish
WJM826T	Stagecoach South	WYV17T	East London	XMS423Y	Fife Scottish	YJV806	Cheltenham & G
WJM827T	Stagecoach South	WYV18T	East London	XNV878S	United Counties	YLJ332	Stagecoach South
WJM828T	Stagecoach South	WYV19T	East London	XNV879S	United Counties	YNA363M	Midland Red
WJM829T	Stagecoach South	WYV20T	East London	XNV880S	United Counties	YNG208S	Cambus
WJM832T	Stagecoach South	WYV21T	East London	XNV885S	United Counties	YNG209S	Cambus
WKO129S	Stagecoach South	WYV22T	East London	XNV886S	United Counties	YNG210S	Cambus
WLT380	Cumberland	WYV23T	East London	XNV887S	United Counties	YNG212S	Cambus
WLT415	Western Scottish	WYV24T	East London	XNV888S	United Counties	YPD129Y	East Midland
WLT439	Western Scottish	WYV25T	East London	XNV889S	United Counties	YPD133Y	East Midland
WLT444	Western Scottish	WYV26T	East London	XNV890S	United Counties	YRN813V	Ribble
WLT447	Western Scottish	WYV27T	Western Scottish	XNV891S	United Counties	YRN814V	Ribble
WLT461	Selkent	WYV28T	East London	XOV753T	Midland Red	YRN815V	Ribble
WLT465	Western Scottish	WYV29T	Western Scottish	XOV754T	Midland Red	YRN816V	Stagecoach South
WLT491	Selkent	WYV30T	East London	XOV755T	Midland Red	YRN817V	Ribble
WLT501	Western Scottish	WYV31T	East London	XOV756T	Midland Red	YRN818V	Ribble
WLT512	United Counties	WYV32T	East London	XOV760T	Midland Red	YRN819V	Ribble
WLT526	Western Scottish	WYV33T	East London	XRM772Y	Bluebird Buses	YRN820V	Ribble
WLT528	United Counties	WYV34T	East London	XRR175S	Cumberland	YRN821V	Stagecoach South
WLT538	Western Scottish	WYV35T	East London	XSJ651T	Western Scottish	YRN822V	Ribble
WLT546	Western Scottish	WYV36T	East London	XSJ653T	Western Scottish	YSD350L	Western Scottish
WLT575	Selkent	WYV37T	East London	XSJ654T	Western Scottish	YSD819T	Western Scottish
WLT613	East London	WYV38T	East London	XSJ655T	Western Scottish	YSD820T	Western Scottish
WLT682	United Counties	WYV39T	East London	XSJ656T	Western Scottish	YSF98S	Western Scottish
WLT697	Western Scottish	WYV40T	East London	XSJ657T	Western Scottish	YSF100S	Western Scottish
WLT706	Cumberland	WYV49T	Western Scottish	XSJ658T	Western Scottish	YSO33Y	Bluebird Buses
WLT713	Cheltenham & G	WYV56T	Western Scottish	XSJ659T	Western Scottish	YSO34Y	Bluebird Buses
WLT720	Western Scottish	WYV63T	East London	XSJ660T	Western Scottish	YSO35Y	Bluebird Buses
WLT727	Western Scottish	WYV66T	East London	XSJ661T	Western Scottish	YSO36Y	Bluebird Buses
WLT774	Western Scottish	XAP643S	Fife Scottish	XSJ662T	Western Scottish	YSO37Y	Bluebird Buses
WLT794	Western Scottish	XAP644S	Stagecoach South	XSJ665T	Western Scottish	YSO38Y	Bluebird Buses
WLT809	Western Scottish	XCC94V	Stagecoach Transit	XSJ666T	Western Scottish	YSO39Y	Bluebird Buses
WLT824	Cumberland	XDU599	Stagecoach South	XSJ667T	Western Scottish	YSO40Y	Bluebird Buses
WLT830	Western Scottish	XDV602S	Cheltenham & G	XSJ668T	Western Scottish	YSO41Y	Bluebird Buses
WLT874	Western Scottish	XDV606S	Cheltenham & G	XSJ669T	Western Scottish	YSO42Y	Bluebird Buses
WLT886	East London	XDV607S	Cambus	XSL596A	Bluebird Buses	YSO43Y	Bluebird Buses
WLT908	United Counties	XFF813	East London	XVV540S	Red & White	YSX926W	Red & White
WLT978	Western Scottish	XFF814	East London	YAJ154Y	Stagecoach Transit	YSX929W	Fife Scottish
WPR152S	Stagecoach South	XFU125V	East Midland	YAJ155Y	Stagecoach Transit	YSX930W	Fife Scottish
WPW200S	Cambus	XFU126V	East Midland	YAJ156Y	Stagecoach Transit	YSX932W	Red & White
WPW201S	Cambus	XFU127V	East Midland	YAJ157Y	Stagecoach Transit	YSX933W	Red & White
WPW202S	Cambus	XFU128V	East Midland	YAY21Y	Kingston-u-Hull	YSX934W	Red & White
WSU293	Midland Red	XFU129V	East Midland	YBO16T	Midland Red	YSX935W	Red & White
WSU450	Stagecoach South	XGR728R	Midland Red	YBO18T	Midland Red	YTS820A	Bluebird Buses
WSU451	Stagecoach South	XGS736S	East Midland	YBO147T	Red & White	YTU353S	Cambus
WSU452	Stagecoach South	XGS762X	Stagecoach South	YCD73T	Stagecoach South	YVN520T	United Counties
WUH166T	Red & White	XJJ650V	Stagecoach South	YCD74T	Stagecoach South	YVN521T	Stagecoach Transit
WUH167T	Red & White	XJJ651V	Stagecoach South	YCD76T	Stagecoach South	YVN522T	United Counties
WUH168T	Red & White	XJJ652V	Stagecoach South	YCD77T	Stagecoach South	YVN524T	United Counties
WVM884S	Western Scottish	XJJ653V	Stagecoach South	YCD82T	Stagecoach South	YVV896S	Cambus
WVM888S	Western Scottish	XJJ654V	Stagecoach South	YDC21Y	Stagecoach Transit	YWC16L	Busways
WVT618	Stagecoach South	XJJ655V	Stagecoach South	YDC23Y	Stagecoach Transit	YWC18L	Busways
WWY130S	Cambus	XJJ657V	Stagecoach South	YDC24Y	Stagecoach Transit	YWY830S	Cambus
WYJ169S	Stagecoach South	XJJ658V	Stagecoach South	YDC25Y	Stagecoach Transit	YYS174	Western Scottish
WYV3T	East London	XJJ659V	Stagecoach South				

ISBN 1 897990 23 5
Published by British Bus Publishing Ltd, January 1996
The Vyne, 16 St Margarets Drive, Wellington,
Telford, Shropshire, TF1 3PH
Fax/Ansrwephone: 01952 255669

Printed by Graphics & Print
Unit A13, Stafford Park 15
Telford, Shropshire, TF3 3BB

The 1996 Stagecoach Bus Handbook